Female Genital Mutilation

To the tireless voices of Tanzania and Kenya
who teach "Do no harm."

39.95

Gn

Female Genital Mutilation

Legal, Cultural and Medical Issues

ROSEMARIE SKAINE

392.1
SKA

McFarland & Company, Inc., Publishers

Jefferson, North Carolina, and London

HUNTINGTON BEACH PUBLIC LIBRARY
7111 Talbert Avenue
Huntington Beach, CA 92648

ALSO BY ROSEMARIE SKAINE
AND FROM MCFARLAND

*The Cuban Family: Custom and
Change in an Era of Hardship* (2004)

Paternity and American Law (2003)

The Women of Afghanistan Under the Taliban (2002)

Women College Basketball Coaches (2001)

*Women at War: Gender Issues of
Americans in Combat* (1999)

*Power and Gender: Issues in Sexual
Dominance and Harassment* (1996)

LIBRARY OF CONGRESS CATALOGUING-IN-PUBLICATION DATA

Skaine, Rosemarie.
    Female genital mutilation : legal, cultural and medical issues
/ Rosemarie Skaine.
        p.   cm.
    Includes bibliographical references and index.

    ISBN 0-7864-2167-3 (softcover : 50# alkaline paper) ∞

    1. Female circumcision.   I. Title.
    GN484.S485   2005
    392.1— dc22   2005013929

British Library cataloguing data are available

©2005 Rosemarie Skaine. All rights reserved

*No part of this book may be reproduced or transmitted in any form
or by any means, electronic or mechanical, including photocopying
or recording, or by any information storage and retrieval system,
without permission in writing from the publisher.*

Cover photograph ©2005 PhotoSpin

Manufactured in the United States of America

*McFarland & Company, Inc., Publishers
  Box 611, Jefferson, North Carolina 28640
  www.mcfarlandpub.com*

Acknowledgments

People from many parts of the world enabled and facilitated the writing of this book. I greatly appreciate what they have done.

Dr. Les Huth, Professor Emeritus, Director of the Walter Cunningham Memorial Teacher's Project, Wartburg College, Waverly, Iowa, provided an interview and gave encouragement and guidance for my visit to Tanzania. M. Neil Williams, M.D., retired general surgeon and missionary physician, Cedar Falls, Iowa, gave an interview and provided helpful resources. Jon Heinrich, Director of Missions, Trinity Lutheran Church, Grand Island, Nebraska, arranged interviews with people from Sudan and provided one himself.

James C. Skaine, Professor Emeritus, Communication Studies, University of Northern Iowa, assisted with editing and proofreading. I appreciate his traveling with me to Africa and assisting with the interviews there.

Richard L. and Nancy L. Craft Kuehner and William V. and Carolyn E. Guenther Kuehner gave love and support. Nancy was inspiring and Carolyn helped locate research sources in Grand Island, Nebraska.

John R. Brownell, Attorney, Lauritsen, Brownell, Brostrom Stehlik, Thayer and Myers, and Mercedes Ayala, both of Grand Island, Nebraska, were supportive in many ways.

The Inter-African Committee on Traditional Practices Affecting the Health of Women and Children (IAC), Geneva, provided research material and granted permission to reprint their poem "I Am a Girl Child." Mrs. Berhane Ras-Work, President of IAC, Donika Lafratta, and Anh Nguyen provided timely assistance.

H.B. Shakir, Adventure Tours and Safaris, Arusha, Tanzania, made our safari (journey) in Africa pleasant and productive. His extensive planning, assistance, and management made my research endeavors with the Maasai and with others in Shirati and Arusha, Tanzania, and in Kenya most productive. He also arranged for Mr. Virji Rizwan, Outdoor Expedition Safaris, Ltd., to assist me in Kenya. Chris, our driver and guide in Kenya, gave us a safe and informative experience.

James Emanuel Sichilima from Adventure Tours was excellent as our guide, driver, and interpreter. James contributed to the success of my research through his skill in the languages of Swahili, Maasai, and English.

My research with the Maasai near Mto Wa Mbu, Manyara, Tanzania, was facilitated by the government Uwane (Councilor) Sevingi R.S.A. He accompanied us to see the Maasai and explained their lifestyle and the efforts of government through education to stop circumcision of women and to reduce the number of herds. He gave us a tour of the new school for the Maasai and presented plans for a secondary school at the site for Maasai children. Olaiguenani Landari and his cabinet were most hospitable and informative when I visited their Maasai boma. The Laibon of another Maasai boma was cordial and open to questions and agreed to permit me to have a productive interview with the women of his boma.

Anne Domatob, Rosemary Wellington, and Winnie Muritu of the United Nations Children's Fund (UNICEF) Eastern and Southern Africa Regional Office, Nairobi, Kenya, were warmly supportive of my research. They advanced it by providing UNICEF's special report on female genital cutting (FGC).

Mary Eliakimu Laiser, Head of the Women's Department, and Hulda, Mary's coworker at the Arusha Diocese of the Evangelical Lutheran Church in Tanzania (ELCT), gave me informative and inspiring interviews. Mary prepared an excellent report on female genital mutilation (FGM) just for our interview. Charles H. Sweke, M.D., C.I., Ord., Ph.D., consultant obstetrician and gynecologist, Selian Lutheran Hospital, Arusha, Tanzania, also granted me an interview.

Esther Kawira, M.D., F.A.A.F.P., Medical Officer in Charge, Shirati Kanisa la Mennonite Tanzania (KMT) Hospital, Shirati, Tanzania, assisted in many ways. Her interview was most helpful. Her generosity, spirit, and enthusiasm inspired me. She provided guidance and invaluable research contacts. Josiah Kawira and the Rev. Manaen Kawira also assisted with my research. Rebecca Nice, Telford, Pennsylvania, and Amanda Wagler, New Hamburg, Ontario, Canada, medical students serving at Shirati KMT Hospital, gave valuable input and were involved with several interviews.

Professor Patroba E. Ondiek, Ph.D., Director/Program Coordinator of the Rorya Human Immunodeficiency Virus/Acquired Immunodeficiency Syndrome (HIV/AIDS) Prevention Organization and Program Coordinator for Save the Children of Tarime (Sachita), both in Tarime, Tanzania, was generous and insightful in the interview he granted me. Kebwe Stephen Kebwe, M.D., District Medical Officer (DMO), Bunda, and Regional Chairman, Mara, IAC, Bunda, Tanzania, gave generously of his time for an interview and shared the video of the Kilimanjaro IAC conference. Thanks to Juliet Chugulu, R.N., R.M., M.Sc., Kilimanjaro Christian Medical Centre, School of Nursing, Chairperson, Kilimanjaro IAC (KIAC), Moshi, Tanzania, for her insights and perspectives and to John Wachira, M.D., urologist, Doctors Without Borders, serving in Kenya, Uganda, Tanzania, and parts of Somalia, for providing a forthright interview. Dr. Esther Kawira assisted in securing this interview.

Organizations and individuals contributed to the success of this book. Sonia Palmieri, Inter-Parliamentary Union (IPU), Genèva, Switzerland; the Kilimanjaro Inter-African Committee on Traditional Practices Affecting the Health of Woman and Children (KIAC), Moshi, Tanzania; Mona Bur, International Network to Analyze, Communicate, and Transform the Campaign Against FGC/FGM/FC (INTACT), Cairo, Egypt; and The Research, Action, and Information Network for Bodily Integrity of Women (RAINBO), New York, all provided data that furthered my research.

Informative and inspiring interviews were given to me by persons from south Sudan residing in Grand Island, Nebraska: William G. Riek, President, Sudanese Refugee Community Organization (SRCO) and Refugee Advocate, Community Humanitarian Resource Center (CHRC), Grand Island, Nebraska, and nurse and ophthalmic assistant in Sudan; Aban Laamatjok and Jenty Nawal Chacha Kosta; and Mut B. Ruey and Nyarieka Ruey. Other Sudanese refugees shared their knowledge but asked that they not be named.

Colleen Renk Zengotitabengoa, M.A., J.D., staff attorney, and Lisa Johnson-Firth, L.L.B., J.D., Director of Legal Services, Tahirih Justice Center, Falls Church, Virginia, were most helpful in their interviews and through the resources they provided. Kirsten Aghen, M.P.H., Office on Women's Health, U.S. Department of Health and Human Services (DHHS) gave enthusiastic support and assistance. Toure Fatima, Program for Appropriate Technology in Health (PATH), provided valuable information. Sandra Jordan, Global Health Office of Population and Reproductive Health (GH/PRH), Director of Communications and Outreach, U.S. Agency for International Development (USAID) gave timely assistance.

Christopher M. Schulte, graduate student, art education, University of Northern Iowa, Cedar Falls, Iowa, drew three maps that have been included in the book.

Larry A. Phillips, Cole Photography, Waterloo, Iowa, provided excellent and creative photos for selection for use on the cover.

David Bramley, World Health Organization (WHO), Department of Health Information Management and Dissemination, Geneva, Switzerland, expedited the permission process to use the map of FGM prevalence around the world. Jason Crase, editorial specialist, Division of Publishing and Production Services, Department of Marketing and Publications, American Academy of Pediatrics, Elk Grove Village, Illinois, expedited the permission process to use illustrations depicting types of FGM.

Israel Msengi from Tanzania, a graduate student in the School of Health, Physical Education and Leisure Services, University of Northern Iowa, Cedar Falls, translated literature from Swahili into English. Israel and his wife, Clementine, from Rwanda, provided materials for use in the cover photos.

Dr. Jerry Domatob, professor, Communication Studies, gave scholarly guidance and inspiration. Frida Domatob Fokum assisted me through insightful discussions we had. Dr. Richard Frankhauser and Dr. John Keiser, Covenant Clinic, Medical Associates, Cedar Falls, Iowa, and Dr. Douglas L. Stanford, OB-GYN Specialists P.C., Waterloo, Iowa, were most supportive of my research. Capt. Jim Castleberry, Hall County Sheriff's Office, Grand Island, Nebraska, and Pastor Martin Schmidt, Senior Pastor, Trinity Lutheran Church, Grand Island, Nebraska, assisted me in the early stages of my research. Kathleen Sheldon, an independent scholar with a research affiliation with the University of California at Los Angeles (UCLA) Center for the Study of Women, generously shared her research on FGC. Dr. Alma Gottlieb, Department of Anthropology, University of Illinois, Urbana-Champaign, gave guidance. Dr. Lee G. Burchinal with the private University of Sudan and Associate Editor of the *Ahfad Journal* in Arlington, Virginia, provided research material.

Robert Kramer, Professor Emeritus, Center for Social and Behavioral Research and Department of Sociology, Anthropology, and Criminology, University of Northern Iowa, advanced the book through his expertise in technology. David and Darla Kelly's help made possible the Africa trip.

Cass Paley, my friend of yesteryear, came and gave without taking. His gifts continue to give.

Contents

Preface

The more you know about something, the better off you are. It is good to know a lot about anything that comes your way and to have an inquiring mind. It is good to have an open mind about female circumcision, where the reaction of a Western person might be automatic horror and revulsion. One should hold back from that and read [this] whole book that will include the entire spectrum of things. Then have a realistic and balanced view of it.

Esther Kawira, M.D. F.A.A.F.P., Shirati, Tanzania[1]

As I wrote this book, I found myself on a journey that reminded me of the one I made when I wrote my first book *Power and Gender*.[2] Alice Walker and Pratibha Parmar, in their book *Warrior Marks: Female Genital Mutilation and Sexual Blinding of Women*, wrote:

I believe we are destined to meet the people who will support, guide, and nurture us on our life's journey, each of them appearing at the appropriate time, accompanying us at least part of the way. I think specific human beings, sometimes only in spirit, will present themselves in such a way that their presence will shape and reshape our hearts until we are more fully who we are ... we must adhere to our own peculiar way, that is the only chance we have to meet those spirits who wander along our road; we must persist in being true to our most individual soul.[3]

So it was for Alice Walker when she approached Pratibha Parmar about creating a film that also became a book. Walker says that she gained a new appreciation for the word "grief" and welcomed her readers to a hazardous journey, one "guaranteed to work the heart into a bolder shape."[4]

I invite you to journey with me as we relive stories told by spirits that wandered along my road and worked my heart into bolder shape.

Female genital mutilation (FGM) has received global attention and has been written about extensively. When we read about FGM, we find

1

that controversy abounds. Although FGM has been defined by the United Nations and there is no disagreement on its definitions, *what* to call it is vigorously debated. Scholars do not agree on the name for it, so the practice is referred to as mutilation, cutting, circumcision, excision, surgeries, or operations. I use the term *female genital cutting* (FGC) most frequently, but I cannot deny that my cultural bias makes me favor the term *female genital mutilation*, which is the most well known and commonly used term. The Inter-African Committee on Traditional Practices Affecting the Health of Women and Children (IAC), for example, adopted the term FGM in 1990 at a meeting in Addis Ababa, Ethiopia.[5] However when I interviewed members of cultures who practice the procedure, I found that they use the term *female circumcision*; therefore, so do I. I agree with Nahid Toubia, M.D., when she stated,

> Efforts to empower women cannot begin with using language that offends them.... We accept that the term female genital mutilation has been too widely used to be rolled back. In fact, we prefer to retain the term FGM at the policy level to remind everyone of the effect of this practice on girls and women. However, we advocate the use of the term female circumcision when dealing with affected individuals, parents, or other community members. Consider what an African woman may feel when a stranger asks her if she is "mutilated" or whether she plans to "mutilate" her daughter. It is important that we respect the feelings and beliefs of individuals even as we inform them of facts contrary to these beliefs.[6]

As I visited with Africans during my trip to Kenya and Tanzania, I used "circumcision," when I talked with the Maasai and others. However, professionals working with the issue preferred FGM but used cutting and circumcision as well. So in this book I will use whatever term is used by the source I am citing.

FGM occurs in many parts of the world, but most of it is found in Africa. FGM is a cultural practice thought to be centuries old, even though its origins appear to have been lost in the past. International efforts to eliminate it also have a long history. Christian missionaries and colonial administrations in Africa attempted to prevent the practice as early as the seventeenth century.[7] FGM was first mentioned in a resolution adopted by the United Nations Commission on Human Rights in 1952. Since then, it has remained an international concern.[8] Growing African activism against FGM has increased international awareness,[9] which caused the United Nations to assume an active role in the campaign to eliminate the practice.[10]

One contemporary view holds that FGM is psychologically, socially, and sexually harmful and that its effects are negative. Fran P. Hosken said that some Middle-Eastern and African women feel compelled by tradition to mutilate their own children so that they will be eligible for marriage, the only career option.[11] Hosken concluded that men controlling women goes on in every society, but the means of control vary. Mutilating the genitalia of female children alters their natural personality development and renders them subservient to men. When women say that "it is required by our traditions," the control over women is complete. Women have internalized the need.[12]

Challenge and change coexist with cultural tradition. Efforts to eradicate FGM are underway within and outside of practicing cultures. Why does the practice continue despite the efforts inside and outside of Africa to end it?[13] The answer is found by exploring African themes such as relationships, social codes, cultural and commercial customs, traditions, and proverbs.

Molefi Kete Asante said, "The critic's chief problem is finding a place to stand — so to speak — in relation to Western standards, imposed as interpretative measures on other cultures."[14] In this book I seek to explore the human condition and to recognize feeling, knowing, and acting. This book recorded the voices of African women and men and African authors involved in the debate and reached the conclusion that eliminating FGM is a social movement that is gaining momentum.

Related problems have surfaced in the United States; I addressed these briefly. Rigid concepts of gender established by sex have had a detrimental effect on how society responds to "intersexed individuals" (those with ambiguous genitalia). In far too many instances, pediatric genital surgeries were performed with the intention of having the patient conform to established definition of gender/sex.[15]

The practices of body cutting, tattooing, and piercing in the United States popular culture present provocative questions. Are they harmful cultural practices on a continuum with other practices such as private self-mutilation, transsexual surgery, and cosmetic surgery? Do they duplicate spiritual practices of other cultures?[16] Or are they merely lifestyle indicators or fashion accessories?[17] How fraught with medical concerns are they?[18] Sheila Jeffreys suggested that these harmful cultural practices are sought or carried out on groups, including women, who occupy a despised social status.[19] Not only does culture in the United States have its own controls over sexuality but, because of immigration, it must also assimilate other cultures' controls, such as those on FGM.

Recent controversy about FGM has a distinctly modern cast. Global communication and multinational corporations have brought an increase in migratory habits. Immigrants, refugees, and tourists intersect the world.

The first and third worlds no longer are distinctly separate. Current debate focuses on the nature of universal human rights. What are the rights of minorities and women? What is the meaning of and how workable is a multicultural society?[20]

Chapter 1, A Traditional Practice, focuses on the basics of understanding the practice. A discussion of the definition and types of FGM is followed by an exploration of the common justifications for the practice. An overview of the psycho-social-sexual effects is presented.

Chapter 2, Prevalence, co-authored by James C. Skaine, is critical to understanding the existence of the practice over time. A worldwide incidence overview reveals its increasingly global nature. Incidence in Africa and incidence by type are presented. Incidence in other countries makes FGM significant in matters of immigration.

Chapter 3, Globalism and Law, presents global laws, efforts by country, and practical issues. The laws of the United States are discussed. An examination of efforts in Canada and the Eastern world shows how extensive and global the issue has become.

Chapter 4, Legal and Practical Issues in the West, discusses nations in the West that legally ban FGC through examining the issues of definition, enforcement, and multicultural challenges. Medicalization is explored. A possible relationship between circumcision in other cultures and genital piercing and other forms of cosmetic surgeries in Western countries is also examined.

Chapter 5, Tradition and Change in Practicing Cultures, examines the debate versus the practice, rights versus rites, and religion versus tradition.

Chapter 6, Challenging the Change and the Challenge of Change, reminds us that even as understanding of FGM increases and as some programs meet with success, the practice continues. Ethical, political, and legal considerations continue to provide fuel for the debate, and there are continuing global efforts and growing unity within Africa to end FGM.

Chapter 7, The Maasai and Female Circumcision, contains interviews that I conducted when I visited the Maasai in Tanzania in 2004. The men talk about male circumcision and the women talk about female circumcision. Another interview with a Laibon, a traditional witch doctor, is featured. A government official explains efforts to build educational facilities for the Maasai.

Chapter 8, Meeting the Challenges in Tanzania, demonstrates firsthand how professionals and individuals are bringing progress through their programs. Featured are interviews conducted while I was in the Arusha, Kilimanjaro, and Mara regions of Tanzania in 2004.

Chapter 9, The Changing Status, analyzes the critical role of culture. The relationship of programs and changing attitudes is illustrated by Tostan, an excellent program that achieved its goal.

Chapter 10, A Compendium of Change, summarizes the concept of moving from tradition to social movement to social change to cultural evolution. In the evolutionary stage, strength lies in our reaching toward the ineffable.

1

A Traditional Practice

The destiny of Africa is intimately linked to the condition of its women. What we do affects us individually and collectively. Any initiative to move Africa forward economically, socially and democratically has to take into primary consideration the challenges women face as victims of harmful traditional practices.

> Mrs. Berhane Ras-Work
> President of Inter-African Committee[1]

Traditional practices passed down through the generations are common in Africa. Some practices affect women and girls negatively. One practice is female circumcision (FC), which has such negative effects that those who oppose it call it female genital mutilation (FGM). Not everyone agrees, however, that FGM is the most appropriate term to apply to this traditional practice.

DEFINITION

FGM "is the collective name given to several different traditional practices that involve the cutting of female genitals."[2] Other terms used to describe the practice are female circumcision, female surgeries, female traditional surgery, cutting, and excision. Which term to use is debated by scholars. Efua Dorkenoo believes that the use of different terms perpetuates much misinformation.[3] Kathleen Sheldon, an independent scholar with a research affiliation with the University of California at Los Angeles (UCLA) Center for the Study of Women, concludes, "'Mutilation' is clearly political, 'circumcision' inaccurate, FG 'surgeries' makes it sound medical.... I have opted for 'cutting,' in part following the suggestion of Claire Robertson and Stanlie James, friends of mine who have recently published a collection of articles on the topic."[4]

James and Robertson identify the difficulties specific terms pose. They believe that FGM suggests all alteration is mutilating and circumcision suggests a "false analogy" to the "more minor operation performed on men." The contributors to Robertson and James's book underscore the debate when they use terms such as female genital cutting (FGC), female genital surgeries, female genital operations, clitoridectomy, and pediatric genital surgeries.[5] Women who have undergone FC may be offended by the term FGM because they do not consider themselves to be mutilated.[6] Anika Rahman and Nahid Toubia found that the terms female circumcision and female genital cutting evolved out of respect and sensitivity to the women who never considered the procedure mutilation.[7] I am amenable to using different terms in specific contexts and will do so throughout the book.

TYPES OF FGM

The World Health Organization (WHO) groups FGM into four categories.

1. Type I, clitoridectomy, involves removing the prepuce with or without excision of part or all of the clitoris.
2. Type II, excision, removes the prepuce and clitoris together with partial or total excision of the labia minora.
3. Type III, infibulation, removes part or all of the external genitalia and stitches/narrows the vaginal opening. (In northwestern Nigeria, infibulation is often performed after a clitoridectomy.[8])
4. Type IV, unclassified, includes all other procedures such as pricking, piercing, or incising of the clitoris and/or labia; stretching of the clitoris and/or labia; cauterization by burning of the clitoris and surrounding tissue; scraping of tissue surrounding the vaginal orifice (angurya cuts) or cutting of the vagina (gishiri cuts); introduction of corrosive substances or herbs into the vagina to cause bleeding or for the purpose of tightening or narrowing it; and any other procedure that falls under the definition given above.[9] (See Figure 1.1.)

In Islamic culture, Type I is also called sunna ("tradition" in Arabic); Type II, clitoridectomy or excision, is called khafd ("reduction" in Arabic); and Type III or infibulation, is also known as "pharaonic circumcision" because it was thought to be practiced in Egypt during the Pharaoh dynasties (2850–525 B.C.)[10]

Figure 1.1— Female Genital Anatomy
as Affected by Female Genital Mutilation

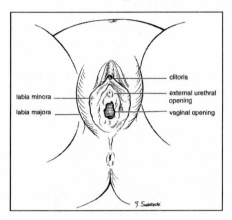
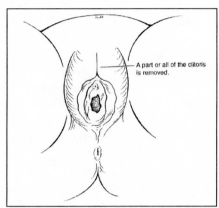

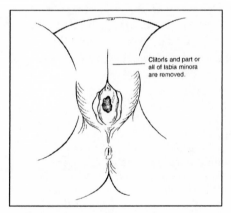
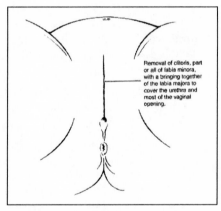

Top left: Normal female genital anatomy. **Top right:** Type I: Clitoridectomy. **Bottom left:** Type II: Excision. **Bottom right:** Type III: Infibulation. Used with permission of the American Academy of Pediatrics. Source: American Academy of Pediatrics, Committee on Bioethics, "Female Genital Mutilation," *Pediatrics* 102, no. 1 (July 1998):153–156. Available: http://pediatrics.aapublications.org/cgi/content/full/102/1/153. Accessed Feb. 4, 2004.

The word infibulation is derived from the Latin *fibula*. The Romans fastened a clasp or fibula through women's labia majora and men's prepuce to prevent sexual intercourse among slaves. Females could not bear children and brought a higher price on the slave market.[11] Infibulation is the most extreme form of FGM because it leaves only a small opening for the passing of urine and menstrual blood. WHO explains that "the opening is often preserved during healing by the insertion of a foreign body."[12]

The Inter-African Committee on Traditional Practices Affecting the Health of Women and Children (IAC) adds that pharaonic circumcision is also called Sudanese circumcision. IAC adds defibulation and re-infibulation as types of FGM. Defibulation is performed to allow intercourse or on a mother who is giving birth to enlarge the passage. According to IAC, the gishiri cut is performed when labor is prolonged. The traditional birth attendant cuts soft tissues with a knife to enlarge the vaginal orifice. The angurya cut is performed on infants to remove the hymen loop. This procedure is based on the belief that if the loop is not removed, it will continue to grow and seal the vaginal opening. Normally, the loop disappears a few weeks after birth. Re-infibulation is performed on women who have lost their infibulation. Young mothers after delivery or wives during a long absence from their husbands are re-infibulated.[13]

While we were traveling in Tanzania we interviewed Professor Patroba Ondiek, Ph.D., Program Coordinator for Save the Children of Tarime, (Sachita) Tarime, who has worked extensively with FGM. He has traveled in countries that performed Type III. He concludes that Type III is "the most terrible," and says it is done in Somalia, Mali, Nigeria, and Ethiopia. He observes, "This is too much. I do not know what they want this lady to do. Why did they do that? It's only for urine, that's all they have left."[14]

Rachel Carnegie, Consultant, United Nations Children's Fund (UNICEF) Eastern and Southern Africa Research Activities (ESARO), explained the suffering when Type III is performed:

> Sometimes the girl's legs are bound together for several weeks so that she cannot move, to allow the wound to close. If the vulva does not heal properly or the opening is thought to be too big, the girl may be operated on again. Later in life, the woman may need to be cut again in order to have sexual intercourse. When it comes to childbirth, she will need to be cut to allow the baby out.[15]

A study reported in 1999 highlights the relationship between type of FGC and the likelihood of associated complications. The study surveyed 21 clinics in rural Burkina Faso and four rural and four urban clinics in Mali. Ninety-three percent of the women in Burkina Faso and 94 percent in Mali had undergone cutting. In Burkina Faso about half had had a clitoridectomy, and in Mali about three-fourths had undergone excision. About five percent of both samples had undergone infibulation. Those women who were infibulated were almost two-and-a-half times more likely to have complications than those women who had excision or clitoridectomy.[16]

INSTRUMENTS AND PRACTITIONERS

The WHO summarized types of instruments as "special knives, scissors, razors, or pieces of glass. On rare occasions sharp stones are used, for example, in eastern Sudan, and cauterization (burning) is practised in some parts of Ethiopia. Fingernails have been used to pluck out the clitoris of babies in some areas in The Gambia."[17]

Traditional practitioners perform most but not all FGC procedures, according to the Population Reference Bureau. Traditional practitioners, birth attendants, midwives, barbers, and circumcisers usually have no medical training.[18]

In urban areas and some rural areas, the richer families use a qualified health professional to perform the circumcision. In these cases, FGC is done with anesthetics and antiseptics. This "medicalization" of FGC is condemned by the WHO and by medical associations.[19]

Karen Hughes summarized Fran P. Hosken's account of a case history in Somalia. Hughes stated:

> The child, completely naked, is made to sit on a low stool. Several women take hold of her and open her legs wide.... With her kitchen knife, the operator first pierces and slices open the hood of the clitoris. Then she begins to cut it out. While another woman wipes off the blood with a rag, the operator digs with her sharp fingernail a hole the length of the clitoris to detach and pull out the organ. The little girl, held down by the women helpers, screams in extreme pain....
>   The operator finishes this job by entirely pulling out the clitoris, cutting into the bone with her knife.... The operator then removes the remaining flesh, digging with her finger to remove any remnant of the clitoris among the flowing blood.... After a short moment, the woman takes the knife again and cuts off the inner lips (labia minora) of the victim.... Then, the operator, with a swift motion of her knife, begins to scrape the skin from the inside of the large lips.... With the abrasion of the skin completed, according to the rules, the operator closes the bleeding large lips and fixes them one against the other with long acacia thorns.... The operator's chief concern is to leave an opening no larger than a kernel of corn or just big enough to allow urine, and later the menstrual flow, to pass. The family honor depends on making the opening as small as possible because with the Somalis, the smaller the artificial passage is, the greater the value of the girl and the higher the brideprice.[20]

Efua Dorkenoo found that the instruments used and those who performed the procedure varied with the region. In urban areas, Western-trained medical practitioners performed procedures with anesthetics in hospitals or in their private offices. She concluded that there is no evi-

Female Genital Mutilation

Table 1.1
Person Who Performed Circumcision on Respondent

Percentage

Country and Year of Survey	Doctor or trained nurse/ midwife	Traditional birth attendant	Traditional circumciser	Some-one else	DK missing	Total
Sub-Saharan Africa						
Benin 2001	0.5	1.5	94.1	-	3.7	100
Burkina Faso 1998/99	0.6	0.2	86.3	0.8	12.2	100
Côte d'Ivoire 1998/99	0.4	-	46.7	47.1	-	94.2
Eritrea 1995	0.2	4	91	0	4.8	100
Guinea 1999	9.4	2.7	87.1	-	0.8	100
Mali 1995/96	2	5.5	82.2	0.1	10.2	100
Mauritania 2000/01	0.9	6	28.3	37.3	27.5	100
Niger 1998	2.6	7.9	-	87.1	2.4	100
Nigeria 1999	12.7	35.8	37.3	0.9	13.4	100
Sudan 1990	35.6	63.9	-	0.3	0.2	100
Tanzania 1996	3.6	8.6	74.2	7.4	6.2	100
North Africa/ West Asia/Europe						
Egypt 1995	17.3	61.8	-	19.2	1.7	100

Source: *Adapted from ORC Macro, 2003. MEASURE DHS+ STAT compiler. Available: http://www.measuredhs.com. Accessed December 18, 2003.*

Circumcised women by person who performed the operation: Among women who report being circumcised, the percent who reported they were circumcised by a doctor or trained nurse/midwife, a traditional birth attendant, a traditional circumciser, or by another person, according to background characteristics.

dence that the less-drastic procedures performed in this manner are "a first step" toward eradication of FGM.[21]

In the findings of the Population Reference Bureau and Demographic and Health Survey (DHS), (see Tables 1.1 and 1.2), Egypt had a greater medicalization, using nontraditional practitioners and medical professionals to perform FGC. The Bureau found Tanzania uses greater medicalization as well.

The Population Reference Bureau attributes the use of medicalization to the programs of the past 20 years that encouraged abandoning FGC by emphasizing the "health risk" or the "harmful traditional" nature of the practice and by using health professionals to deliver the health messages.[22]

Tribes in Mali used a saw-toothed knife. Some tribes in Sudan used a special razor with pieces of glass or scissors; some Eastern Sudanese used sharp stones. Some in parts of Ethiopia used cauterization and some in areas in Gambia used fingernails "to pluck out the clitoris of babies."[23]

In Tanzania, my interviews revealed that a common tool used is the razor.[24] Concern about spreading human immunodeficiency virus/acquired

Table 1.2
Person Who Performed Circumcision on Daughter(s)

Country and Year of Survey	Doctor or trained nurse/ midwife	Traditional birth attendant	Traditional circumciser	Some-one else	DK missing	Total
			Percentage			
Sub-Saharan Africa						
Benin 2001	0.4	1.4	97.8	-	0.4	100
Burkina Faso 1998/99	0.7	0.4	97	0.5	1.5	100
Côte d'Ivoire 1998/99	0.2	-	52.5	45.9	1.4	100
Eritrea 1995	0.6	3.7	95.3	0.1	0.2	100
Ethiopia 2000	0.9	6.4	92.4	-	0.4	100
Guinea 1999	26.9	3.6	69.1	-	0.5	100
Kenya 1998	34.4	11.9	50.3	0.3	3	100
Mali 1995/96	5.2	5.7	87.9	0.1	-	98.9
Mauritania 2000/01	3.2	9.4	34.6	52.4	0.5	100
Niger 1998	0.6	5.2	-	94.2	-	100
Nigeria 1999	33.1	28.8	36.7	0.9	0.6	100
Tanzania 1996	3.6	8.9	77.7	5.5	-	95.7
North Africa/ West Asia/Europe						
Egypt 1995	54.9	32	-	12.8	0.3	100
Egypt 2000	61.4	32.1	-	6.2	0.3	100
Yemen 1997	8.5	67.5	-	23.9	0.1	100

Source: Adapted from ORC Macro, 2003. MEASURE DHS+ STAT compiler. Available: http://www.measuredhs.com. Accessed December 17, 2003.

Circumcised daughters by person who performed the operation: Among daughters who were circumcised, the percent who were circumcised by a doctor or trained nurse/midwife, a traditional birth attendant, a traditional circumciser, or by another person, according to background characteristics.

immunodeficiency syndrome (HIV/AIDS) has caused groups such as the Maasai to use a different razor or knife for every girl in a group to be circumcised.[25]

A traditional circumciser, usually a woman, performs the procedure. The circumciser is often elderly and may have poor eyesight. Usually the girl is held down. Depending on the circumciser's skill and how much the girl struggles, the procedure may take up to 20 minutes. Poor lighting, unhygienic conditions, and crude tools cause the girl to suffer damage.[26] In Bunda District, Tanzania, the circumcisers are women, but they are not the mothers. Dr. Kebwe Stephen Kebwe, District Medical Officer (DMO) for Bunda and the Regional Chairman for Mara of the IAC, Tanzania, said, "If it happens that a mother is a circumciser, she can do it to the children of others, but not to her own. Just like men. There are men who are circumcisers. They circumcise the boys of other men, not their sons."[27]

AGE PERFORMED

FGC may be done in infancy, childhood, adolescence, at the time of marriage, or during the first pregnancy. FGC is most commonly performed between the ages of four and twelve. Carnegie found that the average age is trending younger and concluded that the link is weakening between FGC and initiation into adulthood. This weakening may be because of concerns about legislation against the practice and because some older girls are refusing and running away.[28] My visit with the head teacher at the Esilalei Primary School for the Maasai in the Monduli District of Tanzania substantiated Carnegie's findings. The teacher said that they are finding education is a deterring resource for girls. Education helps them avoid getting circumcised.[29]

The statistics compiled by the DHS show a similar age range when FGC was performed. (See Table 1.3 and Table 1.4.) The median age range FGC was performed on the respondent was 0 to 12.9 years. Women who had the experience of being cut in the zero year (the first year of life) were residents of Ivory Coast, Eritrea, and Nigeria. (See Table 1.3.) The age range FGC was performed on the respondents' daughter was between 0 and 10.6 years. Women who reported that their daughters had the experi-

Table 1.3
Median Age at Circumcision
Among Respondents Circumcised

Country and Year of Survey Sub-Saharan Africa	Median age — years
Benin 2001	7.2
Burkina Faso 1998/99	6.3
CAR 1994/95	10.8
Côte d'Ivoire 1998/99	0
Eritrea 1995	0
Guinea 1999	9.3
Kenya 1998	12.9
Mali 1995/96	5.1
Mauritania 2000/01	0
Niger 1998	5.8
Nigeria 1999	0
Tanzania 1996	12.2
North Africa/West Asia/Europe	
Egypt 1995	9.8

Source: Adapted from ORC Macro, 2003. MEASURE DHS+ STAT compiler. Available: http://www.measuredhs.com. Accessed December 18, 2003.

Table 1.4
Median Age at Circumcision
Among Daughters Circumcised

Country and Year of Survey Sub-Saharan Africa	Median age — years
Benin 2001	6.9
Burkina Faso 1998/99	4.3
Côte d'Ivoire 1998/99	4.9
Eritrea 1995	0
Ethiopia 2000	0
Guinea 1999	7.4
Kenya 1998	10.6
Mali 1995/96	1.9
Mauritania 2000/01	0
Niger 1998	4.7
Nigeria 1999	0
Tanzania 1996	9.4
North Africa/ West Asia/Europe	
Egypt 1995	9.8
Egypt 2000	10
Yemen 1997	0

Source: Adapted from ORC Macro, 2003. MEASURE DHS+ STAT compiler. Available: http://www.measuredhs.com. Accessed December 18, 2003.

ence of being cut at zero years were residents of Eritrea, Ethiopia, Mauritania, Nigeria, and Yemen. These results could occur because of the mass programs to abandon FGC. (See Table 1.4.)

In parts of Sudan where FGM is an entrenched tradition, it is performed early enough to leave time for a proper marriage. Aban Laamatjok, who is from Malakal in south Sudan and is now residing in Nebraska, said:

> The surgery is performed between the ages four to eight, because they think the ages like ten and eleven is very late. So they try to do it earlier. In Sudan, especially in the Muslim communities, most of the young ladies get married early, maybe twelve or fourteen. Then they have to be ready before she gets married, because you will never hear that there is some lady that got married first and did surgery later.[30]

FGM appears to occur at earlier ages also because of parental views and the motives of uncircumcised women. Parents wish to reduce the trauma to their children, avoid government interference, and avoid resistance from their children as they get older. Uncircumcised young adult women may undergo the procedure when they marry into a community that practices it or after the birth of their first child.[31]

So how did this controversial practice, a practice that is not difficult to define but is elusive in the terminology used, begin? How and when FGC began is still debated.

ORIGIN

Differing opinions abound concerning the origins of FGM, but the existence of ancient records could lead to the conclusion that what is known today as FGM did indeed precede even the most early accounts. Scholars and physicians differ as to which groups, ethnicities, and religions first practiced FC and when. The practice predates Christianity and Islam.[32]

The British Museum houses a Greek papyrus dated 163 B.C. that mentions girls in Egypt being circumcised when they received their dowries. In 25 B.C., the Greek geographer Strabo reported circumcision of males and excision of females in Egypt. Herodotus, a Greek historian, reported FC in Egypt in the fifth century B.C. He believed the custom originated in Ethiopia or Egypt, but it was also practiced by the Phoenicians and Hittites.[33] Philo also reported that women at age 14 were circumcised with the onset of the menstrual flow.[34]

The early documents suggest the practice of FC began in Egypt, but there are no engravings indicating its existence.[35] Fran P. Hosken wrote that archaeologists found well-preserved mummies that established clitoridectomy and infibulation had occurred.[36]

The accounts of historian Pietro Bembo, posthumously published in 1550, reported that most likely FC originated in Egypt and the Nile valley, then spread out to the Red Sea coastal tribes with Arab traders, and then spread into eastern Sudan. In the eighteenth century various travelers reported the practice on slave girls taken by slave traders along the Nile.[37]

Hanny Lightfoot-Klein wrote that the historical resources and anthropological findings leave us with not much more than speculation as to how FC began and whether there was one or more places of origin. She suggested the reasons for the practice were population control, primitive man's desire to "gain mastery over the mystery of female sexual function" a reduction of the woman's sexual desire and to keep her monogamous when the early patriarchal family system allowed women one husband and allowed the male many wives, and the Egyptian pharaonic belief in the bisexuality of the gods. The masculine soul of a woman was believed to be situated in the clitoris and the feminine soul of a man was located in the prepuce. A girl is fully a woman and capable of sexual life after circumcision. In order for a girl in ancient Egypt to marry, inherit property, or enter a mosque, she had to be circumcised.[38]

Bettina Shell-Duncan and Ylva Hernlund offer an alternative perspective that emphasizes behaviors that limit fertility as adaptive.[39] Hanny Lightfoot-Klein illustrated this idea with the example that water-poor areas such as Darfur in Sudan could not support even the smallest population increase. Thus, she believes infibulation could have arisen from a serious need for population control that developed because of drought and desertization of previously fertile areas.[40]

Dr. Nawal M. Nour, Director of the African Women's Health Center, wrote that although the origins of FGC are a mystery, the tradition "transcends religion, socioeconomic status, and geography.... The practice survives today, reinforced by customs and beliefs regarding ensuring marriageability, rites of passage, maintaining girls' chastity, hygiene, preserving fertility, and enhancing sexual pleasure."[41]

REASONS

The WHO reported that the reasons for FGM fall into four categories: socio-cultural, hygienic and aesthetic, spiritual and religious, and psychosexual. Socio-cultural reasons include: A girl will not become a mature person unless her clitoris is removed; a woman's external genitalia has the power to blind birth attendants; it can cause the death or physical or mental deformity of the infant; it can cause the death of the husband; removal ensures virginity, a prerequisite for marriage and access to land and security; it allows ceremonial celebrations; it ensures acceptance into the group; and the powerful excisor has strong influence.[42]

Hygienic and aesthetic reasons include: The external genitalia are ugly and dirty and they will continue to grow; and circumcision is linked to spiritual purity and makes the girl beautiful. Spiritual and religious reasons are found in some societies.[43]

Rahman and Toubia wrote that the reasons are complex, related, and interwoven into the beliefs and values of the communities. They said they can explain FGC/FGM, but it is dependent on an entire belief system, not a single factor. They described the four most common justifications for the practice:

1. The custom and tradition of becoming a woman involves this "rite of passage" from childhood to adulthood.
2. The need to control women's sexuality.

3. A cultural practice that sometimes has a religious identification.
4. Social conformity to the community.[44]

Laurenti Magesa placed the rationale for male and female circumcision in historical context. Most African ethnic groups impress the lesson of the concern for life physically on the initiate's body at least once in a lifetime. Others do it symbolically at each time of crisis in life. For those experiencing it as a one-time event, it is the most intense and concentrated moment in the initiation process. Usually, some sort of surgery is done and is "always deliberately intensely painful."[45] Magesa noted the description of the girls' operation among Gikuyu people from Jomo Kenyatta's book *Facing Mount Kenya*. The girls are well prepared by their sponsors. They seek to minimize bleeding. The girls are not to show emotion or fear, lest they be a disgrace to themselves. The girls must be stoic. When the procedure is completed, a ritual takes place representing a celebration of courage, the purpose for inflicting pain.[46] The ritual is described:

> When this preparation is finished, a woman specialist, known as *moruithia*, who has studied this form of surgery from childhood, dashes out of the crowd, dressed in a very peculiar way, with her face painted with white and black ochre. This disguise tends to make her look rather terrifying, with her rhythmic movement accompanied by the rattles tied to her legs. She takes out from her pocket (*mondo*) the operating Gikuyu razor (*rwenji*), and in quick movements ... proceeds to operate upon the girls. With a stroke she cuts off the tip of the clitoris (*rong'otho*).[47]

After the ceremony, the Gikuyu sing while the initiates remain stoic.

Magesa's findings among Bambuti are that the initiates had ordeals beyond the circumcision. Often they were beaten and made to run while still unhealed from the surgery. They could not express emotion or they were whipped more. Magesa found water was withheld from Thonga initiates. In addition, they were served distasteful food and received blows for little reason.[48]

The reasoning for the behavior toward the youth is multifaceted. First, if boys and girls do not have courage, the clan's life force withers and eventually dies. If the young men are not brave, who will defend the people? If the mother cannot bear the pain of childbirth, will there be live births? Second, the pain is to teach self-giving for the sake of the community. Third, the procedure is to tell the initiate to know oneself and that to appreciate the worth of others demands self-denial and suffering. In groups where expression of pain is permitted, even to enjoy pleasure, some suffering is inevitable. Magesa explained, "This is why, then, that in many cases the surgery is performed on the sexual organs or parts of the body that are generally very sensitive, on the one hand and, on the other, are associated in one way or another with fertility."[49] Finally, the operation establishes the identity as a member of the ethnic group and unites the youth with ancestors. Unity is also a product among the initiates because they mingled and shared their blood through the initiation knife or because they shed their blood at the same time.

Magesa found that, among the Zaramo, an initiation ceremony is not conducted and females' period of seclusion is longer, taking from one to three years. During seclusion, instruction is given in fertility, in discipline and cooperation, and in communion and solidarity with the ancestors and the clan.[50]

During healing or afterwards, the last stage of the formal initiation process takes place. The reintegration of the initiates into society signifies physical and moral maturity and approval of the clan's ancestors and ethnic group. They are now part of the community whose entire purpose is to maintain and further life. Integration means they are ready to get married and have children. They have been taught readiness verbally and symbolically during the initiation; thus, they have completed their rite of passage.[51]

Dr. Esther Kawira is the Medical Officer in Charge in the Shirati Kanisa la Mennonite Tanzania (KMT) Hospital, the Swahili name for the Mennonite Church in Tanzania. During her visits to Hargeisa in Somaliland, on two different occasions, she learned specifically about the topic of female cutting.[52] Kawira views infibulation as likely having a different origin and purpose than what Magesa refers to in his book as FC.[53] Kawira wrote:

> Infibulation creates a "chastity belt" of skin. This is not done in the other forms of circumcision. Therefore, the reason given in Magesa's book, as a rite of passage for a young person to prove that they can stand pain without flinching, would not seem to me to be the same in infibulation. Infibulation could be done under anesthesia, and the culture would still be satisfied, because the chastity belt had been created. Perhaps it was usually done without anesthesia, just because traditionally no anesthesia was available. I have heard of it being done in hospitals, under anesthesia, in some current cases.[54]

Kawira related an incident regarding anesthesia that she learned from another doctor currently in OB/GYN training in Boston:

> The doctor tries to do reconstruction of the genitalia and to uncover any remaining stump of the amputated clitoris. But if the woman originally had infibulation done under anesthesia, usually it was done very

thoroughly and nothing is left, whereas those who did not have anesthesia wiggled and resisted, and often ended up not having such a
thorough job done. That also points out that it is done on resisting
girls, not on older ones who are supposed to prove their bravery by
not flinching.[55]

Emmanuel Babatunde believes that cultural practices endure because
they make sense to the cultures' members.[56] Colleen Renk Zengotitabengoa, a staff attorney at the Tahirih Justice Center, finds it intellectually
interesting to think about the role of women and the role of men. She said:

> Men represent the public sphere of politics and economics; and
> women and their bodies represent the private sphere, the family,
> social, the society, the culture, the cultural mores, all of that. FGM is
> just one aspect of a way in which men can require a woman to submit
> to a certain practice, or to dress a certain way, or to act a certain way
> because, if she doesn't, then somehow, she, individually, is letting
> down the culture whereas men are not at all confined by these restric-
> tive cultural practices and norms. It is an interesting intersection
> between public and private sphere and how women are forced by men
> and by their societies and almost the entire world to conform to these
> practices, because if they don't, somehow that means that society has
> broken down and that culture has broken down. It's just a fascinating
> comparison.[57]

Mary E. Laiser, Head of the Women's Department of the Arusha Diocese of the Evangelical Lutheran Church in Tanzania (ELCT) believes that
FGM has been used as "first, a tool to discriminate against women and
second, as a tool to control women's sexuality. A woman could not be married until she was mutilated. It was also expected that she could have less
sexual desires, hence remain loyal to her marital relationship."[58] Laiser
added that most elderly men believe FGM secures marital bonds because
a mutilated woman has no desire for multiple sexual partners.[59]

Cindy M. Little wrote that "it is usually African women, not men, who
insist on circumcising their daughters."[60] She believes the ritual is an
important affirmation of the authority one generation of women has over
another.

Laiser said another reason they circumcise is they have ceremonies,
big ceremonies at which they drink and eat a lot, especially for the girls
and also for the families. So sometimes Laiser's program workers ask them,
"Why do you celebrate? On the other hand, you injure somebody. Is that
a celebration really if some[one] is crying inside and bleeding to death
and here you are outside, dancing and eating and drinking a little brew?"
Laiser said to us, "It's amazing, isn't it?"[61] Laiser added:

We asked them that question but they don't understand because they are that level of people as far as FGM is concerned. The other problem which I have seen myself is ignorance. The people are not aware of the dangers of female genital mutilation. Women are mostly ignorant compared to men because traditionally women are denied the right to education. They favor boys' education more than women's. So they just undergo the operation without knowing what they are putting themselves in.[62]

Kawira said that although some assert that circumcision somehow makes a woman more faithful to her husband,

It might do the reverse as far as making women think that men don't care about them, don't care about them having undergone this pain, or don't care that wives are sexually handicapped as a result. Men and women start out unequal already in the area of sexual relations. Women's sexual response is slower than men's to begin with and circumcision is giving her an added handicap. If you're talking about mutual fulfillment in sex, circumcision would make it much harder for a woman to reach orgasm or for a man to produce that in his partner. In fact, I wasn't sure myself, if a circumcised woman, at least one who had the clitoris removed, actually reached orgasm. A person I talked to said that a circumcised woman can have orgasm but it is much less likely and it takes a lot longer. So, it seems that one effect would be that women would have an inherent dissatisfaction (or even anger) because she knows it has been done to her by a man or by the male society. It would make her and women collectively feel that men didn't care about them, didn't care about what was happening to them, as long as they got their own satisfaction. Over time at least, the effect might be to diminish what we hope would be the natural affection across the genders and make it more difficult, instead of at least starting out the way we were created physically and hoping that the affection can increase over time.[63]

Tribal myths justify circumcision to distinguish the sex of a child, according to Leonard J. Kouba and Judith Muasher. The Dogon and Bambara of Mali believe that when a child is born, it has two souls, male and female, and it is inhabited by an evil power, "Wanzo." They believe, "The boy's 'female soul' is in the prepuce, the female element of the genitals, and the girl's 'male soul' is in the clitoris, the male element."[64] The Wanzo prevents fertility. The prepuce and clitoris are seats of the Wanzo and must be cut off to destroy that power of Wanzo.

Kebwe listed the reasons for circumcision as: It is a rite of passage to adulthood; it enables marriage; and it allows that girl to be much more marketable and to be accepted by the society. He explained that anyone can go to see a circumcised woman officially and talk to her rather than going to someone who is uncircumcised. A circumcised woman stimulates men much more than one who is uncircumcised, and circumcision reduces sexual acts as well as prevents promiscuity. Kebwe added other reasons. One is:

> They believe that, because of the big lips, unfortunately some ladies will get vaginitis because of the bacterial infection or fungal infection, even *trichomoniasis vaginalis*, and then with vaginalis comes itching. They believe with circumcision they are going to eliminate the itching.... Another aspect is they believe that this is one way of making the vagina much more clean. So, they are trying to get cleanness of the vagina. Circumcision is one of their hygienic measures. They also believe that by doing circumcision they are going to increase their fertility. Circumcision is going to make easier the delivery process. Childbirth is going to be much easier. On the contrary, whether there is complication, people do differ. People get cut, they don't have enough [pain] killers. They don't excessively bleed from massive cuts, but some of the women have complications from the [pain] killers. Some of them say this is part of the [pain] killer's mission and they go with the therapy. More important, some of them, they get very severe or extensive tears during delivery. They can get up to third degree tears. Yes, tears of the whole perineum up to the rectum including the sphincter. A very severe tear for some of the girls.[65]

Kebwe added that a very small group of people believe that by being circumcised, they are minimizing the chance of getting tetanus. He says, "Quite the contrary. Some of the men get infected with tetanus after circumcision. Cases have been seen and documented. It is a complication.[66]

Kebwe said that still another reason they circumcise is their motive of gain. The parents get money and presents, the circumciser gets money and the girl gets presents. He said, "The one who feels he is so then can not fear and as one of the strong persons of that society. For some of the people, there is a very bit of pain."[67]

Kebwe said another reason is about the men. He explained:

> Because they still have quite a big say in society, they believe that this is part and parcel of whereby men still have the role. Men in our society still have the final say in the family. Girls are coming now, it is better, in some of the family issues, but mainly men are the ones who make the decisions. So, it is still believed that one of the men's role[s] is to make sure they are shaping the society, the family, the children. So they must be shaped by men who are head of the households.[68]

Sometimes reasons for circumcision take medical professionals by surprise. John Wachira, M.D., a urologist who practices medicine in Kenya, Uganda, Tanzania, and parts of Somalia, said:

> As a urologist, I see the results, usually long after the procedure has been done. I have seen all types, including the most severe form as

done in Somalia. There is one group in Tanzania that circumcises infant girls at about three months of age. I was very surprised when I discovered this. They believe it helps to prevent some childhood diseases. It is here that I treated two small girls who had urethral strictures as a result.[69]

EFFECTS ON WOMEN'S HEALTH

Dorkenoo contends that cutting is not medically necessary, produces great pain, and is extremely dangerous. The suffering of many girls and women is sometimes forgotten in the intellectualized discussions of FGM.[70]

Consequences often include scarring, infertility, painful sexual intercourse, rupture of the vaginal walls, long and obstructed labor, chronic uterine and vaginal infections, bladder incontinence, dysmenorrhea, and obstruction of the flow of menstrual blood. Childbirth presents a possible increase in the risks of maternal death, stillbirths, hemorrhage, and infection.[71] According to the Program for Appropriate Technology in Health (PATH), "the highest maternal and infant mortality rates are in FGM-practicing regions."[72] Although the precise number of girls who die from undergoing FGM is not known, estimates in areas in Sudan are that one-third of the girls will die because antibiotics are not available.

Shell-Duncan and Hernlund maintain that long-term complications occur more often with infibulation. They refer to short- and long-term complications as a laundry list that is repeated in nearly all literature with little attention given to the original sources of the information, that is, medical observations of British colonial surgeons and gynecologists of the 1930s and 1940s.[73]

Charles Henry Sweke, M.D., C.I., Ord., Ph.D., a consultant and obstetrician and gynecologist at Selian Lutheran Hospital in Arusha, Tanzania, very often sees the complications of circumcisions. Complications can present an opportunity for the health professional to educate the woman and her relatives.

> These circumcisions very often cause problems especially during labor and pregnancy. It causes some obstruction of labor.... It is a cause for a fistula, but not a direct cause of fistula in a woman but indirect.... I say indirect especially in those circumcisions which are performed in a terrible way. During the healing processes, there are such terrible scars. So these scars during delivery cause some obstruction in the woman, and, if she doesn't get to be here [at the Clinic], she will get terrible tears and lose a lot of blood. Losing a lot of blood makes this woman in danger. She can either die or she can have the baby die before being delivered. So, it is something which has so many compli-

cations. When they come with these complications, that's when we have the opportunity to tell them. I'm sure these people who brought their close relative with those complications, have grieving to bear. We contribute a little bit in trying to help these people spread it to other people but in a limited manner. So, in fact, we see it very often.[74]

Laiser grouped the complications into three categories: immediate, long-term, and psycho-sexual and psychological problems. She discussed the immediate complications and why they occur:

Right when the operation is being done, there is severe pain because they don't use anesthesia so that you don't feel pain. Because if you are cut and there is no anesthetic that is applied, then you go into shock. Also you hemorrhage, you bleed a lot because of the cutting and there is tetanus or sepsis. When they cut, they don't even know the anatomy of a woman's body. The people who do the operation are people who are not educated enough. They don't even know the body. They just find out by using their fingers and nails so they just hold it and cut it without knowing what they are doing. In fact, at the place where they operate, there are lots of nerves, so when they cut they damage these nerves, because they don't know what they are doing. There is also the problem of urine retention. When you talk to the circumcised, [they tell you that] the pain causes them to retain urine. They don't urinate freely because of the pain.[75]

The second group involves the long-term complications, said Laiser:

After the operation, it doesn't heal and then there are lots of things which happen later after the operation, such as cysts and keloids, which are protruding scar tissue. There is also damage to the urethra causing urinary incontinence and pain during urination. There is also pain during sexual intercourse. There is a problem of urinary tract infection (UTI) and also infertility is a possibility. Some get fistulas, which happen in the woman because of the scar. This is the result of delayed labor and happens between the vagina and the urethra. The other fistula happens between the rectum wall and the vagina wall. A person suffers leakage of urine and leakage of feces. The whole of her life is a big problem. There are problems during child birth. The nurses tell there are multiple tears when they deliver, because now there is a scar, the birth does not come normally and results in multiple tears. The women are repaired and they can go for four months without full recovery. The recovery is very, very slow. And do not forget HIV and AIDS because of the instruments they use. They share instruments. A lot of people share. They ask, "What if we don't share instruments?" Then we tell them, "No, we are not just concerned about sharing instruments, we don't want FGM to continue."[76]

Kawira said that in Shirati, the group of people among whom she works, the Luo people, have not traditionally circumcised anyone, male or female. However, there are groups or subtribes around Shirati that do practice it. Every couple of years Kawira hears of circumcision ceremonies taking place in the area. She shared the effects she sees at the Shirati KMT Hospital:

> Occasionally, a girl will be admitted to the hospital when she is felt to have excessive bleeding. They will bring her in for some kind of homeostasis [stoppage of bleeding] whether suturing or some kind of treatment. Or if they think, in fact, maybe she needs a blood transfusion as a result of having lost what is thought to be a large amount of blood. Those are the medical complications that I've seen of the form of circumcision here, which, according to the WHO list you had, I would call Type II in which the clitoris is excised, as kind of an elliptical incision excising the clitoris and maybe some of the skin on each side. That wound is not normally sutured. It is left to heal by itself, which normally results in a rather thin vertical scar in the place where the clitoris was. This Type II form doesn't affect so much the elasticity of the birth canal, of the vaginal opening at the time of birth. Although in some of the groups maybe more tissue is taken off and it creates a rigidity anteriorly that can split during childbirth when the opening is stretched. So sometimes it can do that, but the more severe form, where the whole opening is stitched shut, is not done here, and so that would not prove an impediment in childbirth here in Tanzania as it can be in places where it is practiced.[77]

FGM has serious health consequences when it involves extensive cutting or removal of parts of the genitalia and when it is performed with unsterilized instruments, without anesthesia, and by inexpert individuals. It produces excruciating pain, hemorrhage, tetanus, septicemia, and even death.[78] More recently, concern has arisen over the possible transmission of HIV when one instrument is used to perform multiple operations.[79]

Girls who have gone through cutting are at risk of complications that last throughout their lifetimes. Nour wrote that the extended kinds of complications are determined by "the severity of the procedure, the practitioner's skill, the instruments used, and the postoperative care."[80]

The WHO reports that Type III causes a direct mechanical barrier to delivery and Types I, II, and IV can cause severe scarring that causes an obstruction during delivery. If infection is present at the time of the procedure in Types I and II, possible vulval adhesions can form that narrow or obstruct the vaginal opening and make labor long. The herbal pessaries used in Type IV and the use of rock salt after earlier pregnancies to reduce the vagina may result in severe scarring and stenosis.[81]

M. Neil Williams, M.D., is a general surgeon who served at the Selian Lutheran Hospital in Arusha, Tanzania, in 1998, 1999, and 2000. He knows firsthand some of the health effects of FC. Williams said that he saw Types

I and II. I asked him what some of the effects are on the health of the women who have had the procedure. He answered:

> Of course, I know some of the health effects. The results of the circumcision vary from woman to woman; by that I mean how well it is done, how much tissue is removed, that can vary. If it is just removing the clitoris, there is not too much scarring or problem with it. But some of the women I have seen come in with the clitoris and some of the labia, upper part of the labia, gone, too, and all of that area is fibrous tissue or scar tissue, which narrows the vaginal opening and interferes with delivery, with childbirth. It makes childbirth more difficult.[82]

I asked if the women are prone to more infections or anything of that nature. He responded, "I never saw in my three terms over there any women who were brought to the hospital with infection following circumcision, although we did see it in men."[83]

When asked if women are at any disadvantage to disease as life goes on, because they have had this done, Williams replied that he didn't think so.

I told him that some authors who have written on the subject have said women who have had the procedure are subject to more UTIs and other infections and asked what he found among his patients in Tanzania. He said:

> The women I saw did not seem to have damage to the urethral opening. I don't know if — I guess that would be hard to evaluate — urinary infections are more common or not. I've never seen female circumcision done. In fact, I have never seen a male circumcision done in Tanzania. I've read a lot about it. I've just seen the results in women that I have examined in pelvic examinations. To me, it was interesting to see the wide range of results. What I mean by that is, in some women, the clitoris is gone but that's all. There is very little alteration. In some women you can hardly tell that anything was done and they said that it had been done. In others, it is very disfiguring.[84]

Williams explained that the procedure varies from tribe to tribe and from place to place in Africa. In the Arusha region in Tanzania, he learned and observed that "They use a razor, that's what they usually use. It is mostly clitoridectomy that I saw. Maybe some of the upper labia. Here again, it does vary."[85] I asked whether anesthesia was used. He said, "They just cut them. The women will scream and carry on and this is expected. In the male, they can't even blink an eye. If they do then the whole family is ostracized."[86]

Diana Kiremi, a young woman of the Il-Purko section, is not typical of the Maasai in Kajiado District, Kenya, her birthplace. She is an expert on the life of Maasai women. She described her circumcision as

... carried out with less fuss than it would have been in a traditional *enkang* [whole enclosure that surrounds the livestock and the Maasai homes]. Her head was shaved in the normal way, but then, instead of being the center of attention of all the women of her family and clan, a relative slipped quietly into her house one night and performed a swift, unceremonious operation with a razor blade. Unlike the boys, no stoic silence is expected of girls, and Diana screamed for all she was worth.[87]

Psycho-social-sexual Effects

Amna A.R. Hassan's study in Sudan analyzed psycho-social-sexual effects of FGM.[88] The WHO stated that FGM may leave lasting psychological effects on women. They may feel incomplete and have anxiety and depression.[89]

PATH found that women's sexuality has not been widely studied. In 1981, however, a University of Khartoum study interviewed 1,545 Sudanese women. Fifty percent of those who underwent the procedure said they did not enjoy sex at all and accepted it as a duty. In 1993, the United Nations Population Fund (UNFPA) conducted a study on Sudanese women. UNFPA found that 5.5 percent of women interviewed experienced painful intercourse and 9.3 percent reported having difficult or impossible penetration.[90]

The Research, Action, and Information Network for Bodily Integrity of Women (RAINBO) found that infibulated women may have difficulties performing sexual intercourse. A young bride may be too shy to discuss the problems. Some women are so traumatized by the circumcision that they hesitate to touch their genitals even for cleaning. This hesitation carries over into a lack of desire for sexual contact after marriage. RAINBO stresses that a loving and caring partner can help a woman overcome these feelings and achieve sexual satisfaction.[91]

The WHO identified the psycho-sexual reasons for FC as: The unexcised girl is believed to have an overactive and uncontrollable sex drive and will thus be a menace to all because the uncut clitoris grows big and puts pressure on this organ; the tightness or narrowing of the vaginal orifice enhances male pleasure and in turn divorce or unfaithfulness is prevented; and if a woman fails to conceive, excising will solve the problem of infertility.[92]

The roles family play are important for why the procedure is performed and how it affects the female's social-sexual construction. Because of lessened sexual desire, a woman will maintain her chastity and virginity before marriage, maintain her faithfulness during marriage, and increase male pleasure. Community roles also play an important part. The procedure is an identification with the cultural heritage and is an initiation into womanhood. It provides social integration and the maintenance of social cohesion.[93]

Laiser believes there are psycho-sexual and psychological problems for circumcised women:

> There are problems with sexual attractions and in intimate relations that leave a lasting mark in the life and mind of the woman who has undergone it. I read this book; the author was explaining her sad story. She told how she was psychologically affected and that she is angry about what has happened to her. She called that woman [circumciser] a vulture. She wanted to kill her. So, these problems would follow a person through her entire life. With the psychological complications, schools are involved. I said to a woman, "You are angry about the whole issue and you are angry about the community, about your family. Why did they allow that to happen to you? There is a loss of trust and confidence. You feel incompleteness. You get anxiety and trauma if you are not counseled or if you don't meet other people who console you, so that you let go. You feel suffering the whole of your life, and you just feel that you are not complete. You feel that you are different."[94]

Laiser added that there is another issue, the cyclical nature of poverty:

> Poverty is an issue because money is being used unnecessarily to pay the person who operates on the girls. The other problem is that the circumcised girl gets sick and so they go to the hospital to treat her as a person who has had an accident, but it was not an accident; it was just done to them. So it causes poverty in the family. The money which would have been used for other purposes is used to treat a person who is not necessary to be in that situation.[95]

Hulda, Laiser's co-worker in the Women's Department of the Diocese, added more on how circumcision contributes to poverty:

> They make their celebrations a very big deal. They use a lot of money instead of educating their children, taking their children to school, by using the money for the celebration. We find ladies coming to this office seeking money to take their children to school, but they have money to spend for these celebrations. So, I want the schools to introduce health education and teach both men and women, girls and boys, plainly the effects of circumcision and the advantages of the other side, of not being circumcised. If both men and women know the good of not being circumcised, they will learn what Mary Laiser is emphasizing in this war of FGM and this practice will be abolished completely. So, my need is to introduce this education on circumcision to girls and boys and for men to say no to circumcision and girls to say no to circumcision. It comes down to a family issue on circumcision, to encouraging the health facilities in the villages and trying to give them

strong lessons on this issue and encouraging the leaders not to. This health education is to be introduced widely in every place.[96]

EQUALITY AND FEMALE GENITAL CUTTING

The broader issues of equality of women include FGC and are very important, stated Lisa Johnson-Firth, Director of Legal Services at the Tahirih Justice Center in Falls Church, Virginia:

> [Female genital cutting] is a very visible symptom of the inequality of women. When looking at it, we always need to be brought back to, how did something like this come about, what was the origin of it, and what other things in our society can we look at to see the gross inequality of women and then, as a rule, or generally, how can we work to raise the status of women generally so that we are not dealing with FGM, we don't have women's sexuality curtailed when they're too young to even understand what that is, or that women are getting equal pay in the United States or they're not feeling like they need to have breast augmentation to be a whole human being. All of these issues, I see them as interlinked, and you can draw upon this one, but the bigger picture is, it is only one symptom among hundreds. Even to look at this in isolation from other symptoms like the fact that in many other countries that you've traveled to, these women are living in the depths of poverty and dealing with husbands who may be alcoholics or who take all the family money and spend it at the bar or on prostitutes, would be to miss the bigger picture. This concept that FGC is one symptom, a very important one, but it's one of this broader issue of women's status needs to be raised on whole.[97]

RELIGION AND FEMALE GENITAL MUTILATION

Although some argue that religious beliefs are connected to the practice of FGM, Laiser does not agree, "There is no religion that requires this practice to be done. Neither the Holy Qur'an nor Holy Bible prescribes it. In fact in Tanzania, religious organizations are among the active actors campaigning to eliminate the practice."[98]

Hulda said, "What we want to believe is, for Christian families, the opposition to circumcision is a bit easier than for non-Christians."[99]

Laiser believes that traditions are stronger than people's faith, regardless of what religious belief people practice:

The problem with culture and tradition is that they are stronger than the faith itself. Sometimes I think if only they go out strong in their faith and like the way they are stronger than their tradition, then a lot of things would be easier. But the traditions are stronger. They are very, very strong even in Christian families because the problem with our families' setting is the extended family and also clan families. All the settings have leaders and they have their constitution, even though it is not written but they have it in their minds. So they sit down and discuss, what do we do with this? They put groups in classes to meet with the families. This extended family and clan family all have leaders. The leaders decide what is to be done in their particular families. So it is not an easy thing to let go of traditions because, even if they are Christian, there is this clan whereby the clan leaders sit out there and decide for their families. It has happened to a few families who are Christian but who are also lucky to have an extended family who are Christian and at the same time went to school. If they went to school and are Christian, the percentage who do not circumcise is higher. In most people, the traditions are stronger than their faith.[100]

The reasons given for continuing FGM are evolving. It is not apparent that it is primarily a religious practice, although some do believe that it is a religious practice. Wachira's views of the reasons for the practice of FGM in Africa tie the past to the present and explain the relationship between culture and African religion:

At present, the reasons are purely cultural, not connected with any present-day religion. It is done as part of the culture, or in the name of preserving culture. In the distant past, African religion and culture were not separate.

In my own tribal group, the Kikuyu, there were four important life stages, namely birth, initiation into adulthood, marriage, and death. Circumcision was done as a rite of preparation for adulthood, and having it done was a sign that one had become an adult.

Not all groups in Africa do circumcision, not even of males. But when children began attending boarding schools, they were with others from various tribes. Among boys, some who were not circumcised were teased by their peers, or even by boys younger than they, that they were still little kids. So this led to some of them having it done in a medical setting, not as part of their own tribe's tradition. So, one could call these modern cultural reasons, rather than historical cultural reasons.

Some girls missed being circumcised because they were away at boarding school during the time when their peers were going through it.

Reasons that are often given now for female circumcision, namely to decrease promiscuity or increase faithfulness of women to one husband, were not there in the beginning. The original reason, as I said, was as a rite of passage to adulthood. Some blood had to be shed, and not just from any part of the body, but from a very sensitive part.

Now, the whole adulthood initiation has lost direction. Only a few tribal groups still do the initiation ceremonies. But many groups still hang on [to] female circumcision for what I see as cultural reasons, in the name of "not losing our culture," without even thinking about what the original reasons might have been.[101]

CHANGES IN FEMALE CIRCUMCISION

Dr. Esther Kawira believes that life is very complex and it is good to know as much as possible, because circumcision is not a single issue. Like many things in life, it is very complex. She explained:

> You see something which seems to be harmful to women and yet women are the ones who do it. The women are the ones who perpetrate it and girls run away from their parents in order to have it done as if they're disobeying an order not to get their ears pierced or something. It seems that the girl would know that this is not the same thing as piercing your ears. Then there must be a lot more going on. Some of the reading that I've done has suggested how it is a small part, though maybe the most memorable part, because of the pain, but a small part of initiation ceremonies in which a person changes from a child into a responsible adult. If anybody is trying to change that, they have to consider all the other things. If you say don't circumcise, does that mean don't do anything to help young people grow up into responsible adults? What are you putting in its place? That all has to be considered. In each place that it is done, the issues are different. What it means to those people is different and so it has to be addressed on a case-by-case basis, area-by-area basis, based on what people believe about it, why they think it is, and how strongly they feel about having it continue.[102]

Kawira said that we know historically that there was foot binding of women in China and asked in what ways would this be parallel and the battle against this be parallel. She reasoned, "When Christianity and missionaries came to China, they were opposed to it and tried to work against foot binding. How did it go out? There might have been some religious influence, but it might have also been modernity. When they came into contact with the modern world, women realized that it wasn't done in much of the rest of the world. In fact, they were being looked down upon for that in some sense."

Kawira said that she learned from her colleague, Kebwe, that various groups are working to eliminate circumcision. Among those groups are the Seventh Day Adventist Church. This church is very strong and well known in Tanzania. This and other Christian denominations believe the body is sacred. God made us a certain way, and we shouldn't destroy any part of it. The body as God's Temple is the basis of their opposition to circumcision, said Kawira.[103] She said that the practice is widespread in Islamic areas:

> The people where the extreme form is done are mostly in Islamic countries. They tend to think there is something in their religion that prescribes it. But, in fact, Islam doesn't promote it either, it just happens to be that way in some Islamic countries. Those who really know Islam, know there is nothing in Islam that requires this to be done to women. I am wondering if it is mixed up in those places, it's not so much a historical tradition as somehow mixed up as part of their religion by now that they think it needs to be done to be a good Muslim.[104]

Kawira said that a person does not have to be a Christian in the West to oppose circumcision. People worldwide oppose it on humanitarian religious grounds. She said she asks herself, "Now what is it? Am I just against this because I'm a woman and I can imagine how painful it is? Christianity would honor the integrity and the health of the human body, and that would be in that category, just as we try to get people not to damage their bodies through additions or any kinds and substances that would harm the body physically."[105]

MEDICALIZATION OF CUTTING: NIGERIA, AN EXAMPLE

The Population Reference Bureau reports an increase in the use of medical professionals in some countries to perform FGC. This discouraging trend represents a growing recognition of health risks and heightened concern for HIV transmission. Egypt, Kenya, Mali, and Sudan, for example, are experiencing a trend for medicalization.[106] Mairo Usman Mandara wrote, "... a central question remains: Should medical practitioners intervene to prevent the medical complications that may arise from female 'circumcision?'"[107] Those individuals opposing circumcision believe medicalization will institutionalize the procedure and undermine efforts to eliminate it. People who practice circumcision are heard but not seen. African medical practitioners' views have not been heard widely.

Mandara's research at Ahmadu Bello University Teaching Hospital in Nigeria demonstrates that the practice is becoming increasingly medicalized. Twenty percent of the doctors believed that medical treatment should be given during the period of transition while they gradually try to change attitudes. Most opposed medicalization, but those who supported it believed it ethical to minimize pain and prevent complications. The majority of medical doctors supported the 1996 position of the WHO and, Mandara concludes, would regard medicalization as unethical.[108] WHO advocated, "A major effort is needed to prevent the 'medicalization' of all forms of FGM."[109] The WHO holds the position that willful damage to healthy organs for nontherapeutic reasons "violates the injunction to 'do no harm' and is unethical by any standards."[110]

Kawira said that medicalization apparently is done for health reasons and perhaps to be more humane. Some scholars believe that medicalization is a step away from circumcision and a step toward not doing circumcision at all. Kawira agreed, "Yes, it is a step towards not doing it at all, for females anyway. For males, the debate continues as to whether or not there are medical benefits (less cancer of the penis, less urinary tract infection, less HIV transmission, etc.) to warrant continuing it, albeit in a medical setting."[111]

Wachira lends his support for the idea of medicalization of circumcision, at least for the more minor type:

> Rather than trying to fight female circumcision directly and totally, it would make more sense, rationally, to promote "medicalization" of female circumcision. One doesn't have to just totally oppose minor cutting that would produce bleeding. It could still be done as a cultural rite, for girls to prove to their peers and to adults that they are brave, strong, and can stand pain (if that is indeed part of the reason they even escape from their parents or schools to have it done nowadays). But it should be done in a safe sterile manner, as a relatively minor cut of the labia rather than cutting off of the clitoris or labia.[112]

OTHER PRACTICES OF GENITAL CUTTING

As late as the 1930s in the United States and Europe, removal of the clitoris or prepuce was done to treat clitoral enlargement, redundancy hysteria, lesbianism, and erotomania.[113] PATH points out, "Until the 1950s, FGM was performed in England and the United States as a common 'treatment' for lesbianism, masturbation, hysteria, epilepsy, and other so-called 'female deviances'."[114]

CONCERNS ABOUT MALE CIRCUMCISION

Although Wachira agrees that some of the immediate effects of FC are pain, bleeding, and a chance of infection (including HIV infection) if it is done in an unsterile manner, he believes, "Long-term effects in the milder types of female circumcision are few, as far as things requiring surgical correction. Actually, I see and treat many more complications related to male circumcision than to female circumcision."[115]

Sweke believes that in Tanzania, FC is not done as a medical procedure but circumcision for men is done in hospitals in a good way. He said:

> [Male circumcision] is also in our program and is to encourage these people [to do it sanitarily], because they do it themselves even for boys. Just look at it, it is a terrible thing for both the girls and men because circumcision with knives, especially nowadays, with having this HIV-AIDS, is a big problem, because they use only one knife for all of them. So if one of them is infected, you can just imagine how they spread this disease. HIV-AIDS is one of those spreading diseases for both men and women. So, for boys, we encourage them to come and do it in the hospital. Some are coming. We are doing circumcisions for men, but we don't do it for women, because we are completely against that. So, they don't even bring a single girl because they know we won't do it. So it is done only traditionally. And this is done with the most ineffective training. When HIV/AIDS started, at first it was thought it was just a disease which occurred in town for prostitutes and now we find that even in the village [where] you are not having prostitution at all, but just simply because of circumcision when it is done using a single knife for all and they do it in groups.[116]

CONCLUSION

Reasons for the practice of FC have evolved from when they were first noted on a Greek papyrus dated 163 B.C. No religion requires this practice. Cultural reasons often are given for performing it. In early times, religion and culture may have been one and the same. PATH found that today the most common reason given is the belief that it is a good tradition. Even though many reasons exist for the practice, Laiser maintains the main reason is ignorance. Tradition and culture dictate that women should marry rather than be educated. The education of boys is given higher priority than that of girls. The result is a higher illiteracy rate for women than men.[117] Regardless, when the practice is performed, health side effects are many and are often devastating. A practice done in secret without anesthesia and under unsanitary conditions by a circumciser is sometimes now performed openly using anesthetics in sterile conditions by medical professionals. Increasingly, the practice is being abandoned or changed. The change has resulted, in part, from the fear of HIV/AIDS, one of the most deadly side effects. There is also a change in moving to less severe types and in the age at which it is done. On the horizon is more change away from the practice.

2

Prevalence

with JAMES C. SKAINE

As a woman I have no country. As a woman my country is the whole world.

Virginia Woolf[1]

WORLDWIDE INCIDENCE OVERVIEW

In 2000, the World Health Organization (WHO) profiled the prevalence and distribution of female genital mutilation (FGM), which includes female genital cutting (FGC) and female circumcision (FC). The number of girls and women who have undergone FGM is estimated to be between 100 and 140 million. Each year an estimated two million more girls will have the procedure. WHO estimated that most of the girls and women who have experienced FGM live in twenty-eight African countries, but it occurs in many places other than Africa, including Western Asia, minority communities in other Asian countries, and the Middle East.[2] FGM is also practiced in a few ethnic groups in Yemen, India, Indonesia, Israel, Malaysia, Oman, Saudi Arabia, and Pakistan.[3] In increasing numbers, FGM is found in Europe, Australia, Canada, New Zealand, and the United States, primarily among immigrants from the countries in which it is practiced.[4] (See Figure 2.1.)

In 2001, WHO updated the estimated prevalence of FC/FGM. The update reflected that most of the girls and women who have experienced FGM live in twenty-eight African countries. They noted that their information came from a variety of sources of varying quality and they organized it according to the reliability of estimates.[5] (See Figure 2.2.)(See Table 2.1.)

Figure 2.1— Countries Where FGM Is Found

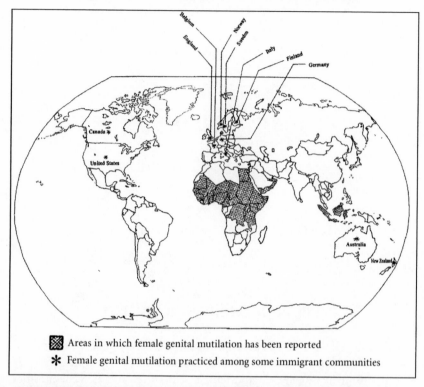

Areas of the world in which Female Genital Mutilation has been reported to occur. (Map by Christopher M. Schulte, with permission from WHO Department of Health Information Management and Dissemination.) Source: WHO, 1997, "FGM — A Joint WHO/UNICEF/UNFPA Statement," 6.

Table 2.1
United Nations Estimated Prevalence Rates for Female Genital Mutilation, updated May 2001
Most reliable estimates: national surveys*

Country	Prevalence %	Yr. of Survey	Country	Prevalence %	Yr. of Survey
Burkina Faso	72	1998–99	Niger	5	1998
C. African Rep.	43	1994–95	Nigeria	25	1999
Côte d'Ivoire	43	1994	Somalia	96–100	1982–93
Egypt	97	1995	Sudan	89	1989–90
Eritrea	95	1995	Tanzania	18	1996
Guinea	99	1999	Togo	12	1996
Kenya	38	1998	Yemen	23	1997
Mali	94	1995–96			

Other estimates

Country	Prevalence Percentage	Year[♦]	Source
Benin	50	1993	National Committee study, unpublished[1,2]
Chad	60	1991	UNICEF sponsored study, unpublished[1,2]
Ethiopia	85	1985; 1990	Ministry of Health study sponsored by UNICEF; Inter-African Committee study[2]
Gambia	80	1985	study[1,2]
Ghana	30*	1986; 1987	two studies[1,2] on different regions; divergent findings
Liberia	60**	1984	unpublished study[1,2]
Senegal	20	1990	national study[1,2]
Sierra Leone	90	1987	Koso-Thomas O. *The circumcision of women: a strategy for eradication.* London, Zed Press, 1987.

*Anecdotal Estimates****

Country	Prevalence Percentage	Source
Cameroon	20	[1,2]
Democratic Republic of the Congo	5	[1,2]
Djibouti	98	[1,2]
Guinea-Bissau	50	[1,2]
Mauritania****	25	[1,2]
Uganda	5	[1,2]

Source: World Health Organization, 2001. Available: http://www.who.int/docstore/frh-whd/FGM /FGM%20prev%20update.html. Accessed June 8, 2004.

1. Toubia, N. 1993. Female Genital Mutilation: A Call for Global Action *(http://www.rainbo. org)*. *(Some figures are unpdated in the 1996 Arabic version of the document.)*

2. World Health Organization. 1998. *"Female Genital Mutilation. An Overview."*

3. Obermeyer, C. M. 1999. *"Female Genital Surgeries: The Known, the Unknown, and the Unknowable."* Medical Anthropology Quarterly; 13(1):79–106.* *One study found prevalences ranging from 75 to 100% among ethnic groups in the north; another study in the south found FGM only among migrants; the 30% comes from reference 1.*

Source for all above estimates, with the exception of Somalia and Togo: National Demographic and Health Surveys (DHS), available Macro International Inc., Calverton, Maryland. Available: http://www.measuredhs.int. For Somalia, the estimate comes from a 1983 national survey by the Ministry of Health, Fertility and Family Planning in Urban Somalia, 1983, Ministry of Health, Mogadishu and Westinghouse. The survey found a prevalence of 96%. Five other surveys, carried out between 1982 and 1993 on diverse populations found prevalences of 99–100%. Details about these sources can be found in reference #3 below. For Togo, the source is a national survey carried out by the Unité de Recherche Démographique (URD) in 1996 (The unpublished report is Agounke E, Janssens M, Vignikin K, "Prévalence et facteurs socio-économiques de l'excision au Togo, rapport provisoire," Lomé, June 1996. Results are given in Locoh T. 1998. "Pratiques, opinions et attitudes en matière d'excision en Afrique." Population 6: 1227–1240.

♦Year refers to the year of the survey, except for Somalia, where years refer to the publication date of the MOH report. Note that some DHS reports are dated a year after the survey itself.

**A limited survey found that all but three groups practice FGM, and estimated prevalence at 50–70%; the 60% comes from reference 1.

***These estimates are based on anecdotal evidence. They are cited in references 1 and 2 above.

****A national survey has carried out by the DHS and the report is forthcoming.

Note: For published studies year refers to year of publication. For unpublished studies, it is not always clear whether year refers to the year of the report or the year of the survey. Where no year is indicated, the information is not available.

Figure 2.2 — Estimated Prevalence (in Percent) of FGM Among Female Populations in African Countries

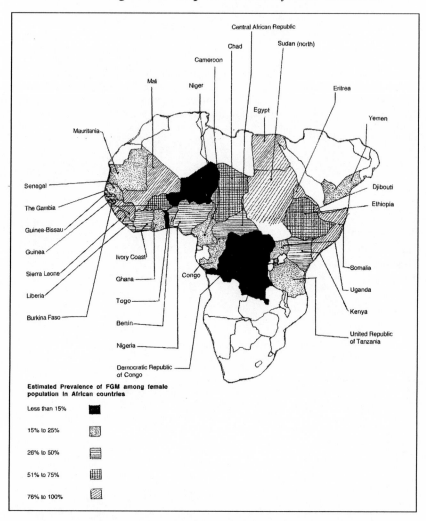

Map by Christopher M. Schulte. Estimates are from the following sources: Toubia Nahid. *A Technical Manual for Health Care Providers: Caring for Women with Circumcision.* New York: RAINBO, 1999, p. 25. U.S. Department of State, Office of the Senior Coordinator for International Women's Issues, Office of the Under Secretary for Global Affairs. "Chart: Overview of Practice of Female Genital Mutilation," Sec. K., Feb. 1, 2001. Updated June 27, 2001. Available: http://www.state.gov/g/wi/rls/rep/9305.htm. Accessed Apr. 20, 2004. World Health Organization "Female Genital Mutilation: A Teacher's Guide," Geneva, WHO/FCH/GWH/01.3; WHO/RHR/01.16, 2001. Accessed June 22, 2004. Available: www.who.int/frh-whd. World Health Organization "United Nations Estimated Prevalence Rates for FGM," updated May 2001. Available: http://www.who.int/docstore/frh-whd/FGM/FGM%20prev%20update.html. Accessed June 8, 2004.

Amnesty International stated, "There are no figures to indicate how common FGM is in Asia. It has been reported among Muslim populations in Indonesia, Sri Lanka and Malaysia, although very little is known about the practice in these countries. In India, a small Muslim sect, the Daudi Bohra, practice clitoridectomy. In the Middle East, FGM is practiced in Egypt, Oman, Yemen and the United Arab Emirates."[6] Data for Asian countries are not included in U.N. Demographic and Health Survey (DHS).

In 2000, the DHS reported that in Egypt, 97 percent of 15,648 women among ever-married women aged fifteen to forty-nine had been circumcised. The survey found 78 percent of the daughters aged eleven to nineteen of the women surveyed had been circumcised. In Yemen, 23 percent of women who have ever been married have undergone FGM, according to a United States Agency for International Development (USAID)-funded 1997 Demographic and Maternal and Child Health Survey.[7] (See Appendix 1.)

The U.S. State Department believes that incidence is small or information is not available for Malaysia, Oman, Saudi Arabia, Israel, Pakistan, or the United Arab Emirates; therefore, their report does not discuss further these countries. The Department reports that FGM "occurs in some Middle Eastern countries: Egypt, the Republic of Yemen (primarily coastal areas), Oman (in limited numbers throughout Oman but more widespread in the southern coastal region), Saudi Arabia (among a few immigrant women and among some Bedouin tribes and residents of the Hejaz), and Israel (among a very small number of women in a few Bedouin groups in the south)."[8]

The U.S. State Department reports that where FGM occurs in some Muslim groups in Indonesia, the most common form is a symbolic pricking, scraping, or touching of the clitoris. A relatively large study in Indonesia released in 2003 provided more insight. The study covered several major ethnic groups from the western to the eastern parts of the country. The study surveyed 1,694 households and found that 97.5 percent of the girls had been circumcised.[9]

The findings indicated in part that Muslim communities support the continuation of the practice of FC. They perceive it as both a societal custom or tradition and a religious duty. Extensive medicalization of FC has begun in some parts of the country and has been established in "Padang (92 percent of 349 observed cases) and Padang Pariaman (69 percent of 323 observed cases) and there is an increasing tendency towards medicalization in Kutai Kertanegara (21 percent of 215 observed cases), Sumenep in Madura island (18 percent of 275 observed cases), and Serang (14.5 percent out of 344 observed cases)."[10]

Indonesia practices two types of FC. The symbolic type accounts for about 28 percent of all the cases of FC in the study. There are two harmful forms involving incision (49 percent) and excision (22 percent). Findings showed that parents and religious leaders viewed FC as a tradition. Findings did not reveal any clear immediate or long-term physical or psychological complications for girls or women.[11]

The Indonesian study showed that midwives tended to perform more invasive forms of FC, such as more incision and excision in sixty-eight to 88 percent of cases, compared to forty-three to 67 percent by traditional providers.[12]

The report found no evidence that girls who were circumcised were damaged or that it is done without consent or without health benefits or religious mandate. It is classified as a violation of the rights of the child as stated under the Convention on the Rights of the Child, ratified by Indonesia in 1990.[13]

FC is reported by medical professionals to be practiced by a very small number of Malay Muslims in rural areas in Malaysia. It resembles a symbolic prick or a tiny ritual cut to the clitoris, or the blade is simply brought close to the clitoris. It also occurs to a small extent among the Bohra Muslims in the largest cities of Sindh and Punjab provinces in Pakistan.[14]

The Center for Reproductive Rights (CRR) reported sporadic practice in some nations in the Middle East and in a few ethnic groups in India and Sri Lanka.[15]

FGM is reported to be practiced in all Western African countries. The United Nations reports that prevalence rates range from five percent of the women in Niger to 94 percent in Mali. At least half of all women have had the procedure in the majority of surveyed countries. The DHS conducted in 1995 show that in Eastern Africa some countries have a prevalence rate near or above 90 percent. In Central Africa, available data revealed rates ranging from five percent in the Democratic Republic of Congo to 60 percent in Chad. In Egypt, 97 percent of the women have undergone the procedure.[16]

The CRR found that FC/FGM is prevalent in "about 28 African countries and among a few minority groups in Asia."[17] In African countries prevalence varies widely from approximately five percent in the Democratic Republic of Congo (former Zaire) and Uganda to 98 percent in Somalia. Many immigrant women in Europe, Canada, and the United States have undergone this practice. Estimates are that 15 percent of all women who have had the procedure have undergone the most severe form, infibulation. This form includes the stitching and narrowing of the vagi-

nal opening. Infibulation accounts for about 80 to 90 percent of all procedures in Djibouti, Somalia, and Sudan.[18]

Baseline Information, 1990s

In 1995, the Egyptian DHS showed that 97 percent of women had
undergone some form of FGM. Not much was known about the severity
of the procedure or the accuracy of women's self-reporting. A clinic-based
study revealed some of the missing information. The study was conducted
by the Egyptian Fertility Care Society, with support from Macro International and the Population Council's Asia and Near East Operations
Research Project.[19]

The study found that Egyptian women accurately report their FGM
status with a 94-percent agreement between medical examination and self-
reporting. Results also showed that the practice varies widely. "Sixty percent of the 1,339 women studied had both the clitoris and labia minora
partially or completely removed, while 24 percent had either their clitoris
or labia minora removed. Nine percent had the most severe form of FGM,
infibulation. The study found that a woman's type of FGM does not depend
on her sociodemographic group."[20]

The Egyptian DHS showed "support was widespread for the practice,
and 92 percent of women with daughters said their daughters were or
would be circumcised. Of the eight percent of women with daughters who
said they would not have their daughters' genitalia excised, more than 40
percent cited medical complications as the reason."[21]

In West Africa, surveys conducted since 1990 found 94 percent of
women aged 15 to 49 in Mali, 43 percent in Côte d'Ivoire, 72 percent in
Northern Ghana, and 20 percent in Senegal have undergone the practice. The age for FGM varies. Most girls are excised before age ten, but
in Mali 44 percent of girls undergo circumcision before they are one year
old.[22]

One DHS indicated that women's attitudes are a factor. (See Table
2.2.) The data do not include all countries where FGC is practiced. In the
fifteen countries reported, the belief of whether the practice of FGC should
continue ranges from a low of 3.4 percent in Benin to a high of 81.6 percent in Egypt. Thus, all women do not believe that the practice should continue, but many do.

The U. S. Population Reference Bureau points out striking contrasts
in some countries between high prevalence and low approval for the practice. (See Table 2.3.) In Burkina Faso, 72 percent of women ages 15 to 49
have undergone FGC, but only 18 percent approve of the procedure. Twelve

Table 2.2
Percent of Women Who Report the Practice of
Female Circumcision Should Continue — by Age Groups

Country and Year of Survey								
Sub-Saharan	*Age in 5-year intervals*							
Africa	*15–19*	*20–24*	*25–29*	*30–34*	*35–39*	*40–44*	*45–49*	*Total*
Benin 2001	4.2	4.0	2.5	2.7	2.6	4.4	3.2	3.4
Burkina Faso 1998/99	18.2	17.2	20	17.2	16.9	17.1	21.2	18.1
CAR 1994/95	27.6	30.6	30.2	30.5	30.2	31.2	35.5	30.2
Ivory Coast 1998/99	25.8	27.2	25.3	29.2	32.5	31.6	38.0	28.4
Eritrea 1995	40.9	49.0	59.0	60.9	68.2	66.6	71.2	56.8
Ethiopia 2000	53.4	57.0	58.5	65.2	63.6	66.3	66.7	59.7
Guinea 1999	60.5	65.7	72.1	69.9	70.7	72.8	71.5	68.3
Kenya 1998	20.6	19.5	20.2	17.1	19.4	20.5	21.9	19.8
Mali 1995/96	70.0	75.9	78.2	77.0	76.9	75.4	74.7	75.3
Mauritania 2000/01	58.0	59.9	61.7	59.2	54.1	62.7	60.8	59.4
Niger 1998	7.3	8.1	9.6	9.9	9.4	10.5	11.5	9
Nigeria 1999	6.3	13.2	15.4	19.2	17.5	22.3	29.9	15.4
Sudan 1990	77.1	74.4	76.7	78.9	81.2	82.2	81.3	78.5
North Africa/ West Asia/Europe								
Egypt 1995	84.8	83.9	81.7	79.2	81.3	80.8	82.2	81.6
Yemen 1991/92	22.2	20.1	21.2	20.5	20	21.9	21.2	20.9
Yemen 1997	17.5	22.3	19.2	20.2	22.5	20.8	23.4	20.8

Source: Adapted from ORC Macro, 2004. MEASURE DHS STAT compiler. Available: http://www.measuredhs.com. Accessed August 1, 2004.

percent do not know whether FGC should be continued. Eritrea has a similar picture. Ninety-five percent have been cut, yet only 57 percent approve of the practice.[23]

Attitudes are more consistent with the high prevalence of the practice in Egypt and Sudan. In Egypt in 1995, 97 percent had been cut and 82 percent approved of the practice. Approval declined to 75 percent in 2000. In north Sudan, 89 percent have been cut and 79 percent support FGC.[24]

Younger women are more likely to oppose the practice, which indicates that they have not been circumcised and perhaps will not sustain the African cultural context of FGC. In most of the surveyed countries, women ages 20 to 24 show greater support for ending FGC. However, results in Mali showed little difference among younger and older women's views toward FGC. (See Table 2.4.) In Eritrea, 47 percent of women ages 20 to 24 support the end of FGC compared with 26 percent of women 45 to 49.

Table 2.3
Women Who Have Undergone Female Circumcision and Who Approve or Disapprove of the Practice

| | *Percent of women ages 15–49* | | |
Country	*Have undergone circumcision*	*Approve of circumcision*	*Disapprove of circumcision*
Burkina Faso	72	18	57
Egypt	97	82	13
Eritrea	95	57	38
Kenya	38	20	73
Sudan	89	79	21

Source: *Adapted from Figure 6, U.S. Population Reference Bureau,* Abandoning Female Genital Cutting, *Aug. 2001, p. 12.*

Table 2.4
Older and Younger Women Who Oppose Female Circumcision

| | *Percent of women* | |
Country	*Ages 45–49*	*Ages 20–24*
Burkina Faso	52	59
Central African Republic	49	57
Egypt	13	11
Eritrea	26	47
Kenya	69	76
Mali	11	13
Sudan	19	26
Yemen	47	46

Source: *Adapted from Figure 7, U.S. Population Reference Bureau,* Abandoning Female Genital Cutting, *Aug. 2001, p. 12.*

Moderate to high disapproval is expressed by younger women in Burkina Faso, the Central African Republic (CAR), and Kenya. In Sudan, younger women express greater opposition. According to the Population Reference Bureau, this finding suggests "that younger generations may have greater access to anti-FGC information and are less influenced by tradition."[25]

The data for Egypt shown in Table 2.4 are from the 1995 DHS, but an Egypt DHS study and a nationally representative 1999 survey of adolescents found there may be signs of attitude change. The national study surveyed 1,500 adolescents; 1,200 were girls and 300 were boys. Egyptian daughters were at least 10 percentage points less likely to undergo FGC than were their mothers. The survey also showed that daughters whose mothers had higher education levels were 34 percent less likely to undergo FGC than those daughters with mothers who had been to vocational school and 64 percent less likely with mothers who had a secondary education or higher. The national survey is further supported by the findings from the Egypt DHS, which show a six-percentage-point decline in the proportion of women with daughters who report that they had a daughter who was already cut or who planned to have a daughter cut, from 87 percent in 1995 to 81 percent in 2000.[26]

The prevalence of FGC of women with at least one living daughter in 14 African and one Asian countries shows Mali with the highest percentage of 73.6 and Benin with the lowest at 6.2 percent.[27] (See Table 2.5.) The attitudes vary considerably among women who have had one or more of their daughters circumcised. Three countries— Egypt, Mali, and Sudan — show women who have had one or more daughters circumcised to be highly supportive. In Kenya and Eritrea, about two-thirds approve and in Burkina Faso, only 28 percent of mothers in this category approve.[28]

Other indicators of whether the African cultural context will be sustained can be examined by residence, educational level, religion, and harmful effects of FGC. The Population Reference Bureau found that in all of the countries surveyed, lower approval exists for FGC among women in urban areas. This suggests that living in an urban area provides greater access to education and diverse ideas and practices.[29]

Table 2.5
Percentage of Women with at Least
One Daughter Circumcised

Country Sub-Saharan Africa	Percentage
Benin 2001	6.2
Burkina Faso 1998/99	39.8
Cote d'Ivoire 1998/99	24.4
Eritrea 1995	71.4
Ethiopia 2000	47.8
Guinea 1999	53.9
Kenya 1998	11.3
Mali 1995/96	73.6
Mauritania 2000/01	66
Niger 1998	4
Nigeria 1999	20.2
Sudan 1990	25.7
Tanzania 1996	6.7
North Africa/West Asia/Europe	
Egypt 1995	49.7
Egypt 2000	49.4
Yemen 1997	19.7

Source: ORC Macro, 2003. MEASURE DHS+ STATcompiler. Available: http://www.measuredhs.com. Accessed December 18, 2003.

Table 2.6
Attitudes Toward Female Circumcision of
Women Who Have Had at
Least One Daughter Circumcised

Country	Percent of women ages 20–39 Approve	Disapprove	Don't Know
Burkina Faso	28	59	12
Egypt	92	4	4
Eritrea	69	27	3
Kenya	61	37	2
Mali	83	10	8
Sudan	91	9	—

Source: *Adapted from Figure 12, U.S. Population Reference Bureau,* Abandoning Female Genital Cutting, *Aug. 2001, p. 16.*

Table 2.7
Women Who Support Female Circumcision
by Urban or Rural Residence

Country	Percent of women ages 15–49 Urban	Rural
Burkina Faso	11	20
CAR	26	34
Egypt	63	85
Eritrea	36	67
Kenya	12	22
Mali	65	80
Sudan	72	82
Yemen	32	46

Source: *Adapted from Figure 8, U.S. Population Reference Bureau,* Abandoning Female Genital Cutting, *Aug. 2001, p. 14.*

Egypt, Mali, and Sudan have high national approval for FGC, but there are disparities in the attitudes between urban and rural dwellers. In Egypt, 63 percent of urban women approve compared to more than 85 percent of rural women. Mali and Sudan have similar results: More rural than urban women approve the practice. (See Table 2.7.)

In Eritrea, an even wider gap in attitude exists between urban women with 36 percent and rural women with 67 percent approving of FGC. Burkina Faso has a higher prevalence rate in urban than in rural areas, but 11 percent of urban women support FGC compared to 20 percent of the rural women. (See Table 2.8.) The Population Reference Bureau concluded, "It appears that social pressure to comply with the practice is high, but attitudes are changing."[30]

Table 2.8
Women's Attitudes Toward Female Circumcision
by Urban or Rural Residence, Burkina Faso and Eritrea

| | *Urban* | | | *Rural* | | |
Country	*Undergone cutting*	*Approve cutting*	*Total*	*Undergone cutting*	*Approve cutting*	*Total*
Burkina Faso	82	11	72	70	20	18
Eritrea	93	36	95	95	67	57

Percent of women ages 15–49

Source: *Adapted from Figure 9, U.S. Population Reference Bureau,* Abandoning Female Genital Cutting, *Aug. 2001, p. 14.*

Women with a secondary education show high levels of disapproval for FGC in half of the countries surveyed, according to the Population Reference Bureau.[31] Results in Eritrea, Kenya, CAR, and Burkina Faso showed 80 to 90 percent of women with a secondary education oppose FGC. Results in Sudan, Egypt, Mali, and Yemen show that only 45 to 63 percent of the more educated women oppose the practice. (See Table 2.9.)

RELATIONSHIP OF INCIDENCE IN AFRICA AND ASIA TO INDUSTRIALIZED NATIONS OVERVIEW

Anika Rahman and Nahid Toubia wrote that as recently as the 1950s, physicians in the United States and the United Kingdom performed FC/FGM to "'treat' hysteria, lesbianism, masturbation and other so-called 'female deviations.'"[32] Although little data are available, African immigrant communities in Europe, Canada, Australia, and the United States also show women who have undergone the procedure. Judicial cases in France lend some documented evidence; otherwise no systematic records have been located. Rahman and Toubia listed in their compilation of country sections what they refer to as "existing sporadic and incomplete data." (See Appendix 3.)

Several governments in Africa and in industrialized nations have taken steps to eliminate the practice of FC/FGM in their countries. Even though these steps reflect change, the question arises whether these steps affect incidence. Do the penalties invoked serve to discourage the inclination to perform the practice?

The probability is high that immigrants from the Asian and African

Table 2.9

Women Who Oppose Female Circumcision Level of Education

Percent of women ages 15–49

Country	None	Primary	Secondary
Burkina Faso	53	70	90
CAR	47	59	84
Egypt	11	18	47
Eritrea	24	61	80
Kenya	56	72	83
Mali	9	17	47
Sudan	18	16	45
Yemen	47	46	63

Source: *Adapted from Figure 10, U.S. Population Reference Bureau,* Abandoning Female Genital Cutting, *Aug. 2001, p. 15.*

countries who practice FC/FGM will carry the practice over to industrialized nations.[33] Probability is also high that the female immigrants will have had the procedure and, thus, increases in the number of women or girls in the receiving industrialized country who have had the procedure can be expected. The overview of industrialized countries in Appendix 3 indicates, for the most part, that the two authors found that either enforcement information is not available or no known investigations, arrests, or prosecutions have occurred.[34] In the United States there were no prosecutions under criminal law as of 2003. In Australia, a case of child abuse was heard in Magistrates Court in Melbourne in December of 1993. Action was brought against a father of two girls who were infibulated. Information on the outcome is unavailable.[35] France had twenty cases involving the practice that have been successfully prosecuted under existing laws. Furthermore, Sweden and the United Kingdom report one incident each. The efforts to eliminate the practice in Africa and in industrialized nations range from laws criminalizing FC/FGM to education and outreach programs. These efforts will be addressed in Chapter Three, FGM and Globalism: Laws and in Chapter Four, Legal and Practical Issues in the West.

A 1998 study showed that the number of migrants coming from countries where women are at risk of FGM is the highest in Britain with more than 300,000 individuals; France with 200,000; followed by Italy with 133,847 and Germany with 77,795. Furthermore almost 50 percent of healthcare providers have seen FGM complications and more than 90 percent would not perform the procedure. The British Medical Association estimates the number in the United Kingdom to be 3,000 procedures every year.[36]

Overall, of the original 28 African countries where prevalence of FC/FGM exists, eighteen of the countries have a prevalence rate of 50 percent or higher. In Asia, prevalence is documented among the Daudi Bohra Muslims in India and in Muslim ethnic groups in Sri Lanka. In the Middle East, reports indicate that in Yemen and Oman the practice exists.[37]

RELATIONSHIP OF INCIDENCE IN AFRICA AND ASIA TO THE UNITED STATES: OVERVIEW

In 1999, Nahid Toubia wrote that almost half of all new African immigrants were women and girls, and thousands of refugee families were being resettled. As African immigration increases, circumcised women come in larger numbers to North America, Western Europe, Australia, and New Zealand. African immigration in the United States has nearly tripled in the past three decades, to almost 25,000 per year in the 1990s.[38] Toubia lists fourteen states and the District of Columbia as having the largest African-born populations as of 1999. California and New York have the largest number, falling between 55,000 and 65,000. Texas and New Jersey have the second largest number, ranging between 25,000 and 30,000. Massachusetts and Maryland have between 20,000 and 25,000. Illinois, Virginia, Georgia, Florida, and the District of Columbia have between 10,000 to 15,000. Michigan, Ohio, Pennsylvania, and Delaware rank last having African-born populations of between 6,000 and 10,000.[39]

Immigrants, refugees and asylees need to be considered when determining the number of African women and children in the United States. The U.S. Census Bureau will have a household breakdown by gender and age of the foreign-born population by late summer 2004.[40] According to the Office of the United Nations High Commissioner for Refugees (UNHCR), as of January 1999, data by sex were available for 4.2 million of the 11.5 million refugees, about one-third of the total refugee population. Women made up 50 percent of the group. Furthermore, women represented 53 percent of the refugees in Eastern Europe, 51 percent in Asia, 47 percent in Latin America and the Caribbean, and 50 percent in Africa.[41] Women and girls often become refugees as a result of violence, including sexual violence. Gender-related persecution is often grounds for seeking asylum and refugee status. FGM is one ground. Australia, Canada, France, the United Kingdom, and the United States have formulated guidelines for gender-related crimes.[42]

Women make up a smaller proportion of asylum applicants. Fifteen percent in Italy in 1992; one-third in the Czech Republic, the Netherlands, and Switzerland in 1995/1996; and a little more than one-third or 38 percent in Canada in 1993 and in Sweden in 1997 were women.[43]

Available data show there are usually as many women as men among UNHCR-assisted refugees. In 1998, in the region of asylum of Northern Africa, the UNHCR assisted 168,000 people, 51 percent of whom were women. In sub–Saharan Africa, the UNHCR assisted 2,000,000 people, 50 percent of whom were women.[44] The Census Bureau notes a trend over time in immigration. More men in the past emigrated than women. Currently, women emigrate in similar numbers.[45]

The United States Department of Homeland Security, Office of Immigration Statistics breaks down immigrants admitted by selected class of admission by region and country of last permanent residence. These data represent only refugees and asylees who got green cards. Unfortunately, according to U.S. Citizenship and Immigration Services (USCIS), data from the former U.S. Immigration and Naturalization Service (INS) are such that USCIS cannot add together data on different legal statuses because many individuals would be counted more than once. Their data systems are organized by application rather than being person based.[46] Using this data, when we follow the reasoning that at least half of the immigrant population from the listed countries are women, we can safely assume that once those women reside in a new country, they will have followed tradition. Egypt is used as an example. Women represent half, or about 3,118 of Egypt's total migrating people, 6,235. (See Table 2.10.) Ninety-seven percent of the women in Egypt are circumcised. When women migrate from Egypt, it is safe to assume most will be circumcised.

Data maintained by the U.S. Office of Refugee Resettlement (ORR) are limited to refugee arrivals in the United States. Legal authority does not rest with their office to track other non-refugee immigrants to the United States. That authority rests with the Department of Homeland Security. Yemen, India, Indonesia, Israel, Oman, Saudi Arabia, and Pakistan are not designated by the U.S. Department of State under the Refugee Admissions Program. The countries fall within the Presidential Determination for fiscal year (FY) 2004 Refugee Admissions.[47] Data were not received on Burkina Faso, Central African Republic, Chad, Guinea-Bissau, Mali, Mauritania, and Tanzania.

INCIDENCE BY TYPE

According to Communicating for Change, a Web site with a distinctly African perspective, in about 85 percent of the 28 countries, genital muti-

Table 2.10
Immigrants Admitted by Selected Class of Admission and Region and Country of Last Permanent Residence Fiscal Year 2002

Country Africa, Asia	Total
Benin	924
Burkina Faso	78
Cameroon	948
CAR	9
Chad	19
Congo, Democratic Republic	90
Ivory Coast	1849
Djibouti	105
Egypt	6235
Eritrea	409
Ethiopia	6315
Gambia	456
Ghana	4693
Guinea	61
Guinea-Bissau	767
Indonesia	2245
Kenya	7305
Liberia	1473
Mali	130
Mauritania	99
Niger	1223
Nigeria	7469
Senegal	543
Sierra Leone	902
Somalia	431
Sudan	898
Tanzania	542
Togo	701
Uganda	583
Yemen	1323

Source: *U.S. Department of Homeland Security, Office of Immigration Statistics, 2002 Yearbook of Immigration Statistics, Table 9, Oct. 2003, p. 34. Available: http://uscis.gov/graphics/shared/aboutus/statistics/Yearbook2002.pdf. Accessed July 12, 2004.*

lation takes the form of clitoridectomy (removal of all or part of the clitoris) or excision (cutting of all or part of the labia minora). About 15 percent of the cases of genital mutilation in Africa are of the most extreme form, infibulation (removal of all or part of the external genitalia and the stitching and narrowing of the vaginal opening).[48]

The WHO reports that Type II is the most common form of FC/FGM, accounting for 80 percent of all cases. Type III, infibulation, involves 15 percent of all cases.[49] Janice Boddy's ethnography found that the more extreme forms are practiced in Sudan among the Zar Cults.[50] Raqiya Haji Dualeh Abdalla's work revealed that Type III is also practiced in Somalia.[51]

Incidence of Type by Country

The Office for International Women's Issues of the U.S. Department of State has compiled findings of incidence by type of FGM (see Appendix 1). Three countries—Ethiopia, Mauritania, and Indonesia—practice a form of Type IV. Type III is found in the eastern part of Chad that borders Sudan, Afars and Issa in Djibouti, a few ethnic groups in southern Egypt, Eritrea, all areas of Ethiopia bordering Sudan and

Figure 2.3 — Estimated Prevalence by Type of FGM
Among Female Populations in African Countries

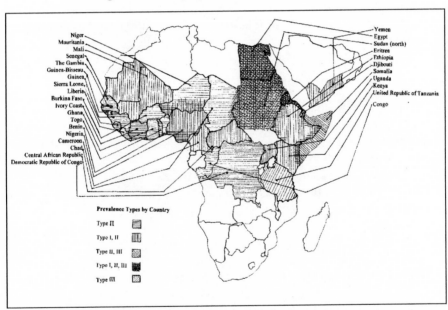

Map by Christopher M. Schulte, adapted and updated with permission from Fran P. Hosken. Estimates are from the following sources: Hosken, Fran P. *The Hosken Report: Genital and Sexual Mutilation of Females*, Fourth revised edition. Lexington, Mass.: Women's International Network News, 1993, p. 43. Toubia, Nahid. *A Technical Manual for Health Care Providers: Caring for Women with Circumcision.* New York: RAINBO, 1999, p. 25. U.S. Department of State, Office of the Senior Coordinator for International Women's Issues, Office of the Under Secretary for Global Affairs. "Chart: Overview of Practice of Female Genital Mutilation," Sec. K., Feb. 1, 2001. Updated June 27, 2001. Available: http://www.state.gov/g/wi/rls/rep/9305.htm. Accessed Apr. 20, 2004.

Somalia, a small percent of Gambia, Ghana, Guinea, the far eastern areas of Kenya bordering Somalia, the southern part of Mali, Nigeria, Senegal, Somalia, northern Sudan, Tanzania, and a small community of East African immigrants and refugees in the Republic of Yemen.[52] (See Figure 2.3.)

Some countries perform only one type; others have a combination of types. Several countries practice only Type II. Benin, for example, has a high rate of prevalence of 30 to 50 percent but performs only Type II. A similar situation is found in Burkina Faso, with a prevalence of two percent of Type II only. The 43 percent in Côte d'Ivoire practice only Type II. The 80 to 90 percent in Sierra Leone practice Type II alone. Countries like the Democratic Republic of the Congo and Niger practice Type II but have a low rate of five percent. Togo has 12 percent.[53]

Amnesty International's findings are very similar. Amnesty International bases its estimates of incidence on the 1997 U.S. Department of State's findings and some of the same sources as the State Department, such as the WHO.[54]

A Longitudinal Analysis of Incidence

A longitudinal analysis of incidence can determine whether change in the incidence of FC/FGM has occurred, but longitudinal data are available for only a few of the practicing countries. An analysis of that data is nonetheless informative.

Sometimes change is not measured in incidence alone but by type of FGC performed. Although Tanzania practices primarily Type I, in some places the medical community is seeing less of a cut, according to Stephen Kebwe, District Medical Officer for Bunda and Regional Chairman for Mara of the Inter African Committee in Tanzania.

In 2000, using a 1997 source, the United Nations reported that "recent DHS surveys found almost no decline in rates of female genital mutilation, especially where overall prevalence is high."[55] The report found that prevalence rates declined slowly but continuously in the CAR and Kenya. In the CAR, fewer women aged 20 to 24 than women aged 45 to 49 had undergone FGM, 43 and 53 percent respectively. In Kenya the corresponding figures were 32 and 48 percent.

In a 2003 draft report, the United Nations Children's Fund (UNICEF) in Nairobi, Kenya, reported that the average prevalence rate of FGM/FC among the practicing countries in the East and Southern African Region is about 74 percent. The range is from 18 percent in Tanzania to 98 percent in Djibouti. They wrote, "There has not been significant change after a decade of intervention. In some high prevalence countries like Egypt, the situation has worsened, going up by a third of a percent to 97.3 percent and up by almost one percent in Sudan to 90 percent."[56]

These statistics are accompanied by reports that a large number of girls in these countries are withdrawn from school to undergo the practice so that they might qualify as wives. The stopping of their education also stops their progression to high academic levels. In turn, high school dropout rates are high. There is a reversion to illiteracy, which is related to high mortality rates and low living standards.[57]

Nigeria

The 2003 Nigeria DHS collected information on the practice of FC in Nigeria from all women aged fifteen to forty-nine. The 1999 data were only from currently married women. About half (53 percent) of Nigerian women had heard of the practice. Of women who reported they were circumcised, half could not identify the type of procedure. For those who could identify the procedure, 44 percent reported cutting and removal of flesh. Four percent reported their vaginas were sewn closed (infibulation).[58]

In Nigeria, FC occurs mostly before the first birthday. Three-fourths of the women were circumcised by age one. Twenty-one percent were circumcised at age five or older. Infibulation is usually carried out at a later age.[59]

Of the women who had at least one daughter, ten percent had a circumcised daughter and three percent intended to have a daughter circumcised.[60] Two-thirds of the Nigerian women who had heard of circumcision believed the practice should be discontinued, and 21 percent believed it should be continued. Half of the women believed that men want it discontinued and one-fifth believed men want it continued.[61] When men who had heard of the practice were asked the same attitude questions, almost two-thirds were against the practice continuing and one-fifth favored it continuing.[62]

Women and men who said they thought circumcision should continue believed it was a benefit because of chastity before marriage and better marriage prospects. One-fourth of the men said there is greater sexual pleasure, but only five percent of the women cited this reason. One-fourth of the women and one-fifth of the men believed circumcision aids safe delivery.[63] Sexual gratification was the most common reason given by women and men who did not support FC.[64]

THE SIGNIFICANCE OF
INCIDENCE AND IMMIGRATION

Because we live in a global community, the significance of incidence related to immigration cannot be denied. My own country, the United States, has become a multicultural nation and the impact of customs of other cultures, including cases of those practicing FGC, has given rise to legislation and social action. Other industrialized nations have passed legislation and have programs directed at FGC. (See Appendix 3.) In countries that have outlawed FGC, legal issues such as asylum seeking and constitutional issues arise.

In 1996 Congress directed the Secretary of the Department of Health and Human Services to "compile data on the number of females living in the United States who have been subject to female genital mutilation (whether in the United States or in their countries of origin) including specification of the number of girls under the age of 18 who have been subject to such mutilation."[65] The results were to help the Department to meet other requirements of legislative language, so that they could identify the communities in the United States that practice FGM, develop outreach and education targeting these communities, and educate healthcare professionals and students about FGM/FC and their complications.[66]

In 1997, Wanda K. Jones et al., Public Health Reports, stated that determining prevalence and incidence of FGM/FC in the United States is a challenge derived from the complex issues of immigration and acculturation. The authors are members of the Centers for Disease Control and Prevention (CDC). They used two sources to derive their estimates, the 1990 U.S. Census based on a five-percent sample of total households in the United States and Toubia's country-specific prevalence estimates.[67] The important assumption the researchers made is that immigrant populations resemble those in their homelands in observing cultural practices of FGM/FC, no matter what year they came to the United States or where they settled. When applied to the U.S. population, the census sample estimated that 271,000 females living in the United States in 1990 reported their country of ancestry as one where FGM/FC is practiced. Girls under eighteen years represented approximately one-fourth of 77,000.[68] (See Table 2.11.)

When the authors applied country-specific or regional rates to the 271,000, an estimated 168,000 girls and women had or may have been at risk for FGM/FC; of these, 48,000 were under 18. About three-fourths of the 48,000 were born in the United States.[69]

States with large African immigrant populations had the greatest

Table 2.11
Women and Girls in the United States
from Countries with Higher Than 5% Prevalence
of Female Genital Mutilation/Female Circumcision
(FGM/FC) and Those Estimated to Have or Be
Potentially at Risk for FGM/FC, by Age Group,
Based on 1990 U.S. Census Data.

| | Age Group | | | | | |
| | Under 18 | | 18 or Older | | Total | |
U.S. Women and Girls	*No.*	*%*	*No.*	*%*	*No.*	*%*
Reported ancestry or place of birth as country with prevalence of FGM/FC higher than 5%	77,000	28	194,000	72	271,000	100
Estimated to have had or to potentially be at risk for FGM/FC	48,000	29	120,000	71	168,000	100

Source: Wanda K. Jones, Jack Smith, Burney Kieke Jr., and Lynne Wilcox, "Female Genital Mutilation/Female Circumcision: Who Is at Risk in the U.S.," Public Health Reports, 112 no. 5 (Sept. 1997):368.

number of girls and women at risk for FGM/FC. More than three-fourths (77.1 percent) of the 168,000 lived in 12 states: New York, California, Texas, New Jersey, Maryland, Florida, Illinois, Georgia, Virginia, Pennsylvania, Ohio, and Massachusetts and the District of Columbia in 1990. About 89 percent of the girls under age eighteen in this group lived in twenty-one states and the District of Columbia in 1990.[70]

The authors wrote that one of the limitations of their study is that it relied on the 1990 census, which was seven years old as they wrote and is now 14 years old as I write. Significant numbers of immigrants from countries with high prevalence rates of FGM/FC have come to the United States since then, and it is expected that immigration populations would reflect those high rates.[71]

In addition to legislation in individual countries, a variety of international organizations address FGC. Among them are the United Nations; International Planned Parenthood Federation in London; Inter-African Committee on Traditional Practices affecting the Health of Women and Children (IAC), with a main office in Switzerland and other national offices; and the Program for Appropriate Technology in Health (PATH) in Washington, DC. These organizations provide advocacy, communication and training materials, documentation of FGC, and contacts of national implementation partners.[72] The great number of human rights instruments signifies that FGC has a universally recognized human rights perspective.[73] Immigration has brought the issue to the doorstep of many Western countries that have dealt with it through legislation, social action, and medical care.

CONCLUSION

Information comes from a variety of sources of varying quality. The WHO organized prevalence data according to the reliability of estimates. The U.S. Population Reference Bureau wrote that the key to the abandonment of FGC is, in part, an understanding of its prevalence. They believe one of the signs of progress is how much more information we now have.[74] In like spirit, UNICEF wrote that "with the foregoing information, it is necessary to foster change both in the methodology and practice that will bring about the positive change."[75]

3

Globalism and Law

God's creation is all one all over the world.
> William G. Riek, President, Sudanese Refugee
> Community Organization (SRCO) and Refugee
> Advocate, Community Humanitarian Resource
> Center (CHRC), Grand Island, Nebraska[1]

Opinion of the world outside of Africa "about female circumcision is readily available," wrote Jessica A. Platt.[2] Bettina Shell-Duncan and Ylva Hernlund believe, however, that Western discussion has been excessive. They seek to reexamine the issue and to create a more balanced perspective than just presenting opposing views.[3] Just as scholars increasingly strive for a balanced view, they also work to include authors of other cultures. Many authors, myself included, have worked to record the voices of African people and to find, as did Christine J. Walley, "there is no unified voice for African women."[4] When I was planning my trip to Kenya and Tanzania, a friend who works for United Nations Children's Fund (UNICEF) told me, "Whatever view you are looking for, we have it all. We have people who are for cutting. People who are against it."

Nyarieka and Mut Ruey are from Miywut in south Sudan and live in Grand Island, Nebraska. Nyarieka believes, "The global society should step in and produce talk—if there's any possibility that they could stop that surgery."[5] Mut, her husband, also believes that the global society should step in and say, "This is not right. You are not going to do anything that would harm a person as a human being.' So we may have to go further to stop female circumcision. The United Nations and all the churches all over the world should come out and say this is not right. You cannot do anything like this because there is no function to perform that kind of surgery."[6]

When I was in Kenya and Tanzania, I found Africans, women and men, open to discussing female circumcision (FC). For them, female gen-

57

ital mutilation (FGM) is both a social and personal issue. I found much African activism against FGM in Kenya and Tanzania. These activists are part of a larger group of African activism called the Inter-African Committee on Traditional Practices Affecting the Health of Women and Children (IAC). In Africa, many governments have enacted laws against FGM and have established educational programs to encourage people to obey the laws. The philosophies of African activism and of the governments are based on international human rights standards.

GLOBAL LAWS AND GLOBAL EFFORTS

The IAC, with the collaboration of local nongovernmental organizations (NGOs), conducts extensive educational campaigns to eliminate FGM in more than twenty African countries.[7]

Second, various national and international development agencies provide technical assistance, advocacy, and funding. Some of these agencies are the Program for Appropriate Technology in Health (PATH); Research, Action, and Information Network for Bodily Integrity of Women (RAINBO); Equality Now; the Focus Project; the Center for Development and Population Activities (CEDPA); the Population Council; the United States Agency for International Development (USAID); the Wallace Global Fund; and the Women's International Network. Agencies affiliated with the United Nations that work to eliminate FGM include UNICEF, the United Nations Population Fund (UNFPA), and the World Health Organization (WHO).[8]

FGM violates human rights, and human rights conventions protect women and children from cruelty and violence. Eradication of FGM is also included in resolutions and action plans at various international conferences.

A Human Rights Issue

Social entities in different countries often do not know or understand the Universal Declaration of Human Rights and so substitute their own cultural beliefs for international human rights standards.[9] In 1979, the WHO organized a seminar in Khartoum, Sudan, to set a direction for renewed international initiatives. The interest of NGOs resurfaced during the U.N. Decade for Women, 1975 to 1985.[10] NGOs meeting in 1992 in Bangkok held the position that universal human rights afford protection to all of humanity. Cultural practices that minimize the universally accepted human rights, including women's rights, are not to be tolerated.[11]

International Human
Rights Standards

The term "human rights" is not defined in the United Nations Charter, as Platt correctly noted, even though human rights is its focus. Human rights were defined in the Universal Declaration of Human Rights proclaimed on December 10, 1948. "The Declaration defines human rights as the inherent dignity of every human person that is inalienable and imprescriptible."[12] In addition, "human rights are defined as universal, acquired at birth by 'all members of the human family whatever the political, jurisdictional or international status of the country or territory to which a person belongs.'"[13] Certain limitations on the exercise of human rights are set, "solely for the purpose of securing due recognition and respect for the rights of others and of meeting the just requirements of morality, public order and the general welfare in a democratic society."[14]

The Universal Declaration does not specifically address violations of human rights and cultural and religious practices, including the practice of FC. However, as Platt noted the Declaration is used by the United Nations' conventions and human rights legislation to support the ending and prohibiting of FC in the international community. The use of the Declaration in conventions and legislation is evident in The International Covenant on Civil and Political Rights,[15] The Convention of the Elimination of All Forms of Discrimination Against Women,[16] The Committee on the Elimination of Discrimination Against Women,[17] and The United Nations Convention on the Rights of the Child.[18]

Anika Rahman and Nahid Toubia maintain that one of the most influential instruments of the twentieth century is the 1948 Universal Declaration of Human Rights.[19] Other instruments important for human rights are the 1966 International Covenant on Economic, Social and Cultural Rights; the 1984 Convention against Torture and Other Cruel, Inhuman or Degrading Treatment or Punishment, prohibiting all acts of torture and cruel, inhuman, or degrading treatment or punishment; the 1995 Platform for Action of the United Nations Fourth World Conference on Women in Beijing, China; the 1994 Programme of Action of the United Nations International Conference on Population and Development; the 1997 Joint WHO /UNICEF/UNFPA Statement; the International Planned Parenthood Federation Charter; and Amnesty International.[20]

Early international human rights law does not specifically address FC/FGM. Interpretation is based in broad rights, for example, the right to life, liberty, and security. The specific inclusion of traditional practices such as FC/FGM in human rights instruments is a recent development.[21]

More recent universal and regional human rights instruments that specifically address FC/FGM and/or traditional practices include the 1990 African Charter on the Rights and Welfare of the Child; the 1990 U.N. Convention on the Rights of the Child; the 1993 Declaration on the Elimination of Violence Against Women; the 1993 Forty-Sixth World Health Assembly Resolution on Maternal Child Health and Family Planning for Health; the 1994 Programme of Action of the U.N. International Conference on Population and Development in Cairo, Egypt; the 1995 Beijing Declaration and Platform for Action of the U.N. Fourth World Conference on Women in Beijing, China; the 1997 Dakar Declaration by the IAC; and the 1998 Banjul Declaration (also African Charter on Human and Peoples' Rights).

Even though the more recent human rights instruments specifically address FGM, Rahman and Toubia wrote that more legal philosophy on interpretation is needed.[22] Rachel Carnegie stated that in addition to recognizing the practice of FGM as abuse of human rights and detrimental to the health and well-being of women and girls, it is critical to have continued international-level actions that press governments to take action.[23] International enforcement remains limited to international criminal courts but, as Rahman and Toubia pointed out, human rights principles are monitored by the United Nations and can be enforced at the national level.[24]

Platt found that the worldwide religious and cultural biases that accompany FGM have encouraged the international community to restrict all forms of FC. These restrictions are found in the International Covenant of Civil and Political Rights,[25] the Women's Convention,[26] the Committee on the Elimination of Discrimination Against Women,[27] and the Convention on the Rights of the Child.[28]

Although FGM is a harmful and sometimes fatal practice, it is defended in societies that practice it on cultural, religious, and/or traditional grounds. These grounds should be respected, according to the USAID Office of Women in Development, but "practices which harm or kill women should be effectively curtailed at international, national, and grassroots levels."[29] This position is supported by the United Nations Special Rapporteur on violence against women, by the United Nations High Commissioner for Refugees, and in various universal declarations.

Some recent human rights instruments have general clauses that address FGM/FC through the word, "traditional," for example, the 1990 U.N. Convention on the Rights of the Child,[30] the 1993 Declaration on the Elimination of Violence Against Women,[31] the May 1993 Forty-Sixth World Health Assembly resolution,[32] and the 1995 Beijing Declaration and

Platform for Action of the U.N. Fourth World Conference on Women in Beijing, China.[33]

Other human rights instruments specifically mention FGM: the 1994 Programme of Action of the U.N. International Conference on Population and Development in Cairo, Egypt;[34] the United Nations High Commissioner for Refugees in May 1994; and the U. S. Board of Immigration Appeals in June 1996, which explicitly recognized FGM as "persecution";[35] and the 1995 Beijing Declaration and Platform for Action of the U.N. Fourth World Conference on Women in Beijing, China.[36]

Regional Efforts

International instruments are usually stated briefly but are forceful. Regional and national governments interpret them in an ongoing process that is key to the development of human rights. International-level bodies also help interpret human rights at high-profile conferences. Regional interpretations have led to requiring governments to take appropriate measures to eliminate harmful cultural practices and include the 1990 African Charter on the Rights and Welfare of the Child, the 1997 Dakar Declaration by the IAC; and the 1998 Banjul Declaration. The result is that nation-states have banned the practice of FGM.[37] The United States prohibits FGM with a punishment for violators of a five-year prison sentence.[38]

COUNTRY LAWS

The Feminist Majority offers a succinct summary of legislation and the year it was enacted. (See Table 3.1.) The dates the legislation was enacted show that prohibiting FC/FGM is very recent, which may account for the more excessive Western-based discussions observed by authors Shell-Duncan and Hernlund.[39] In the same vein, recent African activism and efforts of industrialized nations to address FC/FGM may result from recent legislative efforts. All legislation has passed between 1994 and 2003 except for Guinea. Guinea enacted its laws in 1965.[40]

In 1999, Susan Izett and Nahid Toubia wrote, "There is no clear evidence as to whether passing laws prohibiting FC/FGM has a direct or indirect impact on behavior."[41] Sudan's law of 1946 has little impact. Recent laws such as those in Burkino Faso in 1996, Ghana in 1994, and Côte d'Ivoire in 1998 have yet to be evaluated. They found no information yet available on the effect of laws in Western countries where immigrant populations now reside. In addition, Izett and Toubia concluded that studies are needed on the impact of criminalization of FC/FGM as a

Table 3.1
National Efforts to Eliminate Female Circumcision/Female Genital Mutilation (FC/FGM) and Countries That Have Prosecuted Cases of FC/FGM

Legislation/Decree	*National Efforts to Eliminate FC/FGM* *Year Enacted*
African Nations:	
Benin	2003
Burkina Faso	1996
Central African Republic	1966
Chad	2003
Côte d'Ivoire	1998
Djibouti	1994
Egypt Ministerial Decree	1996
Ghana	1994
Guinea	1965
Kenya	2001
Senegal	1999
Tanzania	1998
Togo	1998
Nigeria, multiple states	1999–2002
Industrialized Nations:	
Australia, 6 of 8 states	1994–1997
Belgium	2000
Canada	1997
New Zealand	1995
Norway	1995
Sweden	1982, 1998
United Kingdom	1985
United States, Federal law	1996
16 of 50 states' law	1994–2000
Countries that have prosecuted cases of FC/FGM	
African Nations	
Burkina Faso	
Egypt	
Ghana	
Senegal	
Sierra Leone	
Industrialized Nations	
France	

Source: Feminist Majority, "Female Circumcision/Female Genital Mutilation (FC/FGM): Global Laws and Policies Towards Elimination," Nov. 2000, Item: F027. Available: http://www.crlp.org/pub _fac_fgmicpd.html. Accessed June 15, 2003.

tool for social change. Thus, although law may initiate the process of change, continued progress will depend on other influences.[42] I believe that law is both a social product and a social force; therefore, social change and the law are interdependent. Laws might not be the first step in a social movement, but then again they might. Either way the law is an important contributing factor to social change, but it is certainly not the only component.

African Nations

The Feminist Majority and the Ministry of Health reported in 2000 that nine African Nations had laws that criminalize FC/FGM: Burkina Faso, Central African Republic (CAR), Côte d'Ivoire, Djibouti, Ghana, Guinea, Senegal, Tanzania, and Togo.[43] In 2003, the U.S. Population Reference Bureau reported the addition of Niger, bringing the total to ten African nations with laws criminalizing the practice.[44] Penalties range from a minimum of six months to a maximum of life in prison.[45] The Female Genital Cutting Education and Networking Project indicated that Burkina Faso has prohibited FGM in a draft constitution.[46] The Harvard University Cyber Law reported that legal means are also in effect in Egypt, Madagascar, South Africa, and Uganda.[47] For a complete summary of laws and outreach on a country-by-country basis, see Appendix 2.

Some countries also impose monetary fines, according to the Feminist Majority. In Egypt, the Ministry of Health issued a decree declaring that FC/FGM is illegal and punishable under the Penal Code. The Feminist Majority and the Ministry of Health reported that, as of June 2000, there had been prosecutions or arrests in Burkina Faso, Egypt, Ghana, and Senegal.[48] The Ministry of Health reported that, as of January 2003, there had been reports of prosecutions or arrests in Sierra Leone.[49]

Dr. Fareda Banda, Lecturer in Law at the University of London, reported that the WHO has identified the following trends in law reform:

> Prohibit all forms of FGM (Burkina Faso, Guinea, Ivory Coast and Djibouti) or only the most drastic types (Sudan); Constitution of the Republic of Uganda, adopted 22 September 1995; The Constitution of the Federal Democratic Republic of Ethiopia; 1994 Constitution of the Republic of Ghana approved on 28 April 1992. Other countries which could be added to this list would include Ghana (Ghana Criminal Code Amendment Act.[50]

The Female Genital Cutting Education and Networking Project reported that in 1946, Sudan's Ministry of Health launched a campaign against the practice and was successful in getting a law passed prohibiting infibulation but allowing sunna. However, enforcement was weak.[51] The Project found that in 1982 Kenya's President Moi condemned FGM and called for prosecution for those individuals who practiced it. In 1990, legislation was passed banning it, but various forms continue to be practiced in Kenya.[52]

The Female Genital Cutting Education and Networking Project indicated that "the position in Egypt is not clear."[53] The educated people abide by President Nasser's ban in 1958. Some say a partial clitoridectomy is permissible. Confusion has led to the practice of excision and infibulation. Mostly, legislation has not been effective in reducing or eliminating FGM, but that may be due to problems of enforcement. The Networking Project pointed out that in 1991, Côte d'Ivoire advised the United Nations that FGM can be prohibited through the country's criminal code.[54]

The advantage of passing laws is that national and international interventions are justified because FGM violates human rights. More controversial is the passing of national legislation. Banda believes, "It is still too early to judge the effectiveness of national laws because they have been passed recently. However, some positive impacts have been noticed such as giving legitimacy to programmes against FGM and fostering inter-agency collaboration, where the judicial systematic role is standard setting and sanctioning, if necessary."[55] She said that sometimes there are disadvantages to passing national legislation. In some situations, the practice goes underground, resulting in no access to medical assistance and lowering the age of initiates.

In spite of the high prevalence of FGM in Egypt, as early as 1959, Ministerial decree prohibited it and made it punishable by fine and imprisonment. In 1997, the Court of Cassation upheld a government ban on FGM. The Health Minister issued a decree in 1996 that prohibits medical and nonmedical practitioners from performing FGM in public or private facilities, except for medical reasons certified by the head of the hospital's obstetric department. Some provisions of the Penal Code on "wounding," "intentional infliction of harm leading to death," might be used. The government is committed to eliminating FGM. There are reports of the prosecution of at least thirteen persons in 1995 and 1996 under the Code. Outreach campaigns have been in progress since as early as 1982; the Population Crisis Committee and Cairo Family Planning Association produced material on harmful effects and carried out training for health professionals. The National Committee of IAC is active. The USAID, in cooperation with the Egyptian government, is funding projects to eliminate FGM.[56] (See Appendix 2.)

Middle East

Yemen

Yemen has no law prohibiting FGM. In 2001, a Ministerial decree prohibited the practice in both government and private health facilities. Some government health workers, including the Minister of Public Health, actively and publicly discourage this practice. Women are doing research to launch a public campaign against the practice. In 2001, FGM was publicly discussed for the first time through a conference sponsored by the Ministry of Public Health.[57] (See Appendix 2.)

Oman and United Arab Emirates

There is no law in effect against FGM in Oman and the United Arab Emirates.[58]

South Asia

In India, although the Daudi Bohra practice clitoridectomy,[59] the Inter-Parliamentary Union (IPU) reported that India has not adopted any law on FGM.[60] The IPU also reported that in Indonesia, according to a university study reported by the WHO, certain forms of FGM were practiced in parts of the country in the past and various noncutting rituals involving the clitoris reportedly persist. The IPU reports having no information on the existence of specific legislation.[61]

Hospitals in Indonesia offer circumcision for girls. In the past, midwives and traditional healers have performed the circumcisions. Circumcision is symbolic. Local healers cut a tumeric root and rub it on the baby's clitoris while those in attendance chant and pray. In the cities where Islamic influence is stronger, circumcision involves drawing blood by putting a pin in the clitoris.[62]

The IPU reports no problems in Malaysia. The country does not have any laws on FGM.[63]

Industrialized Nations

The Center for Reproductive Rights (CRR) reported that the following industrialized countries that receive immigrants from countries where FC/FGM is practiced have passed laws criminalizing the practice: Australia, Belgium, Canada, Denmark, New Zealand, Norway, Spain, Sweden, United Kingdom, and the United States. In Australia, six out of eight states have passed laws against FC/FGM.[64] All eight states have anti-FGM positions under the criminal laws of Australia and under other laws such as the Common Law, Community Welfare Act, the Children's Services Act of 1986, and the Family Law Act.[65] An in-depth analysis of the laws and outreach efforts of the practicing countries and the industrialized nations receiving immigrants is provided in Appendix 2.

Nonpracticing Countries

The Danish criminal code makes FC/FGM a crime. German penal code considers FC/FGM serious and grave bodily harm. In Italy there is no law criminalizing FC/FGM, but the penal code's provisions covering personal injury could apply.[66] In an effort to control FGM, a Florence physician has developed a "symbolic alternative."[67] The Netherlands has no law, but penal code provisions are applicable to FC\FGM. In 1993, the government officially condemned the practice.[68] In 2004, the Dutch Opposition Labour Party (PvdA) called for a new law to be introduced to provide for exception for the performing of FGM on girls over twelve who come from countries where the procedure is traditionally done. It also asked that possible risk for FGM in the country of origin be considered grounds of asylum.[69] New Zealand passed an amendment to the Crimes Amendment Act of New Zealand making FGM a crime in 1995, effective January 1, 1996. In 1995, Norway enacted a law specifically criminalizing FC/FGM.

The United Kingdom's Prohibition of Female Circumcision Act of 1985 makes FC/FGM an offense.[70] Section 2 of the Act "does not render unlawful a surgical operation which is necessary for the physical or mental health of the person on whom it is performed. In determining whether the operation is necessary for the mental health of a person, no account is to be taken of any belief of that person or any other person that the operation is required as a matter of custom or ritual."[71] In 1995, the British Medical Association estimated that between three and four thousand girls had the procedure each year since the law passed in 1985. Critics of the ban say that the number did not decrease. As of 1997, there had been no prosecutions, but information had been disseminated about the ban.[72]

In 1982, Sweden became the first Western European country to outlaw all forms of FGM. It banned health professionals from performing the operation. The law was revised in July 1998 and it made penalties more severe. Australia passed legislation making FGM a crime in six of eight states and territories: Australian Capital Territory, Northern Territory, New South Wales, South Australia, Tasmania, and Victoria.[73]

In 1999, Nahid Toubia stated that passing laws criminalizing and prohibiting FGM in a Western host country is a political statement and is unnecessary because the countries all have child protection and assault laws. She wrote that the most glaring evidence is that the only Western country that ever prosecuted a circumciser or parent is France, a country that has no specific anti-FGM laws.[74] France sets forth a decree in the Code of Medical Ethics forbidding mutilating procedures.[75]

France has relied on existing criminal legislation to prosecute both the practitioners of FC/FGM and parents who procure the service for their daughters.[76] From 1983 to 1999, France prosecuted twenty-six FGM cases. Twenty-five resulted in convictions. The defendants were the parents, usually the mothers. In three trials a practitioner was charged.[77] Holly Maguigan suggested that the French experience may imply that special statutes defining FGM as a crime are not necessary to obtain a conviction and that a strong prosecution policy may not reduce the number of procedures performed. The French government has begun an education campaign to reduce FGM.[78]

In 1999, a woman was convicted of carrying out excisions on forty-eight girls between the ages of one month and ten years. An international organization, Campaign Against Sexual Mutilations (CAMS) tried to stop excisions.[79]

In February 2004, for the first time, a French court sentenced a Mali mother who lived in Paris for complicity in the FGM of her daughter. Activists believe that legislation has reduced excision of babies and toddlers, but the procedure is increasing among adolescents during visits to their countries of origin or before a forced marriage.[80]

The law in Canada went into effect in 1997. Canada Bill C-126 is legislation that would result in an act to amend the criminal code and the Young Offenders Act. Under Section 268, FGM is considered an aggravated assault punishable by imprisonment for a term not exceeding fourteen years. By definition, aggravated assault is committed when one "wounds, maims, disfigures or endangers the life" of a complainant. "Wounds" and "maims" are defined to include "... to excise, infibulate or mutilate, in whole or in part, the labia majora, labia minora or clitoris of a person...."[81] There are limited exceptions. Consent is no defense. The criminal code also makes it a crime to take a child who is a resident in Canada out of Canada to have FGM performed in another country.[82] This amendment is preventive because it allows intervention before harm is done to the child.[83]

In the United States, Toubia worked with other African-American physicians and attorneys to send suggestions to Congresswoman Patricia Schroeder and the congressional women's caucus in 1993, when they were drafting the bill for an anti-FGM law. Their suggestions were included and directives were given to the Department of Health and Human Services (DHHS) to undertake education and outreach to the communities and training to health personnel. In 1995, the organization RAINBO (which Toubia helped start), began to think it needed to expand its first objective for social change in Africa to include programs to serve the African immi-

grant community in the United States and other host countries. Toubia
believes that the health community must help circumcised women in addition to stopping circumcision.[84]

The Federal government, more than a dozen states, and New York
City have criminalized the practice. In 1986, ten years before the U.S. law
was enacted, Holly Maguigan reported that there was only one prosecution in the United States. In DeKalb County, Georgia, a Somalian immigrant nurse was charged with assault. Although she was acquitted, it was
claimed that she had excised the genitals of her two-year-old niece. The
prosecution did not prove the identity of the practitioner.[85] In 2003, an
Ethiopian man was charged for allegedly circumcising his toddler daughter with scissors in 2001. The practice is conducted underground in the
Atlanta area.[86]

Although no statistical studies reveal the prevalence of FGM in the
United States before the law was enacted, evidence existed that physicians
and families practiced it in secret within immigrant communities. Detroit,
Atlanta, New York, and Los Angeles reported the practice within immigrant communities. The WHO and other health groups reported that
wealthy immigrants had paid Western physicians in the United States and
Europe to perform FGM on their daughters. Researchers believed that
immigrants sometimes brought excisers to continue the practice outside
of Africa.[87]

The U.S. law was enacted September 30, 1996, and provides, in part,
that "whoever knowingly circumcises, excises or infibulates the whole or
any part of the labia majora or labia minora or clitoris of another person
who has not attained the age of 18 years shall be fined under this title or
imprisoned for not more than five years, or both."[88]

The U.S. Department of State commented, "The law provides that no
account shall be taken of the effect on the person on whom the operation
is to be performed, of any belief on the part of that person, or any other
person, that the operation is required as a matter of custom or ritual."[89]
Attorney Lisa Johnson-Firth, Director of Legal Services at the Tahirih Justice Center, clarified, "A surgical operation is not in violation if it is medically necessary and is performed by a licensed person or is performed for
medical purposes connected with the birth process."[90]

Johnson-Firth noted the first incident to be charged under U.S. law
occurred on February 5, 2004.[91] Authorities arrested a couple in the
Canyon Country area outside Los Angeles, California. Todd Cameron
Bertrang, forty-one, and his companion Robyn Faulkinbury, twenty-four,
both of Santa Clarita, had struck a deal with undercover Federal Bureau
of Investigation (FBI) agents to circumcise two girls they believed were

the agents' eight- and twelve-year-old daughters. Although no circumcisions occurred, Bertrang allegedly offered to perform two procedures for $8,000 in July 2002. Bertrang and Faulkinbury were charged with conspiring to violate the Federal act on FGM.[92]

Nawal M. Nour, M.D., M.P.H., stated that Federal law made it a Federal crime to perform female genital cutting (FGC), but the law needs to go further. Nour told of Somalian families who return to their country to circumcise their daughters. Europe is further ahead on FGC issues. Britain's FGM Act of 2003 "not only makes it a crime for anyone to advise, assist or perform FGC in the UK, it is also a crime for UK nationals, permanent residents and non-UK nationals to advise, assist or perform FGC outside the UK."[93] Nour argued that the United States has a legal precedent in that it is "a crime to transport U.S. national or permanent resident girls under 18 to other countries with the intent to engage in prostitution or illicit sexual conduct."[94] Nour believes that returning to their country of origin to circumcise their daughters is increasing at an alarming rate and the United States and Africa must find a way to stop it.

William G. Riek agreed that some Sudanese families are sending their children to be circumcised in Sudan, but he believes this practice will not continue.[95] Professor Patroba E. Ondiek, Ph.D., who is the Program Coordinator for the NGO Save the Children of Tarime (Sachita) in Tarime, Tanzania, observed circumcision in the United States, "I had a friend who would call a black doctor, an African American. Yes, and he would do it. Yes, they have sterilized instruments. They take much better care."[96]

State Laws

In addition to the Federal law introduced by Representative Pat Schroeder and passed by Congress in 1996, state laws criminalize FGM. From 1994 to 2000, sixteen of fifty states had laws criminalizing FGM:[97] California,[98] Colorado,[99] Delaware,[100] Illinois,[101] Maryland,[102] Minnesota,[103] Missouri,[104] Nevada,[105] New York,[106] North Dakota,[107] Oregon,[108] Rhode Island,[109] Tennessee,[110] Texas,[111] West Virginia,[112] and Wisconsin.[113] Michigan's[114] house bill was referred to the Committee on Judiciary and Civil Rights in September 1996, where it died.[115] In New Jersey,[116] the general assembly of the 1996–1997 session passed a resolution, but it failed to pass the Senate.[117] Most of these laws prohibit subjecting girls under eighteen to FGM. Four states—Illinois, Minnesota, Rhode Island, and Tennessee— prohibit FGM regardless of age. Equality Now stated that as of 2003,

"There have been no prosecutions for FGM under U.S. Federal law or any state law, to date.[118] The first incident occurred February 5, 2004, in California. (See earlier discussion.)

States that have prohibited FGM even on women over eighteen include Illinois, Minnesota, Rhode Island, and Tennessee. States that explicitly hold parents and legal guardians liable for FC/FGM if they knowingly consent to the procedure include Colorado, Delaware, Maryland, New York, Oregon, and West Virginia. California, Colorado, Minnesota, New York, and Oregon have additional provisions for education and outreach to relevant communities. California punishes doctors and parents. Parents can receive one year plus the regular penalty for child endangerment.[119]

ASYLUM LAW

U.N. Initiatives on Asylum

Women have been recognized as refugees under the 1951 U.N. Convention relating to the Status of Refugees (U.N. Refugee Convention) on the basis that the women would be at risk of FGM if they returned to their country. Amnesty International says that it is important to remember that these cases are few in number:[120] "The U.N. Refugee Convention describes a refugee as ... owing to well-founded fear of being persecuted for reasons of race, religion, nationality, membership of a particular social group or political opinion, is outside the country of his nationality and is unable, or owing to such fear, is unwilling to avail himself of the protection of that country...."[121]

Amnesty International explained that "under this definition, women from a particular country or ethnic group who are at risk of FGM can be properly construed as a 'particular social group.'" This group can consist of large numbers of women. Nationality and political opinion are also used as grounds.[122] Australia, Canada, Sweden, and the United States have granted asylum to members of families on the grounds of the U.N. Refugee Convention.[123]

U.S. Asylum Law

"U.S. asylum law is an imperfect tool," wrote E. Dana Neacsu. U.S. asylum law has progressed toward recognizing that human rights violations of women merit asylum protection. In the 1995 Immigration and Naturalization Service (INS) adopted the first guidelines for when an asylum seeker may qualify for asylum on grounds of gender-based violence.[124] In 1998, INS announced how it intended to implement the Illegal Immigration Reform and Immigrant Responsibility Act of 1996 (IIRIRA)[125] as it pertained to FGM. Visa recipients are to be notified prior to their entry to the United States of the severe harm to the physical and psychological health of women and girls and potential legal consequences for performing FGM on a child or adult or by allowing it to be performed on a child in the United States.[126] In 2000, the draft regulations addressing membership in a particular social group demonstrated that U.S. asylum law progressed toward "the recognition that violations of the human rights of women are a deserving basis for asylum protection."[127]

Although the proposed regulations were withdrawn,[128] what constitutes a reasonable possibility of persecution is spelled out in the law. The asylum applicant will have a well-founded fear of future persecution if he or she can establish: (1) a persecutor seeks to overcome others by means of punishment of some sort; (2) the persecutor is already aware, or could become aware, that the alien possesses this belief or characteristic; (3) the persecutor has the capability of punishing the alien; and (4) the persecutor has the inclination to punish the alien. Thus, an alien who claims that punishment on account of one of the reasons enumerated in the definition of "refugee" occurred at the hands of local officials must show that redress from higher officials was unavailable or that the alien has a well-founded fear that such redress would be unavailable.[129]

An illustration of reasonable possibility of persecution is when the Board of Immigration Appeals (BIA) held that FGM, as practiced by the Tchamba-Kunsuntu tribe of northern Togo, constituted persecution for the purposes of asylum and that

> [Fauziya] Kasinga was a member of a particular social group that consisted of young women in her tribe who were both opposed to FGM and who had not yet undergone the procedure; that Kasinga had a well-founded fear of persecution; that the persecution Kasinga feared was "on account of" the social group to which she belonged; that Kasinga's fear of persecution was countrywide; and consequently that she qualified for and should be granted political asylum.... Violence that is directed at a person because she is a woman does not satisfy the criteria of persecution based on race, religion, nationality, or membership in a particular social group or political opinion, which is necessary for a discretionary grant of asylum.[130]

In addition to the concept of reasonable possibility of persecution, the United States has implemented the 1984 Convention against Torture and Other Cruel, Inhuman or Degrading Treatment or Punishment.[131]

The Convention prohibits all acts of torture and cruel, inhuman, or degrading treatment or punishment.

The Tahirih Justice Center in Falls Church, Virginia, assists women who have migrated to the United States. The Center's mission is to help women and girls who are fleeing gender-based persecution seek justice. Johnson-Firth explained that the Center was founded in 1997 by Layli Miller-Muro after the *Kasinga* case. As a student attorney she handled the case of Fauziya Kasinga.[132] Johnson-Firth explained that the Center does not take a political stand on FGM/FC but offers legal assistance:

> We're very sensitive to the cultural relativism issues here and so for us, as a Center, to take a stand on whether it's right or it's wrong, we wouldn't do that. We wouldn't involve ourselves in the political aspects of it. Women have sought us out and we are simply enabling them to access U.S. laws that would offer them protection and would enable them to stay here. We are involved in the education. We talk about it. We let the public know about it. What the effects of it could be, but we're not an organization that would likely be out there setting up programs to help cultures eradicate this process.[133]

Johnson-Firth said that the Center is an information center that addresses the practical aspects of helping immigrant women. She said, "No one at the Center favors the practice, but we don't really need to address that in our work. We're just helping them access safety here in the United States."[134]

Colleen Renk Zengotitabengoa, staff attorney at the Center, handles the FGC cases at the Center, in particular, those cases related to asylum issues. Most of her clients come from French-speaking West and Central Africa. She uses the language of her clients, and most of them refer to FGC as excision. She explained how the clients find the Tahirih Justice Center:

> They find us at various stages of their application process for asylum. Sometimes they find us right away and we help them submit their very first application. Sometimes they find us after they have already submitted an application with or without the help of an attorney, and that application has been referred from the Asylum Office. They don't call it a denial, but it is not a grant of asylum; they are referred to an immigration judge. Often we get cases at that stage because their previous lawyer may or may not have done a good job or they may or may not also have the means to continue paying a private attorney, and our legal services are provided free of charge. We also have a specialty in gender-based asylum, so there is that something that many private members of the bar might not be able to bring to an asylum case based on FGM.[135]

Renk Zengotitabengoa explained what happens once a client finds the Tahirih Justice Center and comes for help and they take the case:

I meet with them over the course of usually many months and work
on a statement from them, with them, in their words, although I'm the
one who is usually drafting it. It is their history, their story. What happened to them? How were they subjected to FGM if they already have
been or how did they come to learn that they would be subjected to
FGM? Why do they fear it? How did they escape? What were the pressures from their family, from their society, from their culture, from
their country? What in their knowledge is happening in their country
to prevent it or to prosecute those who do practice FGM, if there is
anything in that regard. And, usually, we end up with a statement that
is anywhere from twenty to thirty pages long describing their whole
history. In addition to that, we try to gather as much other evidence in
support of the application as we can. Statements from other friends or
family members who may or may not have gone through this already
or who aware of the cultural practices within their ethnic group. Medical reports from a doctor who has examined the client saying that she
has or has not been circumcised. Then, probably the bulk of our asylum application will be the country condition research. That consists
of scouring all the information that's out there. One, about FGM and
the harmful side effects—physical, psychological, and sexual—that
can occur from the practice as well as the country's specific information. What are the prevalence rates of FGM in their country, particularly among their ethnic group? Are there any programs in their
country that are working to eradicate it? Is it against the law in their
country? If it is against the law, are there any prosecutions? Is it really
in effect or is it just in name only? We usually try to present as comprehensive an application as we can.[136]

Renk Zengotitabengoa shared the details of asylum law, for example,
how they argue FGM under the asylum law in the United States:

In order to be eligible for asylum, in their application, in the procedure, they have to meet the refugee definition as it is incorporated into
U.S. law. It is very similar to the U.S. international definition for a
refugee. That definition says that someone who is outside of their
country of nationality or class residence and they have been persecuted
or they have a well-founded fear of persecution on account of one or
more of the statutorily protected grounds which are race, religion,
nationality, membership in a particular social group, or political opinion; that their persecution or their fear of persecution is at the hands
of their government or at the hands of a group that their government
is unable or unwilling to control. In those five statutorily protected
grounds, there is no ground that is specific to gender. Oftentimes
making a case for asylum based on gender is like putting a square peg
in a round hole. It is something people who are practicing anything
having to do with gender within the context of asylum law have been
struggling with. Typically, what happens is we fit our arguments into
the category of membership in a particular social group. And that is
indeed what the Board of Immigration Appeals did when they decided

the *Kasinga* case. They said that she was eligible for asylum and they defined her social group as young women of her ethnic group who feared FGM and who were opposed to the practice as it was practiced by their ethnic group. More often than not, we use some statement like that specific to our cases, but very much along the same lines as the *Kasinga* reasoning. Then essentially, we have to make an argument that if they have been persecuted in the past, in other words, that they have been already circumcised, they are eligible for asylum. We argue that someone who has been persecuted in the past is eligible for asylum per se because FGM is such a severe form of persecution in the actual cutting and all of its lifelong consequences. It happened in the past, but it was so severe that that person is therefore entitled to a grant of asylum because of what happened in the past. There is this bifurcated analysis within the refugee definition about past persecution or a well-founded fear of future persecution. So it's either in the past or there's this fear of persecution in the future or it could be both. Depending on the particular facts of the case, if it's already happened to them, then there's an analysis of their persecution that they've suffered in the past. Or if they've escaped before it happened, why they have a well-founded fear of it happening in the future. That analysis, that well foundedness of their fear, is split up into two parts, which are a subjective fear and an objective fear. And the objective fear, we make an argument through the country condition research, how FGM is X percent prevalent in their country, so objectively there is a good chance that this would happen to her. Subjectively, that is when we use a lot of the information from her about her own family. How many sisters of hers were circumcised? Did she know anybody who died from it? Her aunts? Her grandmothers? Everybody in her community? How much in her own knowledge is she aware that it happened, and that informs her subjectiveness of her fear.[137]

Renk Zengotitabengoa has a recommendation for the Tahirih Justice Center:

> We've talked about supporting an amendment to the Immigration and Nationality Act that would make FGM persecution per se. Because even though there is this precedent case, the *Kasinga* case, and people are granted asylum based on the reasoning contained in that case, the immigration laws don't say that automatically you are entitled to asylum if you had this done or if you fear having it done.[138]

Layli Miller Bashir holds that women's fear should classify them as a social group, thus satisfying the asylum law.[139] However, the United States showed a reluctance to make use of asylum law before the *Kasinga* decision.[140] Stephanie Kaye Pell found there was little relief for those seeking relief under U.S. asylum law.[141]

The United States is not alone. John Tochukwu Okwubanego maintained that little has been done by most global components—the church,

Islam, the international community, and the United Nations—leaving an international apathy.[142]

Peter Margulies contended that legal changes "are irrelevant unless they are adhered to and legitimated by people in their day-to-day practices."[143] Women should be able to live in their own countries without fear.

Daliah Setareh wrote that U.S. immigration policy needs to recognize the "unique violations" inflicted upon women. Only then could asylum be considered an "adequate remedy." Essential to achieving gender equality is a statutory definition of refugee that includes the violations women endure.[144]

Susannah Smiley stated "Most American courts have been unwilling to create a blanket rule acknowledging that women comprise a particular social group. The courts, maintaining a relativist stance, agree that for purposes of asylum law, mere social or legal discrimination does not rise to the level of persecution."[145] She theorized that, "because most cultures around the world treat women as second-class citizens," the U.S. courts are concerned that if they adopt a different position, the country might be overwhelmed with potential female asylum seekers.[146] Smiley believes the courts should take note that FGM is a human rights violation that happens primarily to women, which should be a consideration in what makes an act persecution. Gender discrimination is not yet considered grounds for asylum, but some U.S. and Canadian courts often hold particularly egregious gender-based violence as forms of persecution.

Rahman and Toubia pointed out that FC/FGM "presents an unusual issue with respect to the Women's Convention's definition of discrimination against women. Since both men and women undergo types of circumcision, can FC/FGM be regarded as a 'distinction' based on sex?"[147] The authors answered, "Yes." There are certain similarities in male and female circumcision in that healthy tissue is removed and surgery is performed without consent of the child. However, most forms of FC/FGM are severe and its social message defines women and girls as subordinate to men.

Weisblat's position that "women refugees do not get a fair chance at asylum eligibility" is insightful.[148] First, even though INS Asylum Gender Guidelines exist, no clear definition exists of what acts constitute persecution. Second, there is a lack of guidance on "when a nongovernmental actor in the domestic setting is acting in the private sphere or committing a public act."[149]

Patricia A. Armstrong believes that although it has been slow to recognize FGM, the U.S. judiciary has made progress.[150] In spite of the need for improvement, in the *Kasinga* decision the United States followed Canada's lead. The BIA ruled for the first time that FGM is "a form of persecution that could be a basis for a discretionary grant of political asylum."[151] U.S. asylum law has undeniably advanced in recognizing that the violations of the rights of women are a deserving basis for asylum protection.

Renk Zengotitabengoa talked about the law and returning people to their home country for FC:

> There is also a little bit of a movement to have a Federal law passed that would make it a crime to send someone back to their home country. Often that is what will happen: a girl will be sent home for summer vacation and while she is at home, the family will arrange for her circumcision. There is some talk recently about having a law passed that would prohibit that, which would be in line with some other countries' laws, notably the United Kingdom, France and Australia.[152]

Johnson-Firth explained that the United Kingdom, France, and Australia are a little ahead on this issue because they have greater immigrant populations from countries where circumcision is performed. She saw first hand what is happening in the United Kingdom:

> I was just in England and dealt with this issue a little bit. Because it is against the law in the UK to remove a girl, to take her back home for FGC, teachers are told to look out for it and report it if the child goes to school and says that they are going on a vacation for a couple of weeks to their home country. Removing a child to her home country is happening here in the United States; it's just very underground.[153]

In February 2004, the first anniversary of Zero Tolerance Day in the United States was observed on Capitol Hill. At the observance, the 1996 law was assessed. The Congressional briefing that was part of the observance revealed there has been little follow-up of the programs to combat FGC. Immigration from practicing countries continues to grow, and it is reported that young girls are being taken back to their country of origin to have the surgery performed. Data have not been compiled on the number of women living in the United States who have been subjected to FGC or who are at risk. The programs initiated in the late 1990s that address individual and health provider needs had not been evaluated.[154]

The Congressional briefing identified successful international strategies but believed the programs needed to be scaled up for meaningful inroads to take place. Much of the work had been done in West Africa, with fewer initiatives in East Africa. The briefing brought out that more comprehensive programs are needed in reproductive health programs, for example, in the training of health providers. Medicalization is not an effective means to eradicate FGC because it tends to perpetuate the practice. Medicalization is seen as a violation of bodily integrity that undermines the health and human rights of women and girls. Finally, not all countries had enacted laws to prevent FGC.[155]

The data in Appendix 2 show that the countries represented have not only passed legislation but have other active outreach programs. The people I interviewed in Tanzania and Kenya indicated that the law alone is not enough because elimination of FGM/FC cannot be forced, but the law supported by educational programs will bring about change.

Karen Musalo wrote that "the term 'particular social group' and the determination of what is commonly referred to as 'nexus,'— the shorthand term used in the refugee adjudication context to describe the required causal connection between persecution and a [Refugee] Convention reason — may be among the most thorny interpretive issues in refugee law."[156] Since 1999, tribunals in the United Kingdom, New Zealand, and Australia have issued decisions that address social group and nexus with interpretations that are inclusive of women's claims. In June 2002, the United Nations High Commissioner for Refugees (UNHCR) affirmed the approach of these three countries when it published guidelines on social group and gender claims. However, the position of the United States on gender claims has been characterized "as being out of step with evolving jurisprudence, and inconsistent with international norms."[157] Musalo maintains that these countries have a unifying rationale that could help bring the United States into step with their positive adjudicatory trends.

The United Kingdom, New Zealand, and Australia and the UNHCR guidelines uphold the idea that a social group may be defined by gender, and if the role of the state as well as the individual persecutor is considered, nexus can easily be established. This approach is compatible with the underlying principles of the refugee protection regime: "to provide surrogate protection when the individual's country of nationality fails to do so."[158]

Musalo concluded that the position of the United States is contradictory and unsteady. The *Kasinga* case broke new ground because it contextualized the claim within the country and society of the asylum seeker. In the *Matter of R-A-* case, however, the position was reversed. Musalo suggested that when the BIA revisits the *Matter of R-A-*, "it can reach a protection-oriented decision by applying its own *Matter of Kasinga* precedent in a manner consonant with the rationale developed in its three sister-states, as well as the UNHCR. For the United States to do otherwise would be a regrettable rejection of well-developed refugee norms as well as international principles of nondiscrimination on the basis of gender."[159]

Other Cases Cited for Seeking Asylum in the United States

When we think of asylum in relation to FGM, the plight of women usually comes to mind. We do not usually think of a male seeking asylum on the basis of being subject to persecution related to FGM. So it was with Azeez Jimmy Imohi, who applied for asylum in 1994 on the basis that his return to Nigeria would infringe on his reproductive rights by putting at risk any female children he might have. His "asylum application alleged that he had been subject to persecution in Nigeria because he had founded a grass roots organization known as 'People Against Female Circumcision' (PAFC)."[160]

Imohi alleged the elders of his community threatened his life and his aunt's. He claimed that he could not be silent on the subject of FC. The BIA found Imohi's testimony unbelievable and denied his application for asylum and his request for a withholding of deportation. The Court upheld the BIA's decision.[161]

Sometimes interpretation of U.S. law must be disappointing to noncitizen parents, as was the case for Ruth E. Obazee. That Obazee, an alien's U.S. citizen daughter, would be subjected to FGM if the alien were returned to Nigeria did not entitle the alien to asylum. If the alien were deported, her daughter did not have to be deported because the child could remain in the U.S. with her father, a U.S. citizen.[162]

Sometimes aliens will apply because they fear persecution on the basis of gender due to prior subjection to FGM. In the case of Helen Seifu, the court did not find that a reasonable person in her circumstances would fear FGM because she had already undergone the procedure.[163]

Asylum Laws in Other Countries

Three countries beside the United States that have granted asylum under the U.N. Refugee Convention, according to Amnesty International, are Canada, Sweden, and Australia.[164] In 1993 Canada granted refugee status to a mother from Somalia, Khadra Hassan Farah. She fled her country with her ten-year-old daughter, Hodan, out of fear that Hodan would be forced to undergo FGM. The immigration officials ruled that Hodan's "right to personal security would be grossly infringed" if she were returned to Somalia.[165]

In 1997 two families were granted asylum in Sweden on the grounds that the female members would be in danger of FGM if they returned to Togo. The families were not considered refugees under the U.N. Refugee Convention but were granted residence permits on humanitarian grounds.[166]

The Australian Government's Guidelines on Gender Issues for Decision Makers, 1996, and the French Refugee Appeal Commission recognize that FGM may be classified as persecution and give rise to a claim for refugee status.[167]

CONCLUSION

FGM is an ongoing global concern. Because it occurs in so many parts of the world, governmental and nongovernmental bodies that address global issues are concerned. International human rights standards are being applied at the regional and national levels to combat FGM. Laws put into effect are aimed at the eradication of FGM. Evaluating the effectiveness of these laws is necessary to eliminate the practice. Although the success of eradication does not rest solely in laws, law is both a social product and a social force. Asylum is a key issue in industrialized nations. Asylum law in some countries is more advanced. Those countries lagging behind must work to have a more coherent legal theory.

4

Legal and Practical
Issues in the West

The theory of universalism holds that there are human rights
so fundamental to every human being that they transcend all
societal, political and religious constraints.

Robin M. Maher[1]

Nations in the West that legally ban female genital mutilation (FGM)
are faced with issues of definition, enforcement, and multicultural challenges. Sweden and the United States, for example, have laws against performing FGM and both face the challenge of immigrant populations
desiring to have genital plastic surgery. Voluntary genital cosmetic surgery
is under examination in Sweden. Is there a relationship between circumcision performed in other cultures and genital piercing and other forms
of cosmetic surgeries in Western countries?

Medicalization of FGM challenges the United States when immigrant
families must turn to private means to have the procedure done, including sending their daughters back to their home country. In the United
States, reinfibulation after childbirth is not against the law, but are there
ethical concerns? To what extent does the U.S. FGM law apply?

The practical issues of FGM in Western countries are imminent, and
education is critical. As new generations of immigrants grow up in their
new cultures, assimilation may take care of some of the legal and educational urgency in the West.

LEGAL ISSUES

Sweden

The 1982 Swedish law banning FGM also makes illegal any operation on or change made to a woman's genitals even if the woman has consented to surgery. The law was intended to eliminate FGM. In 2004, plastic surgeons reported a marked increase in women requesting genital plastic surgery. The reasons women request the surgery include esthetics and increased sexual pleasure. Young Muslim women request hymen reconstruction because they are expected to be virgins at the time of their marriage. The National Board of Health said cosmetic surgery may be illegal because the law bans all forms of FGM but makes no mention of voluntary cosmetic surgery. The Board will present a report to determine whether a new law is needed to the government sometime in 2004.[2]

The United States

Academic scholars Stanlie M. James and Claire C. Robertson echo the caution of legal scholars Joan R. Tarpley and E. Dana Neacsu that relying on one's own cultural milieu is difficult when judging another's claim of discrimination. James and Robertson noted the worsening and "lamentable tendency" of some Western media and feminists to sensationalize the issues of clitoridectomy and infibulation. Opinions in the West vary but few people consider themselves in favor of FGM. Some individuals hold the extreme view that all aid to a country practicing FGM should cease. The Women's Caucus of African Studies Association maintains that this approach is unsound. The challenge is in finding the appropriate and effective way to achieve the goal of eliminating the practice. They urge staying informed as the best means.[3]

Federal Legal Considerations

Several incidents propelled the subject of FGM into the foreground in the United States. One development was the novel and hour-long television documentary by Alice Walker with Pratibha Parmar "Possessing the Secret Joy and Warrior Marks." Two other events increased awareness in the United States. In 1994 Lydia Oluloro, an illegal immigrant from Nigeria, was successful in fighting deportation orders by the U.S. Immigration and Naturalization Service (INS). In 1995, Kasinga from Togo initially lost her bid for asylum claiming that FGM was persecution.[4] She later prevailed.

News of alien parents who have no standing to remain in the United States continue. On December 31, 2003, the Seventh Circuit held that Nigerian citizen Doris C. Oforji could not establish a derivative claim for asylum based on hardship to her citizen children who had the right to remain in the United States in the event of the alien's deportation. Her request for asylum was denied. The court held that Oforji's claim to derivative asylum under regulations implementing the Convention Against Torture lacked legal support.[5] The court said, "Oforji failed to state a claim for asylum based on 'derivative asylum' or 'constructive deportation'."[6] In 1997, Oforji testified that if she returned to her country, her two daughters born in the United States would be circumcised. Oforji had undergone the procedure required by the Ogoni tribe in Nigeria; to refuse is punishable by death. The court concluded there was no legal basis for Oforji to have her own deportation suspended because of her fear for her children if they returned with her. As United States citizens, the children had the right to stay without her. If they stayed, Oforji would have to choose a form of guardianship for them, a choice undesirable for her. Thus, the court said, "Oforji is in effect requesting that we amend the law to allow deportable aliens who have not resided here continuously for seven or ten years to attach derivatively to the right of their citizen children to remain in the United States."[7] Because the father was not a part of the family unit, Oforji was left with the choice of leaving her children in the United States with a guardian or having them return with her to Nigeria and its possible threat of FGM.

In 1996, the American Bar Association (ABA) discussed legal responses to FGM in the United States. The ABA found that although reliable statistics had not been compiled, strong anecdotal evidence suggested that FGM is being practiced in immigrant communities throughout the country. The ABA explained:

> A number of physicians have reportedly been asked by immigrants to perform the procedure on their daughters; in all cases, the physician has refused to do so.
>
> However, it is believed by the American College of Obstetrics and Gynecologists (ACOG) that a few U.S. physicians do perform the procedure, albeit with the disapproval of their colleagues. There are also reports that women have asked physicians to reinfibulate them following childbirth, citing concerns about retribution from their family or husband if it is not done.
>
> This evidence, together with the number of women and children showing up at U.S. hospitals with complications from the procedure, has led the ACOG, the American Medical Association, and the Union of American Physicians and Dentists to resoundingly condemn the practice. Unfortunately, and despite this opposition, there is no way to stop parents from performing FGM in the privacy of their own homes.[8]

The ABA reported that, in response to these reports, Congresswoman Patricia Schroeder introduced Federal legislation to criminalize the procedure in the United States. The United States has now criminalized the performance of FGM.

In 2000, James McBride addressed constitutional questions raised by the Federal Prohibition of Female Genital Mutilation Act, sponsored by Congresswomen Patricia Schroeder (D-Colo.), Barbara Rose Collins (D-Mich.), and Constance Morella (R-Md.) and added to the U.S. Code, Titles 1, 8, 18, and 22.[9] McBride contended that FGM was associated with the Islamic religious ritual of *khitan* and with the widely practiced and legally sanctioned male circumcision and that the statutes gave rise to First Amendment concerns of freedom of religious traditions and Fourteenth Amendment concerns of equal protection.

Controversy surrounds the Religious Freedom and Restoration Act of 1993. Its goal was to reestablish the standard of "compelling state interest" in judicial review of free exercise cases. This standard had been struck down by the Supreme Court in 1990 and again in 1997 by the High Court in *City of Boerne v. Flores*. Before 1990, the standard allowed the state to abridge the free exercise of religion only if it showed a "compelling state interest." The Court recognized such an interest was the welfare of children. Parents were free to become martyrs, but they were not free to make martyrs of their minor children. McBride concluded that the new laws did not violate free exercise or the equal protection rights of parents and the children they wished to "martyr."[10] The assumption underlying these issues is "that FGM is truly a religious practice."[11] He added that this assumption is disputed by different religious backgrounds— Islam, Christianity, and African faiths.

The criminalization of FGM also raised concerns of equal protection under the Fourteenth Amendment. The assumption was "that male circumcision and FGM are legally (if not strictly speaking medically) analogous."[12] Critics of this position contend that male circumcision is not analogous with FGM and that the appropriate analogy of FGM would be castration. McBride concluded, "If these assumptions hold true, state intervention to ban the practice in the United States would be subject to scrutiny by the Federal courts under existing First Amendment free exercise jurisprudence and Fourteenth Amendment equal protection analysis."[13]

In March of 1999, the American Academy of Pediatrics (AAP) announced that there is no weight of medical evidence in favor of routine neonatal male infant circumcision. Babies being circumcised do feel the pain. The AAP claimed they would no longer recommend circumcision as a routine neonatal operation and stated that circumcision should be an "ethical" choice.[14]

The Federal Prohibition of Female Genital Mutilation Act of 1995[15] made it a crime to practice FGM on persons under eighteen years of age, unless the procedure is necessary to protect health. The penalty is a fine and/or imprisonment for up to five years.[16] Congress directed government departments to work to eliminate FGM. The Department of Health and Human Services (DHHS) was to compile data on the extent of FGM in the United States, to engage in education and outreach activities in relevant communities, and to develop recommendations for medical students on the complications of FGM. The U.S. INS in cooperation with the Department of State must provide information on the harmful effects and legal consequences of FGM to all aliens issued U.S. visas. Congress also enacted legislation requiring U.S. executive directors of international financial institutions to oppose nonhumanitarian loans to countries that have not taken measures to prevent FGM.[17]

In addition to Federal legislation and directives, some states have passed laws and New York City has passed a local law.[18]

PRACTICAL ISSUES

In most industrialized countries where FGM is not allowed, some immigrants will seek to honor their cultural practices. Others will work against FGM. Those advocates face a challenge. "African women campaigning against FGM in the West have the triple burden of having to confront gender oppression, white liberal guilt, and racism within the community."[19] In reviewing Joan R. Tarpley's legal analysis, E. Dana Neacsu concluded that it "shows how difficult it is to rely on one's own cultural milieu when judging another's claim of discrimination deserving asylum relief."[20] Tarpley wrote that when people know that FGM is practiced by some black people on black girls, racist remarks occur. Evoking a strong sense of pride in their African heritage, black people become defensive. Racist remarks also set off guilt feelings in liberal whites "who may mean well but confuse the whole issue by condoning FGM within a naive concept of multi-culturalism."[21]

Holly Maguigan believes it is not advisable to enact special statutes that define FGM as a crime. She wrote that reliance on criminal prohibitions to change conduct and to exert social control is a well-established aspect of U.S. social policy. This reliance "persists even in the face of evidence that it is not an unmitigated success."[22] The state and Federal statutes share a common definition of the conduct not allowed, but differences exist in definitions of offenses, persons liable, statutory limitations, and sentences. Criminal sanctions do not give sufficient attention to the penalties faced by convicted immigrant parents, primarily mothers.[23]

Maguigan concluded that criminal sanctions should be in the background as a way to eradicate FGM in the United States. She believes they will drive immigrant parents to get the procedure performed in secret. Parents will be discouraged from getting needed medical assistance. They will also fear being removed from the United States.[24] Other Western nations have failed to create educational programs regardless of what law is in effect. The greatest success, however, has been in countries that do not criminalize FGM. Criminal sanctions in other countries have been ineffective, and Maguigan said the United States should acknowledge that these sanctions would be equally ineffective if we prosecute women in the name of keeping women and girls safe from violence without efforts to abolish FGM in a nonpunitive way.[25]

Allan Rosenfeld, M.D., wrote that the debate has evoked questions yet to be resolved. These questions concern the right of an individual or group to preserve their cultural beliefs and practices in a host country. Do members of the cultural group have the right to alter a child's body in the name of tradition? Should adults have the right to choose and consent to ritualistic altering of their bodies? While the debate goes on, "circumcised women and girls in host countries are faced with healthcare providers who have little if any information on FC/FGM and who are not trained in the management of its complications. Fortunately, one thing that is not under debate is the right to health and to receiving appropriate healthcare services."[26] Donna E. Shalala, Secretary of the U.S. DHHS, wrote that most healthcare providers will not encounter FGM until they see a woman who is pregnant or in labor, and then they will also confront medical decisions that have to be made quickly and that they have not ever before considered.[27]

Results of a nursing science study revealed that most Somali women living in the United States are frustrated because they can not circumcise their daughters. Healthcare providers face the dilemma of "whether the failure to perform the procedure will harm a woman's self-esteem and cultural identity or affect her social integration." The decision to have FGM performed is made by a woman on behalf of a child.[28]

The law alone will not bring cultural change. Education and economic independence for women will make acculturation easier, wrote Rita Morris. She proposes that working with the Somali people to discourage harmful practices is critical. Once they are in high school, Somali girls will realize that their peers are different. They are vulnerable to sexual identity problems.[29]

Immigrants

From 1997 to 1999, a nationwide project was conducted among 162 Canadian immigrants from regions in Africa where practices of excision and infibulation were still in effect. The study's conclusion was that gender identity is inextricably linked to notions about the ways in which girls, women, and virginity are socially constructed. The acculturation process and the integration within a host society is complex. Conflicting identities available to women result.[30]

Of the 130 million women worldwide who have undergone female genital cutting (FGC), about 190,000 females in the United States have either undergone the procedure or are at risk. The African Women's Health Center opened at Brigham and Women's Hospital in 1999. Its purpose is to offer specialized, holistic, and comprehensive care to African refugee women living in the United States. In 2001, there were eight hundred patient visits and thirty-three defibulations were performed on infibulated women who had long-term complications. Many of the Center's patients have undergone FGC and are living with its complications. The Center is committed to worldwide eradication of FGC. Not only is the Center the first of its kind in the United States, it is the only African health practice that focuses on FGC. The Center is under the direction of Nawal M. Nour, M.D., M.P.H., a board-certified obstetrician and gynecologist. Dr. Nour was born in the Sudan and raised in Egypt and England.[31]

As we examine the comparison of the practical approach versus the legal approach to circumcision, perhaps medical professionals should bear in mind that a circumcised woman's circumciser might have left an intact clitoris. The prevention and abolition of FGM and adequate medical care for "the already wounded" were the primary aims of a 1996 conference in Brighton, United Kingdom. During one session, Dr. Harry Gordon displayed photographs of FGM on a screen. He shared his discovery, "You see there, this rosy protrusion that had been hidden under the scar? It's a clitoris intact."[32]

In 80 percent of the 150 defibulations Gordon had performed, he found an untouched or mildly bruised organ in cases in which professionals would automatically assume the organ had been amputated. The physician gave as the reason, "I suppose the midwife wanted to avoid damaging her reputation by losing too many patients, since severing the clitoris—as opposed to 'merely' slicking [the] labia—places girls at greatly increased risk of bleeding to death. And also, she might have thought no one would know the difference."[33]

Nahid Toubia reported a similar circumstance in a case of the defibulation of a Sudanese woman living in the United States. During defibulation, the physician noted that the clitoris was only partially removed and care had been taken not to injure the tissue.[34]

Clitoral survival may have been a circumciser's practical way to handle a sociocultural requirement in Dr. Gordon's example, but it is good news for women requesting defibulation. The discoveries were not intended to distract from the urgency of abolition efforts, wrote Tobe Levin, who attended the conference.

Genital Cutting in the United States

Cutting of genitals in the United States has long been considered to have no relationship to FGM, but the questions should be asked: Is licensed medical cutting of one with ambiguous genitals without the woman's consent a form of FGM? Is popular culture's involvement in genital piercing also a form? Is the trend of Hollywood and mainstream middle-class culture toward cosmetic surgery a form? Are these cuttings a form of FGM only if there is no consent? Are some cultural pressures to conform leaving little choice not to cut?

Intersex Movement

The recent television documentary, "Opposite Sex: Rene's Story," portrayed the struggles of an adult woman with ambiguous genitals who decided to have surgery to become a male. One transsexual panelist said that as a society we need to recognize that gender is a continuum and that gender does not mean only two—male and female. To some, society has a third sex, the intersexual. The adult transsexual along with family, physicians, and enlightened scholars can contribute to making a difference. However, sometimes genitals are surgically reconstructed to assign a particular gender to a patient who is less than 2½ years of age.

The issue of gender-assignment surgery raises the question: Does what is proposed to be done or is done to people with ambiguous genitals bear a relationship to FGM? Cheryl Chase responded, "One of the forms of power that maintains gender boundaries in the United States is the surgical 'correction' of infants whose genitals are deemed by medical professionals to be socially unacceptable."[35] She observed, "Media and scholarly discourses continue a long tradition of making Africans into the 'other,' suggesting that ethnocentrism is a key factor in the sometimes purposeful maintenance of ignorance about U.S. genital surgeries."[36] One of the tenets of her essay is "the double standard regarding representations of genital cutting, depending upon who is cutting and where in the world the cutting is done."[37]

Although intersex surgeries affect children of both genders, Chase wrote that U.S. law on FGM is clear but the law was never intended to protect about "five children a day in the United States who are subjected to excision of part or all of their clitoris and inner labia simply because doctors believe their clitoris is too big."[38] The medical profession holds that a large clitoris or a small penis with a urethra placed other than at its tip is a "psychosocial emergency."[39] The surgery is performed because of the belief that the child would not develop into an emotionally healthy adult or be accepted by the mother and peers. This model of treatment for intersexual infant children was established in the 1950s.[40]

The positive part of the stories of discontented intersexuals is that much progress has taken place. Social justice movements helped make it possible for intersexed people to speak out. In 1999, a *Journal of Urology* article recommended ending feminizing surgeries because of tissue atrophy. The same year, the *Journal of Pediatrics* advocated not castrating micropenises.[41] Another positive effort is that in 1994 the Intersex Society of North America began a newsletter by and for intersexuals, *Hermaphrodites with Attitude*.[42] The Intersex Society of North America recommends a new model of treatment. The model is based on the avoidance of unnecessary surgery on infants and children.[43]

Western Hollywood and Mainstream Middle-Class Culture: Cosmetic Surgery

Virginia Blum's new book, *Flesh Wounds: The Culture of Cosmetic Surgery*, argues that we need to face that we are a "makeover-mad world."[44] The obsession has migrated from Hollywood to mainstream, middle-class American culture, wrote Blum.

In 1959, a medical journal article revealed how American medicine condoned female circumcision.[45] In 2004, Lisa Johnson-Firth raised the issue of body modification through plastic surgery and clitoridectomies in relation to FGM:

> When you are talking about FGM and the ways that women abroad may feel compelled to modify their bodies for social acceptance, it can't be lost that American women do the same things through plastic surgery. But even more poignantly, 2,000 girls in the United States a year have clitoridectomies, so that their clitorises are of the appropriate socially acceptable size in this country. And that's recommended by

doctors and parents. That is another interesting twist of this. We actually have a history of doing this to women in this country to curb lesbianism or masturbation or whatever, but now, we are doing it so that girls are socially conforming from their parents' standpoint.[46]

Johnson-Firth does not believe that genital piercing in popular culture is in the same category with FGM. She explained:

> The reason I'm drawing the line with clitoridectomies performed on young girls is because it occurs before they are of age to know what effect this will have on their own sexual feeling later on in life. It's done by their parents and their doctors. They have no choice. In FGM/FGC, I see that as analogous because most often it's happening to girls who don't have a choice, whereas body piercing I would generally say that, although that sounds excruciatingly painful to me, most of the people who do that are doing it of their own free will. It's not that we as a society are expecting them to do that. Maybe it could be argued we as a society are not expecting women to have breast augmentation either. I do see it as a little bit different. It's the consent issue so I would draw the line on it personally.[47]

The-Clitoris.com maintains, "There are many social and cultural traditions and practices that have a negative impact on the clitoris and female sexuality."[48] The first tradition is FGM. The second tradition is the clitoridectomy performed in the United States. The third is the denial of the existence of the clitoris. Most societies deny the existence of the clitoris.[49] Therefore, perhaps societies offer psychological surgery excising the clitoris. Perhaps an analogy can be drawn to cosmetic surgery and genital piercing — society plays a role, this much we cannot deny.

Western Popular Culture: Female Body Piercing — Fashion, Fad, or Mutilation

Authors L. M. Koenig and M. Carnes reviewed the available literature on body piercing. They concluded that it is "an increasingly common practice in the United States, it carries substantial risk of morbidity, and most body piercing in the United States is being performed by unlicensed, unregulated individuals."[50]

Victoria Pitts found a substantial rise in body modification in the 1990s. The types included the renaissance of tattoos, the rise in body piercing, the emergence of neo-tribal practices like scarification and flesh hanging, and the invention of new high-tech forms such as subdermal implants.[51] The same sex history of body modifications played a significant role in the rise of the body art movement.[52] Other authors found that "body art" is more popular than ever before because it is supposed to increase individuality. The many side effects include infections, especially hepatitis B and C.[53]

Pitts's research found that, on the one hand, body modification practices have been described as self-harming, mutilative, and self-objectifying. On the other hand, subcultural discourse provides the view of "positioning women's body modifications as rebellious acts of 'reclaiming' the female body."[54] Willfully and playfully constructed, body modifiers violate gender norms, explore taboo aspects of embodiment, and provoke attention and can be seen as examples of women's strength and independence. No universal standard exists by which to measure these practices.[55]

Is body modification self-mutilation? The view of some radical feminists is that body alteration is an instance of patriarchal mistreatment of women's bodies. The patriarchy is willing to make literal use of the female body, and some women are willing to happily endure the pain to shape the body. This view holds that the female body should be spared interference, alteration, and pain.[56]

What are the causes of body modification? For some, it arises out of the experience of being sexually abused as a child. Body modifiers maintain that a violated female body can be rewritten, while radical feminists argue that body modification is a replay of the violence once suffered. Others modify their bodies in reaction to society's norms about how they should look, think, and act.[57]

Pitts maintains "that women are not choosing whether or not to be modified and marked, but are negotiating how and in what way and by whom and to what effect."[58] Body modification in postmodern culture might be understood as an expression and reception of meaning or a form of self-determination in an increasingly wider number of cultural and technological options.[59]

Jean-Chris Miller wrote that body art is "all about expressing one's own personality,"[60] but the trendiness is for more than style. She explained, "But, of course, the *real* purpose of those piercings is to increase sexual stimulation. C'mon, do you really think someone would have a twelve-gauge post inserted through a sensitive body part if there wasn't a *big* payoff?"[61]

Although body piercing is not a new cultural phenomenon, it appears to be on the increase. Along with this increase, there is a developing industry of body modification in which cutting, tattooing, and piercing are performed in studios for profit. S. Jeffreys offers a feminist understanding of the industry and places it on a continuum of harmful cultural practices that include self-mutilation in private, transsexual surgery, cosmetic surgery, and other harmful Western beauty practices:

The ideology created by industry practitioners, that "body modifica-tion" replicates the spiritual practices of other cultures, reclaims the body, or is transgressive, ... Such harmful cultural practices of self-mutilation are sought, or carried out on, those groups who occupy a despised social status, such as women, lesbians and gay men, disabled people and women and men who have suffered sexual abuse in child-hood or adulthood.[62]

In the sense that body modification may replicate the spiritual practices of other cultures, there may be a relationship between body modification and FGM.

Genital Piercing

It isn't enough to understand why women pierce. If we look at the more elaborate types of genital piercing, the question could be posed, "Are we so different from tribal customs of other countries?" The Internet has ample information on types of body modifications, including female gen-ital piercing. On one Web site, six types of female genital piercing are listed: Clit Piercings, Triangle Piercings, Inner Labia Piercings, Hood Pierc-ings, Outer Labia Piercings, and Other Female Piercings.[63] Although the Body Modification Ezine (BME) body piercing site stresses safety, the piercing of these areas leaves open the question of safety. This is particu-larly so in two of the more extreme piercings listed under Other Female Piercings: the Princess Albertina (a transurethral piercing) and the Isabella (a deep clitoral/hood piercing).

The Princess Albertina is not done often. BME explained, "This extremely rare piercing enters the female urethra and exits at the top of the vagina. A woman must have a large urethra to be able to get it, and should be warned that a piercing in this location can increase their risk of bladder infections."[64]

Also rarely done is the Isabella, which is deep clitoral shaft piercing. BME explained, "This extremely deep clitoral shaft piercing starts below the clitoris and just above the urethra, and then goes up through the cli-toral shaft and exits at the top of the hood. Because this piercing inter-sects the shaft of the clitoris, some piercers maintain it has the risk of nerve damage. Either way, it is an extremely rare piercing."[65]

Is the culture of the United States so different from others with the practice of body piercing? In an interview, I asked physician Dr. M. Neil Williams, "What is your opinion of women, and men for that matter, in the United States popular culture who engage in genital piercing? Wouldn't that be a cultural behavior?"

He replied, "That's a cultural behavior. It's a bad idea. I can't imagine that can be very comfortable, for one thing. There again you have all the problems of infection, bleeding, scar tissue build up, and that kind of thing. I know even with ear piercing we find lots of complications: cyst formation, infection, chronic problems."[66]

I asked Dr. Williams why he thought people in our popular culture do body piercing. His reply, "They want to be different."[67] Results of one study confirm his observation.[68]

I asked, "Is piercing something physicians would help young men and women do or is this something they do at piercing places? If someone would come to a regular physician and ask them to do piercing, would they do it?" Dr. Williams's answer helps to understand piercing, and ear piercing in particular, in the context of time:

> When ear piercing became popular, it was done in doctors' offices and I did a lot of them — piercing the lobe of the ear. I didn't promote it, but if a woman asked for it, I thought, well, this is fairly harmless, why not do it under sterile conditions. Doctors don't do it anymore. Most places that do it, do it under fairly good sterile conditions and are careful about it. It's a very simple thing. But when it comes to other parts of the body like the tongue, I can't imagine that. People even do it to themselves or split the tongue. That's even worse when they divide the tongue. I don't understand why people do that or why young people go through that. It certainly does have health considerations, primarily infection.[69]

Health Issues

Body piercing raises concerns about health-related issues such as HIV, substance abuse, hepatitis, dental problems, and reproductive complications. In Sheffield, United Kingdom, a study of nine piercing establishments found that there was a general lack of knowledge about possible serious complications from ear piercing.[70] J. Niamtu wrote that earlobe repair is a common request in cosmetic facial surgery and the increase in piercing will bring more piercing-related complications to the cosmetic surgeon.[71]

Tattooing and body piercing are on the rise, especially among college students. In one study, more frequent health problems and impulsive decision making were noted for those with body piercing than those with tattoos. Three cases of hepatitis were reported.[72]

The other side of the increase in body art, at least in tattooing, is the skyrocketing rate of removal. Laser removals increased 27 percent from 2001 to 2003, according to the American Society for Dermatologic Surgery. The Academy says the number of tattoo studios in the United States increased from three hundred to more than four thousand in the past twenty years, and about ten million Americans have a tattoo.[73]

"The practice of oral tissue piercing, until recently, has been limited mainly to various native tribes in Africa. However, in recent years, body piercing (including oral tissue piercing), has become increasingly popular in the United States and Europe."[74] One reason that body piercing is popular is jewelry. One site, Painless Pleasures, offers a variety of jewelry for placement in the tongue, navel, belly button, nipple, nostrils, and eyebrows. Furthermore, the site offers tips for safe sex after genital piercing.[75]

Metallic piercings can cause adverse reactions including allergic reactions.[76] A thirty-one-year-old woman experienced chronic pelvic pain. Medical analyses revealed that her multiple body piercings "revealed an umbilical adhesion from the small bowel to the anterior abdominal wall."[77]

Of great concern is the risk of HIV. One study focused on "the relationship of alcohol and drug use to tattooing and body piercing — an often overlooked HIV risk behavior."[78] These authors concluded, in part, that "The popularity of tattooing and piercing and the risk involved with these activities make them an HIV risk behavior worthy of address."[79]

Similar studies have been conducted focusing on the relationship of body modification in adolescents and alcohol and drug use. This study concluded that in one-third of their sample, body modification was associated with self-reported problem alcohol and other drug use.[80]

Oral piercing has been found in a number of studies to create various dental problems such as gingival recession and mucogingival defects.[81] In the case of one woman who did not remove her jewelry before surgery, tongue piercing produced difficulty in breathing.[82] Other side effects include chipped or cracked teeth. The most common gingival problem was trauma to the lingual anterior gingiva. Two patients reported a salivary flow-stimulating effect.[83]

CONCLUSION

Law in the United States initially raised constitutional concerns. In all countries, laws prohibiting FGM challenge actual practice. Immigrant populations best represent this challenge. How their rights are balanced with the laws of their host country is a timely concern. Will there be a move toward true multiculturalism or will the need for FGM fade with each successive generation? Meanwhile, the law alone is not enough. Law combined with education appears to be the best approach.

Although no universal standard exists by which to measure the practice of body modification, the question of the relationship between some forms of body modification and FGM remains.

5

Tradition and Change in Practicing Cultures

Mama, wenzangu wametahiriwa likizo hii mimi nitatahiriwa lini?
Daughter: Mama, my colleagues have been circumcised. When am I going to be?
Mwanangu usitahiriwe ni mateso ya ajabu maisha yako yote.
Mother: No, don't be circumcised, my daughter, you will suffer your whole life.
Usimtahiri Mwanamke Mpe Elimu
Don't Circumcise a Woman! Give Her Education!
Message on poster, Tanzania[1]

Continuing with the culture that is good without cutting. That means that there are certain good things the community may permit in their own cultural setting that may continue without cutting.
Mrs. Juliet Chugulu, Moshi, Tanzania.[2]

Molefi Kete Asante wrote in 1988 that it is conceivable that Africans are experiencing "the birth of a collective Afrocentricity, not realized since ancient time."[3] The Euro-American response to the rise of African spirit will be positive, said Asante. Afrocentricity will reinterpret history and present a new way of looking at race and power relationships. The way a person becomes Afrocentric is the only way to break though or take transcending action, which takes people from the traditional to the revolutionary consciousness. In its most elemental state, it is called "the eradication, blotting out, of the old and opening up to the new."[4] Asante explained that when each person chooses to become Afrocentric, the person experiences "a certain tearing away from mental and psychological habits that held you enslaved to Eurocentric concepts. This is a violent process. It is a separation and all separations are violent. We move away from the lifestyles of oppression and victimization."[5] Asante's titles for these two sections are appropriate to the change taking place in Africa today, "Seizing the Time" and "The Transcendent Process."[6]

Tradition and change are clashing over female genital mutilation (FGM) in African culture. Change that reduces or eliminates FGM generates enthusiasm among African anti-FGM activists. The professionals I interviewed during my visit to Kenya and Tanzania in 2004 were passionate about and dedicated to breaking through, bringing people to a new level of consciousness, and removing traditional FGM from their countries. However, these professionals are the first to recognize that for some African citizens, a difference still exists between the debate about and the practice of FGM.

DEBATE VERSUS PRACTICE

The answer to the remaining difference between the debate and the practice, say these professionals, is education, not force. They caution that changing a culture takes time and, while the change is in progress, other ways of celebrating culture must be substituted for time-honored traditions.[7]

The Debate

Ellen Gruenbaum maintained that for those people outside of the cultural context where circumcision is practiced, understanding is more than just knowing the facts or arriving at a position for or against.[8]

Before cases of FGM became high profile in industrialized nations, the subject of FGM was somewhat taboo for those outside the cultures that practiced it. Gruenbaum pointed out that because most people are shocked when they first learn about female circumcision (FC), it leads them to consider the subject taboo. She adds, "But female circumcision is not a secret at all. In Sudan everyone knows about it." When she discussed with a Sudanese legal scholar the subject of circumcision being taboo, the scholar said, "It's not a secret; we celebrate it."[9] I interviewed Maasai in Tanzania who also celebrate it. The Maasai men and women openly and freely discussed female circumcision. In my interviews I learned that they do not want to lose the celebration and rewards. They are not in favor of not circumcising in general. Girls who are allowed to attend school learn about not being circumcised and are not totally in agreement with their elders.[10]

Humanitarian Values and
Cultural Relativism

Claudie Gosselin maintains there have been two lines of division that have resulted from the debate over cultural relativism, and the debate has become polarized. The lines are accentuated in growing international focus on human rights, especially after the 1993 United Nations Vienna Conference, and on women's human rights since the 1995 U.N. World Conference on Women at Beijing.[11]

Cultural relativists believe Westerners should stay away from FC altogether. Those who advocate global campaigns to eradicate circumcision do not reflect current realities, according to Gosselin. These campaigns are based on human rights, Islamic revivalism, and feminism.[12]

Sondra Hale, a researcher in Sudan and Eritrea, asked the reader to step back and ask why "the idea of 'female circumcision' is the *only* idea an American may hold about Africa or the middle east."[13] She asked, "What do our points of view reflect about the politics of knowledge?"[14] She listed eleven positions taken in the insider versus outsider debate. The last two are her position:

> In some areas of Africa, for example, people have a lot more to worry about than these practices (e.g., drought, starvation, war, disease, infertility, high infant and mother mortality, and abject poverty—not to mention economic exploitation and neo-colonialism). We should stop using cultural excuses for crimes against women and children.[15]

Hale asks those of us involved with the subject of FC not to have what the feminist poet Marilyn Frye called, "arrogant perception." It is not so much what we know, but what we do with the knowledge.[16]

Anke Van Der Kwaak, a researcher in Somalia, said it another way. Although Westerners may have clear perceptions about infibulation, "we should try our notions with patience. Without subscribing to cultural relativism, we should leave much to the people themselves."[17] Van Der Kwaak cautioned that, although we in the West may have sincere intentions, we should be careful not to march to the sound of a drum Somalian women cannot hear.

Christine J. Walley, a researcher in Kenya, offered a position to resolve understanding "female genital operations in 'either/or' terms, in other words, in terms of *either* cultural relativism *or* politically-informed outrage."[18] She asked if the polar viewpoints held by people in Europe and the United States—moral opprobrium or relativistic tolerance—are enough to form a feminist and humanist political response to the issue of female genital operations. She suggested that the positions represented in the debate share an unacknowledged common thread, "This commonality is a hardened view of 'culture' based on a rigid essentialist notion of the difference that can be historically linked to the colonial era."[19]

Richard A. Shweder, an anthropological researcher, encourages listening to the multicultural voices of feminism. Some cases may be less one-sided than we think.[20] Shweder and other anthropologists find an inconsistency between what they see in the field and what they read in the scholarly literature. Shweder bases his research, in part, on the works of medical anthropologist Carla Obermeyer. Obermeyer suggested that claims of the anti-FGM movement are exaggerated and do not match reality. Obermeyer also reported that publications lack evidence of the devastating effects of FGM and that methodological flaws are apparent in some studies.[21]

Shweder proposes that prevalence rates suggest circumcision is routine and normal in many groups and that for both sexes the best predictor of circumcision is ethnicity or cultural group affiliation, just as other approval ratings of the custom are high. In the mid-1980s, most women in Africa had voting rights. They could influence policy decisions regarding harmful practices, yet they upheld the mores of their communities. This, too, says Shweder, lends support to show that circumcision of women is a poor example of patriarchal domination.[22] According to Shweder circumcision is a poor example of gender inequality or discrimination against women because in Africa it is more a case of the society treating boys and girls equally by introducing them to society in parallel ways.[23]

Isabelle R. Gunning, an African-American feminist and professor of law at Southwestern University School of Law, wrote, "American culture has a long tradition of racialized and racist 'us'–'them' imagery which intertwines with our colonial/ imperial heritage."[24] Gunning agreed with Sondra Hale that the popularization of female genital surgeries (FGS) in the popular consciousness can be characterized as an "arrogant perception." The approach to the problem is not that the issue is presented as negative but that it denigrates all other cultures, typically African, ignoring FGS's existence in Arab and Asian countries. Nor is enough attention given to the strength and ability of African people, especially its women, to struggle against their own problems.[25]

The 1980s global debate was led by feminists such as Janice Boddy, Kay Boulware-Miller, Mary Daly, Efua Dorkenoo, Fran Hosken, Hannie Lightfoot-Klein, and Alice Walker. Efua Dorkenoo directs the Foundation for Women's Health, Research and Development (FORWARD) International, the most active nongovernmental organization (NGO) working on FGS outside of Africa.[26] Dorkenoo's *Cutting the Rose* is an effort to gather support for a global effort to eradicate FGM. She also highlights that African feminists are divided on the issue of circumcision.[27]

The issue of FC became part of a global debate in the United Nations World Conference on Women in the mid-1980s in Copenhagen. Gosselin wrote that at this conference Western and African feminists were bitterly divided. For author Angela Gilliam the debate epitomized the division in the women's movement "between those who believe that the major struggle for women is increasing their access to, and control over, the world's resources and those who believe that the main issue is access to, and control over, orgasms."[28] The debate in Copenhagen gave insight into the division. FGM is a human rights issue that is campaigned against as violence against women. Gosselin said FC is unlike any other gender-specific violence. It may be a global issue but it basically is an African occurrence. Thus, she believes this is why the issue pits the West against Africa.[29]

Since the 1993 United Nations Conference in Vienna, FGM has been presented as a violation of human rights. Nahid Toubia argued for this position. Kay Boulware-Miller's work opposes FGM because it "violates the rights of the child or the woman's right to sexual and corporeal integrity."[30] Gosselin wrote this reason alienates many African women because the research of Lightfoot-Klein, Gruenbaum and her own in Mali demonstrates that circumcised women do experience sexual satisfaction.

Gosselin wrote that the "right to health" argument is more culturally sensitive and less problematic. However, she also believes that this approach tends to reduce women and girls to their genitals. Although health consequences may often be exaggerated or misreported, they are undeniable, according to Nahid Toubia, a prominent writer and physician wrote Gosselin.[31]

Gruenbaum wrote that when FC becomes known, people outside the cultures often conclude that continuing the harmful practices violates humanitarian values. She posed the question, "If these practices are based on deeply held cultural values and traditions, can outsiders effectively challenge them without challenging the cultural integrity of the people who practice them?"[32] She questions whether it is permissible to try to change another culture's beliefs and practices. Even if it is permissible, how effective will the change be? She suggests that viewing cultural differences naively from one's own cultural perspective is not preventable and is not necessarily harmful, but some views lead to misconceptions and negative judgments. These views contribute to prejudice. Too often people "latched onto some single cause" against FC.[33] She concluded that without understanding the views of those people who practice circumcision, real change will not occur.

Gruenbaum's philosophy is that a culture should be judged within its own context rather than by the values of others. This position is not the "ultimate ethical stance," but is a beginning to avoid negativism.[34] No clear rule exists for a person to decide when to apply a universal moral standard and when to view the world through the moral values of one's culture. Gruenbaum concluded that this dilemma is at the core of the controversy over FC, "Assertion, appeals to reason, or complex logical arguments cannot easily dislodge beliefs rooted in culture, faith, emotion, a different philosophical perspective or lack of knowledge."[35]

Hope Lewis asked, "Is 'cultural relativism' a smokescreen that enables governments and non-state actors to legitimize the oppression of women?"[36] Furthermore, she questions whether the international human rights system is accessible to women affected by FGS or if it is merely a collection of irrelevant theoretical constructs. She concluded that a fruitful by-product of a better understanding of the FGS controversy is a more profitable engagement between African-American and African feminists who support the eradication of FGS, even though it is not likely to result in a universally acceptable resolution to the debate.[37]

Two prominent African female professionals active in confronting FGS are Nawal El Saadawi, an Egyptian physician, and Nahid Toubia, a Sudanese surgeon. These physicians combine their training in Western medicine with their understanding of the cultural and political perspective of the communities from which they came. Awa Thiam, a Senegalese political activist, wrote a condemnation of FGS in her 1978 book *Black Sisters: Speak Out*. African women living in the West who have also been active are Sella Efua Graham, a Ghanaian nurse in London and author Efua Dorkenoo.[38] African organizations, such as the Association of African Women for Research and Development (AAWORD) and the Inter-African Committee on Traditional Practices Affecting the Health of Women and Children (IAC) also work against FGS.[39]

M. Neil Williams, M.D., a retired general surgeon and missionary physician who has served among the Maasai on three different occasions, discussed the medical ethical issues of a female immigrant wanting to be circumcised:

> Ethically there is no need, no health or hygiene reasons to have it done in a female, where you can make that argument in males that removing the foreskin promotes better hygiene and so on — the usual reasons given for circumcision — which may or may not be true. It is not an ethical problem except from the standpoint of disfiguring and result-

ing in a defect for sexual pleasure or sexual gratification. It is ethically wrong from that standpoint.[40]

I asked Williams if ethical issues would be raised if an American physician refused a woman's request for the procedure knowing that she would find someone else to do it where conditions might not be as sanitary, instruments might not be as clean, and the woman might suffer more. Would a physician ask him or herself whether he or she should do it? He replied, "Certainly from that standpoint, any physician would advise against having it done in the home — it is a surgical procedure — and it would be just like having abortion done in a clinic that is not legitimate or does not have good medical, surgical sterilization and other practices."[41]

I asked Williams what a caring physician does when an immigrant woman comes to him or her and says, "I want to have this done. I don't have a sanitary way to do it, but I am going to do it." He replied:

> I don't know what you can do other than try to discourage her from doing it. If I was the physician in that situation, I would not feel that I am ethically or morally bound to do it just because I'm afraid that she might do it. If she is determined to do it, there is nothing you can do to stop it. I doubt that you would find any physician in this country that would do it. A plastic surgeon might, or a gynecologist, that's another possibility.[42]

Williams sees the practice of circumcision for women as harmful. He believes we should discourage any harmful cultural practice and does not see this effort as imposing our cultural values upon another culture. He explained:

> Female circumcision is harmful and is degrading to women and it may result in complications in childbirth and, certainly, may have some effect on their enjoyment of sex with their husband, which interferes with that union of man and wife and must, in some way, help produce some estrangement or lack of companionship or union. Whatever we can do to discourage the practice should be done, either legally or through changing cultural mores. That is happening, especially among Maasai that have become Christian. Not that we want to impose our cultural norms on them, but any cultural practice that is harmful, we should try to discourage or change.[43]

Radhika Coomaraswamy, the United Nations Special Rapporteur on Violence Against Women, wrote that in the everyday life of women across the world the "tension between the rights of groups to practice their culture and the rights of women under international human rights norms plays itself out."[44] The FGM controversy is one example of this tension. Coomaraswamy wrote that in 1990 Fuambai Ahmadu, an African scholar from Sierra Leone, spoke with emotion at the American Anthropological Association:

> It is difficult for me, considering the number of ceremonies I have observed, including my own, to accept that what appear to be expressions of joy and ecstatic celebrations of womanhood in actuality disguise hidden experiences of coercion and subjugation. Indeed, I offer that the bulk of Kono women who uphold these rituals do so because they want to ... embrace the legitimacy of female authority, and particularly, the authority of their mothers and grandmothers.[45]

Coomaraswamy found that African feminists and physicians such as Nawal El Saadawi and Asthma El Dareer, Western feminists Alice Walker and Fran Hosken, and the human rights group Equality Now presented a view contrasting with that of Fuambai Ahmadu.[46]

Coomaraswamy wrote that the FGM debate has become one of colonialism and imposed Western values. Feminist pioneers believe that an important element in eliminating the practice is imposing criminal sanctions. However, Western feminists are challenged by African scholars' view that FGM is "being human the African way." The African way, they say, is that FGM is the rite of passage to womanhood linked to symbolic birth and ideas of being a woman. In turn, individual African women disturb the African scholars' "romanticization of FGM as a celebrated practice of being a woman the African way." One example is how women activists in Kenya, Senegal, and Egypt conduct door-to-door campaigns against FGM. Another is the case of Fauzia Kasinga, who, with the help of her mother and sister, fled from Togo to the United States to seek asylum.[47]

The insider/outsider differences blur as immigrants bring FC to non-practicing countries, Gruenbaum wrote. The world becomes more connected and the health of women and girls is a global issue.[48]

The African Immigrant

When we discuss change in countries that practice FGM, we have to consider also the change facing those immigrants. My hometown of Grand Island, Nebraska, is a microcosm of the United States in that it is multicultural. Some scholars believe that the benefits of a diverse society will not be realized until the larger society recognizes that multiculturalism rather than assimilation is more desirable.[49] These scholars point out that more research is needed on multiculturalism as opposed to assimilation. Even so, what are the implications of multiculturism? If we as a society were to benefit, would we not expect those who practice FGM to forego the practice once in the United States? How then do immigrants who believe in circumcision cope?

Countries other than the United States experience immigration. Attorney Lisa Johnson-Firth, Director of Legal Services at the Tahirih Justice Center in Falls Church, Virginia, poses thought-provoking challenges within the United States. She asked that we be aware that despite our advances and the feminist movement in the United States, women are under extreme pressure to conform to societal images of women. Women's advances in the United States are recent history. In 1920, women gained the right to vote. She stated:

> It was only in the 1950s that doctors stopped performing clitordectomies to prevent women from masturbating, from being promiscuous or demanding on their husbands, or from becoming a lesbian. And, although we may not practice the extreme of FGC [female genital cutting] on our daughters, 2,000 American girls each year are at risk of losing a part of their clitoris because doctors and parents deem their clitoris to be socially non-conforming in that it is larger than the accepted 3/8 inch at birth. Furthermore, what does it say about our culture and the equality of women when in 2002[,] 237,000 women had breast implants, known to have severe physical complications; 106,000 women had face lifts; 230,000 women had liposuction; and nearly a million got themselves injected with Botox, a highly toxic substance.[50]

Johnson-Firth wrote that these figures do not include the number of teenage girls in the United States or other indicators of low self-esteem arising out of the patriarchal nature of the U.S. society. She points out that holistic change is needed to help women who suffer inequality under the law. Suffering exists for women in cases of unequal pay, no access to education, sex-selective infanticide and feticide, domestic violence, rape, and honor crimes. She concluded, "The eradication of FGC, just one extreme symptom of the global inequality of women, cannot occur until the foundations of sexism are eradicated for all women worldwide."[51]

My interviews with Sudanese refugees in Grand Island, Nebraska, were made possible through Jon Heinrich, Director of Missions at Trinity Lutheran Church. Heinrich stated that the Sudanese migrated to Grand Island in 2002. Between five hundred and six hundred Sudanese lived in Grand Island in August 2003. He explained that for the most part, the Sudanese who come in contact with Trinity Lutheran Church are Christian.[52] I asked Heinrich if he thought it possible that as time goes on the church might be asked to face the issue of FGM with the Sudanese community. He responded: "I don't have a good sense of that. I just don't know if that would be an issue or not. A lot of the families tell me it's not practiced anymore among the American Sudanese. So, that would make me think that it wouldn't be an issue, but I suppose that there is always the potential out there that it could be an issue."[53]

Heinrich said I should ask one of the church's pastors to answer the theological question I posed: "What might the church's role be if, say, in the future someone did come to you with a firm resolve to have this procedure done on their daughter?"

I had observed in some of my interviews with the Sudanese that the women did not speak because they did not know English. I asked Heinrich why the women don't know the language like the men do. He said he believed that:

> Some of that goes back to Sudan. It is a pretty male-dominated culture. Some of it goes back in time that the men didn't want the women to learn a lot of English. In some of their political things, with some of the men, not all of them, that's a very controlling thing: if you speak English and they don't, then you can manage these other people. And you can do that under the guise of being helpful, but it gives you quite a bit of power and control if you can help them with language.[54]

Heinrich added that the church has tried at times to help the women learn the language but they are very busy with their children and their jobs. He thinks that, as the children go to school and have to learn English, the mothers will become more involved in the language. Assimilation will come.

Heinrich said he thinks much about culture and other cultures like the Sudanese. "In terms of our perspective of them, it is important to remember that just because it is different, doesn't make it wrong. It is a cultural thing. It's their culture. We do it this way, they do it that way. That is a cultural product."[55] Heinrich stressed that his statement "should not be construed as condoning practices which are morally wrong. Female circumcision is not a good idea in my opinion."[56]

In an interview with Sudanese refugees from South Sudan, we asked Jenty Nawal Chacha Kosta from Juba and her husband Aban Laamatjok from Malakal, "What will people do that come to the United States believing in this custom and want to have this procedure done on their children? Will they send their children back to Africa to get it done or will they try to have it done in the United States?"

Aban answered, "There are Muslim societies and communities here, like where we were in DC. There we have a large group of Sudanese Arabs. They perform this by themselves here, because they know that they cannot do it in the hospitals. And some of them will have the chance to go back to Africa to Sudan, Saudi Arabia or Egypt. They send their daughters back there and they perform this surgery and they come back."[57]

Aban explained, "How long a daughter stays in Africa when she is returned there for the surgery depends. One month is enough time to recover."

We asked whether they knew of any individuals who changed their minds about having the surgery done once they came to the United States or whether they knew of anyone who changed their ways of looking at the tradition once they were in our culture. Aban said they did not know any person in particular, but:

> What we know is some of the Sudanese Muslims are here from the big cities, like the capital, Khartoum. Most of them no longer perform this surgery once in the United States—even in Sudan in their communities. But those who are moving from the countryside and rural areas, most still believe in this surgery. But in big cities where there is education and the government is near, people start to give it up. They realize it is a wrong act because they realize the disadvantages for their daughters. But those who are coming from the far villages, they are still performing surgery, because it will take time for them, even if they are in the United States, to change their minds and learn to adopt new things, and to discover that this is kind of surgery is not good.[58]

Jenty believes, "The Muslims who are here now, many of them forget about those things and don't do it anymore."[59]

Aban added, "Some of them still do it here. Some go back."[60]

We asked if in the United States the surgery would be done by a religious leader or if it would be done by somebody else in the community. Aban replied, "Some of them would be done by a religious leader and some of them by someone else who has some qualifications to do it."[61]

Jenty added, "These kind of people who can do that are the religious people. The Arabs who are religious can have their own doctors and have money. They can go to Sudan, do it there and come back."[62]

Aban explained, "They know also that this surgery is against the law. So, even while they perform it, they are still doing it in secret here, because they know that if they are caught, they might go to prison or something or they may be deported. So they are doing it in a secret way."[63]

We asked, given the secrecy, if there still is a celebration with circumcision done in the United States. Aban answered:

> No. If they do, it would be in a limited way. It is not like in Sudan. In Sudan, you just declare this surgery in the open. But here you cannot do like that.
>
> They say we will have a dinner. They will invite only the close family and friends, those who they trust. They cannot go and report this surgery. Because if they know that someone is opposing it, they will never let him know what is going on. Even if you are a friend of the family, you will just say, "Our daughter, she is married and she had

surgery." And they will give any name of any other surgery, just to prevent saying. Because if you were to ask, "Where is Nanny?" "She is sleeping inside. She's sleeping." They will never go into detail and tell you actually what happened.[64]

Mut Ruey, who is from south Sudan and resides in Grand Island, told us, "Those who are doing that kind of circumcision are Muslim, and the Muslims are in northern Sudan. In south Sudan, they do not do that kind of surgery."[65] He then spoke to the issue of whether some people from Africa might return their children to the homeland for circumcision:

> If I wanted to send my children back to Africa, in Sudan — as long as they are dependent on me, I may say, "O.K. I want you to stay in Sudan for seven years, maybe two to three years. So after two to three years, you can come back." So, whenever they feel like they don't want to come back, it is their choice. But they don't have a choice to say that "I'm not going back to the United States," while they are still under me. So, I would say, "Come back to the United States."[66]

William G. Riek is the President for the Sudanese Refugee Community Organization (SRCO) and the Refugee Advocate for the Community Humanitarian Resource Center (CHRC) in Grand Island. Riek obtained information about FC from Muslims from Sudan. He said,

> They say that they do surgery or circumcision particularly on the female because it deals with sexual desire. Men have formed an impression, too much desire for young ladies is not favored, this way they circumcise women to control sexual activities. They put it this way — circumcision is a cultural and Islamic practice. The Arab culture controls the ladies in the ways that they want, for example, women are to be good Muslims, to cover their heads, to dress like the Muslims want.
> Circumcision doesn't seem like it does something bad. But when the lady wants to give birth, there is a little problem. It is not easy to have labor or contractions like normal ladies that have had no operation.
> Here in the United States circumcision is not allowed for women. The Arabs do it tribally and, according to them, they have it done in Sudan by some midwives and some nurses. They have knowledge.[67]

Riek explained more about attitudes in the United States. He said, "Generally, the Muslims say they do not do it so much, maybe they do it privately. What I know is they send children back to the country to do it the traditional way. It's not so functional here, someday they will forget about it, they do not have good enjoyment to do it because they do it privately. Circumcision is not allowed."[68]

Riek explained that the Muslim population from Sudan circumcises three ways. The first way is by cutting all of the vaginal area, or as Riek explained "cut all of it from the root. All of the clitoris is removed. The upper part of the vagina is stitched to make the opening small and tight. The operated part of the vagina will remain until the time women give birth. At that time, the stitched area is opened to allow the child to come through the birth canal. As soon as the child is born, the vaginal areas are stitched again."[69]

In the second way, Riek said:

> A little adjustment is made. It is very easy for them to make an adjustment or a little incision or not to cut at all, for example, shaving the area. Whatever is done, is done without removing the clitoris. Even in Sudan the milder form is sometimes done. The operation is the same anywhere they are. They don't do it for all the people here because the culture in which they are living does not allow this. Or no insurance.[70]

Riek said that some in the Muslim population do it illegally. If they do it in the United States privately, the circumciser is a midwife or nurse who is known for performing circumcision. If they know a medical person, that person will perform the circumcision for them. Because insurance does not cover this procedure, Riek said, "People pay the bill themselves or send their daughters back home to have it done."[71]

The third way the Muslims from Sudan circumcise is to "cut the top part of the vagina, leaving the remaining parts uncut."[72]

The Muslim population that Riek visited said the side effects include no satisfaction or enjoyment during sexual intercourse, infection from unclean instruments, pain before the wound is healed, and complications at labor or while giving birth.[73] Riek said, "Generally, difficulty in birth is related to delay. The area the child comes through, he's so big for that area, they do the operation like they do for all to get the child out.[74] They may have infection because it is a wound, and if they cannot treat it so it will heal, they will have difficulty."[75]

Riek explained why circumcision is done among those of the Muslim faith, "The operation is performed to control the woman's desire for sex and to keep the vaginal canal tight during sexual acts. Women feel little or nothing in the way of sensation during sexual intercourse, but the big thing is culture. In their culture you are dealing with Islamic religion."[76] He explained more about a Sudanese Muslim's view of circumcision in the United States:

> The man would not see another young woman. He will still be satisfied by his woman. But when the young women become mature, they don't like circumcision because they are not satisfied and do not enjoy sex acts because they feel no sensation. By now, in civilizations of the world or in free countries, the women decide not to continue the practice in their young daughter, as they do back home. At home in Sudan,

the circumcision time is at the age of seven years old for girls and boys. They celebrate the circumcision day as a big cultural event.[77]

In Practice

Patrilineal Nature of Practicing Cultures

Although many believe that male domination is a common characteristic of African society, Emmanuel Babatunde chooses to place men and women in positions of prominence in the various areas of life.[78] He is outraged over clitoridectomy and does not believe cultural differences are excuses for violations of human rights. If one is interested in helping both genders, reducing the practice to male chauvinism limits the wider cultural understanding needed to eliminate it.[79] Efua Dorkenoo is one who believes that the patrilineal nature of all ethnic groups in Africa that practice FGM is alike. These societies are male dominated. The male controls the resources and power.[80] Charles Henry Sweke, M.D., Ph.D., consultant obstetrician/gynecologist at the Selian Lutheran Hospital in Arusha, Tanzania, spoke about male power:

> There is a program in Tanzania to fight against FGM. It is to make our women feel they have a choice. I have the impression that they don't like circumcision. But because it is something traditional, and, as I say, in Africa, men are more powerful, everything which is in fact, wouldn't be condemned by men, they are being advised to fight against it. As long as men are coming up and helping us, trying to give confidence to their women that even if they're not circumcised, they are to be considered just like other women. They are going to be married. This would be very good. It's a bit difficult. I'll give an example: telling somebody who is blind that this is a correct way is just wasting their time because he or she doesn't see. That is, this correct way is also a big step for someone who does. Because we are trying to tell them about the complications for those who have any other complications before, it's different. But we are trying our best and we are going to succeed.[81]

Mary E. Laiser, Head of the Women's Department of the Arusha Diocese of the Evangelical Lutheran Church in Tanzania (ELCT) analyzed the psycho-sexual dominance of men over women in Africa:

> Circumcision has been used to discriminate against women, and also to control women's sexuality. The story in former times was that there was a war and in order to control the women, they discussed circumcising them to control their sexuality when they are away in the war. But then we used to ask them, "Is there still a war? It's over, the war is over, why are you continuing to do circumcision?" And another funny

thing is they teach the women — the ones that are operating — but they don't want to let go of that operation, even though it is bringing a lot of suffering to women, they still continue it. The whole issue is of discrimination and control of the woman's sexuality. Like there is if a woman could not be married until she is circumcised. Who marries that woman? A man. And if a man says, "I won't marry a woman who is circumcised," then it will have an impact. But because it is a tradition which is very strong, then it is not easy.[82]

Laiser said there are men who say that they want to marry a woman who is not circumcised. "Young men, who were born outside the country or outside the community, like the Maasai people who are going to school outside the region, outside the Arusha region, have come across girls who are not circumcised, so that now they know the difference. So they come home, silently they don't marry their girls at home, but they go outside the community and marry outside girls."[83] Change is beginning, Laiser added, "But quietly. They don't mention why they are doing so. But we have tried to find out and we thought that's the result."[84]

Efua Dorkenoo wrote that it is inaccurate to "paint a picture of the all-encompassing subjugation of women" in male-dominated societies.[85] In interviews with James Emanuel Sichilma, our driver, guide, and interpreter in Arusha, Tanzania, we found a variation in the way one male uses his power to help women. He said, "Actually, I don't like circumcision. I don't like it because it's very bad, it's pain for the woman. I know the woman suffers when having a baby."[86]

Sichilma directly affected his wife's situation and is working vigorously to spare his daughters. He told about using his power with his wife's family:

> My wife didn't get circumcised because, when she was a very little girl, she was out of the home. She didn't live with her parents. She lived in the city, and so circumcision has not happened to her. But, in the traditional practice, I heard that even though I am already married, circumcision can take place. I refused to have my wife's family do that to her because it's not good. I told her that, and her family agreed with me that my wish is okay.[87]

He has some concern for his daughter and is working to prevent her having to be circumcised. "And I try to tell my wife, do not bring the tradition of circumcision to my daughter, because it is not good."[88]

James Skaine asked him, "If you visit your wife's family, is it possible that someone would want to circumcise your daughter while you were visiting your family?"

Sichilma answered, "Nobody can say straight away because all of them know these things are not good and they do it confidentially. They don't want anyone to know about it. And I'm of a different fabric from them, so it's difficult for them to tell me. If they ask my wife, 'You need to do this and this and this,' my wife can say, 'Ah, but my husband....' They cannot interfere in this situation."[89]

Sichilma works in society to change thinking. He said:

> My friend asked me what I'm doing here in Shirati. I told him that we are doing research about the people who are circumcised and to encourage them not to be circumcised. I asked him if they bring their daughters to the circumciser. He says not yet, but his wife was already circumcised. But before he married her, she was not circumcised. When he married her, he was told to bring her to the circumciser. I tried to tell him that it was not good to circumcise the woman because so many bad things can happen to her. He agreed with me and said that he would never circumcise their daughters. I tried to tell him a lot of things about its history.[90]

Although the African males are a very powerful group, I sensed, while in Africa, that definite change is occurring. Some males have joined other advocates and say that circumcision of women should stop. Sichilma is not a traditional African male, nor were other males we met while in Tanzania and Kenya. Progressive in their thinking, these males worked to eliminate the practice of FGM.

Other Family Roles

On balance men hold the power. How did this balance come about? Other family roles also play a critical part in families that practice FGM. That woman was the slave of man at the beginning of society is an absurd notion that has come down from the period of Enlightenment of the eighteenth century, according to Friedrich Engels. Weak and unstable pairing in a family could not create an independent household. Thus the communistic household from earlier times that implied the supremacy of women and exclusive recognition of a natural mother prevailed. It was not possible to determine the natural father, so this position was granted women.[91]

In prehistoric times, Engels maintains, women held a free and highly respected position among all savages and barbarians of the lower and middle stages and partly of the upper stage. When wealth increased, descent according to the mother's right had to be overthrown so that inheritance was in favor of the father's children. As the three epochs of civilization evolved — the world of antiquity, serfdom in the Middle Ages, and labor in modern times — three forms of servitude were their companions: open, latterly, and disguised slavery.[92]

The exploitation of one class by another is the basis of civilization, wrote Engels. Each new emancipation of one class means a new oppression for another class. This state is not how it should be and as a result the following declaration is made: "The exploiting class exploits the oppressed class solely and exclusively in the interest of the exploited class itself; and if the latter fails to appreciate this, and even becomes rebellious, it thereby shows the basest ingratitude to its benefactors, the exploiters."[93]

The Role of Women

Perhaps Engels's nineteenth century philosophy may explain why some women no longer wish to practice circumcision. Even so, some women may not express a lack of appreciation toward the exploiting class(es), let alone rebel. The women in Africa who do not wish to end FGM may not wish to do so because they are dependent upon males.

Sweke shared his perceptions of African women and their attitudes toward change:

> When we talk to women, they are really supporters. Bright women are the ones who really are stuck, because they consider how it is: "for years and years, our queen mothers have been doing this and now these people want to throw away our culture." They raise some resistance. But, to the young generation, not being circumcised is really positive and organizations which are trying to help, might make the result positive.[94]

Some women who do not wish to continue to carry out circumcision fear for their daughters and seek asylum in another country. One such case was analyzed by Patricia Dysart Rudloff. Lydia Oluloro of Nigeria did not believe that the Nigerian government would help her protect her daughters from FGM, a Yoruba tribal custom. She sought asylum in the United States.[95] James A. Lazarus wrote that the tribal or customary law is perhaps the most pervasive law existing in Nigeria, and it supports the practice of polygamy and FGM. The *Oluloro* immigration judge remarked that "although the Nigerian government does not promote FGM, Nigerian State Department reports indicated that FGM is ... common and is deeply ingrained in the cultural tradition."[96] On this basis another case, *In Re Anikwata*, reasoned that if Anikwata were forced to return to Nigeria, Anikwata "cannot be expected to overcome such indoctrinated traditions and institutions."[97]

Other Roles

The Excisers Jane Wright maintained that the length of the procedure depends on the child's age, "the struggles of the girl, the degree of mutilation and the skill of the exciser."[98] Society itself and unenforced legal efforts play an important role in perpetuating the existence of excisers. Legal efforts to discourage excisers often are not effective, but the exciser's role is undergoing change. In Djibouti an exciser was counseled to stop cutting after one of her circumcised girls was hospitalized as a result of the procedure.

Enforcement

Thirteen countries had no information available on enforcement. In six countries where FGM is known, no arrests or prosecutions have occurred. The absence of political will to interfere in a private matter deeply embedded in cultural traditions works to protect the excisers.[99]

On the other hand, African activity persists in efforts to discourage excisers from continuing their practice. In 2004, in Kajiado District, Kenya, the government issued a two-week ultimatum to traditional circumcisers now operating to discontinue the trade or face arrest. The district commissioner warned community nurses that if they secretly cooperated with circumcisers they would face consequences. [100] A few days earlier, two hundred female circumcisers from Kenya's Rift Valley Province "abandoned their tools of trade and vowed to fight the deeply rooted custom."[101] Their decision followed NGO-conducted seminars to mark the March 8 International Women's Day. As children are taught their rights, they resist FGM, but adults then lower the age at which it is done. Many women have been sensitized to the dangers of FGM, but they have not abandoned the practice. Instead, they pay a lot of money to medical professionals to perform the procedures on their daughters. In some areas, parents still insist on drawing blood by piercing the girl's genitals as a symbolic alternative.[102]

In January 2004, a Circuit Court at Bawku sentenced a woman, aged seventy, to five years in prison for circumcising seven girls at Yelogu in the Bawku East District. The judge said he was compelled to sentence the woman in spite of her seventy years because she said she knew that circumcision was an offense but performed it anyway. Thus, the judge hoped that her sentence would serve as a deterrent to other practitioners.[103]

In 2002, Communicating for Change, a Lagos-based NGO, met to commemorate World Health Day. The event featured the film *Uncut: Playing with Life.* Stella Iwuagwu, a woman who had been circumcised as a baby and suffered later in life during labor, said the film "exposed the barbarism involved in female genital mutilation."[104] We can see role change by the efforts of women who circumcised other women. The film depicted the life of a one-time traditional female circumciser in Benin, Stella Omoregie. At one time, Omoregie visited Lagos and watched the film but remained unmoved by its message. However, she was moved by another drama presentation because it reflected her own life. In the drama, a woman who had been circumcised bled to death. Committed to ending FGM, Omoregie never circumcised anyone again. She began crusading against the practice. She also "was one of those who actively pressured the Edo State House of Assembly to pass a law banning the practice in the state."[105]

In 2003, the IAC wrote about Madam Tolla C, a woman who was an exciser for 50 years in the Koldo Region, Senegal. She agreed to stop circumcising even though it was a means of subsistence for her family. She now works to convince parents not to cut and excisers to abandon the practice.[106]

Professor Patroba E. Ondiek, Ph.D., the Program Coordinator for the NGO Save the Children of Tarime, (Sachita) in Tarime, Tanzania, told how his program deals with the circumcisers and how it tries to reach them to change their thinking:

> At first, we deal with the young people. We teach them. But the circumcisers could not allow us to go to them, because when they circumcise, they are given something. Some get money, some get cows. Oh, yes. It was an economic part which was becoming difficult to get rid of. Then we realized that this circumciser, and the women who circumcise are controlled by the cultural leaders. So, you can go to the circumcisers, we have been talking with them. When we tell them all the reasons that have been given for not performing circumcision, they say, "Why haven't you talked to the cultural elders, because they are the people who give the cows? We do the job, but they give the money. Talk to the elders." To get to the elders, that has been a problem because they defend their culture, and they strongly believe that, in this culture, a girl who has not been to school is forced to believe that unless she's circumcised locally, traditionally, she won't get married. So, the cows are sold, look around, but by educating them, they now understand. We have to educate these people. Yes, they will understand.[107]

Ondiek spoke of a five-day seminar Sachita organized for parent-child communication in Tarime:

> We invited the parents to this seminar, with their own daughters, each parent was coming with each of two daughters, two was maximum, you could bring one. So that they were being trained together. So that we can make the parents see what we are telling them to do and their own daughters in the same halls. So that in the future, they won't fail to tell the father or mother, "Mommy, I can't. I just can't, following

the training we had there." And the father says, "Sure, my daughter." But then those two can agree. They are getting an education.[108]

Laiser shared her experience with traditional birth attendants who are also circumcisers:

> I have one very old lady who was a circumciser long ago, but she no longer does it. I normally visit her and talk to her, but I never asked her about tools. Because when you tell them that recently in 1998 there was a law to ban female circumcision, the circumcisers are scared about the law. So whenever you go to their house, they think you are going to arrest them or you are going to report that they are doing circumcision. The minister of education started a system to change traditional birth attendants in the villages or the communities. Some communities don't have health centers close to their villages. So they taught traditional birth attendants to assist women during labor time. They give them rules, they give them tools to do it. But, surprisingly, some of the traditional birth attendants are circumcisers also. So women suffered because of them. Those women who escaped circumcision during their childhood, suffered circumcision during childbirth. So the traditional birth attendant does the two jobs. They do both. They deliver the baby and then they cut them. So a woman during healing time is surprised and asks, "Why is it taking too long to heal?" only to realize that she has been circumcised.[109]

Sometimes it is not from the community but from the mother-in-law, Laiser said. In Tanzania, sometimes it is the extended family that comes to the delivery. The extended family is not the nuclear family in the West. Laiser told how the extended family operates:

> All the people in the extended family have a say in what happens in a family. So the family member can set something, normally, there is a leader of the family. This leader gives rules according to what they discuss in the community. So they say, "This lady is not circumcised. Let's see, where will she go during delivery? If she delivers at all, then we will arrange for that to be done to her." So what do we do? If you do not [know] what to expect, you never know if you are safe from the new family of your marriage. Then they do it. The mother-in-law is very strong: "No, I don't want an uncircumcised lady in my home. That is what I think. And this one, I know she's uncircumcised, she's still a child, she['s] still stupid, so what we want is to have her circumcised."[110]

Functional Aspects   Rituals, says Laurenti Magesa, serve a functional aspect. Traditionally, the ritual of circumcision represents a celebration of courage, self-giving and self-denial, and suffering. The girl's identity is established and she experiences the unity of the clan and its members. She is now ready to move into adult womanhood.[111]

Rights versus Rites

An Example, The Kétu's Balance

FC among the Kétu, a subgroup of the Yoruba in Nigeria, is related to procreation because it is marriage oriented. The purpose of marriage is to create, especially sons to continue the patriline. There is no wide variation in age at which time the Kétu circumcise. They always do so at about age twenty "as a preamble to marriage and procreation."[112] Babatunde reasoned that since the purpose of marriage among the Kétu is procreation and not just loving companionship, "every attempt would be made to streamline this aim by cutting away what may distract attention from that aim."[113] Viewed this way, circumcision is necessary to demonstrate that the sexual act is a means to an end—circumcision being the means and children, society's highest good, being the end. The primary purpose of the Kétu fertility rites is to enhance fertility in the woman, fertility being basic to the survival of the society.[114]

Reasons for circumcising differ in various societies, as does the type and time of the operation. Why, in the face of social change, does circumcision continue? Among the Kétu, the answer is within the meaning held by the participants. Even though the Kétu society has an ideology of male dominance, it also believes females are equally prominent in specific areas. Division of labor is according to the sexes, but the female's position is not one that is inferior. Rather, the separation of roles creates a need of mutual dependence and respect. Thus, the Kétu continue circumcision because it satisfies powerful motives of both men and women.[115]

However, Kétu men explain circumcision as a way of controlling women's sexual behavior. In their society, the women justify circumcision on a deeper ritual level. The women explain that the excised part is given back to the "source of fertility." This gift is to ensure that the giver may receive blessings that make her fertile. Then the birth of the child gives her passage from an unclassified and asexual youth to a secure sexual and complete adult woman.[116]

Most African development programs place population control as a high priority. However, African societies fear infertility. It is natural, then, for those societies to establish a relationship between fertility and circumcision. This concern and the resulting relationship make the rite important. Babatunde explained that "the excised part is given or sacrificed to the ancestral shrine in the belief that the ancestor will present them to the source of fertility so as to obtain blessings of fertility for initiates.... In Sierra Leone, the excised part is ritually cooked and served in a sacrificial meal to the initiates upon graduation, and a small quantity of the meal is served to certain favored men as a protection against infertility."[117] The practice continues in the Yoruba rural areas and urban centers and among people with formal education.

Kay L. Levine agreed that the practice of FGM "falls within the purview of cultural requirement defenses."[118] Parents subject their daughters to the procedure to mark them, culturally, as marriageable virgins and to prevent them from becoming social outcasts. "The crucial point is that the cultural logic dictates that the surgery be performed."[119]

Balancing Cultural Values and Autonomy Against International Standards and Human Rights

Strategies to eliminate FGC are a bitterly contested debate. Kay Boulware-Miller wrote that the meaning of FGC and its importance varies from one culture to the next. Cultures that view it as a problem may not give it high priority even though the international health community gives it high priority.[120] The cultural relativism approach raises questions. The questions evolved into the cultural relativists versus the universalists debate.

The universalist position is "that certain individual rights are so fundamental to humankind that they should be upheld as universal rights whose breach is subject to condemnation and, in certain instances, punishment through legislative force."[121] Although FGM is increasingly seen as a human rights violation, the practice of FC is not universally recognized as such. Thus, the debate centers on balancing cultural values and structure against international human rights.[122]

Boulware-Miller's presentation of the problems of the health approach include that women already know of the health risks and those risks do not alter the importance of the procedure; that FGC reflects the position of women; and that the approach is futile and cultural pressures to be marriageable will prevail.[123]

Cutting Without Ritual

Ylva Hernlund examined an alternative ritual to circumcision in Gambia. She believes that alternative rituals can contribute to the elimination of FGC, can empower women, and can allow other "individuals and communities to avoid the accusation that to give up female 'circumcision' is to give up one's 'culture'."[124] Some trends concerning attitudes toward and talk of circumcision in Gambia were noted by Hernlund.

Before the 1980s, circumcision was not often discussed in public. Media coverage has made Gambians aware that the local practice has become part of a global debate. Some of the people of Gambia are aware that the ritual may not deal properly with the new and present world. Because of the element of celebration, some believe that it makes no sense to have cutting without ritual.[125]

Others express the opinion that continuing circumcision has not so much to do with marriageability but with ethnicity, religion, proper child-bearing, and maintaining cultural tradition.[126] Traditionally, the Gambians circumcised with ritual and a long period of seclusion. Hernlund pointed out that the trend is for girls to undergo the procedure with little or no teaching or celebration. The reasons given for cutting without ritual include avoiding lavish expense; school-aged girls had no time for lengthy seclusion; girls taken against their will and girls "considered too old"; a circumciser is one who had agreed not to practice; and the orthodox interpretation of Islam of cutting without ritual.[127]

Ritual Without Cutting

In Gambia, Hernlund typically heard, "I am just as good a Mandinka as those people. You can get rid of this one thing and still have your culture."[128] In ritual without cutting, it is important that villagers in other roles such as the circumcisers be allowed to retain or regain their important roles and high status in a community. Replacement rituals allow roles to be retained. For example, in 1996, the Foundation for Research on Women's Health, Productivity and the Environment (BAFROW) Youth Advocacy Group encouraged communities to return to having prepuberty rituals to stress traditional values. Hernlund favors alternative rituals.

In 2003, Kenya designed a new plan to replace FGM. The plan involves a week-long program, known as Ntanira Na Mugambo or Circumcision through Words. The program educates young women about their health and bodies and emphasizes self-esteem, communication, and problem solving. A graduation ceremony that inducts the participant into womanhood is held at the end of the week. Each woman participating in the ritual also finds support and encouragement from her "godmother," a friend or relative who helps her through the week. By 2003, nearly three hundred women had completed the program since it began in 1996.[129]

RELIGION VERSUS TRADITION

FGM Is a Cultural Tradition

FGM "was, and remains, a cultural, not a religious practice," writes B. A. Robinson.[130] John Wachira, M.D., a urologist, agrees that at present the reasons for circumcision are now cultural, but the practice has evolved from a basis in religion to culture. Dr. Wachira said, "In the distant past, African religion and culture were not separate."[131]

The Religious Debate

Anika Rahman and Nahid Toubia wrote "it is important to note FC/FGM is a cultural, not a religious practice."[132] The practice predates and is not a requirement of Christianity or Islam. FC/FGM is strongly identified with Islam in African nations, and many Muslim community members advocate the practice. It is not known in many Muslim countries outside of Africa.[133] FC is not practiced by all Muslims or by all Arabs. North African countries, Turkey, and Iran ignore the practice. Egyptian Christians and Ethiopian Jews most likely practice circumcision in Israel today, as do Africans living in France. According to Sami A. Aldeeb Abu-Sahlieh, Sudan, Somalia, and Egypt are among the largest Arabic countries practicing FC. Arabic countries that practice circumcision are Yemen, the United Arab Emirates, Bahrain, Qatar, Oman, some areas of Saudi Arabia and Mauritania, Indonesia, Malaysia, Pakistan, and India.[134]

Rahman and Toubia point out that the debate over interpretation of the Qur'an and the hadith continues even though neither has a direct requirement for FC/FGM. The procedure is practiced by Jews, Christians, Muslims, and indigenous religious groups in Africa.[135]

Abu-Sahlieh sees no valid distinction between male and female circumcision and he believes, "A God who demands that his believers be mutilated and branded on their genitals the same as cattle, is a God of questionable ethics."[136] Rare medical circumstances may dictate the necessity of circumcision, but arbitrary mutilation of children, boys, or girls, is not appropriate, he concluded.

Jewish Beliefs

Because the Bible does not mention FC, whether the Jews practiced it is also controversial. Strabo mentions female excision in several separate passages. In one, he described the customs of the tribe of Creophagi, "The males have their sexual glands mutilated and the women are excised in the Jewish fashion."[137]

Abu-Sahlieh found that even though Philo mentions FC, he denies that Jews practiced it. Legend is that Sara circumcised the servant Hagar. They say descendants of Ishmael's family circumcised both the Abyssinians of Tigré males and females before entering Jerusalem. The Falasha practiced circumcision in Jerusalem in the time of Solomon. Outlying tribes of Eastern Jews around 1000 practiced FC to reduce sexual sensitivity. It was believed that an uncircumcised woman would have orgasms sooner and oftener than a circumcised man. Frequent intercourse was not good for her health. In Ethiopia, women performed excision, but men did it when women were not available.[138]

In 1959, a Jewish physician wrote that Jews and Western physicians practiced FC in the United States.[139] Abu-Sahlieh pointed out that Jews are angered by the allegation and make efforts to correct it. It is possible that Rabbis would have to admit women into the inner circle of Judaic religious practice if they admitted FC is performed. The Bible does not mention FC, but then the Bible does not report all customs the Jews practiced. Interpretation plays an important role and the debate continues.[140]

FC was performed among the Jews in Egypt before Christ. The Copts maintained the practice through their conversion to Christianity and then to Islam. In the sixth century Aetius of Amida, the Byzantium court physician, wrote that the reasons for the removal of the clitoris are that because it grows, it is "unseemly and shameful," and that the rubbing of women's garments arouses them.[141] Removal was done at the time of marriage. Aetius also described the removal procedure. "They cause the girl to be seated on a stool, and a strong young man standing behind her, places his forearms beneath her thighs and buttocks, holding fast her legs and her whole body. The operator standing front of her seizes with a wide-mouthed forceps her clitoris, pulling it out with his left hand, whilst with his right hand he cuts it off with the teeth of the forceps."[142]

Abu-Sahlieh reported that at the end of the thirteenth century, Athanasius, the bishop of Qus in Egypt, said that circumcision was not allowed. Catholic missionaries worked to forbid the practice in Egypt, where it was done by women with a knife or razor when the child was about eight years old.[143] Abu-Sahlieh pointed out that currently Copts work to stop FC because their holy books do not mention it and the procedure is damaging to health.[144]

Some Jewish individuals deny the practice of FC. Abu-Sahlieh asked the reader to consider that if these denials are set aside, "we find that some contemporary Jews have instituted a ceremony for baby girls parallel to the ceremony of male circumcision."[145] The ceremony's purpose tries to correct an inequality between men and women represented by male circumcision. In the ceremony, the girl is admitted to Abraham's alliance with a Hebrew name. God changed the name of Sarai, the wife of Abram, to Sarah and Abram to Abraham, but circumcision on Sarah was not performed.

Some believe that Sarah celebrated her new name by immersing herself. Others suggest that washing the girl's feet is done, because Abraham washed the feet of his guests. Whatever method of immersion is used, it is a symbol of the woman's rebirth.[146]

The Koran is the first source of Islamic law and does not mention male or female circumcision. Abu-Sahlieh wrote, "an extensive interpretation of verse 2:124 shows some barely traceable indication of it."[147] "When Abraham was put to the test by his Lord, through certain commandments, he carried them out. God then said: 'I am appointing you a guide for the people.'"[148]

One of the sayings of Muhammad commands Abraham to circumcise males as a test. Abraham was a model for other Muslims. In sunnah of Muhammad, the second source of Islamic law, there are sayings relating to both male and female circumcision. In a debate between Muhammad and Um Habibah, female circumciser of female slaves, Muhammad asked her whether she had continued to practice circumcision. Her response was, "Unless it is forbidden ... and you order me to stop doing it." Muhammad replied that it was allowed, saying that when she cut, not to overdo it. The practice brings more radiance to the face and is more pleasant for the husband. Abu-Sahlieh explained that FC or *makrumah* means meritorious action. Thus, he concluded, "it is better to do it although it is not obligatory from a religious point of view."[149]

Supporters of circumcision believe Muhammad's narrative is not credible. Abu-Sahlieh wrote that arguments against circumcision can summed up this way, "Can one imagine a God who demands that his believers be mutilated and branded on their genitals the same as cattle?"[150]

Support for this argument in the Koran is easily found. Verse 4:119 does not allow man to change God's creature, "[The devil said]: 'I will mislead them, and I will create in them false desires; I will order them to slit the ears of cattle, and to deface the fair nature created by God.'"[151] Male and female circumcision supporters forget this verse completely as well as verse 32:7, "He perfected everything He created," wrote Aldeeb Abu-Sahlieh.[152]

Muhammad's response to farmers who had been told not to pollinate their date trees, and whose trees did not bear dates that year, was, "You know your worldly business better [than I do]."[153] The Sheikh Hassan Ahmed Abu-Sabib from Sudan came to the conclusion that FC should be banned because medical science had proved it harmful. He then cited the Koran at 1:195, "Do not throw yourselves with your own hands into disaster," and the saying of Muhammad, "Who harms a believer, harms me and who harms me, harms God."[154]

These arguments, said Abu-Sahlieh, have only been used against FC and could be used against male circumcision. As for Muslim law, the female has no foreskin and, thus, no impurity, making circumcision only advisable. Fatwa or religious decisions in Egypt have varied. In 1949 it was declared that abandoning FC is not a sin. In 1951, the same body did not recognize abandoning FC as an option and stated that it was advisable to curb "nature." In 1981, the same body was adamantly opposed to abandoning FC.[155]

Not circumcising females has serious consequences. They are ill regarded by their countrymen. However, religious reasons are given *a posteriori*, said Abu-Sahlieh. Beneficial results, real or fictitious, are conferred upon the religious norms. He says it is recourse to reason to justify reason, proving that God hurting people, in order to brand them like cattle, is not accepted anymore.[156]

Christians

FGM existed before the introduction of Islam or Christianity and is not mentioned in the Bible.[157] As early as the seventeenth century, Christian missionaries and colonial administrations in Africa attempted to prevent the practice. These efforts met with resistance because they were seen as a colonialist attempt to destroy the local culture.[158] Jessica A. Platt wrote, "Christian groups promote traditional customs and support circumcision as a link to Africa's past ... regardless of the debate concerning whether African religion truly dictates the practice of female circumcision, a majority of the people in Africa believe it does."[159] These elements combined make the following account of Mary Nyangweso's experience with the Nandi culture relevant to the Christian religion and circumcision.

Examining the Meaning of the Christian Gospel as it Relates to Nandi Culture In spite of condemnations and various efforts to stop the practice, FC persists among a number of African groups, including Christians. Nyangweso examined how FC is interpreted through the gospel message, especially Christ's redemptive message in relation to the Nandi culture. Recognizing the complexity of culture, she suggests change through a theological basis in the Kenyan Nandi female initiation rite.[160]

The importance of Christ's redemptive message for the Nandi culture of FC is that it relates to female suffering. Christ is the center of Christianity. His redemptive message extends to all those under any form of oppression. She portrays Christ as a mediator, as a way to atone for sin, and as a liberator. Eight percent of the Nandi profess Christianity and have high regard for their cultural ways. Because they highly regard their Christian faith, it is important to have a Christian reaffirmation of their traditional ways.[161]

Nyangweso believes that scientific knowledge characterizes Christianity. Science either invalidates or disproves some traditional practices. The Nandi need to reconsider FC in light of scientific knowledge. Because Christ mediates, the act of mediation between ancestors and God—communion with the ancestors—is outdated. The Nandi will receive blessings by praying directly to God or through Christ. Christ and atonement are the belief that Christ is the last who shed blood in suffering for the sake of humanity's salvation. Thus, the concept of atonement calls for the end of the Nandi's bloodshed. Christ's liberating spirit is seen through him in his way of relating to women in the Scripture and recognition that women, too, should live a fulfilling life. Thus, Nyangweso suggested the initiation rite can continue but the actual circumcision can be replaced by some other symbolic act not harmful to women's bodies. This symbolic act can come from the culture itself or from, for example, reading the scripture to initiates.[162]

Islam

The Practice Predates Islam FGM is widely practiced in countries where the predominant religion is Christianity, in multifaith countries, and in Muslim countries. Robinson concluded that associating FGM with the religion of Islam is incorrect. The procedure predated Islam and is practiced in countries such as Ethiopia and Kenya where Christianity is predominant.[163]

FGM is practiced in Muslim countries in or near Africa, but FGM is rare or nonexistent in other Muslim countries such as Iran, Jordan, Lebanon, Syria, and Turkey. The Maghreb countries of Northwest Africa do not practice it, and it is but occasionally performed in Indonesia and other predominately Muslim countries in Asia.[164]

Multifaith countries that practice Animism, Christianity, and Islam also practice FGM. Examples of multifaith countries are Ethiopia, Eritrea, Sierra Leone, and Sudan. FGM was once practiced by Ethiopian Jews, but it is not today.[165]

Although FGM is not a religious custom, Muslims often justify it with two controversial sayings of the Prophet Mohammed that seem to favor sunna circumcision, said Robinson. Robinson attests that other scholars disagree and stated "even if true, they only permit the practice; they do not mandate it."[166] The procedure began between one and two thousand years ago during what Muslims call "al-gahiliyyah" (the era of ignorance). The Old Testament of the Qur'an, Hebrew Scriptures, and the New Testament of the Christian Scriptures do not mention FC. The Sunnah, the words and actions of the Prophet Mohammed, has references to FC, wrote Robinson. Some scholars do not believe these references are credible or authentic. They see passages in the Qur'an that by implication oppose FGM. Robinson explained the reasoning for this belief:

> God apparently created the clitoris for the sole purpose of generating pleasure. It has no other purpose. There is no instruction in the Qur'an or in the writings of the Prophet Mohammed which require that the clitoris be surgically modified. Thus God must approve of its presence. And so, it should not be removed or reduced in size or function. The Qur'an promotes the concept of a husband and wife giving each other pleasure during sexual intercourse. For example: "It is lawful for you to go in unto your wives during the night preceding the (day's) fast: they are as a garment for you and you are as a garment for them." (2:187) "... and He has put love and mercy between you." (30:21)[167]

Mutilated genitalia reduce or eliminate a woman's pleasure during sexual intercourse, Robinson maintains.

Johnson, in her study of the Mandinga of Guinea-Bissau, found circumcision to be a cleansing rite. The rite defines women as Muslim and enables them to pray in an appropriate manner. Thus FC is related to the construction of religious identity. At this point, religious and ethnic identity fuse. Becoming a Muslim is an important part of being Mandinga. Religious identity is constructed locally in ways that differ from global doctrines and texts.[168]

The Tug of Tradition

In May 2003, a mother from Somalia, Africa, who lived in Copenhagen, Denmark, was faced with the decision whether to have her four-year-old daughter circumcised. In March 2003, the Danish government introduced legislation making it a crime to take girls or young women to another country to be circumcised. The mother did not believe in the procedure due to her many problems resulting from her own surgery. An estimated 17,300 Somalis live in Denmark. Increasing numbers disapprove of FC, but many others still feel the tug of this tradition. As a result some Somali parents circumvent the law by taking their daughters to Somalia or an Arab state for the surgery.[169]

The tug these parents feel is not unique to the Somalis who migrated to Denmark. For example, in France, rough estimates suggest that thirty-thousand women and girls may have suffered the procedure. In Paris, a woman of Mauritanian origin received a three-year suspended sentence in March 2003 for having her French daughter circumcised in Africa.[170]

The Scars of Tradition

The scars of the tradition of FGM range from psychological stress or physical pain to medical complications, including human immuno-deficiency virus/acquired immunodeficiency syndrome (HIV/AIDS).

While these parents in Copenhagen, Denmark, often feel the tug of tradition, others feel the scars of the tradition. Amina Kamil Jibrel offers counseling to other Somali women in Copenhagen. One woman, Rahmah Ali Kudar, described the pain of her circumcision as so intense that she passed out. Charles P. Wallace reported, "Even 23 years later, she is still dealing with medical complications from the operation. She has trouble menstruating; there were severe difficulties during her pregnancy; she spends hours on the toilet to pass urine."[171]

One certain scar of tradition is HIV/AIDS. Ethiopia's situation is not very different from other African countries but serves to illustrate the high toll of AIDS. Ethiopia's population is ever increasing, standing at the second most populous country in Africa. Of the approximate seventy million people, more than 2.2 million are infected with HIV and about 219,400 have full-blown AIDS. The highest rate of infection is among the fifteen to twenty-four year old age group. Fifty-eight percent of those infected are women. The HIV/AIDS awareness level for women is eight percent versus 23 percent for men. "With each new case, the cycle of poverty is exacerbated," reported the *Addis Tribune*.[172] The article painted a bleak picture:

> Significant barriers face women in Ethiopia, including the widespread prevalence of social and cultural practices, which are discriminatory or harmful, such as marriage, abduction and female genital mutilation (FGM), which affects 80% of all women.
> Young women in Ethiopia are at a high risk of contracting HIV in part because they are disempowered socially and economically, and as well because of widespread and socially acceptable patterns of subjugation including widespread genital and other traditional forms of mutilation at a young age, abduction of under-aged girls, rape and forced marriage.
> Although women are responsible for at least half of all subsistence agricultural production and form 80% of the agricultural labor force (1994 Census), their contribution has not been recognized and it remains in statistics compiled at all levels.[173]

Although the National Policy on Ethiopian Women developed in 1993 is aimed at promoting equality between women and men, much still remains to be done in redressing the status of Ethiopian women, the article concluded.

CONCLUSIONS

FGC as a traditional practice is undergoing change. Although debate and the practice still continue, the hopeful sign is that culture can maintain its rights while changing its rites, for example, culture without cutting. Some argue that FGC is a religious matter, but close examination shows that this practice predates Islam and is not mentioned in either the Bible or the Koran. Thus, FGC remains a practice with a long history as a tradition in cultures in change. As Chugulu said so well, "The culture will continue, retaining its good things, casting off the harmful practices."

6

Challenging the Change and the Challenge of Change

Give the spirit the time to ripen.
Village Chief, Bougouni, Mali[1]

WHY DOES FEMALE GENITAL MUTILATION CONTINUE?

Why does the practice of female genital mutilation (FGM) continue? Understanding of FGM has increased and some programs have met with success, so why do people still do it? The Program for Appropriate Technology in Health (PATH) includes varied reasons for supporting FGM, "'good tradition,' a religious requirement(s), or a necessary rite of passage to womanhood; that it ensures cleanliness or better marriage prospects, enhances male sexuality, facilitates childbirth by widening the birth canal, prevents promiscuity and excessive clitoral growth, and preserves virginity."[2]

In 1998, a report by PATH used the term "the mental map" to refer to countries confronted with complex and culturally entrenched beliefs about FGM. The mental map includes:

> Myths, beliefs, values, and codes of conduct that cause the whole community to view women's external genitalia as a potentially dangerous, that if not eliminated, had the power to negatively affect women who have not undergone FGM, their families and their communities. To make sure that people conform to the practice, strong enforcement mechanisms have been put into place by communities. These include the rejection of women who have not undergone FGM as marriage partners, immediate divorce for unexcised women, derogatory songs, public exhibitions and witnessing of complete removal before mar-

125

riage, forced excisions and instillation of fear of the unknown through curses and evocation of ancestral wrath. On the other hand, girls who undergo FGM are provided with rewards, including public recognition and celebrations, gifts, potential for marriage, respect and the ability to participate in adult social functions.[3]

Like PATH's mental map, the National Committee on Traditional Practices in Ethiopia (NCTPE) found several similar issues that were stated at most project sites in the Harari Region. Their results included the community, especially men, believe female genital cutting (FGC) marks, preserves, and identifies virginity. Cutting makes a girl decent, disciplined, calm, and respected. An uncut girl will go look for a man before marriage and bring into the world an illegitimate child and shame. Men will not marry uncut girls. They are perceived as "open" and used by all men. The uncut girl and her mother are criticized, insulted, accused, discriminated against, and isolated if there are no plans to perform the surgery. The uncut girl will have no moral for love. It is tradition. It is Islamic law and keeps women clean for prayer and fasting. Girls compete and ask for the surgery because they will be demoralized, outcast, and isolated if not operated upon. A mother will impose FGC on her daughter because the mother wants social respect.[4]

PATH also found that agencies and groups working on prevention only reach a small percentage of the people who traditionally practice FGM. Strategy needs to be reoriented. Currently, prevention is "based on the message that FGM is a harmful traditional practice that has negative health consequences for women and girls. This message does not address the core values, the myths, or the enforcement mechanism that support the practice."[5] PATH concludes that if the mental map is to be understood and dismantled, programs are to be tailored to the audience, and monitoring the target audience's behavior change are some of the remaining challenges to change.

Mary E. Laiser, Head of the Women's Department for the Arusha Diocese of the Evangelical Lutheran Church in Tanzania (ELCT), shared some observations of her audience about the challenge to change:

> People are asking us about medicalization also, especially when we mention HIV and AIDS. Female genital circumcision can cause HIV/AIDS because of the sharing of the instruments. Then they said, "Oh, if that is the reason, why don't we use separate instruments? Like other circumcisers introduced the razor blade, one single razor blade for one person." And they were telling us, "We started to do that long ago. So every girl who comes to my house brings [a] razor blade, a new one." They both said, "A new one, so we are safe." No, look at these complications because HIV and AIDS is only one complication. What

about the severe pain? And what about hemorrhage or bleeding which causes anemia and a person can die from that. Then they really die in the villages, but they don't want to accept it. In this region, you will find that people are not ready to accept the problems that we are facing as a nation, they refer back to their forefathers. Their mothers survived FGM. They say that people survived it, so we don't really accept the complications you are telling us about. In other places, they don't even listen to us. They tell us, "We don't want to listen to you. You came all the way to tell us about the conditions of FGM." It is amazing. They are suffering but they don't want to accept it. And when you go to the hospitals, you find the problems. Nurses and midwives know a lot about women who come there to deliver and suffer complications. So we give them some of the information from the hospitals and ask them, "What happens when they come for delivery? Do you see any problems?" They say, "Yes, there are problems. They don't heal. They take longer during labor compared to those who are not circumcised."[6]

Ethics and Politics

The World Health Organization (WHO) is unequivocally opposed to the medicalization of FGM. WHO reasons that whether the procedure is performed in a hospital or in the bush, FGM is deliberate damage to healthy organs for no medical or scientific reasons. "Performing FGM violates the ethical principles 'do no harm' and 'do not kill'."[7] According to the WHO, the ethical principles at stake are "respect, autonomy, beneficence, non-maleficen[ce], justice, veracity and fidelity and obligation, responsibilities and accountability."[8]

Salem Mekuria critiqued certain "crusaders in the West."[9] Chris Lowe suggested "an approach for engaging with the ethics and politics of genital mutilation and surgery."[10] Lowe wrote that this approach is the one advocated by Seble Dawit and Salem Mekuria.[11] In a later article, Mekuria expanded on this approach. Lowe's summary of that article includes the crusade of the West, gender oppression worldwide, sustaining African cultural context, the need for African women to assume leadership, and the need for men and women to be involved.[12]

Gender Oppression Worldwide

Lowe suggested that the continuum of gender oppression is not limited to Africa alone. FGM should be placed as a part of the continuum rather than in isolation.[13] The continuum of gender oppression includes "the murder of female children, less health care for girls, less nutritious foods, less schooling, harder work, child marriage and early pregnancy, breast implants/reductions, anorexia nervosa, and the millions of dollars we spend on cosmetics and harmful diet programs."[14]

Sustaining African Cultural Context

African forms of FGM need to be understood in their particular social and cultural contexts. It is not enough to condemn FGM as patriarchal because women are the "direct agents" of and sometimes share the ideologies that sustain it. Nor is it enough to not recognize women's role in FGM as well as acknowledge that women are disempowered because their sexuality is repressed and their human rights are violated.[15]

Lowe summarized Mekuria's point to sustain African cultural context this way, "In particular, the ways that FGM harms women and denies them power and agency need to be related to the ways that women (or some women) negotiate limited areas of power out of them, as well as the implications of the practices in cultural conditions for social respect."[16]

Ethics, religion, and reaction to harm resulting from the practice also influence participant's attitudes. An example of the ethics of the limits of cultural independence is shown by the Sudanese government's plans to legalize FGM in 2003. The government's actions came just a few months before FGM was rejected at a 190-country strong world summit. The United Kingdom has had a recent debate on children being taken abroad for the procedure. Although the United States later backtracked, about the same time "the American embassy in Nairobi said that Somali refugees who had rushed to circumcise their daughters before being moved to the United States would probably be barred from emigrating.[17]

Several groups expressed concern. The Sudanese Women's Rights Group (SWRG) based in the United Kingdom issued a press release expressing grave concern. The Sudanese Ministry of Religious Affairs and Endowment and an Islamic university held a workshop that recommended "that female circumcision should be legalised, awareness about its importance in society should be raised, and the Islamic University should establish centres all over the country for training practitioners of female circumcision."[18]

"The obvious ethical question that underlies the considerable risks of FGC and its known consequences is why parents want it for their daughters."[19] The answer may be marriageability or economic security for the girl and her family. R.J. Cook et al. wrote that if this reason is true, then it raises the issue of why it is so. The authors reason that FGC is common because marital virginity is required and is related to family honor and purity.

Religious reasons are the least substantiated, wrote Cook et al. Instead support is from pragmatic roles that involve decreasing women's sexual desire. The wider role of FGC is for men to control women's sexuality. FGC is unacceptable because it harms women's health and integrity and denies women's dignity, which includes their sexuality.[20]

The Population Reference Bureau found, "While many religious groups practice FGC, women's attitudes reflect the cultural rather than religious nature of the practice."[21] There are, however, differences among women of Muslim, Christian, and traditional religions in their opposition to FGC. In the largely Islamic countries— Egypt, Eritrea, and Mali — Muslim women are less likely than the Christian women to oppose FGC. Kenya has a large Christian population, but Muslim women are as likely as Christian women to oppose FGC. (See Table 6.1.)

The International Federation of Gynecology and Obstetrics (FIGO) Committee for the Ethical Aspects of Human Reproduction and Women's Health designates all types of FGC as violent.[22] In 1994, FIGO passed a resolution opposing medicalization of FGC. The argument against FGC as an authentic medical procedure "is one of principle, pitched at the societal or macroethical level."[23] The difficult challenge could arise when an adult patient who is infibulated is deinfibulated to give birth, then requests to be reinfibulated after the delivery. Regardless of other reasons to reinfibulate or not to reinfibulate, "the same professional objection applies as to initial FGC, namely that it is a medically unnecessary, socially contrived procedure which should not be given respectability by medicalization."[24]

Even if risks of physical and psychological harm were not an issue, performing FGC remains a violation of a woman's human rights. Suppression and control over women's sexuality are demeaning to women and deny an aspect of their humanity.[25]

The harmful physical health effects were demonstrated in findings of the Population Research Bureau. Twenty-seven percent of women in the Central African Republic (CAR) reported side effects after cutting com-

Table 6.1
Women Who Oppose Female Circumcision by Religion

	Percent of women ages 15–49					
Country	*Muslim*		*Christian*		*Traditional Religions*	
	Undergone cutting	*Disapprove of cutting*	*Undergone cutting*	*Disapprove of cutting*	*Undergone cutting*	*Disapprove of cutting*
Egypt	98	11	88	39		
Eritrea	99	18	92	51		
Kenya	28	75	38	74	31	54
Mali	94	13	85	27	90	4

Source: Adapted from Figure 11, U.S. Population Reference Bureau, Abandoning Female Genital Cutting, *Aug. 2001, p. 15.*

pared to five percent in Egypt. In both countries, the women reported bleeding the most common and pain the second most common side effect.[26]

Female circumcision (FC) is surrounded by legal and ethical issues. Cindy M. Little believes that change will not come easily because it is understood as a necessary ritual and not viewed as a human rights violation. Despite serious health consequences, it is viewed as a cultural right. "It would not be prudent of an organization to believe they could change the ontology of a culture. It will take more than education to change a deeply imbedded cultural practice."[27]

Little pointed out that in 1998, the WHO stated that "some women may not change their attitude towards female genital mutilation unless they receive the signal of approval from influential women within their support network."[28] She concluded that this support certainly may be the case for implementing education and change in the practice because often it is the women in a community who exert pressure on girls and young women to have the procedure. Thus, the importance of Mekuria's point that a need exists for African women to assume leadership is well taken.

Need for African Women and Men to Assume Leadership

Women should assume a central leadership role and be as closely linked to the community as possible in efforts to eliminate FGM. Male involvement is critical in encouraging the abandonment of FGC. Men are not always a target audience of the campaigns but are becoming more so. The U.S. Population Council studies in Mali and Burkina Faso indicate that men recognize that FGC will not be abandoned without their involvement. In Burkina Faso, fathers play the most critical role in determining whether to have their daughters cut.[29]

ENTRENCHED AREAS AND CAMPAIGNS WITH PROMISE

The U.S. Population Reference Bureau reported on four promising community-based projects in Egypt, Senegal, Kenya, and Uganda. Preliminary data suggest that these particular community-based projects may be success stories.[30] These efforts and other undertakings are offered here to demonstrate that progress and promise are present in countries where prevalence rates of FGC are high.

Egypt

In 1995, the WHO found that 95 percent of Egypt's women were circumcised.[31] The Coptic Evangelical Organization for Social Services (CEOSS), which is a half-century old, works to help rural women in the Coptic Christian community. In 1995, it established an anti-FGC program to address all family members. It focuses on girls ages seven to thirteen who are at risk of excision and their mothers.[32]

The PATH/WHO review of the CEOSS program found it succeeded in reducing the rate of excisions in eight of twenty-two communities in Minya Governorate; the FGC abandonment rate was more than 70 percent in the eight villages. These positive changes occurred over seven years.[33]

Since 1998, the Center for Development and Population Studies (CEDPA) has been working to end FGM in Egypt. The cornerstone of CEDPA's work is the invention and use of the "positive deviance approach" to FGM abandonment. The FGM Abandonment Program has been expanded into twenty-four Egyptian communities through support from the United States Agency for International Development (USAID)-funded Enabling Change for Women's Reproductive Health (ENABLE) project. The program is based on Save the Children/U.S. nutrition work in Vietnam. In the case of FGM, "'positive deviants' refer to those individuals who have decided that the practice of FGM is wrong and harmful, despite the fact that the majority of people around them perform the ritual on their girls."[34] This program has three phases. In Phase I, CEDPA trained partner organizations to help identify positive deviants in the community. Phase II focuses on designing more effective ways to combat FGM. Phase III expands the scope of the program. The project has enabled people to openly talk about FGM for the first time. CEDPA has also developed education and communication materials.[35]

Preliminary analysis of Phase II shows that more than 73 percent of families visited said they would not circumcise their daughters. Because prevalence of FGM is so high in Egypt, it is safe to say that community interventions are making a significant impact on people's perceptions of FGM. The results indicate a higher success rate with Christian communities than Muslim communities.[36]

Phase III finds this program expanding. In June 2003, CEDPA completed a training of trainers for two partner nongovernmental organizations (NGOs). The NGOs identified four local NGOs and eight communities in Qena and eight communities in Alexandria in which to launch the program. Training for girls, who are at risk began in January

2004. In addition, the program is planned to be implemented in the Assuit Governorate.[37]

Egypt designated the year 2003 as the "Year of the Girl" to spread the culture of children's rights, including eradication of FGM.[38] In a 2003 update on Egypt, the U. S. Population Reference Bureau reported there may be some signs of change in attitudes. In 1999, Egyptian women were at least ten percentage points less likely to undergo FGC than their mothers. Girls who were more highly educated than their mothers were less likely to become circumcised. Another result showed "a six percentage point decline in the proportion of women with daughters who reported that they had a daughter who was already cut or who planned to have a daughter cut — from 87 percent in 1995 to 81 percent in 2000."[39]

Kenya

Persistence in performing FC is found in some areas despite the campaigns. In 2001, Kenya was an example of a country where FGM was heavily entrenched. The *Africa News* related the story of seventeen-year-old Nanyu (not her real name). Nanyu wanted no part in the festivities taking place on the day on which she would be the center of attraction. Nanyu became one of the sixty-four girls from the district who rejected the traditional rite of passage. She enrolled at a government institution. There the girls were "taught the principles and values of womanhood and responsible lifestyle."[40] The project, Promotion of Initiatives to Overcome Female Genital Mutilation, is sponsored by the German Technical Cooperation (GTZ). The project coordinator, Ms. Jane Kamau, said the practice is very prevalent, "As we take these sixty-four girls through an alternative rite of passage, we are told that there are more than fifty more who are being circumcised in various homesteads today since this is the season."[41]

The battle, far from being won, continues and a long drawn-out war lies ahead, remarked The *Africa News* article. In 2001, statistics bore out the persistence of FGM:

> In Kenya, the practice is prevalent among the Kisii, Kuria, Maasai, Kalenjin and a section of communities living in Taita Taveta. North Eastern Province has about 100 per cent prevalence with Kisii following closely with 94 per cent.
> Ministry of Health statistics indicate that even in communities that have greatly yielded to the fight against FGM such as the Kikuyu and the Kamba, 18 per cent of the girls still go through the cut.[42]

Some groups continued their work against FGM. In 2003, religious leaders in Kenya formed a committee to work against the practice. These groups represent the Anglican, Methodist, and African Independent Pentecostal churches and the Supreme Council of Muslims in Kenya.[43] In Boni, a youth organization organized a workshop to demonstrate the harmfulness of FGM. They stressed that Kenya's Children Act banned FGM for girls under eighteen. A Boni participant told how about twenty girls are circumcised with the same kitchen knife. She blamed illiteracy and poverty. At the end of the workshop, the Boni women decided to launch an anti-FGM campaign to free their community.[44]

In 2004, the British Broadcasting Corporation (BBC) reported that Kenyan men are rejecting their "mutilated" wives and girlfriends for sexual partners in Uganda, where FGM in uncommon. The men hope their actions will serve as a warning to parents and clan leaders.[45]

In 2004, Kenya's Centre for Human Rights and Democracy (CHRD) and parents of missing girls were "locked in a dispute" over FGM.[46] Forty girls fled from their homes in Marakwet District in the Northeastern Province to escape FGM. The Centre claimed that the parents of the girls harassed its staff. The parents were demanding their daughters' return. Although the Centre helped the girls flee from their homes in November 2003, it said that it turned the girls over to a Marakwet-based NGO.

In 2003, teachers in the north of the Rift Valley Province did a study on performance of circumcised girls. They found these girls, "lack the will to study hard, suffer from an inferiority complex, are shy and lack confidence and are submissive."[47] The study compared the behavior of the circumcised girls to other girls in areas where most girls were uncircumcised, like Nairobi, and found the girls who were not circumcised were more vibrant and confident.

In 1996, the Maendelo Ya Wanawake Organization (MYWO) and PATH developed the first alternative rites of passage program, Ntanire Na Mugambo or Circumcision by Words. The MYWO formed in 1952 to improve living standards of families and communities in Kenya. The Alternative Coming of Age Program encouraged abandonment of FGC in seven of sixty-three districts in Kenya.[48] This program collects the traditional wisdom given to girls at the time of circumcision and adapts the messages to encourage the positive traditional values without the physical and psychological effects of FGC. It includes a five-day seclusion period to teach adult values and behaviors. The seclusion is followed by a one-day coming-of-age ceremony that includes feasting, gift giving, and presenting graduation certificates.

The Circumcision by Words ceremony began with twelve families in Gatunga, Tharaka Nithi. Fourteen rites of passage have taken place in Kisii, Meru, Narok, and Tharaka districts. In 2000, four years after the first ceremony, almost three thousand girls have gone through the alternative rite-of-passage ceremonies. The success of this program is attributed to build-ing on positive community values that underlie FGC, dialogue, and mem-ber participation.[49]

Attitudes are gradually changing in Kenya. A 1991 survey showed that 78 percent of adolescents had undergone FGM compared to 100 percent of women over fifty. Also in 1991, a study showed that 62.3 percent of women over age fifty had Type II FC, while only 38.9 percent of girls ages fifteen to nineteen had Type II. PATH attributes the decline in Kenya to secondary education's disapproval, girls' refusal, greater access to health education, modernization, fear of laws, public ridicule, and the realiza-tion that FGM has no effect on girls' behavior.[50]

Uganda

In 1995, male elders in the Sabiny community in Kapchorwa decided to resolve to replace actual cutting with gift giving and other festivities. Their decision was a result of the U.N. Population Fund REACH program. The Reproductive, Education and Community Health (REACH) program used community seminars and workshops, trained adolescents as peer educators, trained traditional birth attendants and health workers, and established a cultural day to celebrate values. The percentage of women and girls cut in the two-year period 1994 to 1996 decreased by 36 per-cent.[51]

OTHER AREAS AT TURNING POINTS

Gambia

More than 70 percent of Gambia's girls and women have undergone either a clitoridectomy or excision between the ages of five and eighteen, according to the Foundation for Research on Women's Health, Productivity and the Environment (BAFROW). In 1999, BAFROW found that thirty of 101 circumcisers in three administrative divisions of Gambia had stopped practicing. In 1997, in Niamina District only twelve girls were cut com-pared to ninety-two in 1996. Similar results were found in Fulladu Dis-trict. In 1997, 190 girls were cut compared to 412 in 1996.[52]

Somalia

Ninety-five percent of Somalia's girls undergo FGM at age seven. Most are infibulated. "In Somalia the husband uses his fingers, a knife, or a razor to enlarge the opening of his wife."[53] The reopening is a reinjury to the genital area.

In 2004 in Berbera, the mayor made a speech at a meeting to honor six circumcisers who had volunteered to disarm. He said, "I want to make it clear that we, in the regional authority, are with you in this war."[54] Also present were the mayor's colleagues from city hall, doctors, and sheiks. The mayor's speech, or any man speaking on FGM, in Somalia a few years ago would have been "unthinkable."

Also at the meeting was a midwife. In 1985 a midwife, Zahara Abdillahi, went to Yemen to work. Abdillahi told what she saw, "I saw that a woman who had not been mutilated had no problem — she gave birth perfectly. I had never seen such a thing before. That is when I became active in this work."[55]

Abdillahi returned to Borama, Somaliland. There she; an Italian woman circumciser who was as a health worker in a tuberculosis (TB) hospital, Annalena Tonelli; a sheikh, Haji Mohammed Sayeed; and a social worker opened an office against FGM in 2001. Knowing that traditionalists liked to dismiss the campaign as "pernicious work" of outsiders, Tonelli set up teams and found financial support but remained in the background.[56]

In 2000, Sheikh Mohammed Sayeed met with mosque leaders in Hargeisa to discuss whether FGM was sanctioned by Islam. Two groups were formed — the traditionalists and the activists. Sayeed believed FC kills people because his wife had six full-term babies who were stillborn. Her birth canal was too tight. Sayeed says, "Are you better than God that you tamper with His work? Allah opened the mouth. Would you cut and stitch that too?"[57] As circumcisers learned from Sayeed's work that it was against Islam, they said, "If this is not in Islam, we are ready to give [it] up. But our problem is that this is our living. How shall we survive?"[58]

The teams provided funds for new businesses and school fees for the children. Twenty-four circumcisers initially gave up their work. One challenge remained: reducing the supply of services is only half the answer; the demand for circumcision must also be reduced.

The experience in Somalia consistently met those forces that challenged change. In 2004, when Annalena Tonelli was murdered at the age of sixty, they were able to continue their programs because of her ability for organization.[59]

Mali

Ninety-four percent of women in Mali have undergone FGC. Global Health Programs and the PRIME II project along with political support from the President of Mali, Alpha Oumar Konaré, and the Ministry of Health work to end FGC. In 2001, the president called a special meeting to educate himself and his cabinet. The meeting was hosted by the National Action Committee to Abandon Harmful Practices (CNAPN). After the meeting, PRIME II with USAID/Mali funded and produced a video featuring physicians, an anthropologist, and opinions of men and women interviewed on the streets of Bamako. This video was distributed to all government officials.[60]

Circumcisers are entrenched, and the efforts to reduce the number of traditional excisers have failed in Mali. The result of public campaigns has been a trend to increased medicalization by trained professionals. Thus, PRIME II has focused on primary care providers. Their campaign's first goal is to train 150 providers and their supervisors about the complications arising from FGC.[61]

In 2000, the three-year Project PASAF began to assist the CNAPN in the Bougouni region. As of June 2002, Project PASAF was successful in making alliances with local NGOs and raising the awareness of political leaders.[62]

CNAPN recognizes that the decision to abandon FGC "must be made by the *very communities that practice it.*"[63] They provide community members an opportunity for reflection and dialogue along with the information needed to make intelligent decisions. More than twenty-five villages in the Koulikoro and Kayes regions have openly abandoned FGC. Villages in Bougouni in the southwest have declared a moratorium on excising for ten years. PATH concluded there is a long way to go in Mali and that the campaign is in the beginning stages, but because people are talking, change will occur.[64]

Ethiopia

In 1998, the NCTPE found 73 percent of the women had undergone FGC. In 2000, the Demographic and Health Survey (DHS) showed that 80 percent of the women had been circumcised. In the Harari region 95 percent of the women were circumcised.[65]

PRIME II's objectives were to educate women of reproductive age on the harmful effects of FGC and to target people who have critical leadership or influential roles within the community. Their program was aimed at fifty community members in five sites in the Harari Region. Members were from the community at large and from leadership with an equal number of men and women, and there were an equal number of married men, married women, and unmarried women without children.[66]

PRIME II found evidence of religious reasoning, but people were unable to state it. Religion is misinterpreted, especially by women. The mother, without the knowledge of the father, decides and performs FGC. Infibulation is considered a sin, but sunna-FGC (Type I) is supported. The remaining findings of PRIME II are not unlike other results throughout Africa.[67]

The U.N. Population Fund (UNFPA) estimated that between fifty-thousand and one-hundred thousand women may be affected by obstetric fistula in the whole of Africa. This condition is a result of long labor. Internal ripping of tissue occurs, creating a hole between the bladder and vagina and rectum. The reasons why FGC is resistant to change are very apparent in the story of a thirteen-year-old girl who developed a fistula. Meseret from the Lalibela district in northern Ethiopia became ill with this condition. She married at twelve and became pregnant at thirteen. After six days of labor, her child was stillborn. Journalist Sonny Inbaraj wrote, "The girl's husband quickly rejected her. She had given him a dead baby and now she stank badly. He sent her home to her family."[68]

After selling a cow to pay for a three-day bus ride to Addis Ababa, the capital, the family arrived at the hospital with no money. Fortunately, the hospital offers free surgery and a free bed. The hospital treats twelve-hundred women a year, a fraction of the fistula cases in Ethiopia. The positive side of Meseret's plight is that when surgery is done properly, the success rate is up to 90 percent and there is usually a possibility for more children. Poverty and stigma keep women "invisible" to policy makers. The girls are illiterate. They cannot communicate or say they have a problem and need help.[69]

Although UNFPA began fistula prevention programs in 2002, President George W. Bush withheld thirty-four million dollars of funding. The President was alarmed by reports that UNFPA was supporting forced abortions in China.[70] Thus, the misguided policy makers add themselves to the long list of reasons that change is challenged. Along with misshaped policy, change is challenged by unaltered village culture, poverty, and stigma.

Guinea

Amido Diallo, a Guinean public servant, spoke of the sorrow he felt at the funeral of his fourteen-year old niece Kadiatou. She died when her Aunt Fatima had her, without her parents' knowledge, undergo genital cutting.[71]

The government of Guinea has made the eradication of genital cutting a national policy. To support the government, USAID/Guinea worked with local organizations to arrange a public ceremony to raise awareness of the problem and to urge that the practice be stopped. It was at this ceremony that Diallo publicly spoke about the tragedy of his niece and called for the practice to stop. The event's success attracted pledges from other districts. A similar ceremony has taken place in another region.[72]

The WHO reported a 99 percent prevalence rate of FGC in Guinea in 1997.[73] From October 1998 to February 1999, the DHS conducted a qualitative research study on FC, or FGC in Guinea. Circumcision before marriage is a common practice in the Republic of Guinea. The study sought to gather information on events related to coming of age among girls, such as information on social preparation for marriage and adult life and about FGC itself.[74]

Four hundred twenty-two women, seventy-six men, and twenty-two female FGC specialists including traditional practitioners and other healthcare people were interviewed. Four different types of FGC were practiced. Most of the Sosso women interviewed said that circumcision was an important event, whereas only a few Guerze women said that it was. Less than half of the Fulani and Malinke women cited it in the context of growing up. The majority of the women using Sosso, Fulfulde, and Maninka languages had undergone some type of cutting. Seventy-seven of one hundred eight or about three-fourths of the Guerze-speaking women had experienced cutting.[75]

Types practiced in the Sosso and Fulfulde regions were "total removal of the clitoris and the labia minora, total removal of the clitoris (clitoridectomy), partial excision of the clitoris, and pinching and nicking."[76] The Guerze- and Maninka-speaking women reported one type, complete removal of the clitoris and labia minora. The study also found that FGC is increasingly performed within the medical system and is taking a less-severe form.[77]

The women from all areas said that they continued FGC because of tradition. They believed the tradition was of no benefit, but peers would laugh at an uncut woman. They reported that FGC promoted abstinence because the removal of the clitoris reduced desire for men. Except for women who lived in urban areas, the majority believed the practice purifies and socializes unmarried girls through the training received during seclusion. Women were divided as to the role of religion.[78]

Men interviewed believed that FGC should continue because "it is part of their cultural heritage; it regulates sexual relationships between men and women; it is a physical ordeal that serves to socialize a girl and prepare her to become a good wife, an exemplary woman."[79]

Several factors contributed to this program's success. It concluded that having a sensitivity to language and allowing discussion of FGC as one element in a girl's preparation for adulthood permitted women to be more comfortable when speaking of their own experiences. The study recommended an expansion of the awareness campaigns to include religious units, elders, and leaders; to replace media messages with participatory programs; to demedicalize the FGC information campaigns; to train people familiar with language and culture to help; to integrate the younger generation in the movement; and to have more studies.[80]

Sudan

The PATH reported in 1997 that a four-percent change in attitude in Sudan is significant considering how deeply entrenched FGM is there. In 1981 a study showed 82 percent of the 15- to 44-year-old women supported FGM. In 1989 to 1990, only 78 percent favored the continuation of FGM. Sudan restricts the types of FGM, resulting in legitimizing and medicalizing the practice instead of eradicating it.[81]

Different forms of pharaonic and clitoridectomic circumcision are practiced in Sudan. A variety of surveys shows prevalence at about 90 percent. In 2002, findings of a study on sexual experiences and the psychosexual effect of FGM/FC on Sudanese women showed that the majority (69 percent) had fearful and painful expectations of their first sexual intercourse. After the first time, 77 percent enjoyed all sexual experiences. Of the 77 percent, six percent never reached orgasm in their sexual lives. The study investigated three hundred Sudanese women with sexual experience who lived in the cities of Khartoum, Khartoum North, and Omdurman in Khartoum State.[82]

The study found that the NGOs succeeded only in breaking the silence around the issue of FGM/FC and that not enough attention had been given to the spread of FGM/FC. In addition, the practice of cosmetic recircumcision had not been addressed as a serious issue.[83]

More revealing are the findings from Alison T. Slack's research. A woman's infibulated area must be penetrated by her husband on her wedding night. The opening is small and often keloid scar tissue has built up. In Sudan, the procedure is carried out in secret and reflects negatively on the husband's potency. One of the few local health clinics or a midwife might open the woman. Without exception, Sudanese women who were interviewed reported going through, "a great deal of suffering during a process of gradual penetration which lasted an average of two to three months. Quite a few suffered tearing of surrounding tissues; hemorrhage was common, as were infections and psychic trauma.[84]

We asked Jenty Nawal Chacha Kosta from Juba and her husband, Aban Laamatjok from Malakal in south Sudan, whether any African tribes in the south practice circumcision other than the ones who are Arab or Muslim. Aban replied that the women did not except for Arab or Muslim women.[85] Jenty expanded upon his response:

> These are women who are Muslims that come from the north and wandered into the state. Even now people are trying to stop it, because now many of the Arab women are dying especially during delivery. It's not good. It does not help. That's why maybe in some years to come, they are going to change this system. Circumcision, especially for women, is not good. For men, it's a different thing. For women, they used to cut the clitoris, and you know in biology they say it is not helping in delivery and also sometime it helps for if you are approaching someone sexually, it helps women to get their fluid. Now for them they don't have the vaginal opening. Sometimes women die, because the child cannot come out and if you want to force a child out, you cannot, the vaginal opening is not there any more.[86]

We asked why the surgeries are done. Jenty replied, "It's a custom of Islam actually. You have to be circumcised."[87] Aban added:

> Female surgeries in Sudan, and the girls who practice this surgery also, are in the north of Sudan. All of them are in the north, because they consider it as a part of cleanliness. It's part of Islam.
> It is based on religion, Muslim, Islam. Most important, it's not mentioned in the Koran, Sunna or all of the Islam books, but it is a part of tradition. They took it out of the part of tradition. It just moved from part of the tradition and became part of the religion. But it is not in the Koran. It's not like a prayer or like a high pilgrimage to Mecca.[88]

Aban explained that most who practice circumcision in the south are the minority Muslims:

> They move from the villages, from their tribes and settle in the biggest cities in the south like Malakal, Bentiu and Wau. They found communities there and most of them, they found Muslim. They lose their tribal cultures. Adult workers who come from the north, because they are Muslim, they need to follow the practices in the north. Those people who practice female surgeries in the south are in the minority."[89]

Aban said the government is trying eradicate the practice. "It is permitted by the laws in Sudan. But people especially in the countryside — for them the belief is part of the religion. So, they don't care about what the government is trying to say that this will harm the women."[90]

In an interview with another south Sudanese couple living in Grand Island, Nebraska, Mut Ruey and his wife Nyarieka Ruey, Mut agreed that government does not always know when circumcision occurs:

> They circumcise because of religion or custom that they have used for
> a long period of time. It is still done, but they don't do it in a public
> place, like taking the girl or woman to the hospital. They do it in a
> private place with the person like the pastor. Islamic custom calls this
> person differently, he is not a pastor, but someone who has a back-
> ground of religious experience. They do it without the government
> having any knowledge that they are doing it.[91]

Aban believes the effort to eliminate circumcision will take time:

> You cannot fight against this practice while the people there are illiter-
> ate. You need to educate them first. When you address them about
> these kinds of practices that it is not good for the health and is also not
> a part of religion, they will have the ability to understand and to
> respond. But even what the people know about their religion, Chris-
> tianity or Islam, is limited. Muslims don't read, they don't write — so it
> is very hard to change them.[92]

Understanding the traditions that are there and that are ingrained in
people is basic to change. Aban continued:

> They used to say, "Our fathers, our mothers have been doing this for
> hundreds of years. So, why now do you come and tell me that this is
> not good and this will affect my health?" They cannot believe you. You
> cannot convince them. They will say, "Look to my mother, look to my
> grandmother, they are still in good health. What happened to them?"
> They take that as a good example. While you are talking, you don't
> have a good material example that you can show them that it would
> harm.[93]

Aban added, "You cannot do this kind of surgery in the hospital,
because all of the hospitals are controlled by the government and because
the government is trying to eradicate this practice. We have local doctors
who do the surgery. Actually they did not study medicine, but they do this
in the communities and the countryside."[94]

There are people assigned to do the surgery. Jenty said that these are
"people who are tribal leaders."[95]

Aban explained their role. "We call them *sheikh*. They are, in Islam,
like elders in the church and sometime[s] it is the pastor who knows better about the religion, who knows better about the work, who knows better about anything. They are the most respectable, the most powerful,
even holier than everybody — so if they say anything, people will follow
them and will never follow the government on anything.[96]

We asked if a celebration or ceremony accompanies the female
surgery. Jenty replied, "Yes, they have a celebration. They have a small
party."[97]

Aban described the party. "If we did this surgery, for example, to my daughter, we'll have a big party starting out, and we'll invite the relatives, friends and neighbors. All the people come and share in that and they are happy. They will announce the daughter is circumcised."[98]

Jenty explained about the *henna*, "They put little things on the body in our culture, Sudanese culture, called *henna*. They put *henna* before you are coming out. Before they don't come out, they put *henna* on their legs and hair. It is like a tattoo."[99]

In addition to the *henna*, says Aban, "the one who is circumcised will wear a special dress, and it is a big event. It is just like a marriage. It is something to honor. The one who is circumcised, they are honored by something. They cut off something which is not clean."[100]

We asked if the circumcision itself is done in private. Aban replied that it is. He said, "If this is done in our compound here, we would have like a *sheikh* who is doing this in this area perform the circumcision."[101]

Jenty and Aban told us that either a man or a woman can perform the surgery, but that mostly men do so. An advantage of FC is that it prevents women from committing adultery. Aban says that this belief is held mostly by Muslims, but most Africans try to prevent the girl from having sex until she gets married. "The Muslim[s] say this kind of surgery will reduce the desire to have sex before she gets married. And if she commits adultery before she gets married, she will be found out and this will cause her to be stoned or be killed and will bring shame to her family. This is the primary reason they are performing this kind of surgery."[102]

Neither Nyarieka nor Mut Ruey saw that FC has any advantages. Nyarieka said, "As for myself, I don't like it at all. But I heard that it happened in northern Sudan. But we in south Sudan do not practice it. We do not perform it at all. There is no advantage to the woman. The disadvantage is, if they do that to the woman, it will harm her. Nothing will function by the way that we do things."[103]

Mut noted, "To my knowledge, there isn't any advantage at all. A disadvantage to circumcision is the woman does not ever feel comfortable like the way she used to."[104]

William G. Riek, President of the Sudanese Refugee Community Organization (SRCO) and a refugee advocate for the Community Humanitarian Resource Center (CHRC)in Grand Island, Nebraska, was a nurse in south Sudan. He explained that in Sudan, he was a salaried assistant and treated mainly eye problems caused by the tropical, hot climate. He said there is some change taking place away from FC in north Sudan:

> Now, it is not like before. They have changed because a lot of problems occurred and they get advice from doctors and from countries of the world. To prevent health problems from occurring, they limit the cir-

cumcision of women. Because when the women are circumcised, they have internal bleeding or big swelling or germs affecting them. The result is death sometime[s]. People have no interest in that anymore.[105]

Riek explained that circumcision still continues for boys and that the Islamic faith tends to circumcise whereas the Christian faith does not:

> The Arab boys in north Sudan — let's say among the Muslim people — they do circumcision, all of them. They put it as the rule of Islam for the little boys, but not for some of the little girls. They are careful not to do that. Some understand that circumcision is a problem for girls. When you come to the south or in the Christian areas, we do not have circumcision, generally. Among some of the people, maybe fifteen percent used to be circumcised. Not all female, maybe one percent of female is still circumcised. The fifteen percent of the boys who are circumcised are those who adopted the northern culture, those who relate to the Arab culture. Muslim[s] sometimes, whether they are in the north or the south, will follow what Islam says to do. Generally, in South Sudan, we are Christian, and culturally, we don't use circumcision at all. We used to say, "It is something not correct by God; we don't want that."[106]

Because Riek is a nurse, he believes there may be circumstances where circumcision is done for reasons related to health. He said, "I may choose to be circumcised myself, if I have a problem in that area. People may say, 'This will be treated by circumcision.' Maybe I will accept because of the condition. Some people circumcise because they have a problem to be treated by circumcision."[107] Other than for health-related reasons, Riek said, "We don't want it at all in the culture, and we don't want it in Christianity. If, according to Sharia, someone wants it, he can do it. If someone does not want it, he may not use it."[108]

We asked Riek whether he was saying that the health problems came because they had the surgery. He clarified:

> When I say it affects the health of the person, I mean, during the operation. Germs can enter the wound when it is cut. It happened to some that they formed a big swelling and it attacks the body when they get infected by the germs because, maybe the tools are contaminated. For some, it causes long term bleeding and they get dehydrated. Some go back before they heal, but the problem depends on the kind of surgery they had.[109]

Men and Women Need to Be Involved

Mekuria advocates that both women and men need to be involved to bring about change. A mixed-gender effort would enable an understanding of the reasons why the practices are believed to be necessary and valuable. In addition, it would increase understanding of women's perceptions of the consequences if the practices are not carried out. For both genders "in particular localities, it would widen [the] range of possible terms for interpreting and debating the choices involved."[110]

THE CONTINUING GLOBAL EFFORTS TO END FGM

African Unity

The Inter-African Committee on Traditional Practices Affecting the Health of Women and Children (IAC) consists of twenty-six African countries and four affiliated European countries. In 1997, the IAC passed the Declaration on the Importance of Adopting Legislation Against Female Genital Mutilation.[111]

IAC Declaration

On February 6, 2003, the IAC declared an International Day of Zero Tolerance. The declaration involved 250 women from thirty countries in Europe, North America, and Africa. Among those women attending were the first ladies of Nigeria, Mali, Guinea, and Burkina Faso. The declaration stated in part, "It is heartening to note that harmful traditional practices in general and female genital mutilation in particular are receiving gradual regional and international focus."[112]

The Role of Religious Leaders

There are many examples of success with religious leaders. In the years 2000 to 2002, the IAC reported specific successes. In December 2000, the IAC reported that dialogue with religious leaders was among the highlights of their achievements. They had been successful in consultations for analyzing religious misconceptions. Misconceptions have been a major justification for the perpetuation of FGM. Religious leaders from Iran, Egypt, Ethiopia, Sudan, Gambia, Senegal, Nigeria, and other countries confirmed that Islam and Christianity opposed the practice of FGM. The campaign in partnership to set up a network of religious leaders is advancing satisfactorily.[113]

In December 2000, the Committee reported the findings of a four-year study conducted by Sudan National Committee on Traditional Practices (SNCTP) and sponsored by Save the Children, Sweden. The study had a sample population of 1,230. Regarding religious leaders and FGM, it found that leaders "did not agree on 'Hadeeth' and that the religious concept was left to the development of knowledge and 'Ijtihad'."[114]

In 2000 the committee organized a follow-up symposium for religious and traditional leaders in Arusha, Tanzania. The Symposium was a follow-up of the first Religious Symposium held in Banjul, Gambia, in July 1998. Twenty-three leaders from ten African countries attended. Many other religious meetings were held during the year.[115]

In 2002 the IAC reported that during their visit to Somaliland in 2001, they found the prevalence rate of FGM was about 98 percent. There was also "a tendency of shifting from the practice of infibulation to sunna. Religious leaders advocate the sunna type, but condemn infibulation."[116]

Another action of unity among religious leaders occurred in 2003, when the Kenyan bishops joined other faith groups in forming a committee to help end FGM. Other members included the Anglican Church of Kenya, the Methodist Church, the African Independent Pentecostal Churches, and the Supreme Council of Muslims in Kenya. The committee released a statement, "By being silent on the subject of female genital mutilation, faith-based organizations have propagated the continuation of the practice."[117]

MEDICALIZATION: A STEP AWAY OR A STEP TOWARD FGM

In some societies, FGM is performed by physicians in a clinic or hospital to alleviate some of the disastrous side effects. In others, it may be another way to continue to have FGM performed on women and girls. This approach is called medicalization of FGM. Due to numerous health concerns and immigration, health clinics and physicians are faced with women and girls either requesting the procedure or requesting healthcare resulting from having had the procedure. As a result, much literature has been generated to help educate healthcare professionals on FGM itself, the techniques of defibulation and reinfibulation, care for the childbearing woman, and the importance of clear communication styles.[118]

In the United States, more than 168,000 women and girls have undergone FC.[119] A large number of these women do not consider themselves "mutilated." Most of the women from their communities have undergone circumcision and do not believe they are being selectively tortured. Many female immigrants are surprised to learn that most women in the United States are not circumcised. Dr. Nawal M. Nour, Director of the Obstetric

Resident Clinic and the African Women's Health Practice at Brigham and Women's Hospital, wrote:

> Women who have undergone FC/FGM have voiced concern that we are not sensitive when broaching this subject. Many patients have seen physicians gasp in horror and question the patient as to whether she has been burnt or tortured. Others have been told that they have to undergo a C/S [cesarean/section] because of their scar. Women have found themselves obliged to educate their healthcare providers about this practice.[120]

Most appropriate for the United States and other countries where FGM is against the law is how to respond to requests for circumcision. The Research, Action and Information Network for Bodily Integrity of Women (RAINBO) provided the following example of an appropriate response:

> I understand that female circumcision is commonly practiced in your culture and is an old custom. Recently there have been many studies and information to show that this practice is harmful to women. Because of that the United States government and the United Nations decided that female circumcision must be made illegal. As a healthcare provider in the United States, I will be breaking the law if I perform this procedure. If you get it done by someone else, both you and the circumciser will be subject to imprisonment and possible deportation.[121]

Concern for preservation of cultural identity challenges change even in countries where FGM is prohibited by law. Some physicians who work with immigrant populations have voiced concern about the adverse effects of criminalization of the practice on educational efforts. "These physicians emphasize the significance of a ceremonial ritual in the initiation of the girl or adolescent as a community member, [and] advocate a lesser procedure, such as pricking or incision of the clitoral skin, as often sufficient to satisfy cultural requirements."[122] The Committee on Bioethics of the American Academy of Pediatrics opposes all forms of FGM and advises physicians to "consider their role in perpetuating this social practice with its cultural implications for the status of women."[123] It is unclear whether lesser procedures would be exempt from the law.

Not all aspects of FC are against the law in the United States. Dr. Nawal Nour pointed out that some women will request immediate reinfibulation after delivery. This procedure may create long-term complications. Dr. Nour wrote that reinfibulation "should be strongly discouraged. However, given that a patient may only feel comfortable being infibulated, her request must be respected."[124] Dr. Nour wrote that this request is not a legal impossibility because reinfibulation is not included as a Federal crime and can be performed in the United States.

RAINBO's African Immigrant Programs work on reproductive health and gender issues for immigrants and refugees. They provide education. They explain that defibulation permits the baby's head to come out during childbirth. RAINBO recommends that women should have their scars opened before or in the early stages of pregnancy. Some women feel unnatural or uncomfortable if they are not stitched. Others believe their husbands will dislike them being left open. These women request reinfibulation after birth. The health risks for reinfibulation are the same as for the initial infibulation. RAINBO pointed out "In some European countries doctors are forbidden by law from re-stitching. In the United States and some other countries there is no such law."[125]

On February 6, 2004, USAID sponsored the first anniversary symposium to review the advances and challenges in abandoning FGC. The symposium, Translating Zero Tolerance into Zero Cutting, included a Congressional briefing. Participants included Dr. Abdelhadi Eltahir, Senior Technical Advisor for USAID; Nawal Nour, M.D, M.P.H., Director of the African Women's Center at Brigham and Women's Hospital, Boston, who was the 2003 winner of the MacArthur Genius Award; E. Anne Peterson, M.D., M.P.H., Assistant Administrator of the USAID Bureau for Global Health; Mrs. Fatoumata Diakité, a member of the IAC; Dr. Nahid Toubia, Founder and President of RAINBO; Molly Melching, from the Tostan Program, Senegal; and Kerthio Diarra, a member of the Senegalese women's group in Malicounda Bambara.[126]

Dr. Nawal Nour discussed the African Women's Center and its work with immigrant women in the United States. The majority of the Center's women come from Sudan, Somalia, and Ethiopia.[127] Dr. Nour reported that during workshops several glaring issues have surfaced:

• Circumcised women have poor access to healthcare and little exposure to reproductive health issues.
• There is a dearth of culturally competent health[care] and service providers who understand the complexities of FGC.
• The African Community and medical community seem unfamiliar with U.S. law.
• There is a growing population that is traveling to Africa to perform the circumcisions on their daughters.[128]

Nour said the biggest question that she constantly faces is, "What can we do to prevent this practice from continuing and to ensure a healthy life for those who have already been circumcised?"[129] She offered the following suggestions:

• [The] African community needs more education and outreach. We evaluated our workshop six months later and had a comment section. Unsolicited, 20 percent in the comment section requested more workshops. Molly Melching's work in Senegal demonstrates how persistent outreach can change attitude.

• Health providers need more cultural and linguistic education. Dr. Toubia produced an excellent manual that is now out of print. The American College of Obstetricians and Gynecologists (ACOG) has a terrific slide-lecture kit that has helped medical students and residents in the United States and Canada. More of these manuals are critical.

• Protection of the uncircumcised African here in the U.S. My plea is that the United States government take action to protect the young girls.[130]

Nour advocates treating people with respect and dignity regarding FGC because they want to be seen as healthy, beautiful individuals who contribute to society.

Europe

The Inter-Parliamentary Union (IPU) organized, at the initiative of its Meeting of Women Parliamentarians, in Ouagadougou, Burkina Faso, in September 2001. At its 106th Conference, it organized a panel discussion on "Violence Against Women: Female Genital Mutilation."[131] An agreement was reached for action at the national, subregional, and international levels on recommendations that directly concern parliaments and the IPU. After gathering information, at the 107th Conference in 2002 the IPU established a think tank to be placed within its framework. Its members would be men and women who would meet parliamentarians from those countries where traditional practices are still entrenched.

Parliamentary Assembly of the
Council of Europe Resolution

In 2001, the Parliamentary Assembly of the Council of Europe passed a resolution declaring "genital mutilation should be regarded as inhuman and degrading treatment within the meaning of Article 3 of the European Convention on Human Rights, even if carried out under hygienic conditions by competent personnel." It also condemned the increase in the number of forced marriages and virginity tests. The Assembly called on the governments of member states to introduce specific legislation prohibiting genital mutilation; declare genital mutilation a violation of human rights and bodily integrity; inform all people about the legislation; adopt more flexible measures for granting the right of asylum; adopt specific time limits for prosecution and grant organizations the right to bring action; prosecute the perpetrators and their accomplices; conduct information and public awareness-raising campaigns; introduce sex education classes in schools and in all relevant groups; make sure that any marriages involving young girls under marriageable age are preceded by interviews; and ratify the relevant international conventions.[132]

European Parliament: Report and Resolution

The European Parliament acted upon a report on FGM[133] by making any form of FGM a crime.[134] Any resident of Europe who has taken part in FGM, even if the offence was committed abroad, would be prosecuted and punished. The Parliament wants the authorities of Member States to have the right to intervene where there is a risk of FGM. The roundtable will bring together immigration officials, child welfare professionals, and refugee advocates.[135]

The European resolution asked for States to devise educational programs "to assist and protect victims of FGM and to recognise that people at risk of being subjected to FGM have a right to asylum."[136]

The European resolution was also "urged to provide foreign aid to countries which have adopted measures to punish FGM and to promote programmes to prevent and combat it,"[137] and was asked to make its voice heard in the United Nations.

The United Nations and Other Bodies

Active agencies affiliated with the United Nations continue to work to eradicate FGM. The WHO is also actively disseminating information and passing resolutions.[138] Treaties and other recent international agreements provide standards for laws.

CONCLUSIONS

FGM continues because, as the village chief in Bougouni, Mali, wisely said, we must, "Give the spirit the time to ripen."[139] Countries are confronted with complex and culturally entrenched beliefs about FGM. Current beliefs and behaviors must be understood and dismantled. Programs must be tailored to the audience, and the target audience's behavior changes must be monitored in order to discover some of the remaining challenges to change.

The ethics and politics involved in changing cultures give rise to debates such as medicalization of FGM and the West's participation in the issue. It is important to note that FGM occurs in countries other than countries in Africa; in Africa, however, it is essential to examine to what degree culture will be sustained. During the process of change, it is important for men and women, religious leaders, and village leaders to exert leadership, particularly in countries where the practice is entrenched.

7

The Maasai and
Female Circumcision

> We hope many people will read your book and that some
> will learn about the Maasai. We hope they will get an
> interest in the Maasai and come to encourage and help
> us.
>
> Maasai female village members, Tanzania[1]

The Maasai migrated into East Africa about five centuries ago from
the Sudan border near Lake Turkana.[2] The East Africa Maasai number
approximately one-half million people and inhabit 160,000 square kilo-
meters of semi-arid and arid land in southern Kenya and northern Tanzania along the Great Rift Valley.[3] We visited in the Monduli district in
Tanzania, where Government Councilor (Uwane) Sevingi estimates there
are three hundred thousand Maasai.[4]

The Maasai people "have continued to practice their ancient rituals
and ceremonies; they have continued to maintain their age-set structure
with its warrior caste of haughty, swift and predatory *moran* [warrior]—
storm troopers or commandos of the tribal world."[5] They have resisted,
for the most part, the programs offered by the West. The Maasai exasper-
ated the early colonial officials and have remained obdurate to the cur-
rent-day United Nations' agencies desire to introduce range management,
water conservation, and so forth, wrote Elspeth Huxley. She adds, however, that Maasailand long has had schools and hospitals and has produced
university graduates, professors, and Ministers of State.

The Maasai do not have a well-defined religious system, according to
D. Lee Roper, but the use of proverbs is a major part of their belief system. Proverbs explain the unknown and establish moral guidelines for
day-to-day relationships. Conversations often begin and end with a
proverb. Elders and wives teach proverbs to their children.[6]

The nomadic Maasai are admired the world over.[7] I am no exception. In January 2004, my husband James and I visited two Maasai villages. The research visits were planned and arranged by H. B. Shakir of Adventure Tours and Safaris in Arusha, Tanzania. We were escorted by Uwane (Councilor) Sevingi-R.S.A., a Tanzanian government official from Mto Wa Mbu, and by James Emanuel Sichilma, our driver, guide, and interpreter from Arusha, Tanzania.

Uwane Sevingi-R.S.A. told us about the Maasai:

> The Maasai are one of the major pastoral groups found in Tanzania, and they are thinly spread over the northern part of Tanzania, especially in Ngorongoro and Monduli districts.
>
> Maasai social and economic life centers on livestock. Cattle, sheep and goats form the basis of their subsistence. Milk, meat and blood form their dietary staples but, in reality, agricultural foods frequently supplement their pastoral diet, particularly during droughts and at the height of the dry season. Exchange of livestock for grain has probably always been taking place between the pastoral Maasai and their neighboring societies.
>
> Livestock means far more than food and economic security to the Maasai. Cattle in particular constitute a key value in Maasai culture. The Maasai move from one place to another looking for pastures for their cattle. In an ecological perspective, Maasai society is designed to strike a viable balance between man, livestock and the physical environment, water and pastures.
>
> Because of this situation, it becomes impossible for them to settle on one place for permanency and makes it difficult for government to provide them social welfare. Human population densities are lower but animal-man ratios are relatively higher. Those problems also affect Monduli district.
>
> The government and social groups are trying to recruit on the bases of practical considerations of resource utilization and of congeniality in cooperation rather than as the normative exigencies of kinships and residence rules.[8]

Dr. Les Huth, Professor Emeritus and Director of the Walter Cunningham Memorial Teacher's Project at Wartburg College in Waverly, Iowa, has had many opportunities to be out among the ethnic groups in the rural areas of Tanzania. He spent time in Kenya and traveled extensively in Tanzania. He conducted nine study tours to Tanzania for Wartburg students. Huth's studies have had a concentration on the Maasai people. He says that he has had the good fortune to work with Tepilit Saitoti, a Maasai who studied in the United States and returned to his homeland in Tanzania. Tepilit is the author of two books, *The Maasai* and *The Maasai Warrior*. Huth said Tepilit's life history is unusual:

He [Tepilit] had an eighth grade education and eventually got to the United States. They allowed him to start college and he completed an ABD doctorate from the University of Michigan. He has returned to the Maasai area. He has been featured in two National Geographic videos. He invited us to a celebration of a wedding and he invited us to the initiation of his son into the Maasai society. In those times, I and our students have had discussions with him about FGM [female genital mutilation] and female circumcision and how embedded it is in the culture. Just as an example, he knows that this is against the law, but within the past two or three years his daughter was circumcised. He contends that it was because the daughter was so persistent and said she would be ostracized if he didn't allow her to do this, that he did it.[9]

Huth reflected on the Maasai's practice of FGM:

It is very humiliating to the women who have a concern for it as a practice. What I've seen is that the Maasai, particularly those who are becoming more contemporary, see it as a very poor practice and something that physiologically can be very damaging to the woman. They are not opposed to the Maasai continuing their cultural practices except where the practices start to impact one part of that group in a very negative way. The Maasai people are described by anthropologists as the people that have maintained their culture more than any other ethnic group in the world. Many are very firm in wanting to continue practices. For example, we had Tepilit Saitoti's older sister speak to us about the practice and she just said there isn't anything wrong with it, it needs to be continued, it is our rite of passage and why would they want to take it away from us.[10]

Huth said that, in addition to the fear of being ostracized, there are other reasons why circumcision continues. He said, "The cultural practice of polygamy and of selecting wives contributes to the cultural aspect of it. They would not be selected as a wife if they hadn't gone through the ceremony. They believe this."[11]

One of Huth's study groups had a conversation with a very well educated Maasai woman who indicated that this practice does not go back in history that far. Circumcision came during a time of war. Huth said, "When the men were going off to war, they did this to try to limit sexual pleasure among the women."[12] Huth believes that some of the Maasai women are trying to study circumcision to determine how they can stop the practice.

Huth admires the Maasai for the way they have retained their culture, especially their practices that embody their reconciliatory outlook on life, but he would like to see female circumcision (FC) end. He said:

In the Arusha Lutheran Diocese, their efforts to eliminate or reduce female circumcision need to include a tremendous amount of education of the males. As long as the males continue to believe that this practice is something that women need to be included in the society and don't understand the health and psychological implications for women, it is going to be very difficult for the women to change. If there is a way that education can happen, it would be good. In a way it is kind of sad to say that you need to educate the males so the practice for the females can be what it should be. But that is a reality of the culture and the people.[13]

M. Neil Williams, M.D., is a general surgeon who served at the Selian Lutheran Hospital in Arusha, Tanzania, in 1998, 1999, and 2000. He believes that FC is a cultural rite but that education does make a difference. He said:

> Women that have become educated, especially in the mission schools, object to circumcision. They are usually of different tribes, too. Education of girls among the Maasai is just now really beginning to happen. The Lutheran Church has built a Maasai girl's school — a special school just for Maasai girls — which has just been completed in the last three or four years. I think they have just had their first high school graduating class in 2000 or 2001. It would be interesting to know what percentage of those girls have been circumcised. I don't know the answer to that.[14]

It is not easy, sometimes, to grapple with the basic needs of developing countries. In the United States, we are fortunate to have good school systems. The inspiring aspect of developing schools in Africa is the dedication of those people who work to bring education to the children of their country. Such is the vision of Uwane Sevingi-R.S.A. as he works tirelessly to bring better conditions to existing schools and to build additional schools so that more children can have the opportunity to be educated in the four districts in the Arusha region that he serves. One afternoon we visited a site for a new Maasai school at Mto Wa Mbu ward in Monduli District. The name of the school will be Mto Wa Mbu Secondary School. At the time of our visit, the school consisted of two buildings. At this school the Uwane showed us his architectural plans for the remainder of the school, a secondary boarding school that the Tanzanian government plans to build.

In our conversation with the Uwane, he said that he believes FC is decreasing because of the schools. "Girls know there is a choice even when they return home and are not given a choice. If they go to school, a boarding school, and get away, get an education, to live a life apart, they will be less likely to choose female circumcision."[15] The Uwane has worked with the Maasai for three years. In his work in the government, he finds funding a big problem. He says there is a great need to get spring water to the school by pipe. He also discovered that boys were being educated rather than girls. He believes in reaching the men or men who have been away because, "He can say, 'I don't want your daughter circumcised. I want to marry her but not with her circumcised.'"[16] Then together they can make a change.

For progress with the Maasai to continue, Councilor Sevingi believes funding must be found for the schools. The Tanzanian government pays half of the cost of tuition, and the other half must be paid by parents or raised through campaigns. In Sevingi's Mto Wa Mbu Secondary School Project, students whose parents have no ability to pay and students whose parents have died need help with the secondary school fee. As of March 2004, this ward had fifty pupils.[17]

Another area of need is textbooks for the primary school. The ward has 6,500 pupils, and one book is usual for ten to twenty pupils. Therefore the requirement is 29,800 books, which are available in Tanzanian book shops. Each book costs 3,500 Tanzania shillings (about $3.50 U.S. dollars). The desired ratio is one pupil for one book.[18]

The Maasai will benefit greatly from the Uwane's efforts. His emphasis on education for girls will also benefit them. In a letter he gave me while I was in Mto-wa-Mbu, he wrote:

> Now the government is trying to make sure that every child should go to school, secondary schools should be built in Maasai areas, to stop circumcision to the women and to reduce the number of herds.
> As our visitor, we are very eager to tell you we have many problems in the Maasai areas, the biggest problem is to educate the mass and we are building the secondary school, please go and think how you can help the Maasai in education.[19]

Uwane Sevingi is a truly motivating leader. In an earlier letter he asked that we "... show love and mercy to the People of Mto Wa Mbu, Monduli and other districts in general where Maasai peoples stay...."[20]

Uwane Sevingi's introduction to the Maasai people formed a strong foundation for our understanding. James Emanuel Sichilma's knowledge of the Maasai added to that foundation. James lived among the Maasai as a young boy and that benefited our research. My husband James's lifelong experience in the field of communication was also a great aid in understanding the questions and answers that the Maasai had for us. We visited two Maasai villages in the Monduli District: Kigongoni and Silalei. In the morning, we went to Kigongoni and visited with the leader of the village, Olaiguenani Landari and his cabinet. We sat in the shade of a tree at first. They brought stools for us to sit on.

We began with a very general conversation with the Olaiguenani and his cabinet. During the interview, we communicated in three languages. I asked my question in English to James, our interpreter, who translated it into Swahili for one of the Maasai leaders on the cabinet who understood Swahili and who could then translate my question into the Maasai language for the others. The Olaiguenani and his cabinet would then have a discussion. Our interpreter, James, explained, "You know, this [group] is like his cabinet. So, anything you want to talk about, he will say to the cabinet, 'They want to say this – is it good for them or is it not so good.'"[21]

We waited until they decided on their answer. Then the same cabinet member translated from the Maasai language to Swahili for our interpreter, who translated their answers into English for us. Our interpreter, James, began with the introductory part of the interview. He asked the Maasai to explain how many wives, daughters, and sons each had. He asked the mode of travel they use. James said they asked when we came from America. When the Maasai had their answer formed, they said, "We are a little bit scared to tell the truth about some things, because we are afraid of the political systems. Maybe you come to ask how many wives and how many children we have, so then you will go and talk with the government and say this and this and this."[22]

The Uwane added, "They doubt us." James explained that they doubt us because the government forces the children to go to school. The Maasai don't like to send their children to school because they want their help with the cows. So, this is what they are afraid of.[23] After we reassured the Maasai that I was not the government, they told us about the role of the leader. We learned that the leader of the Maasai can control a very large area sometimes and that he is very much respected by all the people.

They told us that they would like to talk in a very, very friendly way. We learned that the chief leader had seven wives and the first wife had five children. Some men have four wives, some have three and so on. Landari's grandchildren number about fifteen. Some who were already married were not living in this boma (village) but had gone to live with their husbands. Some still remained together in the same boma with their parents.[24]

We asked if the council and Mr. Landari make the rules and laws and if they change the laws from time to time. We asked not just about the family but also how the Maasai community operates. James explained their answer:

> They participate with the Uwane and Olaiguenani on so many things because they are friendly. A kind of a discussion will take place, let's say about the progress of their farming. If during the dry season the Maasai do not have a place to bring their cows to get water, they are supposed to go to the villages. Some of the villagers know that the

Maasai's cattle get their water there. The villagers are supposed to tell the Uwane, Councilor, that the cattle are supposed to come there for water.[25]

Sometimes the Uwane comes to encourage the Maasai to go to school, so the Maasai talk with the Olaiguenani. James said:

> The Maasai say to the Olaiguenani that it is better to do like this, like this, and like this. The Uwane [Councilor] is to only give advice and must proceed very slowly with careful thought. He must go slowly to encourage them and show how the discussion can help them. So, they are talking this, this and this and Olaiguenani is going to encourage the other Maasai to bring the baby to school. Sometime they can invite even him to the traditional celebration. Maybe Olaiguenani here will have a traditional celebration and he will invite the Councilor here to his home and celebrate it.[26]

We asked if the Maasai have to do what the Olaiguenani says they should do when the Maasai come to him. The Olaiguenani said that if someone comes to him for advice, that person must do what he instructs. For example, "Maybe a member of the community abused the older people. And the older people come to the Olaiguenani and tell him about it. The Olaiguenani will tell the community member that because 'you do that, please tell that you made a mistake and be excused for that.' He is supposed to do it, because the older man told the Olaiguenani."[27]

At this point in the interview the Maasai said it would be better to go inside their hut because there was too much wind and it was difficult to communicate.[28] We went inside their hut, where we all sat in a circle and the discussion continued. About midway through the discussion we were asked if we would drink what they give their honored guests, hot milk. A young warrior brought in the hot milk. When we finished drinking the milk, they wanted us to drink more, but it would have been too much so we did not drink a second cup.

During the informal parts of the discussion, Uwane Sevingi explained that the government is working with the Maasai to stop them from having animals sleep inside their huts because of disease. They are making some progress. The government is also working with them to have their young people in school and to stop circumcising their women. We discussed the inside of the hut and family and community member roles while sipping hot milk. James explained the inside arrangement of the Maasai house, "On the left side, the cows are kept. They say that they always serve guests hot milk when they come to visit them. In traditional custom, they very much respect you, so they bring some milk to drink. That place there, their oldest sleeps there; the husband sleeps there; and the mama and the baby will sleep in there. But this house is not yet finished."[29]

James explained that for a long time, the Maasai women endured more hardship than the men because women do most of the building of their houses. There has been some change in that the man can help the woman build the house. All the houses are plastered with cow dung. He explained more about the woman's role, "Right now, the man helps the woman a little bit, but before it was only the woman's job. It was also the woman's job to find and give the baby food. The Maasai allow the woman to take the milk from the cow for the baby. And the man's job is only to take the care of the cow, to graze and to bring it back and control everything."[30]

I asked who does the cooking and if the man ever cooks. James replied, "Never. Never does the man cook. Never does the man come in the kitchen. This is a woman's job. As usual, the man can choose today he is going to sleep at this house, and tomorrow at another house and another day, with another wife."[31]

I asked if the men participate with the women in raising the children:

> They say that there is a kind of participation between the man and the woman. But usually, the woman just does everything. And sometimes when the woman has a small baby and that woman who bears the baby is needed to go to find water somewhere, then the man who has maybe six or seven wives, and maybe the daughters live in another house, so another house's daughters come there to help the mother care for the baby. And while the baby is growing up and when there's quite an age difference between the baby and the adult daughters, the daughters are to take care of them.
>
> But traditionally, if a Maasai has a baby, the baby is not only yours, it's for everybody, especially a boy. If you have boys, and the boys make a mistake which is not good, there are young warriors who can punish. If one boy makes a mistake, sometimes the young warrior will hit all of the boys the same age. He will say, "Your friend made a mistake." So he hits. He goes to another one and says, "Your friend made a mistake." So he hits all of them in order to give them respect for doing right. So everyone is watching another and warning, "Don't do that because he's going to punish all of us." This is their tradition.[32]

The discussion progressed to circumcision. It began with a discussion of male circumcision by the Maasai. Later, one man told of his own experience:

> Even the adults who are already circumcised who are the warriors, they respect by watching. When the uncircumcised boys come back from their circumcision, they are joined together in the group and they stay together and sing. They choose one house and they stay there and sing

all day. If one of the houses far away had a shortage of some kind or if somebody was crying — all of them run there. They think maybe there is something such as a lion came close to the house. They go to fight it. Then they can eat anywhere they want. They can go to another boma to eat and then shift to another boma to eat. Most of the time they are going to eat with the grand woman, the older woman who prepares the food for these warriors. This is their tradition.[33]

My husband James asked the Maasai what preparations they made for circumcising the boys. After a discussion among the Maasai, one Maasai told the story of male circumcision:

> It is special to the boy when they bring him to be circumcised. There are two kinds of Maasai, some are called Arusha.[34] Arusha speak similar to the Maasai, but the traditional Maasai is much deeper than the Arusha. To the Maasai, every boma means that a couple of houses are needed for this man. So, if a Maasai needs to bring his boy to be circumcised, he comes to this house. Maybe the circumcision will be tomorrow. So, today there is kind of a celebration before they do it. During the night the people sing. The kind of song encourages them. It is not very good for them, because if they are not strong, they will be punished. During the circumcision, they are not allowed to cry or to show a sign that they are afraid. So, when they are cutting, there is no pain killer, you stay like this [the Maasai sits with legs apart and hands resting on his thighs], and then they cut. Slowly.
>
> So while they are cutting, the boys must show that they are brave. It's not allowed to show any emotion before they are circumcised. They always circumcise very, very early in the morning. So in the night, they sing. The adult people punish them to encourage [them] to be brave in the heart. When they do that, they are very angry and they are brave.
>
> Early in the morning, the circumciser comes. During the circumcision, one person stands behind the person and they catch him like this. [Demonstrates.] When they are finished cutting, the young men are taken to the river, to a place where there is a bed site and they sleep there. They stay there three to four days. At this place, they eat the sort of thing we call soup. They have meat and sometimes they are given blood; blood and milk mixed together. From there they go out with painted faces and they go stay in the bush.[35]

We received an interesting answer to our question about the age of the young men when they have their circumcisions and initiations. "Always in Maasai, we say, you don't count years. So, maybe these things happen around 15 to 16 years of age."[36] Curious, we asked how the Maasai do count if not by years. "When one elder says this is a good enough time, the boys will go to the circumciser," we were told.[37]

A warrior joined our group. He was introduced and we all exchanged "Jambos" (hellos). The discussion resumed. The Maasai told us about the build-up to the year of circumcision for boys:

There are seasons for circumcision. The exercise can take up to seventeen years. It continues every day, "circumcise, circumcise, circumcise," but until the seventeenth year, they don't circumcise. They are waiting for the little boy to grow up. If you are a boy, it may be five years, seven years, ten years and you are approaching close to the last of the season of circumcision. The boy thinks, another thirteen years he will have to stay as he is until he can become circumcised.

And, as a father, your boys are becoming big and older, maybe more than seventeen years, but you are supposed to wait for the season to appear. But sometimes they say, "Oh, my boy is still older." And while you are not circumcised you are still children, even if you are adult. But maybe the boy who is going to the circumciser is small, but he must give a very big respectful expression, and sometimes he's feeling shy, because all of them respect their elders. If you do not get circumcised, you are just a boy.

You put your head like this, and they put their hand on top of you to indicate that you are a baby, that you are still a child. If a boy is feeling shy about being circumcised, he will plead with his father, "I need to have circumcision earlier." His father is supposed to go to the Olaiguenani and talk with somebody who is a respected talker, to have his son circumcised, but the son must stay a boy.[38]

The Maasai man told how the uncircumcised boy cannot associate because, "While they cut, he is between the warrior and the baby. The younger one is to wait to be circumcised so they can be together. They can perform greetings like an adult but he still waits for the others to indicate that he and the warriors are now together. All males after they are circumcised are Morani."[39]

The Maasai men had more discussion, and when I heard the chief elder say the word, "mama," I knew that he was addressing me or talking about me with the other Maasai. A warrior entered with more hot milk. We tried to thank them in Maasai language but were not clear in our pronunciation, and the Maasai chuckled. Then they resumed the discussion about male circumcision among themselves:

Usually both boys and girls are circumcised in June. They prefer that. If you come in June [which is winter in Tanzania], there are many celebrations. In every boma there will be a celebration of the circumcisions. This time is preferred because the weather is good, because it's cold. The cold is like a pain killer. The cold helps to reduce the pain when you are circumcised.[40]

With our interview almost over, we returned to the subject of FC. The Maasai said, "We have another type of circumcision for the woman. We do circumcise women, but this is special and is done behind a closed door. For that special time, it's not allowed for any man to be around. The person who is the circumciser is a woman too."[41]

I asked at what age the women are circumcised. They said, "With the women, they are growing very quickly, so we do it early, around ten years."[42] Then I asked if the circumcision of women signifies moving into adulthood and if it is comparable to the men's in that it signifies a movement into adulthood. The Maasai men gave me an answer that I would hear again in the afternoon when I talked with Maasai women in a different boma. "We have to make an order to marry, 'I need to marry your daughter.' For placing the order, age doesn't matter. Maybe the daughter is nine or ten years, just to prepare for circumcision later."[43]

The Maasai told us that age does not matter and that the main reason is marriage. One man explained what a man had to do to marry his daughter:

> It doesn't matter what age the girl is, the man just places an order that he needs to marry my daughter, and the father agrees. So, they bring the woman to be circumcised. By that time, they can stay for a short time with their mother until they circumcise the girl. Like with the men, the woman wears some special clothes to show people that she is already circumcised. For that time, it will depend on the husband if he needs to marry, whether he needs to take the baby he has ordered and stay with her in his home until the baby is grown up, or if he needs to leave her with the parents until she is grown up. So, it depends on the husband, however he likes.[44]

I asked if women had a choice whether to have it done or not and if they would still be a welcome member of the group if they chose not to do it. The Maasai responded:

> We actually like the daughter to be circumcised, because while this house in this boma (village) has not circumcised and the other bomas around us are already circumcised, they have a celebration, singing and talking at circumcision, we cannot share this. We cannot sing with them. So every day we think, when will it be my day to circumcise in order to be doing what the others are. We need circumcision in order to share with the others, to celebrate, to prove ourselves.[45]

James concluded that they like it and need it.

James, our interpreter, asked the Maasai whether they had some daughters who are circumcised and if the daughters were there in their homes. One Maasai replied that he had some daughters who were circumcised last year in August and they were still here with him, their father. Some were married, but some were still here. I asked if daughters remain with the family unless they have a husband and if they marry young. James explained that the daughters were already booked to go to their husbands but they didn't go with them and that maybe they would wait and go much later.[46]

I had completed all of my questions. I told the Maasai that we appreciated their time, that their answers were most helpful, that I learned very much, and that I appreciated the opportunity and that they had refreshments for us. James, our interpreter, told the Maasai we were very sorry that they didn't have a woman who could translate for me and that I would like to talk to the woman to ask questions such as how they cook, how they help their husbands, and how they take care of their babies. I would like to talk to a daughter who is circumcised and maybe one of their women could stand between to translate. James asked the Maasai interpreter if he would accompany him to their one woman so the two of them could ask my questions. The Maasai man said that it would be better if I came back the next day. Then they would give me their one mama to talk with me all day or as long as we wanted, but right then they had some traditional meetings to attend. So we thanked him. Afterwards, we took photographs and presented them with gifts of sugar and tea.[47] The next day, however, we had other commitments so we did not return to this Maasai village.

After we visited Kigongoni in the morning, we visited Silalei in the afternoon. James told us the Laibon, the traditional Maasai witch doctor, was in charge. A witch doctor is a positive force for the Maasai. In Tanzania, the Maasai Laibon is looked upon as having divine power and as a healer. D. Lee Roper wrote, "Maasai medicine men are more prophets and religious and political leaders than they are healers."[48] According to Roper, "the medicine men are the most respected leaders of the Maasai people."[49]

The Laibon serves all Maasai villages. He usually has many women around him. James was sure we could talk about FC. We walked up a hill and sat in the shade of a tree. They brought stools for us to sit on, and the Laibon sat on a cowhide rug. Other Maasai sat on the ground around him. James explained that the Laibon was the first to build a house at this boma with his one wife. "Then he married the second wife. They have some adult boys that are already married, and they are living here with him. So, they share life with their baby and their grandchildren."[50]

Uwane Sevingi explained that some people come to the Laibon to get medicine for some diseases. He suggested that we begin with some questions about medicine or traditional medicine. James, our interpreter, asked the Laibon about his role as a witch doctor in helping the other Maasai in so many ways. For example, James explained, if there is no rain, people will come to him and ask if they were to pray somewhere would he help them to get rain. The Laibon answered James's question, "All the people are coming here and asking about that. Then I tell them to bring their honey, kind of a traditional alcohol."[51] James explained that the alcohol is made with honey mixed with some traditional roots. Next, they slaughter the sheep and mix the blood with some other ingredient. Then they go somewhere and hang this with a cord. They believe that can help.[52] Roper says that one of the ways medicine men make their decisions is by basing them on the visions they experience after "getting intoxicated on beer and honey wine."[53]

James asked how long it takes to do this sacrifice. The Laibon said it takes one day. James then asked if there is some special place to do it or if it can be done anywhere. The Laibon replied that they have a special place — just a tree and just this whole area. Furthermore, eight people eat the meat of one sheep and talk of the people they are going to pray for.[54]

James asked the Laibon what he would do if somebody came to him and said the magic made him sick and how he knew that somebody made magic for this sickness. The Laibon answered, "I have special traditional magic for him. I will look how to help him; sometimes I heal by magic. When the patient has magic when he is sick, it's difficult to treat him. It's close; I cannot treat him."[55] So, the Laibon looks to see if the magic is closed or open. If it is open, he knows how to treat it.

I asked what happens when the Laibon thinks he cannot make someone well and whether the patient accepts the situation. My husband James, asked if he makes them all well, if there are some that he can't make well, and what happens to the person that he can't make well. The Laibon answered, "Since I treat the people, I do not have people who do not get well. I hope that the people should get well."[56]

The Laibon is very famous all around the area. We asked him if someone who is sick and came to get something from him would get well? The Laibon answered, "Yes, if they give money to me." We then asked how he would help people who don't have money. He replied, "I help and he gets well. I tell him that he has to go and find the money. When he gets the money, bring it here. He is supposed to get the money."[57]

The time seemed right for me to ask my questions about women's health. I asked about the rites of ceremonial processes that women go through for circumcision; what is done; what tools are used; and if any sicknesses result. James, our interpreter, told us the Laibon was looking for a place for me to talk with the women. The women, James, and I went down the hill to another tree and sat down to have the discussion on FC. The Maasai women had questions for me as well. James said that they asked, "Where has mama come from? She is from America?" I answered. They asked why I suffer for all these things? I answered that I would like to talk with them and understand their traditional activities.[58]

The Maasai gave traditional reasons for FGM. However, Mary E. Laiser said that a reason pertinent to the Maasai is preparation for womanhood. She explained, "A woman is prepared to become a full woman or a whole woman if she is circumcised. For example, in the Maasai community, if a woman does not commit to being circumcised, she is regarded as a child throughout her life. So even if she is old enough to be an adult, if she does not submit to the operation, they regard her as a child."[59]

Because the Maasai culture continues to undergo change, Laiser added, "Young men who were born outside the country or outside the community, like the Maasai people who are going to school outside the region, outside the Arusha region, have come across girls who are not circumcised, so that now they know the difference. So they come home, silently they don't marry their girls at home, but they go outside of the community and marry outside girls."[60]

Dr. Charles Henry Sweke, an obstetrician and gynecologist at Selian Lutheran Hospital in Arusha, Tanzania, would agree with Uwane Sevingi that circumcision for females is being fought against, starting nationally. He said:

> Our government is very active. There are the NGOs [nongovernmental organizations] which are trying to help complete a fight against this. And I would say here in Arusha, in my practice, is one of the tribes which in fact does practice very much circumcision in Tanzania. I would say the effort of the government is trying to do right now is getting really good results, because we are seeing even the Maasai people who are trying to help in fact to fight against this.[61]

Sweke also spoke to the issue of what happens to the uncircumcised woman among the Maasai:

> You see the problem we had before is that these people traditionally for a woman who is not circumcised would most likely not get married. Certainly, every girl would like to get married. I saw on television Maasai people themselves who are trying to convince their people, they are promising them that even those uncircumcised girls are going to be married by the Maasai people themselves. It is a positive thing for which, and as I say to everybody, women are trying to teach them early the disadvantages of having this done.[62]

Sweke believes that African men will play a critical role in achieving success in the campaigns to eradicate circumcision of women. He said:

> Men can help in accomplishing this goal, if at all, as some where now it's right there, girls are going to be married, because that is one thing they are afraid of that "if I am not circumcised, I won't be married by a Maasai man." In our country here, we are afraid to get married just outside the tribe. We have got more than 120 tribes in Tanzania and of course, most of them prefer to be married from the same tribe. So men will help if in fact, if at all, if they insist, because in African cul-

ture, men are the ones who got the say. If at all this say will come from men, this thing is going to go fast. So we expect support from men in this aspect.[63]

James began the discussion by asking at what age the Maasai daughters are ready to go to their husbands. The woman who spoke for the group said, "Like that one is ready to get a husband. If anyone wants to marry a girl like that one, they come and they bring the rings (she shows me the bracelets on her wrist). He has brought some rings to make a booking that she shall be his wife."[64]

The child she pointed to as an illustration was probably five years old or younger. I asked the woman if the girl was already circumcised. She answered, "Not yet for that time."[65] When I asked the age of the young girl, she answered, "We don't have an exact age to book the marriage. Sometime the baby looks like this one, and we book her too, to prove we are waiting, and they do not choose the husband. Sometimes the man is very, very much older. Even old men can marry a very young girl. There is no choice for the woman. The woman has no choice, she is supposed to go with the man who chooses her."[66]

I asked if the young girl goes with the husband when the man gives the mother the bracelets and books the young girl for marriage or if he marries her later. The woman replied, "She lives with her parents until the day she is grown. So the day she is circumcised and after she gets well, she is ready to go to her husband anytime."[67]

I asked her at what age the girls are circumcised and who does it, the old mother or maybe the young one. The woman answered that it depends on the child's age. I then asked how the circumcision is done and what kind of tool or instrument is used. She answered that they used a blade to circumcise.[68]

I asked if this isn't painful or if they have something for the girls' pain. She responded, "When we circumcise, the daughter gets in pain, very much pain. Before we do that, the daughter drinks fresh blood to reduce the pain."[69]

When I asked her why they do circumcision, she answered, "It is tradition to do it." When I asked if everyone does it, she said, "We like it very much."[70] The answer the woman gave parallels that of Diana Kiremi, who graduated as the first Maasai woman to attain a bachelor of arts. Diana wrote that the Maasai offer no explanation for circumcision, only that "it is the custom," and is as ancient as the tribe itself.[71]

I asked the Maasai woman why they like circumcision "very much." The woman repeated her position, "We like it because it is our tradition. We like tradition, so we like the fuller traditional system."[72] The trend in

Tanzania is away from circumcision of any kind or to have only a very small cut. Either way, the ceremony is kept.[73] Therefore, when the Maasai woman spoke of "the fuller traditional system," she meant full circumcision with complete traditional procedures and celebrations.

I asked the Maasai women what follows the circumcision and if there is a ceremony. Her answer was yes, they have a celebration, and I received an invitation to return and be a part of the festivities. "Yes, we have a very, very big celebration. We slaughter our cows, sheep and goats and enjoy. Even if you're not around here, we can write a letter to you to come and celebrate on the day."[74]

James told them that I live very, very far away. They asked "You say very far?" James replied yes. I asked if anyone chooses not to get circumcised. The woman said, "Yes, if they choose, but they like to. Nobody can say that I don't need to be circumcised, because everybody needs to do that."[75]

I asked if the women and girls experience any illness or hardship after the circumcision is done, for instance during or after childbirth. The woman said, "No one has given us any advice that circumcision is not good while we are bearing the baby."[76]

I asked if, when they have a baby, they go to the hospital or have it on their own. The woman replied that they have the baby on their own. We then asked if when they are having the baby it isn't difficult at the place that is expanding in order for the baby to come out because it can break and bleed and some can die from this situation. I wanted to know how many have this problem. She replied, "We have a traditional medicine that we put at this place, and later the mother drinks blood. So, the mother gets well."[77]

I asked why they celebrate and what kind of clothes they like to wear. She responded that they mostly wear very clean clothes, "While maybe the woman takes the baby on the inside while they celebrate, they must wear some special clothing. They can't escape, their skin cannot escape, material is the skin, they are put into one type of clothing. One skin they wear on the skirt, and the second skin is put on top like this. Singing, dancing and celebrating."[78] The circumcised girls and women wear a blue dress to designate they have been circumcised.

The discussion took an interesting turn when the Maasai women asked questions about my own culture. They asked what women do to have a baby in America. I explained that in the United States, most women go to the hospital and have the baby there. A doctor delivers the baby and we usually stay in the hospital overnight. If mothers have trouble, they may have to stay longer to become well and then return home. A few women choose to have their babies in another setting.[79]

They asked if we have a celebration after that. I replied that in our own way, we do. Most people are very happy when a baby comes into the family. Before the baby is born, a baby shower is sometimes held for the mother, and people bring gifts. Usually the husband is not present. The wife is there and her friends bring gifts for the baby. That is one of the ways we usually celebrate.[80]

She asked me if we circumcise while the child is a baby or when the child is an adult. I told the Maasai women that in the United States we don't circumcise women, just men, and not all men. A discussion with much levity followed among the Maasai women. The women asked, "If some men do not get circumcised, how can he be married, to make love." I told the women, "There are no problems that way, that I know of, for those men."[81]

After more discussion among themselves, the women asked if we make any celebration when we circumcise the man, the boy in our country. I replied, "No. Usually, it is done right when the baby boy is born. You do not have to circumcise the baby boy, but it is done for hygiene reasons. The mother has to give permission. She has to sign. It is routine in most hospitals."[82]

The women asked what kind of clothes children wear when they are babies and when they are grown up and which clothes they wear to show people that they are already circumcised. I told them that I don't know of any type of clothing that tells if a male is a man or a boy. They were eager to share more about who wears what type of clothing. They said, "While you are a baby you can wear any kind of clothing, maybe like this one, red or any color, but when you are already circumcised you are supposed to wear like this, blue."[83]

Then the women asked me, "Why are you here? And what are you learning?" I explained that I am writing a book on FC to help educate society about this procedure.[84] Their response was that they hope the Maasai would motivate others to become interested in them. "We hope many people will read your book and that some will learn about the Maasai. We hope they will get an interest in the Maasai and come to encourage and help us."[85]

Then the women talked about the practical problem of having enough corn for the Maasai. James elaborates:

> The shortage of corn affects more than the Maasai. It is also a problem for the other villages. The Maasai are not farmers; they keep the animals. So, they are supposed to go to the village to buy something. There is corn, but it is very, very expensive. They suffer because they have so many children and they don't have enough money to buy it.

Another problem the Maasai have is water shortage. They don't have a place to get the water that is very close to the place where they are living.[86]

The discussion drifted back to circumcision. We asked what instruments are used to circumcise. The women answered that they use iron. They sharpen the iron first. I followed up by asking if everyone uses the same instrument. They said, "For a long time we used one knife for cutting all of the girls, but right now everyone is supposed to have their own tools."[87] We asked how they perform circumcision, if they make stitches, and if they use a kind of medicine to put in the place where they do it. The women said that they just use the local medicine. I asked if the circumcision ever has to be redone, say after a child is born, and if a woman might have to be circumcised again after having the baby if she had some tearing. The women said, "Circumcision is only once. You are circumcised when you are a baby, it is enough."[88]

The conversation shifted back to when children marry. The women said, "This child is the last one to marry. And this is the sixth stage. There's the first, second, third, fourth, fifth, sixth. This is the last one." Then we asked, if the old man can marry more than he has, what happens when the old man says no, he doesn't want more wives, that the number he already has is enough for him. We asked if there is any conflict among women because men can have several wives. James asked the women, "You don't feel bad when you[r] husband is going to sleep in another house?" They answered, "We feel well, we enjoy, no problem."[89]

The Maasai women wanted to know my name and if I am rich. They explained that if I have a lot of children, that means that I am rich. I explained, "It's kind of the other way around in our country. Usually the people who do not have a lot of money have more children. But I am not rich. I would be like middle-income. There is low income and high income. I'm middle. I have two children, two boys, but they are grown up. I'm a grandmother."

The one area of discussion neither James nor I approached is whether being circumcised has an effect on the women's sexual satisfaction. The women were quite interested in the uncircumcised American male's ability to perform sexually. One could conclude that because the women see their male counterparts as enjoying sex, and because the men are circumcised, it is the circumcision that makes them enjoy sex and/or helps women also enjoy sex. Kiremi was not embarrassed to talk about sexual enjoyment, "There's a kind of sensory compensation elsewhere in the area."[90]

The discussion ended and we all walked back to the top of the hill where the Laibon sat with Uwane Sevingi, my husband, and some Morani. We took more photographs, thanked the Maasai for their gracious hospitality, and gave them gifts of sugar and tea.

What we heard in our interview is supported and expanded upon by Aud Talle in his analysis of the roles of Maasai men and women. The interesting part of becoming a Moran is that it "plays a pronounced role in the shaping of female fertility."[91] All of the Maasai culture abides by an age-set system by which women and men are regulated. Men are divided into corporate age groups giving priority to seniority. Power relations between men of different age groups are important, but the system also structures sexual and gender relations on the basis of a patriarchal society. After a male is circumcised, at about sixteen to eighteen years, he enters the warrior or Moran stage for seven to eight years. He lives a life separated from other adult males. During this time he is a defender of the people and livestock and cannot marry or reproduce or associate sexually with married women.

Aud Talle explained how Maasai emphasize physical strength, nutritious food, and good health. A healthy person is sexually active. Because they are not allowed to have sex with mature females, they associate with girls ten years of age and older. The "girls and boys" meet, sing, dance, and have sex. These activities prepare both genders for married life and procreation. The societal meaning to sex play transcends pleasure.[92]

Penetration is done gradually and begins when the girl is quite small, according to Talle. Adult women direct the Morani in how far they may penetrate depending on the size of their genitals. The Morani will choose one among themselves whose penis is small enough to begin opening the girl, but he may not be the one to finally penetrate her. The Morani are very careful not to harm the girl physically. The older Morani or ones with large penises choose not to have sex with very young girls.[93]

According to Talle, the girls comply to being penetrated, but not without fear or anger. She selects usually three boyfriends and makes her choice public at a milk-drinking ritual. At this ritual the Morani reciprocate her milk with their semen, symbolizing a complementary but not equal relationship between men and women.[94]

Although many Maasai brides are children when they marry, their bodies have been made into social entities through sex play with the Morani. The Maasai claim that the semen of the Morani helps the girls to gain health and develop breasts. Talle wrote, "Culturally, then, the services of the young, unmarried men are indispensable to women's physical development and achievement of fertility."[95]

Circumcision is the last step of the "opening process." The change in the appearance of the girl's genitals means that socially and culturally, she is a woman and ready to be married. Talle wrote that recurrent themes in Maasai prayers are that women, by having a womb, embody life and continuity. The access to the womb is through the vagina. Thus circumcision is "charged with meaning and conveys powerful messages of 'ownership and control'." The subordinate men and women do the work, but the elders "are the rightful appropriators of the womb as a 'source of life'."[96]

Circumcision ends the playful times with the Morani. The woman associates only with her husband and members of her age group. She may continue with her earlier lovers clandestinely. Talle insightfully wrote, "the illicit relations between married women and Morani, kindled by the pleasure of evading fathers' and husbands' authority, carries an embryo of revolt against patriarchal power in the Maasai society."[97]

Male bonding through the female body is not new. In the Maasai's age-set culture, it may begin when two Morani share the same girl, sometimes mixing sperm, symbolizing that two Morani operate as one body. Male intimacy is forcefully expressed in this way. A child can strengthen the relationship between the two men when the husband encourages his wife to be impregnated by a certain age mate of his that he admires. At the same time, however, "the act confirms the husband's control of his wife's body."[98] The continuity of the Maasai society depends on fertility that must be molded and controlled, concluded Talle.

CONCLUSION

The Maasai that we interviewed in the Arusha region are fascinating. They are very aware of the influences that ask them to change their time-honored traditions. Through the hard work of Uwane Sevingi, who represents the government; through Mary Laiser and the others who work through the Evangelical Lutheran Church; and through the school teachers, education is changing the Maasai.

8

Meeting the Challenge in Tanzania

You can't deal with this FGM [female genital mutilation] by force, because it is a traditional, cultural behavior for these people since they were born. We are not blaming the culture when there is still circumcising, but right now there is a problem with that culture. And the problem is this disease [human immunodeficiency virus/acquired immunodeficiency syndrome (HIV/AIDS)] which has come and many people begin to know, and when the ngariba, that is the circumciser, will use one unsterilized knife, and cuts about 10 to 20 young girls.

> Professor Patroba E. Ondiek,
> Ph.D., Tarime, Tanzania[1]

Now is the time to change the mode of communication. Rather than talking about the law enforcement when you are telling somebody, "Don't do this,"— You must give him something too. Short of that, eradicating FGM could be quite a big problem. This is a traditional custom which cannot be stopped overnight, it will take time. We have changed the way to prevent getting HIV/AIDS. You can use condoms. Since FGM is still being practiced, if you can use the message of HIV/AIDS together with a message about FGM, a lot of people can really understand much better.

> Dr. Kebwe Stephen Kebwe, Bunda, Tanzania[2]

The 1996 Demographic Health Survey (DHS) conducted in Tanzania found that eight of its nineteen regions have a high prevalence of FGM. Of those eight, Arusha had the highest at 81 percent, and Morogoro had the lowest at 20 percent. (See Table 8.1.)

At least 15 percent of women in Tanzania undergo FGM. The age at which girls undergo FGM varies between six and fifteen years," according to Mary Laiser, Head of the Women's Department of the Arusha Diocese of the Evangelical Lutheran Church in Tanzania (ELCT).[3]

Table 8.1
Estimates of the Prevalence of Female Genital Mutilation
(FGM) in Eight Regions in Tanzania

Region	Percent of Females with FGM
Arusha	81
Dodoma	68
Mara	44
Kilimanjaro	37
Iringa	27
Singida	27
Tanga	25
Morogoro	20

Source: Tanzania Demographic Health Survey 1996 in Mary E. Laiser "Female Genital Mutilation," report prepared for author, Arusha, Tanzania: The Evangelical Church Diocese in Arusha Region, Women's Department, Jan. 2004.

WOMEN ADVOCATES

Juliet Chugulu, R.N., R.M., M.Sc., the chairperson for the Kilimanjaro Inter-African Committee on Traditional Practices Affecting the Health of Women and Children(KIAC) in Moshi, Tanzania, told about the women she has seen in the Kilimanjaro area:

> We have come across women who have been circumcised, who have expressed bitterly while standing up in front of the community and saying, "I don't feel ashamed to say that I'm circumcised, because I don't expect to get married again." When these people say that lady is circumcised, they speak and they say, "This practice must go." Some cry. A lady cried and said, "I went home after having two children. Married to a man from another area where the practice is not done." She went to her grandma. Her grandma told her, "You see you must be circumcised. The ancestors will curse you." And she became circumcised when she had two children. When she went back to her husband, that was the end of their marriage. The man said, "I loved you the way you were. Now I close the chapter." So women stand up and speak, those who have been circumcised.
>   Some of the women who have not been circumcised also stand up and speak for other children. Some women who have been married in areas where circumcision is cherished, some of them stand up and say how they have been discriminated against by the mother-in-law or family members just because they have not been circumcised. And they say, "If I get a baby, my mother in law will not cook for me because I'm not circumcised."[4]

Hulda is an active member of the Women's Department for the Arusha Diocese of the ELCT in Tanzania. Resisting circumcision is not always an easy feat, but in Hulda's case, family support made refusing circumcision possible. Hulda explained:

> Some girls who had money for education escaped circumcision. I felt good because I escaped. Of course, my parents who are Christians could not force you to do something that you don't want. I escaped it.
> So it is possible for girls who are educated. You will find that education is very important in this issue. If you are educated and you know exactly what is good and what is bad about circumcision, you will escape and you will say no to it.[5]

We asked Hulda whether there were any negative aspects in her community because she didn't get circumcised. She replied, "Some of them knew. Because I was the one who went for further education in that area, they could not tell me anything or insult me in any way but when I would go and stand near them, they would just leave me and leave me standing alone. But they can't tell me anything."[6]

They did not socialize, but community members did not come out and say Hulda should be circumcised.

A MALE ADVOCATE

Besides working with people closest to him like his family and his friends, James Emanuel Sichilma of Arusha, Tanzania, works with additional groups. James is an example of how the individual can make the programs to abandon FGM work. He explained:

> That circumcision causes suffering forms my opinions so, first of all, we might ask, are there any units I that can talk with in the government to prepare ways to advocate stopping? We also have singers, especially among the young people, that sing this situation is not good and encourage people to not circumcise. Advocacy can be like joking. When somebody advertises something like a condom or like Coca-Cola, it is a promotion. Advertising encourages every young man to say, "I cannot marry the woman who is circumcised." So, by this way, the woman can say, "Oh, I don't need to do that because I will not have a boyfriend."[7]

James expressed concerns about the tribes in the villages:

> People who do not know anything, they just follow the traditional. We can try to invite the leaders. They can't say no to coming by invitation. You collect many different traditional tribal leaders and bring them far away out of their village, like to a restaurant or a big theater, in hopes of educating them. Maybe at least in one month or two months they can understand the role of these things because you show them pic-

tures and everyday you talk with them. When they come back to their village, they cannot stop circumcision very quickly, but slowly, because the people there respect them, they will try to change the people's behavior. The leaders will tell the village that they need to stop and that female circumcision is not good.[8]

PROGRAMS

Arusha Diocese of the Evangelical Lutheran Church in Tanzania

Mary E. Laiser is Head of the Women's Department for the Arusha Diocese of the ELCT in Tanzania. Laiser said that she handles programs that study women and their issues. One of the issues she addresses is FGM. She believes FGM "is part of the cultural baseness to women. We have so many parts of cultural practices which are injurious to women's development or advancement."[9] Laiser has been addressing it for more than ten years. She has faced many problems because the women and people "out there" do not want to accept the change. She said,

> I came across problems like lack of education in the communities, especially among the women, because one of [the] failures in the culture is also education. Women are not given education. Women are married off at an early age, from 12 to 14 years of age. They are mutilated and after that, they are married off. So, we talk about it and emphasize the importance of education. Education is a key to her life. If you teach her, she will be able to realize everything in her life and she will be able to control her life. But when you look at female circumcision, it's a big change in education to women, because once they are circumcised, then it paves the way to being married because men out there are waiting for her. If she is mutilated, she is ready. She has a ticket to be married. Lack of education is a very big problem.[10]

Laiser works in the Diocese of Sarogin, which works in two regions, Arusha and Manyara. Tanzania is divided into twenty-six regions and each region has smaller parts called districts. Arusha and Manyara have five districts each. The Diocese works in seven districts.[11] Laiser explained how the Diocese is divided to addresses the roles of men and women in relation to FGM:

> We are divided into six areas and fifty-four parishes and more than three hundred congregations in smaller churches. I say women because women from all of the diocese go to the villages to sensitize their women, girls and youth and also other people. We sometimes also send men who are our assistants and we ask them to go out there

to their men because traditionally men and women won't sit together and if they sit together, the women will not talk. They do not choose to. In former times, men were the only people who can talk and meet and make decisions. So when men and women are there, she waits for the men to make the decisions. Not that they don't give positions, they have a lot, but they are not given the opportunity to make decisions. We pick people who are accepted and then we send them. We invite them to have a seminar or if someone has prepared a seminar, we invite them.[12]

Laiser talked about their teaching program. The program teaches those who come to the seminar and then it sends them back to their areas to teach their communities about the dangers of FGM. Laiser explained:

What we are saying is female circumcision is dangerous. It causes a lot of problems to women and we mention those problems. We don't tell them to stop circumcision because if you say stop, they won't stop. What you do is tell them about the dangers and about the problems. They have done this and they don't want to let go, but FGM brings all these problems. If you have to prove it, just check with the women who have delivered and check with the position the women took after they delivered. You will find them in the house for a long time because of the scars or the tears. They say the women show by using their fingers. They say "magical" tears. They can't even explain it. They stitch the tears but sometimes they are not stitchable. It's a problem. They also cause fistulas between the walls of the vagina and the urethra, so that a hole appears and they leak urine or feces. So you find that they suffer for a long time indoors. Sometimes the ladies are isolated. Nobody takes care of them so they suffer silently and they shy away from saying. So you find that the spouses who are separated from them go out with other women.[13]

Laiser said the Women's Department also works with the medical department of the diocese. In their work, she said:

They have started a wing which repairs fistulas. They learned it from abroad because in this country, there was no hospital which could repair fistulas. They knew there was a problem. Some women went to the hospital. We have one hospital in the diocese, Selian Hospital.[14]

The hospital received funds from somewhere. The patients that go to the hospital pay for their bus fare to the hospital, but all the procedures, medicine, and everything are paid by the hospital. So the women are relieved. You should see the three women who were the first to come to the hospital. They were cured. They were happy that they had a life to face. After suffering for a long time, for many years, they were very, very happy. They didn't even know how to express their joy after being cured.[15]

Laiser's recommendations include ongoing sensitization for women who do not yet accept that circumcision causes their suffering and continued educational efforts. She said:

> Women are suffering, especially the women in the villages who live far away from town. We have the administrating needed to sensitize them so that they realize that this is a problem. Because if they are not aware, then they will continue suffering for a long time. It is important to support a good education especially in the villages and all those communities in which female circumcision is still being practiced. So if we promote a good education then we will be sure to get rid of this barbaric act. It is barbaric because it is a denial of women's human rights.[16]

Laiser said that she also recommends a special program for traditional community leaders. She explained:

> In those communities are also their traditional leaders and those people are key people when it comes to traditions. In those areas where FGM is being practiced, the leaders need to have a special program so they know the dangers. Sometimes men do not know the problems women are fac[ing] in female circumcision because they are not the ones who are doing it. They started it long ago. And, after they introduced it, they taught women how to do it. But the men don't do the suffering because it is not they that are being circumcised. The programs for men are important to get them to understand what is being done.[17]

We asked Laiser whether she had found some of the clan leaders beginning to change their thinking about forcing all girls to be circumcised and if there are clan leaders out there who are saying, "Yes, it is voluntary and we will accept that." She replied:

> Not yet. What we are doing is pressuring them and we are still planning for them. We call them "traditional gatekeepers." It is a crucial area when it comes to these traditions—all of the traditions together. They are the ones who are decision makers for the clan. We invite them to our seminars and we talk to them. The problem is that they don't work individually, they work together, so they have to accept together. Even if one individual has opposition to circumcision, he may say "No, I am not in favor of it, but we need to talk, we need to discuss in our meeting." So you find where the problem is, and we pressure them. We talk to them and have them understand the danger, so they may be able to go and defend those people out there. If they don't understand it themselves, they say, "Hmm, we don't see anything bad about it. After all, the women do not complain. We see it as your problem because you have been going out in our communities and you have been spoilers. Here you come and tell us these things. No, we don't see any problem about it." So, it is still a struggle, a big one.[18]

Laiser added that some of the clan leaders are Christian, but they still yield to tradition. She explained:

You find a possible dilemma: maybe he's a strong Christian believer but at the same time, his traditions are very strong. Given the situation that the families are being led by the clan leaders and the extended family leaders, then you find it's a problem. When the traditions are so strong, then they will be honored even when the person is a Christian. If any clan leader says no to female circumcision, then he says that individually, but it is a collective decision. Individually he can decide on faith. You may even find one with girls who escaped circumcision who thinks, "My children did not go through that operation, but we still need to decide when it comes to the community at large, we need to decide together with our colleagues."[19]

Elderly women, the grandmothers, are very, very vocal on the issue of circumcision. Hulda, Mary Laiser's co-worker, said that the grandmothers are the other leaders who must be approached. She explained, "Yes, what I know about this issue of circumcision for girls is that your grandmother can tell you that 'we don't need the complaint. I will cuss you.' They have this strong thing, especially if the grandchild is called by her name. The grandmother holds strong opinions on circumcision. They are leaders who are accepted on this."[20]

Laiser explained how the groups of young and old are targeted for change:

> We target some of the people in our circumcision seminars because we invite different age groups. We invite elderly women. We invite girls and little girls also. We want to have the opinions of all and we want to give information to all. In the beginning, we produced leaflets which told what circumcision is, the dangers of FGM and what is being done. Then we distributed them to the little girls who can read, who are in school. We sent quite a number of them, even to some who went to forcible circumcision afterwards, after they knew all about the dangers and the effects. Unfortunately, they were overwhelmed by their family settings. "I know you taught us, but it was too much for me. I just can't take it, so I had to go." "I had to go." That is what they tell us. We also introduced posters so they could get them and read in a few words to sensitize them and see, "Oh, this is really bad." It helped a lot. But these elderly ladies are really very vocal when it comes to circumcision. They just force them. They circumcise them. I don't know what chance the girls have. Sometimes, a girl agrees that she does not want circumcision. After two or three days here, she is gone and a lady has taken her to the circumciser and had her circumcised. I had the experience of my own at home. I had six laboring girls. I used to talk to them in the evening. I had small books and leaflets. We talked about the effects of FGM. I talked with them and asked them, "What do you think about FGM? I talked with them especially during school holidays, because that is the time when they do it. I told them, "Don't agree to do it because of the pressure. Just read these leaflets and if you have any questions, feel free to come to me." I only saved two, only

two. The rest went. They would wake up early in the morning at five
and then they would go. The two I saved, I found in the morning
preparing to go. "Why are you awake at this hour?" They told me lies.
"Maybe you are going to the circumciser." They looked away and then
I knew that was the plan. But they didn't go. Four went. After one
week, the two did not go and the two are safe today. Whenever I visit,
they say, "We are glad we are safe." "How do you feel?" "Very
happy."[21]

Laiser showed a videotape from Ethiopia that demonstrated the
infibulation practice. Men were in the audience who were interested to
know what female circumcision (FC) was about. She said:

When we showed the video, oh, the video was scary. The operation
was scary because the women tied up a little girl who was about eight
or nine years old. They tied her hands and dropped her hard. The circumciser's fingers and nails were long and dirty. Her mother was there
and she knew what was being done to her girl. They did the cutting
and the girl was crying. The sound was off so we didn't hear the crying, but there must have been a scream, a very big scream, that was
coming out of that video. Just to see that girl and see the movement of
the lips you would guess that she was screaming. Then the ladies cut
her and stitched her by using little sticks. And they left her there.
Some of the people just couldn't watch and one man fainted.[22]

The diocese started a school for Maasai girls. We asked if the girls who
are educated became more effective in resisting circumcision and if there
had been the progress she wanted. Laiser replied:

Yes, it is happening. In a way it is, but the other problem is that when
the community is not aware enough and the girl is alone in a home-
stead or among people who are not educated, then it isn't very easy for
her to escape. They can do it by force. But the school is helping by not
allowing girls to go back home, because once they allow them to go
back home, the first thing they will do is circumcise her by force and
the second thing is to marry her by force. The school doesn't let them
go during vacation, they just stay in school. Those whose family the
teacher knows well and who will not force the girl to do anything like
circumcision or marriage, then they let them go. Most girls are there
until they finish school. When they finish school and they have grown
enough, they will be able to decide on their own, but when they [are]
still very young, they are being ruled by the practices in their families.[23]

The Diocese school enrolls students after the seventh grade. Laiser
explained the school system:

After the seventh grade, they go to secondary school, which has forms:
one, two, three, and four. Then they go to high school, which is form
five and six. So the level is form six. When they do well in their O

level, which is what secondary school is called, then they go to the advanced level which is high school. When they are not able to go to high school, they go to colleges. So it is helping, really. For those who have finished with the school up to form four, up to higher levels, then they are free, because now they can be on their own. They can then face their families and say, "No I don't want to be circumcised."[24]

Bunda District, Mara Region

"Female genital mutilation is a telltale phenomenon, and it has been there since time immemorial being part of the traditional customs of the area. My tribe to which I belong doesn't practice it. Female genital mutilation has been part of the tradition, without it a woman is not a part of that society. And I believe that this is all over,"[25] Dr. Kebwe Stephen Kebwe, the District Medical Officer (DMO) for Bunda and the Regional Chairman for Mara for the IAC in Tanzania, told a group of us. He went on to say that every tribe has its own identity. In the Bunda district, for example, there are about four tribes that practice FGM. In his district, Type II is the most common, followed by Type I and infibulation. Infibulation is found among the immigrant population. Kebwe said the immigrant Somalis perform infibulation. He said, "Sometime they travel very far because of a job. So, in their absence, they have their wives circumcised. It's very disfiguring. It is very brutal. It's very inhuman."[26] Dr. Esther Kawira, M.D. F.A.A.F.P., the Medical Officer in Charge at Kanisa la Mennonite (Mennonite Church) Tanzania (KMT) Hospital in Shirati, Tanzania, was a member of our group. She said that infibulation is likened to a "Chastity belt. Skin bridge — ."[27]

Kebwe said that his district is working on gathering incidence data:

> We don't violate confidentiality but in the delivery registration, there is an added column that asks "Have they been circumcised? Yes or No?" And if you do it the first time they deliver in your facility, then you won't be getting repeats of the same person. The data is collected over several years.
>
> In the past, the delivery register did not have that column. Because of the district initiatives, we decided to add that column purposely to set the permanent system to enable us to make a follow-up. Most of the deliverers conducted a survey of the villages to compare with the ones that had facilities. It is one way of getting information for circumcision. We do it because there is no other avenue that we can use. You cannot ask somebody, have you been circumcised? She says no. During delivery, you can get 100 percent.[28]

Kebwe said there are three main components they press for throughout the nation to condemn FGM: "One, it is public opinion. Second, it is the individual. Third, it is the parents. Public opinion includes peer pressure."[29]

After that kind of grouping, Kebwe said we can go to other components:

> From peer pressure, other girls will practice [FGM] because they say that maybe their companions will not accept them. If it happens that some of the colleagues have been circumcised, then definitely that woman will be now a part of the group. They were peers who were in school together; sometimes they live nearby, they live together. They may belong to the same family. So, if she does not do circumcision, then she may be considered an outcast.
>
> They believe that if one is circumcised, it can replace an evil kind of spirit. You invite the evil spirit if you don't do it, if you are not yet married. Those beliefs are outrageous. Also, society has a wrong belief. What they believe is: if a woman is not circumcised, she can be prone to promiscuity. So she can run here and there for sex and needs sex with a variety of men, which is not true. They think if she is circumcised, then she is going to ignore her sexuality. Their logic is not accurate, because the libido is from the heart sometimes. It is there, whether they are circumcised or not; it's only the stimulation, which is a small part of their sexuality, which does increase, but the contact is for the stimulation. Those are the issues when it comes to the contact. It is so dangerous because some women are circumcised before they have sexual contact. They don't attain the maximum or optimum stimulation when they start practicing sexual coitus. They don't feel it as the one who is not circumcised. As a result, they become much more promiscuous, because they are trying to feel something they are told about by other colleagues. When they go to a particular man and they don't feel it, then they go somewhere else and they don't feel it, "Ah, where is the tickling we are told because of the sensory organ, the clitoris?" The main type of circumcision they do here is the intermediate type of circumcision. The clitoris and labia minora are excised. Once they do that, definitely most of them won't feel it like the one who is uncircumcised.[30]

A medical student in the group asked Kebwe who is more resistant to change and if men are more in favor of this practice or if women are more in favor because they have gone through it. Kebwe replied:

> We see men are more resistant to change. The young girls are divided; some of them do it secretly or they do it for the sake of getting the circumcision price, but some of them run away. They say, "Why do I have to go and have circumcision?" They run away. Some of them refuse and tell their parents they are not going to have it done. We see that as kind of a change, some women have less acceptance. Some men make the change, but the change is very gradual.[31]

Kebwe agreed that if the women would be more willing to change, the men would go along.

Kebwe showed us a video taken at a Kilimanjaro IAC Conference. The video showed the pressures of gifts when they do circumcise. Kebwe elaborated:

> They get a lot of gifts because they are getting a kind of certificate like you get when you graduate. It is a kind of celebration, they are happy, they get their certificate. They believe that one of the certificates they get out of society is when they have been circumcised. There are reservations. Other people believe that once the woman is circumcised, once they bleed, they are rejuvenated. They are getting new blood. The old blood has gone away and now they have been cleansed. That kind of reasoning is bad. The reason peer pressure presses them so hard is the question of marriage. Some of them feel if they don't get circumcised, they won't get married. However, there are other people who put group pressure on a woman to stay uncircumcised. It's two ways. In our society, we are feeling our way toward change but very gradually. On the question of changing traditional beliefs and customs, it is not a one-night show.[32]

It is a criminal offense to perform FGM in Tanzania. In 1998, the Tanzanian parliament enacted a law entitled "Sexual Offences Special Provisions Act 1998." This Act prohibits circumcising girls less than 18 years of age. This provision states:

> Any person responsible for protection or has the duty of taking care of a female child and lead to or cause to or shall cause the circumcision of a female child, then such a person shall be guilty for committing such an act against female children and if accused and found guilty, the punishment shall be sentencing to jail for not less than 5 years or pay a fine that does not exceed three hundred thousands (Shs. 300,000/=). Or both punishments jail and fine together. Also, such a person shall be ordered to pay the victim a compensation that shall be agreed upon by the court for the wounds the victim shall incur.[33]

Law enforcement in Tanzania is having an effect, according to Kebwe. He noted a trend downward of the number of women circumcised since the law was passed. Law enforcement with education is the approach of the many activist groups in the campaign. Kebwe explained that his group is one of the activists, but his group does not have enough associates to go out into the community level in order to develop some findings that can be implemented with the committees that were formed.[34] He explained the campaign:

> We have wards in this district, but we started with only ten wards. We made this campaign at the first level to the ten wards and recruited a peer leader from the committee in three wards. The three wards in total have about eleven villages, two have four villages each, and one has three villages. They bring us reports. I will bring the reports on

committee visits to see what is happening and what they are doing. We
attempt to give them advice At least, they can visit almost every
household to get information to see what is happening in the villages
and also to work it. Plus we do designate a member as chairperson
from the group.[35]

Kebwe continued the description of his work in the villages:

When we go to the villages to work we focus on group discussions. We
do a group setting, one for the elderly, another group for the young
people and one for the boys and girls. The groups are free to meet
together. They can talk very freely about their experience. Another
group that can be together are middle age. So women and men can be
together and, most of the time, they can also be separate. They will be
very afraid to say their opinions. So if you live with twelve groups in
the community, you can get a lot of information. So, that's how we
approach it. We talk with every group separately. They give their
views, and then later, when you conduct a mass meeting, you have the
information from all angles. And now we can talk with them with
great information. That's how we do.[36]

The circumcisers pose a challenge and are also talked with separately.
Kebwe explained, "Mainly, the circumcisers say, 'I know I can talk to you,'
because they are afraid of the law enforcement. Sometimes they can't say
they are still doing it. But the people around the committee say, 'I know
they are doing it but secretly.' But some of them really have stopped circumcising."[37]

Kebwe believes his district's program is very successful, but he does
have recommendations:

First, we hope to get some resources in the community that are the
continual kind that provide certain ability to work with these people
very closely, rather than going maybe once or a couple of visits, then
you are away. The close contact in the community is a very good tool.
It is a good weapon.

Second, change the mode of communication. Rather than talking
about the law enforcement by force you must give that person something too. Short of education, it would be quite a big problem. Circumcision is a traditional custom which cannot stop overnight, it will
take time. In the case of HIV-AIDS, we now change ways to keep from
getting it, for example, the use of condoms. One of the major objectives of the Inter-African Committee is to stop the risk of other harmful traditional customs. So FGM is one of the harmful traditional
customs, and since it is still being done, if you can use the message of
HIV-AIDS together with a message about FGM, we think a lot of people can really understand much better.[38]

Kebwe said that when circumcision is done on men or boys in the
villages, they are told that everyone should insist on having his own knife,

which is safe, but is not the way they used to circumcise with just one knife. They used to line up about eight people and use the same knife. They do it traditionally, but they use separate knives. In some cases, "because there are circumcisers that do not have enough money and only every now and then buy a nice new knife, I tell them, 'You must prepare your own sharp knife.' Some of them have told me that for the circumcision of men, they are going into medical office[s] to do it under anesthesia."[39]

A third recommendation is the involvement of the elders and women. The elderly people are one aspect of the very good projects that work. Kebwe stressed that "You must talk to the elders, they are given very great respect by the society. If you go by force, you can't build a friendship and they can't trust you."[40] Kebwe explained that other leaders can go to a village, talk with the public, discuss and do and, at the end of the day, they leave. And if they leave the elderly people with a commitment, they say they are being respected. The elderly are important people to talk to in order to bring about the elimination of FGM.

Involving women is also wise for success in an anti-FGM campaign. Kebwe said that because women are with their daughters most of the time, they can tell them and also be physically separate from them. He explained, "We must go to all groups separately. This is the kind of thing done from Moshi [KIAC headquarters], we work through public meetings, through leaflets, through audiovisual, all those kinds of things provide constant messages to the public all the time. There must be a constant message, not a seasonal one. If it is seasonal, that can never be preached as their idea. Once you leave, everything will be left."[41]

A fourth recommendation is that campaigners must go around to the schools and the colleges. "Part of the promotion is catching the community. Also the campaign tries to involve the leaders before they go to the public. In the Serengeti district, people are doing so. The committee over there is very active. When the leader goes to the public meetings, he talks of FGM, HIV and other traditional harmful customs."[42]

Getting girls in school and involving the media are two other elements of a successful campaign. Kebwe said, "The mass media people must be part of getting to the community. Some of the teachings we are doing several times have been published in various newspapers. You will see some newspapers in town. So when you are going around to the villages, you are going with the press people, and the various types of mass media, the TV."[43]

The media have published that Type I is more recently done in the first week of birth.[44] In September 2003 in the *Lake Zone News/Announce-*

ment, the community in the Mara region was asked to disclose all people who are still promoting old-fashioned traditions, including girls' circumcision, so that those involved would face the law. The article further stated:

> Dr. Kebwe who is also the head doctor of Bunda district issued this statement following some reports that mutilators in that region [Mihingo Ward, Bunda district] have designed a new strategy where now they circumcise infants right after their umbilical cords fall off.
>   Dr. Kebwe stated that misleading traditions are taking place in that region such as: circumcising girls, poor nutrition, uvula [the small, fleshy, conical body projecting downward from the middle of the soft palate] cutting, removing cartilage teeth, and widow succession as well as marriage between women, must be condemned because they hinder the development of the society.[45]

Kebwe, the chairperson of the IAC in the Mara region, accepted some bicycles for the peer educators in Mihingo Ward, Bunda district. The bicycles were provided by a company in Germany, Raphael Group, to facilitate educators' mobilization of the society to abandon traditions that bring harmful results to human health.[46]

The marriage between women mentioned in the article is not a lesbian marriage. This marriage takes place when "an infertile woman, in order to have children, can pay dowry for another woman to be her wife, officially. And any children that that woman has by whatever man she can get, they become her children and they inherit her property. So, it's done for that reason."[47] This type of marriage is considered a harmful tradition.

An article that appeared in the *Lake Zone News* a year earlier stated the strategy of circumcising infants right after their umbilical cords are cut is known as "tambisa." After the procedure is performed, "the child is then forced to put on a long dress in order to avoid being noticed by the public. Formally, the circumcised girls usually would wear a Khanga (a nice piece of cloth commonly worn around the waist by East African Women to cover the body from the waist all the way down) along with another piece of cloth tied around the neck covering the body all the way from neck to the legs, known as Lubega."[48]

Thus, when Kebwe goes around to the villages, he is going with the press people and the TV reporters to help educate them. We asked Kebwe what the villagers think of the mass media being in their villages, if they mind, and if the media go right into the villages. He responded, "The people are so friendly. They are so friendly, very cooperative, because they want to air their views."[49]

The *Lake Zone News* reported that Ms. Erica Burchord from Germany spoke to peer educators from Mihingo and Mugeta Wards in Bunda in 2002. She spoke out against circumcision and other traditional practices.

She said that polygamy, widows succession, forcing girls into marriages, and refusing to send girls to school have had negative impact to the society.[50]

Kebwe described another use of the media — drama, little plays that people write themselves. Some of them feel that "if we speak loud to these press people, I am sure we are going to be heard much more."[51] The video from the KIAC conference showed a meeting with the villagers, the committee, and the circumcisers. A woman testified that, "I saw why this kind of evil acted like that to me." Kebwe said, "She blamed the circumcision when she lost blood for three days and thereafter, she didn't get any child. She became infertile. So she said to me, 'I believe it is because of the very severe sustained, bleeding,' which is very true."[52]

Kebwe and his committee managed to incorporate circumcisers into the committee because, as committee members, they would talk with village elders and work against FGM.[53] Dr. Esther Kawira saw the efforts of his committee as involving a collective interest. She said that "the circumcisers are trying to destroy their own traditional business. They are getting a new status by being on the committee to make up for lost revenue, or don't they get revenue? They must get some kind of compensation for doing the job, right?"[54]

Kebwe responded, "Yes. If you are doing away with something, you must put something in its place as a substitute. If you don't do that, things are not going to be very different."[55] Kebwe believes if you have a discussion or debate about circumcision instead of confrontation, you can introduce anything. Men, for example, continue to meet because the meeting is for getting together. They say it breaks the habit. He explained:

> We try to see what kind of substitute can be put in the place of circumcision. So, I'm thinking how come if I were going to tell them — you can tell me where the ceremony is and at those ceremonies then you can use that time to discuss a certain issue concerning the society. Because it is part of the society issue if they're circumcised. You say, yes, it's one of the societal roles.[56]

We asked whether Kebwe's committee got much resistance from the circumcisers. Kebwe replied, "No, from the circumcisers, you don't get resistance. Mainly, the resistance is from some of the committee members and of the elders. Yes, those are the two main groups which are very difficult groups."[57]

All in all Kebwe believes the very strong tribes in Tanzania are the Maasai people and the Kuru people. For them, he says, "Change from the traditional is not difficult but very gradual."[58]

Kilimanjaro, Tanzania

Another excellent example of the anti-FGM movement is the campaign of the Kilimanjaro IAC in Moshi in the Kilimanjaro Region, Tanzania. Mrs. Juliet Chugulu works with dedication for the abandonment of FGM. Chugulu wrote her masters thesis for her degree in health education and health promotion on the reasons FGM continues in rural Kilimanjaro[59] in 1999 at a time when little information was available.[60] In addition, Chugulu and her research partner, Rachael Dixey, produced an article that reported on two villages studied in the Moshi Rural District in the Kilimanjaro region. The subjects responded that tradition was the main reason they continued the practice. FGM affected 41 percent of the one hundred fifty women questioned. Health workers and mothers and grandmothers were the most influential in swaying girls to have the surgery.[61]

Chugulu explained that in 2004 quite a number of women had been circumcised in Kilimanjaro area. She does not have the exact figure, but the committee is working on an evaluation of their work. The report is expected to come out soon.[62]

Chugulu said Type I is the most common type of circumcision performed, followed by Type II. She added, "But there are times if you should go to pastoral community, in the process of healing, some of them go to the other type, Type III. But otherwise, only a few people like the Somalis from outside would perform Type III."[63]

She has witnessed many of the side effects of FGM. Some young girls have heart infections because of circumcision. "They do not want to send them to the hospital because of the campaigns, but eventually they go to the hospital," she said.[64] Infections, bleeding, and pain are some of the complications she has seen. Mrs. Chugulu continued, "We have seen a girl about 10 years who developed keloid and after the campaign, her mother brought her to hospital for an operation. In some of the areas we have witnessed mothers speaking about their experiences and experiences of their own children. They have pain. Sometime they have a problem when they are passing urine because of pain."[65]

The video Kebwe showed contained a great deal about the KIAC's campaign in Moshi, so we were eager to hear from Mrs. Chugulu about the campaign's progress. She said in addition to a traditional practices approach, since 1997 the Kilimanjaro committee has trained peer educators and sensitized health workers, religious leaders, and policy makers. She said the first step is a traditional practices approach and that they have given mass awareness seminars to the communities:

To start with, it was not very easy. And we never went with female circumcision as an approach. We used traditional practices as an approach. We go into the community and we ask the residents about the traditions they have in their locality. We ask them which ones they think are good and that they should promote. We ask them which ones they think are not good and should perish. Then, in most cases, female circumcision would come out. And that's where we start our discussion. We ask them if it is existing in their own community and what are the reasons and what could be done. So, we have been advocating for people to understand that it is a problem. And not only female circumcision, we are looking to other traditional practices like early marriage. That goes together with female circumcision. We have been asking the community members to identify their own people who could be trained and then who could do house-to-house campaigns. So we have trained what we call village facilitators. People who have been selected by their own people. They are trained for three days, and then they make their own plan and they move from house-to-house. Whenever they get an opportunity like when they have small gatherings or when there are ceremonies, they also get an opportunity to talk to their own people. And also when they go to the local food shops, they discuss a lot about circumcision.[66]

Another aspect of the campaign is to train youth peer educators. Chugulu said that they have seen that if youth are trained, the village's whole population is involved. Chugulu told about the positive contribution of youth:

After training the youth, they train other youth and they become watchdogs in their own community. Citing from communities where young people have reported those who did circumcise their children, and, in this scenario, we went as far as the police station. The lady went to the police station and the community members decided to help the girls who were circumcised. We have been to the village, but we have not seen the two men or the two girls who were circumcised. They have disappeared from that community to another place. So, we feel the youth have done a lot.[67]

Chugulu said that their campaign has also sensitized some health workers who have been avoided in the community when the committee talks about who does the circumcision. She explained how the health workers are viewed:

[Health workers] are not looked upon as ngaribas (circumcisers), they are just health workers like the health attendants, maternal and child health aides and, that is a small area in Hai district in Kilimanjaro, in a few areas, some ngaribas (circumcisers) have been mentioned, especially in this region, Kilimanjaro. So, we have sensitized some health workers, but not all. We have also sensitized school teachers, especially primary school teachers. We have sensitized traditional birth attendants who have also been some of the people have been engineering the practice.[68]

The Kilimanjaro committee's efforts to educate teachers were undertaken with the financial support of the Women World Prayer Organization of Germany. They produced *A Booklet for Training Community Educators* that includes a map of Tanzania, circumcision demography for Tanzania, anatomy and functions of female genital parts, deceptive ideas and facts about FGM, negative effects of FGM, the law on FGM, responsibilities regarding eliminating genital mutilation practices, and empowerment of women. In addition to health workers and teachers, the Kilimanjaro Committee has talked to religious leaders, Catholics, and Lutherans. She explained:

> In some of the areas where we go, there are many Catholics. And in the past, the Catholics would not mention much about female circumcision. In areas where the Lutherans are present, the practice is there, but they don't approve it. With the Catholics we have pushed in, and we have used the churches for mass campaigns. We have been given a chance by the Roman Catholic priest to discuss about this practice there.[69]

Policy makers are key to the success of the campaign in the villages because from experience the committee realized that, in the villages, "if you want to win, you have to find the key people."[70] Chugulu explained how the committee undertook the challenge:

> Some of the key people are the village government. We have sensitized the village governments. An area where we feel proud when we go to there is a small area in Hai district in Kilimanjaro. It is known as Narumu. There are four villages. When we wanted to start our campaigns, it wasn't easy. We were rejected. From the priest to the village government, but we never faltered. We went there several times. We managed to sensitize all the four villages. We started with the village government, went to a women's group, a youth group, and then eventually, we wanted to meet the clan elders. The elders are very important to reach because they want the practice to continue. And today if you go there, they will say, "Every household knows what is at stake. We know the practice will not disappear overnight."[71]

The Kilimanjaro committee has been successful in sensitizing some areas— so successful that those areas have chosen to celebrate without cutting. She explained:

> The campaigns have been going from house-to-house and the community members have decided to opt for an alternative rite of passage. In those areas, if the community members themselves will say, "Now we have decided we want to have ceremonies without cutting," then they

would to come to us, they would ask us, "What is your part with this?" Then we say, "We will do the teaching, and you will also do the teaching as far as your culture is concerned." But we tell them, "We want to be there, so you do the right thing." We teach girls and these old women who have been identified by the community. We come in and teach them the culture, things which they think are good. We do that for five days. On the fifth day the girls come out, they are set in the rules. In Chagga community, if the girls have a fiancé, the fiancés would come. They would do as they used to do there during those days. They would give them money for those who have fiancés. For those who don't have fiancés, they would dance, they would play, and the elders will drink. They will eat and drink and then they call it a day.[72]

I asked Chugulu whether the committee found some resistance in the early part of the program and whether they find much resistance now. Chugulu responded that, although it was not easy in the beginning, the participants did not resist, then or now. When they started, some of the people could not talk because they did not understand. The committee found basic education encouraged village participation:

We use models to teach so when we went there, we identified, after much indecision, a group of twenty, twenty-five or thirty who are selected by the community. Then we train those people. In the process of training, we came to realize that some women never even knew their anatomy. We taught them the functions of female organs and then we related it to what is done. So, when people could speak their mind, they could contribute. When we started, it was not easy. But now it's easy. We have media people to assist us. They also talk. They report some women who give testimonies. They mention about what girls say. They also write something about what some of the elders think about female circumcision. I'm glad to say that young people have said, "Oh, it is good that you have come, and the campaigns have gone great. We are sure our sisters, we are sure some of us will not be cut because we have been taught.[73]

Chugulu has seen progress in the thinking of the villagers. They have come to the conclusion that the reasons for circumcision don't apply anymore:

Circumcision is a cultural ritual for us. It's not related to religion. It's entirely related to culture, to tradition which has passed from one generation to another. And of course, people have brought some reasons with them, like somebody will become a prostitute if she is not circumcised. On the other hand, when we discuss at length with these people, they just tell you straight that "Now we have seen. In the past it worked, but now it doesn't work." They say. "When a girl is circumcised or she's not circumcised if she wants to have many sexual partners, we see there's no change." And then they also say, "If you don't circumcise, you'll be cursed by your ancestors." They put it as a reason. And another thing is that, you see, with this circumcision in the past, it used to bring people together so that they may drink and eat. Now they say, "Simply because of food, that's why people and our ancestors were entertaining these."[74]

Sjaak Van der Geest's study of proverbs sheds light on why ancestors are given as a reason to circumcise and why change results when ancestors are questioned. He conducted a study in Kwahu Plateau in Southeastern Ghana and found:

> Proverbs used by the elders to extol their own virtues is gradually turning into a rhetorical weapon to defend their traditional position against the undermining forces of a changing society. S. A. Dseagu rightly says that "one of the main uses of proverbs is to preserve the status quo of things." The new generation, however, is hardly interested in the knowledge of the elders and finds their dignified manners pompous and archaic.[75]

Van Der Geest discovered that, "a proverb is no longer understood or recognized when it originates from a period or a culture that is not familiar to those who use the proverb. Proverbs in particular, which may have a life of several generations, are likely to contain such images that are no longer part of the context and life experience of the present generation."[76] In this way, the thinking of those who have long believed in circumcision is being challenged by the Kilimanjaro committee's program and other programs throughout Africa.

Chugulu said that some believe that circumcision is necessary for a woman to have healthy babies:

> Some say if you're not circumcised, you are going to have abnormal babies. Then we ask them, "How come you cherish circumcision and he doesn't? How come his children are okay. How come children from your area have problems? You have an abnormal baby. How come?" We ask them, "Look what is the science?" The Lawalawa disease [yeast infection] is from poor hygiene. When we talk to these people, we ask them, if you are coming, like Maasai, "How come Lawalawa is interested in the Maasai children and why not where there may be in Nyamwez who do not circumcise?" You say, "There is no disease that does not affect anybody. Diseases cannot infect tribes." So you try to correct some of this misconception.
>
> There's the misconception and the reality. We try to convince these people that it isn't true. Even in pastoral communities who have been very, very rigid, we have managed to see some changes. One of the changes is, the Maasai came to say, "We do this practice and it is not very easy to get out of our mind because we are not educated." We managed to discuss with some in one community about the importance of education. They say that the children cannot go to the schools which are far, and we have an agency whereby we have started their

classes, and we supported them and now they have two classrooms. They say education is the only weapon that will assist the community to get out of this.[77]

Chugulu has a recommendation for policy makers and religious leaders that would strengthen the committee's program:

> One of the recommendations that we put forward is we need to have a commitment from policy makers. If the policy makers right from the grass roots to the national level are committed, I am sure we will succeed, because they are powerful, because people listen to them. And then, another recommendation is for the religious leaders because they are the people who have a lot of worshipers. Religion here still is very strong. So, if the religious are made a part of the campaign, then we can expect some changes.[78]

Chugulu believes in the people in the villages and stresses the importance of education and feedback. "In working with people in the community what is important is to educate them. We find that some of them have never been exposed to school, but you sit with them, talk to them, especially by showing them, by demonstration, by giving them a chance, making it so everybody's approach is valued, then you come to realize that these people really can also give you some good ideas."[79]

Save the Children of Tarime (Sachita), Tarime, Tanzania

Working to eliminate FGM in Africa usually involves working to eliminate more than one traditional harmful practice. Professor Patroba E. Ondiek, Ph.D., has combined HIV/AIDS prevention with FGM eradication in the programs in which he has been involved, such as the Rorya HIV/AIDS Prevention Organization, African Youth Alliance/Program for Appropriate Technology in Health (AYA/PATH), in Tarime District; the Catholic Relief Services (CRS); and Sachita in Tarime.[80]

Professor Ondiek is working full time as program coordinator for a nongovernmental organization (NGO), Sachita. Bill and Melinda Gates brought this project into four African countries: Uganda, Botswana, Ghana, and Tanzania. When we interviewed Ondiek in Tarime, he had formed the Rorya HIV/AIDS Prevention Organization. Ondiek explained the plans:

> One center, according to our plan, would be an orphanage that would have a priority for AIDS orphans. Second, have priority for any orphans whether the parents died because of AIDS or not, one to care a lot. There are very poor children from poor families, we want to take care of them there. There we will need to have two nurseries, that is,

the two rooms for nurseries. And then we create one center. Later on, if we succeed, we can bring in second high school in Shirati.[81]

Ondiek had found that more women in his area are now avoiding circumcision, especially the school girls, because:

The ones we are dealing with most are those who are in grade five, grade six and grade seven, because this group can understand English and they can see they are soon going to second high school. So, these ones are really with us. Secondly, the married women, the newly married women, are also understanding the facts. And again some women in the community, some who are circumcised, but now they are saying no to circumcision of their daughters.[82]

CRS and Sachita are expanding their successful pilot program using peer health education to reach fifteen thousand primary school students, teachers, out-of-school youth, and community leaders.[83]

Ondiek explains that Tanzania has ten districts with separate projects. In Tarime, he is working to improve adolescent sexual reproductive health among in-school and out-of-school youth. This program's donor is the Program for Appropriate Technology in Health (PATH) and includes FGM. He explained his philosophy in eradicating FGM:

You can't deal with FGM by force, because it is a traditional, cultural behavior for these people since they were born. They have some economic benefit from it. The government has tried so much to ban FGM, female genital mutilation, which with them, they call it simply female circumcision. But there are twenty-eight countries. I have been to Sudan for a study. I have been to Somalia. I've been to Mali where it is really dire. In Mali, they go in and sew it, just leave it a hole, what happens, the lady gives up having a child. So we have to use strategies which will reach the parents, which will reach the children, will reach the local leaders, will reach religious leaders, will reach actual leaders. So, that they see what we are talking about now. We are not blaming the culture when there is still circumcising, but right now there is a problem with that culture. And the problem is this disease, HIV/ AIDS, which has come when many people begin to know, and when the ngariba, that is the circumciser, those ladies who sometimes circumcise, the ladies are called the ribe, with the local language here. You see, the ngariba will use one knife, one unsterilized knife and she can cut about ten to twenty young girls. Of course, this is the way we tell them, in case, one of these girls is already infected, definitely, this is going to affect other girls. So this is what we tell them. We are not saying your custom is wrong, but it's just the timing, this disease. So, all of you older people, the elders, help us, by telling the young people that we didn't know, our forefathers did not tell us there would be a disease which will get rid of circumcision of women, so that the children will hear them, will understand them more than when we call with the government for this—where are they, where are they hiding?

So, some of them understand this and some circumcisers are very clever because of the way they can get it done. The girls can go in the rooms that they are going to be circumcised. But the ngariba, the circumciser, just does a little cut, just a little tip. But you know before that, they were really going deeply, the removal was total. With just this, circumcision is a zero.[84]

Ondiek said that as he works in his programs to help people, sometimes people say, "But this professor, maybe he is not as you see him, he is FBI." Ondiek responds, "No, I'm purely here to help what we can help, especially dealing with this enemy called HIV/AIDS, especially to our young people. The young people are the future of this country. Yes. There is our time, but if the future generation will not be there, who is going to take [care] of the old ones. Nobody will do that."[85]

Ondiek has designed many programs for health centers—called dispensaries—that are used to teach people how to deal with life planning skills. He talked about harmful traditional practices:

And this one end: we want to reduce as much as possible the prevalence of HIV/AIDS spreading. Because that's one we cannot cure, but we can control. The strand should be very common everywhere. We want in our schools to prevent, if we can, unwanted pregnancies of the young girls. Some of them could go to universities but after they are pregnant, the future is a little black. We are trying [to] reduce incidence of STD, sexually transmitted diseases, if we can. This we can only do if we tell them how to make decisions. Yes, education. But one of the girls whom I had taught for about five days about unwanted pregnancies and STD, six weeks later came to me and said, "Oh, this has really helped me. My boyfriend wanted me to have sex with him. But I told my boyfriend, 'No, no, you know we are told that you see I can get pregnant.'" But the boyfriend insisted. So she said, "No, No, No, you see I am in menstruation." The boyfriend said, "No, you are lying." She said, "O.K. wait. Let me go to the toilet, I'm coming." So when she went to toilet, she tied a red thing upon her. When she came back to the room, she said, "I told you." Everybody laughed. But she has already got the skill how to communicate with the boyfriend to prevent the sex act.[86]

Education and communication provide people with skills that carry over into the harmful tradition of FGM. There are some challenges. Ondiek agrees people are becoming educated, especially some of the girls. "But last year, some girls who had been in training, about five of them were captured. Sometimes circumcisers come with force. Even with some women from other tribes which are not circumcising women, and if this girl is married into a tribe which practices circumcision, they force them to be circumcised. Even those who are thirty or forty years old."[87]

Peer educators are another valuable method. Young women learn from their peers, said Ondiek. He has found:

> In any group of any societal community, you will indeed listen to what your peer tells you more than what Professor Ondiek is telling you. Yes, because when they are up there, they talk among themselves. Even the teachers when they go there, we teach the teachers to go and talk to other teachers. And young people, they do the same. Peer education here is very strong. And those are the people you see a lot. We train them. For example here, you see forty schools and at each school, we choose ten peer educators. We train peer educators, and in each school, we are training two teachers to help peer educators, because this is where now, we use the trainer-trainee system. When we are away like in the field, we will ask the headmasters, the principal, to set a day, maybe in the evening, I mean after school, maybe three times a week, where these ten children or students can bring together and divide the school into ten groups, and they talk to them. They tell them the problems, the dangers of HIV/AIDS.[88]

Ondiek has found peer educators to be very effective, for example, "We have, let's say, forty schools, and I can't go to those schools in a day or in two days. So, I've decided to use what I call peer coordinators who are also in the same community. So this, I told the program donor, the PATH people, that we want peer coordinators, that I need the peer coordinators who are in the community, who can work with peer educators when I'm not there."[89]

Ondiek cannot always be there, and he needs to start collecting data. "So, the problem was they want something, they want to be paid. I say, sure. Yes, right, because they are going to be almost full time. Some of them won't have any other job. So, we agreed to give them $20 a month and they think they are rich."[90]

Ondiek's program is a big undertaking but it is very organized. In July 2001, a Mara elder, Marwa Mohabe, announced that the annual mass circumcision of both girls and boys would take place in private. The district commissioner Paschal Mibiti said that his office and NGOs would try to prevent it by enlisting the help of the village elders. Professor Ondiek, as program coordinator of the Mara NGO Sachita, maintained that efforts would be made to educate and persuade the elders to stop their plan without using police force.[91] He spoke also of people's perception of the government in matters of traditional practices:

> The problem with the government is if we use force, if you bring the policemen, the people are adamant, they don't want to listen. It hurts sometimes during circumcision. They just come to his office, dressed in circumcision [clothing], they are ready to be circumcised. So, they wonder what the officials can do. What can the police do? They're

already circumcised. They are adamant. Force can not work. And they say to me, "You people, go your way, teaching these people the problem so that they can know." But if we go by force, it will never work. This is our culture. The custom has been here for many years. When you come to talk to them, the people are wary. They ask, "Where are you coming from?" If they think you are not from their tribe, they say, "I don't recognize you." It's very, very dangerous.[92]

Josiah Kawira, a member of our group and Projects Officer at Shirati KMT Hospital, said, "They say that they should kill, should shoot us."[93]

Ondiek agreed, and told of one time he went with people he was working with to a village not far from Shirati. "One of the girls said to me, 'Professor, you be aloof. Don't say anything. Listen to what we are about to tell these people.' And that's what I did. Then later, some of the circumcisers say, 'Where do you come from?' I said, 'No. I'm from here. One of your sons, but I was away for a long time.' They did not question me further."[94]

Josiah Kawira said, "If you were from a different tribe, then they would never listen to you."

Ondiek agreed, "No. They will never. They will chase you away. Yes. The strong ones will shoot you."

Josiah said, "So, you pretend that you are one of them."

Ondiek again agreed, "Correct or don't talk, because it's when you talk, they will have a problem with you. But if you talk, telling them, no."

Josiah said, "You are telling them what to do."

Ondiek said, "Yes."

Josiah added, "From another tribe."[95]

Ondiek has ideas and recommendations for his program:

I am focusing on reaching the cultural leaders, to talk to the cultural leaders. And then the cultural leaders talk back against the circumcision, the FGM. Let them now come back into being willing to tell their young people and the middle age people, "You've really seen the problem, these people [program people] have told us the problem." We are asking the government to go slow on force with these people or they won't listen. The period of circumcision is only three months. It's October, November and December. So if they stay away from the area of the circumcision, the circumcisers will not chase them. Those who are in school at the time of circumcision can choose to stay home, that one thing once set up, they will stay there. They can go back when they are ready. Some of the girls who are going to secondary schools will stay in the dormitories there. So that also makes the circumciser forget about them. But if they're around there, the circumcisers are going to get hold of them.[96]

Selian Lutheran Hospital, Arusha,
Working with the NGOs

Charles Henry Sweke, M.D., C.I., Ord., Ph.D., a consultant and obstetrician and gynecologist at Selian Lutheran Hospital in Arusha, Tanzania, sees women with circumcisions of different types. In the area where he works, the Maasai tribe circumcise as a tradition. He said:

> The percentage is very, very high, almost every girl, because they have the tradition. When I see a young girl, or a woman, in their eighteen to twenties, almost all of them are circumcised, because they are circumcised when they are still young. They have no options. They are being sent by their relatives. Here in Arusha, — I am not talking about the whole of Tanzania because we have some tribes who do not circumcise their girls— particularly here in Arusha and in this area, the percentage is very high.[97]

As to the method used to circumcise, he said, "Some are very horribly done, but most of them are not very terrible ones."[98] Sweke said that the hospital doesn't have its own program but that it works together with the NGOs that are trying to fight against FGM:

> For those few women who are coming into our hospital, we counsel them. We try to educate them. For us as doctors, we see the complications of it and we try to educate the few who come to our places. Some people and organizations in Tanzania are really, really active against circumcision. We hope probably in a few years, this thing is going to go away.
>   We are trying to tell people the disadvantages and the complications they get by being circumcised and, in so doing, people are starting to understand. This is being taught even at schools now, at least right here information is being transferred. The good thing is if this thing is being saved for later, beside themselves, it's very good that these girls will all be uncircumcised, for shortly, they are going to get married.[99]

Sweke said that should relieve some of the pressure that a young girl might feel from her family. He said, "I was told that completely these young girls really feel themselves as not part of the community if they're not circumcised. And now, as long as we have all those, there cannot be but a few girls who are not circumcised, but a few who are coming to the clinic are not."[100]

CONCLUSION

The IAC addresses all traditional practices that affect the health of women and children. FGM or FC is but one. Thus, addressing education and FGM or HIV/AIDS and FGM or early marriage and FGM were three of the approaches we learned about while visiting Tanzania. Whatever the traditional practice, working to eliminate it works best through education rather than through force. New ways of celebrating culture are substituted for the harmful practices. Complete eradication will take time.

9

The Changing Status

Education is a key to her life. If you teach her, she will be able
to realize everything in her life and she will be able to control
her life.

Mary E. Laiser, Arusha, Tanzania[1]

The Director-General of the World Health Organization (WHO) said
in 1994, "People will change their behaviour only when they themselves
perceive the new practices proposed as meaningful and functional as the
old ones. Therefore, what we must aim for is to convince people, including women, that they can give up a specific practice *without* giving up
meaningful aspects of their own cultures."[2] The Director-General believes
that many people in practicing societies do not naturally see the link
between female genital mutilation (FGM) and the suffering of the women
and children who undergo it. He believes the first task is to "document
this link" and then to inform people. He says, "Parents are much the same
everywhere: given the chance, they want the best for their children."[3] They
will accept the change once they see that it is in the best interests of their
children.

Long have women's organizations, health professionals, colonial
administrators, social workers, and human rights activists recognized the
adverse effects of FGM. Serious attention to FGM by governments and
bilateral development agencies is more recent.[4] Concerted efforts are in
place in many countries to prevent and eliminate FGM.

The WHO commissioned the Program for Appropriate Technology
in Health (PATH) to review the FGM programs in countries in the African
and Eastern Mediterranean Regions. In 1998, PATH found that "little
attention had been given to the status of FGM programming, the types of
behaviour change strategies being implemented, their successes and fail-
ures, what lessons have been learned, and what support strategies are
required if the elimination goal is to be achieved."[5] PATH identified cul-

tural reasons why the practice continues, but PATH also discovered the emergence of a large-scale information campaign and an increase in government involvement.

CULTURE

Attitudes are changing gradually. People look at FGM from a range of perspectives. How an increasing number of people view FGM can be seen in the change in the rates of prevalence. The rates are declining in some countries as indicated by comparing those rates among adolescents to rates among older women. In 1991 in Kenya, survey results indicated 78 percent of adolescents had undergone FGM compared to 100 percent of women over fifty. In Sudan, the prevalence among fifteen to forty-nine year old women in 1981 was 99 percent; by 1990, it had declined to 89 percent.[6]

In a study at the University of Khartoum in Sudan in 2000, out of five hundred questionnaires, four hundred fourteen (82.8 percent) were returned from one hundred ninety-two females (46 percent) and two hundred twenty-two males (54 percent). Results showed that one hundred and nine women out of the one hundred ninety-two (56.8 percent) were circumcised. Two reasons why the practice continued were confusing religious messages and ambiguous laws.[7] A study reported in 2003 found that at the University of Khartoum in Sudan, four hundred students said they were opposed to the practice. Only five percent of the women questioned supported FGM, while eight percent thought it would improve their chances of marriage. Seventy-five percent of the men, however, preferred to marry an uncircumcised woman. Of the 57 percent of the women who admitted they were circumcised two-thirds said their mother made the decision to have it done.[8]

Studies in Kenya and Sudan found that some of the people are choosing less severe forms of FGM and others are expressing a desire to either modify FGM or abolish it all together. Factors influencing the change include higher levels of education (those with secondary education have higher rates of disapproval), access to health education, modernization, fear of the law, the girl's refusal, and a realization that whether a woman is circumcised has no effect on her sexual behavior. For many women, the presence of medical complications and pain counter the religious basis for performing FGM. In Sudan and Djibouti, the trend has been medicalization instead of elimination.[9]

Reconstructing a Way of Life and the Cultural Codes

Campaigns to eliminate female cutting continue to meet with success and they are causing changes in ways of life, societal roles, and cultural codes. Roles are changing because, as sociologist Charles H. Anderson said, "Roles are reciprocal in that every role assumes the existence of another role or group of roles."[10] Members of a family have many positions—father, mother, grandparent, oldest daughter or son, youngest daughter or son, and so forth. Each family member also has roles. The roles of one member relate to those of other members, for example, a parent's to a child's, and the father and mother have a sex role with each another. Inherent in sex roles is role conflict, stated Anderson. The cultures in which circumcision has been an accepted part of society are pressured to change as sex roles and ideas about sex change. New ideas, such as a female not being circumcised does not mean she will be more promiscuous, are challenging the old beliefs.

The Cultural Ideal: Meanings, Expectations, and Ideals Publicly Expressed

Roles have three patterns: ideal or normative, perceived, and actual. Society specifies the ideal or normative roles.[11] In the case of female cutting, people grew up with the notion that the procedure is necessary because it provides a link to ancestors, it causes a better relationship between spouses, and it promotes better health. A perceived role is the way a person interprets and evaluates the general expectations associated with a role. The perceived role may become clearer as the actual role is performed. Women who do not undergo circumcision in practicing cultures challenge society's meanings and expectations attached to her being female.[12]

The Real Culture and People's Behavior

In Anderson's theory, the ideal of the real culture that says female circumcision (FC) should be practiced is given a definition appropriate to the society's needs. Introduction into the culture of campaigns against the practice challenges that need. The campaigns demonstrate that the need to cut no longer exists and that cutting is detrimental to a woman's health and sexual fulfillment. Struggle occurs within the culture when roles conflict and when they compete or appear to be inconsistent or rationalized.

A Gap Between the Ideal and the
Real in Practice or Perception?

A role contradiction within a culture may result in a particular role being abandoned, wrote Anderson. The resolution of the contradiction may leave "a big gap between the ideal expectations and the real performances."[13] For the husband and wife (or wives), when expectations about female cutting are altered, new ways to trust and to relate sexually have to be found. Economic considerations will have to change and be incorporated into the new way of doing things, that is, not cutting. Some campaigns dedicated to eliminating cutting advocate that the ritual celebration of a girl's entrance into womanhood be continued without cutting or with less cutting. These options are offered to address the confusion created by role contradiction. Agreement within the culture must be achieved, for example, if cutting is eliminated, what is the circumciser's role to be and what is done to ensure that she or he has different and meaningful work.

"It Is the Movement of Real Culture, the Concrete Behavior and Meanings in Use That Really Matter" for the Society

Culture is the way of life that societal members have developed to best adapt to their social and material environments. Anderson makes a distinction between cultural meanings and expectations that are held up as the ideal and the actual culture exhibited in people's behavior.[14] The way of life of societies that traditionally practiced cutting will change if the campaign to eliminate cutting is successful, and new ways of perceiving actual roles will develop over time. Furthermore, some economic resources may no longer be available, which may be the case for the circumcisers. A discrepancy may be apparent between real and ideal components in their situation. In other cases, parents of uncircumcised daughters may continue the tradition of receiving economic benefit from the intended husband as happened when the daughter was circumcised. For these people there may not be as much of a gap between the real and the ideal. Still, as Anderson discussed, a gap will exist to varying degrees. The parents may feel a disconnect with the tradition of linking with the ancestors through cutting, or they may believe their daughters will be immoral and engage in sexual promiscuity. Anderson wrote, "The point to be made here is that it is the movement of real culture, the concrete behavior and meanings in use that really matter for ... the society...."[15]

Anderson believes that, most typically, actual practices draw away from established ideals until the gap is too great to uphold the old ideas that are then replaced by current practices. As sexual experiences become more rewarding and as people learn that fidelity is not dependent upon circumcision, cutting can be replaced by ritual alone. This is not to say that those most directly affected, the husband and wife or society, might not experience strain, guilt, or frustration. There may be moderate to severe strains within individuals and society during the behavioral shift because the ideals may be deeply ingrained within the individual or new laws or standards may have taken effect within the culture. Many cultural standards are written into law, concluded Anderson.[16]

Susan Izett and Nahid Toubia believe existing behaviors should be assessed. When the answer to the question of why circumcision is done is because it is tradition, custom, or the way of ancestors, it means that cutting was the thing to do for a very long time. According to Izett and Toubia, "Individuals or communities will not change their behavior on the basis of a simple rational argument that their existing behavior is wrong. The choice of behavioral alternatives must be motivated by a new set of interests and emerging social consensus and — in the case of gender-related issues— by a restructuring of power dynamics."[17]

Izett and Toubia suggest that before action is taken to stop FC/FGM, questions should be related to what people know about the cut part of female genitals. How do they think the girl will be affected? What do men and women know and what motivates them to continue the practice? For the researcher this means learning about the practice, beliefs, and attitudes and how these factors interact with other social factors to affect behavior. The answers will provide insight that will enhance social change.[18]

The questions Anderson might ask include: Given the trials in reconstruction, what is the individual society's degree of success where attempts are being made to eliminate FGM? How are these societies applying their resources to complement their own strengths to maximize development? How are they putting together elements of resources and strengths to realize their goals? The answers to these questions are found in the efforts of the international working group, the Inter-African Committee on Traditional Practices Affecting the Health of Women and Children (IAC) "Zero Tolerance" program, and specific communities that followed programs that change attitudes. The IAC and the United Nations Children's Fund (UNICEF) have programs in Tanzania and elsewhere that are successful. Tostan is a program that has worked in Senegal and Gambia and has been a model for other programs.

THE PEOPLE OF A CULTURE
LIVE THE CHANGE

One way to assess progress is through the lives of individuals experiencing the change brought about by the programs. The profiles that follow are examples of such individuals: Dr. D. from Bamako, Mali, a physician; circumcised women from Tanzania, Uganda, and Somalia; an impressing woman who was circumcised, then became a circumciser, and later reduced the number and type of circumcisions she performed to help eliminate FGM; a woman from Gambia who laid down her knife as a circumciser and worked to end FGM; and Nafisa, a circumcised immigrant woman who faces challenges in the United States.

A Physician, Dr. D. from Bamako, Mali

Dr. D. from Bamako, Mali, a physician at the Sikoro Health Center, confessed at a PRIME II workshop that before he left home, he agreed to arrange genital cutting for his brother's two-year-old daughter. At the week-long training, Dr. D. learned, "I have seen patients with the gynecological and obstetric complications we learned about this week, but I never made the connection with female genital cutting. I now realize that many of the slow and difficult births in my center are due to scarring from female genital cutting that reduces the elasticity of the vagina, making birth dangerous for both mother and child."[19]

Dr. D. and the Sikoro Health Center hosted a female genital cutting (FGC) awareness day for opinion leaders in Mekinsikoro, the oldest neighborhood of Bamako. One attendant said of the day, "It was once unimaginable that we could organize an event to talk about female genital cutting, but we did it. And what an event it was. Every layer of society was represented."[20]

A Circumcised Woman, a Resident of Mihingo, Bunda District in Mara Region, Tanzania

In 2003, a woman resident of Mihingo, Bunda district in the Mara region of Tanzania, maintained that her infertility resulted from being genitally mutilated. She requested that the government increase pressure on individuals who continue to promote this tradition. Her statement was made during the Mihingo ward peer educators' meeting when they met with the Mara region committee that deals with outdated customs and traditions.[21]

Her request was that the society all over the country of Tanzania, and especially in the Mara region, be educated about the damage that occurs as a result of FGM. As one of the peer educators in Mihingo ward, the woman said that she became the victim of genital mutilation in 1978. Her parents forced her to have the procedure when she was twelve.[22]

After the procedure, she lost a lot of blood. She was unconscious for three days. The mutilators claimed that her mother was an unfortunate woman (a woman with bad luck). When she became conscious again, she noticed that she was at the traditional doctor (an herbalist). She did not feel any better and was rushed to the hospital.[23]

After her recovery in 1980, she could not be sent to back to school. She was forced to marry. A dowry of twenty-eight cows was paid to her parent. She did not conceive since her marriage.[24]

A Circumcised Woman, Doreen Chesang, from Kapchorwa, Uganda

Doreen Chesang from Kapachorwa, Uganda, related her forced circumcision experience to Women's Vision, a program of the Women's Edition Project of the U.S. Population Reference Bureau. In 1995, people in the area along with clan heads had secretly organized to force her into circumcision. In the evening a group of "drunk and energetic men" came to get Doreen and three other girls.[25] She described the night's activities, "… they immediately tied us with strong sisal ropes and undressed us, leaving us with only our petticoats on. The people danced and rejoiced because they had finally captured us. They beat us and forced us to dance throughout the night."[26]

At the surgeon's the next day, the girls were supposed to say that they wanted to be circumcised, but they refused. People then came with knives and swords and said the girls would be pierced to death if they refused. Doreen said, "They continued torturing us.[27] In our desperate situation we were pushed onto the ground and forced to sit down with our legs wide apart. They still battered us. Finally, we were defeated and we surrendered."[28]

She wrote that the pain was so unbearable that she thought that her mother did not love her. She questioned why her mother let her go through the circumcision. Although the police arrested and imprisoned some of the men as a result of court proceedings, Doreen lamented, "Unfortunately, for us, we had already been circumcised."[29]

While Doreen was healing, people threatened her that if the men were not released from prison, she would have to leave the village or die. Later she returned home to ask for school fees and men kicked the door of her hut. Her mother rescued her, but the men set fire to her hut. Doreen sought safety at Peter Kamuron's (Member of Parliament) place. People other than her family paid her school fees and in 1996, a nongovernmental organization (NGO), Reproductive, Educative and Community Health, registered her as a peer educator. This position enabled her to receive money and continue with her education.[30]

A Circumcised Woman Becomes a Circumciser: Marian Dhorre, from Somalia

Although Marian Dhorre from Somalia found the circumcision experience painful, at fifteen she became a circumciser. Her memory of the circumcision was that "six long thorns were fixed across her labia to complete her genital mutilation."[31] During the time of her procedure, she stuffed a cloth in her mouth to avoid screaming with pain. Four days later, she fell and the wound reopened. She suffered from infection and pain while urinating. Her aunt restitched her labia. When she married at age seventeen, she suffered pain during intercourse. On the night of her marriage, her husband had to use force. She did not like sexual intercourse and sometimes avoided it due to pain. After her first baby was born, they divorced. She remarried, had a second baby, and divorced again. She married a third time and has two daughters and two sons. Pain was constant during all six births. Despite these experiences, Marian became a circumciser.[32]

Economic survival is a major reason most circumcisers perform surgeries. Marian Dhorre is no exception. She was trained as a birth attendant at the Hargeisa Midwife Training School. Here she began earning her living by delivering babies. Dhorre noted that one of her friends seemed to be financially comfortable even though they were earning the same amount of money. One day Marian went with her friend. There she began her interest in circumcision. "Marian determined to make herself more money, too,"[33] wrote Hawa Aden Mohamed. One morning Marian circumcised eleven girls.

Workshops and seminars taught Marian the harmful nature of FGM and that Islam did not require it. According to Mohamed, "Marian says she now only performs the 'mild' form of FGM (*sunna*). She argues that if she stopped completely then families would take their daughters to someone else who would do them more harm by infibulating them. She is aware of all hazards of FGM, even pricking, but she maintains that mothers and/or grandmothers always insist on Pharaonic circumcision being performed."[34]

In one case of circumcision, the grandmother accused Marion of theft because the girl had not been circumcised in the "right" way.[35] Marian continues performing circumcisions because of the demand and because she needs the income. Mohamed adds that we see from Marian's story how deeply ingrained the practice is.

Mansata from Gambia Gives Up Her Trade of Circumciser

Mansata inherited her profession from her family; both her mother and sister were circumcisers. From her work, Mansata earned her livelihood and had prestige in the community. When she first heard about the Foundation for Research on Women's Health, Productivity and the Environment (BAFROW) program, she vowed she would not give up her tradition. However, as a result of the BAFROW program she is now the president of the first Former Circumcisers Association of Gambia. The organization seeks to persuade other circumcisers to stop through promotion of education, women's health, and new income alternatives.[36]

Mansata said:

> Once I understood the body, the organs, and their functions, and that the problems we as women had were not natural, I realized that removing the organs, or mutilating them, was actually harmful. I gave up the practice, and I have convinced others to change their actions as well — even my own family.
>
> Changing traditions and behaviors that have such long histories is not easy. When one does not understand a problem it is not easy to appreciate it. If you do not understand your health, you cannot appreciate the problems of FGC; and if you do not continue to educate people they will not understand. All we are seeking is knowledge. Knowledge will change people's attitudes.[37]

Nafisa, a Recent Arrival in the United States from Somalia

Nafisa was a twenty-two-year-old female patient of Dr. Nawal M. Nour. Nafisa was from Somalia and had received the severe Type III genital cutting. She went to an emergency room in a New York City hospital because she was nauseated and vomiting. The vaginal scar was distracting to health workers, who summoned male and female medical students and residents to examine her. Dr. Nour explained Nafisa's reaction, "Humiliated by the experience, she felt that in time, they might refocus on her nausea. Fighting her tears, she lay there while strangers 'examined' her. She saw their shocked and their horrified faces. 'Why were they doing this to her?' she thought. 'Shouldn't she feel safe in the United States?'"[38]

Dr. Nour said that the health workers failed to obtain a critical part of Nafisa's medical history. During the height of the war in Somalia, Nafisa hid in her home with a younger sister. Five men stormed into her home and tried to rape her. Because of the scar, they were unable to penetrate and slit the scar open with a knife. She was gang raped by all five men. Her sister was raped and then killed.[39]

Nafisa never returned to her doctor and one year later became a patient at the African Women's Health Center at the Brigham and Women's Hospital, a Harvard-affiliated hospital. She was diagnosed with post-traumatic stress disorder and depression.[40]

THE RELATIONSHIP OF PROGRAMS AND CHANGING ATTITUDES

In 1977, an international working group on FC was created in Geneva. The group's purpose was to study FGM and work with African women and men. They sent missions to Africa to analyze the procedure in its cultural context and to identify ways to collaborate. It initiated work in Sudan, Egypt, and Kenya. In 1984, it organized a seminar in Dakar, Senegal. Collaborators were the Ministry of Public Health in Senegal, WHO, UNICEF, and the United Nations Population Fund (UNFPA). At this seminar they established the IAC.[41] As an NGO, IAC promotes the health of women and children in Africa and in migrant communities. IAC fights harmful traditional practices including FGM and promotes beneficial ones.[42] The cultural behavioral shift was under way.

On February 6, 2003, the Common Agenda for Action against Female Genital Mutilation was adopted at the International Conference on Zero Tolerance to FGM held at the U.N. Conference Center in Addis Ababa, Ethiopia. The goal of the Common Agenda for Action is to eliminate FGM by 2010 in Africa and in the world. The goal is to be reached by an "intensive, coordinated and integrated approach by all the key players."[43]

This goal and the activities designed to help meet it show the relationship between programs and changing attitudes. The program involves and integrates all groups needed to reach the goal. Strategy for elimination is based on research conducted. Materials are developed and a series of programs carried out to raise awareness for different groups. These programs and groups include workshops; alternative income-generating activities for circumcisers; mobilizing traditional community leaders; organizing youth, religious leaders, and the media; reorienting health personnel to cease medicalization of FGM; lobbying governments for legislation against FGM, a many-faceted approach to all stakeholders; and periodic monitoring and evaluation of activities.[44]

The First Lady of the Federal Republic of Nigeria, Chief (Mrs.) Stella Obasanjo, on behalf of all the First Ladies of Africa signed the Declaration on February 6, 2003, as "The Day of Zero Tolerance to FGM." In her address, she said, "The Inter-African Committee has come to a stage where a paradigm shift would move the gains we have made so far by having a 'Common Agenda,' which will provide a common framework to intensify and collaborate our activities at the different levels while respecting our diversities."[45]

In 2003, the IAC concluded, in part:

> A lot of effort and commitment have been undertaken to eradicate FGC. However, it is known from behaviour change communication principles that to have a complete breakthrough, we must help the individual and each community to respond to the following concerns:
>   a. What will happen to me if I resist FGC or try to do so?
>   b. What do I believe others in my community would do about FGC?
>   c. What do I believe others would want me to do about FGC?
>   d. What are the risks of undergoing FGC?
>   e. What is the threat of refusing to undergo FGC and where can I go for help?
>   f. What are the possible personal benefits of not undergoing FGC?
>   g. What are the barriers I am likely to face (physical, psychological or financial)?
>   h. What ability do I have to resist FGC?

In particular, FGC interventions should address the following:

> a. Loss of cultural identity and dignity
> b. The fear of possible repercussions as a result of contravening customary law, traditional beliefs and breaking oaths (witchcraft, death, famine, drought, etc.)
> c. The fear of having no one to marry and being considered a girl even after growing up
> d. Threat to the special festivities in the community and missing beautiful gifts at least once in a lifetime
> e. The psychological and social sanctions including harassment, loss of school fees, being chased away from home, etc.
> f. The financial gain, reputation and respect attached to the work of the circumciser.[46]

In 1982, the Tostan program began incorporating these principles.

A Program That Works: Tostan.
Literacy Programs and Training Programs

Tostan, which means "breakthrough" in the language of the Wolof of Senegal and Gambia, is a non profit NGO. In 1991, it was incorporated in the United States and based in Thiès, Senegal. "The mission of Tostan is to contribute to the human dignity of African people through the development and implementation of a non-formal, participatory education program in national languages."[47] From 1982 to 1985, Molly Melching and the team developed the Tostan non-formal adult education program in Saam Ndiaye, outside of Thiès. From 1987 to 1989, twenty-seven villages in the Thiès and Kolda regions participated in program experimentation. These programs were conducted with support from UNICEF and the Canadian International Development Agency.[48]

In 2003, the WHO chose the Tostan Basic Education Program as a best practice. In 2003 alone, the Tostan program was implemented in more than four hundred villages. Tostan began its first long-term project outside of Senegal. This program is a three-year initiative in Guinea through the U.S. Agency for International Development (USAID). "First public declaration abandoning FGC outside of Senegal in twenty-three communities of Burkina Faso, as well as three hundred eighty-two villages in Senegal, bringing the total number of declared villages to 1,140."[49] Within intra-marrying groups, the Tostan program has led to coordinated abandonment of FGC and other harmful practices such as early marriage.[50]

The Senegalese Army organized a large Tostan event on FGC and early marriages at the Ourossogui Military Base in the region of Matam, Senegal, on March 22, 2004.[51]

Tostan literally means "breaking out of the egg" in Wolof. Most of Senegal's 7.9 million people speak Wolof. Tostan is among a number of innovative rural development and women's education initiatives that address the problem of female illiteracy.[52] The program offers literacy, but it also offers tools to take on such community issues as health, hygiene, and the environment. According to the World Bank's Africa Region report, literacy is related to life skills with members participating in problem solving. Tostan has been successful in linking basic education and rural development. First, adult learners gain literacy and numeracy skills in their national languages. Second, they receive the means to understand and solve local problems.

The Role of Women

The village authorities in Malicounda had seen the impact of the Tostan NGO training programs on women in neighboring communities. In addition, the authorities were aware that the Tostan NGO helped the Bambara community of west central Senegal create its own center. The popularity of the women's health and sexuality training broke all records. After this training, the now literate women decided they wanted to address the custom of FC in the Bambara, Mandigue, and Pulaar communities. Armed with information of circumcision's effects on health, the women eventually convinced the village council to officially abolish the practice. During the traditional period for genital cutting, May to July 1997, no operations were performed in Malicounda for the first time in its history.[53]

WOMEN REMAKE THEIR CULTURE WITH THE HELP OF TOSTAN NGO, MALICOUNDA, SENEGAL.   With the help of Tostan and UNICEF, twenty Senegalese journalists interviewed the women. The women performed a play to show the reasons they decided against FC and the arguments they used with other villagers. The media generated publicity. Although some surrounding communities of the same ethnic group made threatening comments and criticism, the group from Malicounda went to two neighboring villages to campaign for a local decision to abolish FGM.[54]

IN TURN WOMEN GO TO OTHER COMMUNITIES TO ASSIST THEM IN REMAKING THEIR CULTURES. MALICOUNDA WOMEN WENT TO BAMBARA/ MANDIGUE AND PULAAR.   In Ngerin Bambara, women took the "oath of Malicounda."[55] The President of the Women's Association and daughter of a circumciser whose daughter bled during the procedure said it was time to change. Community members of the second village, Ker Simbara, involved kin in a network of neighboring villages.

The Role of Men and Women Together

Two men who completed the Tostan ten-week training program traveled from village to village educating members on the ill effects of FC. The men helped the women of Malicounda, Ngerin, and Ker Simbara to organize an intervillage conference in Diabougou. In February 1998, three representatives—the village chief and two female representatives from thirteen villages—gathered. They "formulated the 'Diabougou Declaration,' an engagement on the part of 8,000 villagers to cease henceforth genital circumcision of girls."[56]

The Casamance region of southern Senegal heard about the Diabougou Declaration. Another group of villages of Pulaar lineage who practiced circumcision had a conference and formed a similar declaration. The eighteen communities involved met with similar successful results.[57]

The World Bank, Africa Region, reported that the "active learning" engaged in among women by the Tostan program in Senegal resulted in far-reaching cultural change.[58]

Why the Tostan Educational Program Worked

The Tostan program's success is attributed to "Cultural roots combined with the use of national languages, a deep valuing of African culture is the foundation of Tostan's educational program, exemplifying the practical and profound relationship between culture and education."[59] Senegal's official language is French, but the government increasingly encouraged the use of national languages in literacy programs. Learning is easier and pride is inspired in women to speak up. Children who learn French in the schools are more likely to feel a connection within the village household. Intergenerational communication and solidarity is promoted.

Problem solving is the main strength of the program and provides strong motivation to become literate. Problem solving skills deal with hygiene activities, uses of oral rehydration therapy and vaccinations, financial and material management skills, management of human resources, feasibility studies, and income-generating projects. A number of women started small businesses after training. The program also reached out to school children.[60]

The instructional method used a participatory approach. Participants often involved family and community in problem solving. Using this method adolescents learned to produce their own texts. Women were the least-educated group in Senegal, but the program enrollees were one-third male. Both genders benefited.[61]

Tostan's programs were connected to practical needs of life. The program also addressed the problem of boredom in people's lives. Although it was difficult to find and to pay facilitators at first, Tostan graduates are now facilitators and represent most of the staff. The United Nations Educational, Scientific, and Cultural Organization (UNESCO) flyer on Tostan concluded:

> The availability of a comprehensive program that offers participants problem-solving tools and deals with the crucial problems of health, hygiene, and the environment is an asset for many regions of Africa faced with high illiteracy rates, especially among women. More focus needs to be put on implementing these well-studied and tested programs rather than developing new ones.... Tostan has shown that

individuals without any formal education, from villages with minimal resources, can improve their lives and environment through a solid program leading to greater autonomy and self-sufficiency.[62]

In 1995, UNESCO selected Tostan as one of the most innovative non-formal education programs in the world.[63]

Update on Senegal's Campaign to Combat FGM.

In 2001, the U.S. Department of State reported results of the NGO Tostan project assisted by UNICEF and the American Jewish World Service. Following their courses, "The Bambara village of Malicounda abandoned these practices, with the endorsement of the Imam. As of November 2000, one hundred seventy-four villages had abandoned the practice, following completion of the Tostan program. This affects about one hundred forty thousand people. The Tostan program is being replicated in Sudan, Mali and Burkina Faso."[64]

In 2002, Senegal's government said it was launching a major campaign to combat FGM, which had been banned since 1999. The goal was to eradicate it completely by 2005. About 20 percent of the women still underwent the procedure at this time. The new government campaign of about 2.7 million dollars would focus on "social communication, education and accompanying measures."[65] In the southeast, the government has organized ceremonies where people could publicly renounce the practice. In October and November 2001, in the Kolda region, ten people were convicted for performing genital excision on young girls or for assisting to organize operations.

In 2002 and 2003, a grant from the Bill and Melinda Gates Foundation enabled Tostan to reach two hundred and thirty communities in three regions of Senegal. This project's goal is to increase vaccination rates in these regions.[66]

In 2003, Tostan supported a ceremony of residents of ten Senegalese villages in Nemanding located near the Gambian border. The villagers indicated that they planned to abandon FGM. The ceremony followed a year-long program. Local leaders, parliamentarians, and U.N. officials also attended. After similar programs run by Tostan and UNICEF, "708 Senegalese villages have made public declarations abandoning FGM. Together, they represent 13 percent of the population in Senegal that had observed the practice."[67] People are not instructed to stop the practice, according to Tostan Director Molly Melching. Instead, they are taught about human rights and health risks. Tostan labels this phase of the program "kobi." In the Mandinka language kobi means, "to turn over the soil in preparation for planting."[68] Participants usually decide to give up the practice on their own.

Overall, in 2003, Tostan worked in more than four hundred villages in all ten regions of Senegal and in Guinea, reaching at least twenty-five thousand participants. Because of Tostan's important emphasis of sharing new knowledge with other community members, the program will likely reach more than one hundred fifty thousand villagers.[69]

In 2004, Molly Melching, the founder of the program, reported that 1,271 communities in West Africa have vowed to stop the practice.[70] Melching reported at Zero Tolerance Day in Washington, DC, that the project "now employs fifty-seven Senegalese staff and several hundred Senegalese teachers in ten regions of Senegal working in five different national languages."[71] Melching believes that FGC could end within the next five to ten years in Senegal if at least one thousand more villages are reached through the Village Empowerment Program, social mobilization activities led by informed and educated villagers themselves, and public declaration.[72]

Without a doubt education is an important component of eradicating FGC. Before they received the educational efforts by organizations such as Tostan, many women did not know how an uncut vagina looks. They assumed all women are cut. At Zero Tolerance Day in Washington DC, forty-three-year-old Kerthio Diarra from a village in Senegal described, "... and because I had never received any information on the development of a woman's body and knew nothing about how the different body parts work together to assure good health and protection, I did not realize that I had more problems during childbirth than other women have. I just assumed that all women went through the same pain and suffering."[73]

When they attended the Tostan program in Malicounda, Bambara, Diarra and the others learned about human rights, responsibilities, problem solving, hygiene, health, and good management practices. Diarra and the others became knowledgeable of the dangers of FGC and were able to become active in its abandonment.

Other Programs That Are Working

This book chronicles the social change occurring with regard to FGM. The change continues to take place little by little. In 2003, twenty-three villages in Burkina Faso openly stated their abandonment of FGM at a ceremony in Bere. Surveys conducted in Burkina Faso over the past three years indicate the prevalence has declined from approximately 66 percent in 1996 to between sixteen and 43 percent in 2003. Since the law was passed in 1996, about three hundred people have been arrested, fifteen of whom received prison terms of three to twelve months. The other were fined.[74]

In 2003, chiefs of the Upper West Regional House pledged to work with health professionals to assist enforcement agencies.[75]

CONCLUSIONS

As ways of life and the cultural codes are reconstructed, roles are redefined. Programs make this reconstruction possible. The Tostan educational program is one of the most successful. The change can often best be seen through examining the roles of the individuals who are actually living the change brought about by the programs. Mary Laiser's philosophy is well put: Education is the key to life.

10

A Compendium of Change

> I want you to not give up on women's rights, saying that you cannot do women's circumcision, all over the world. And also, I want you to encourage women to say, "This is not right. We don't need it. We don't want it to be done to us."
>
> Mut Ruey from Miywut, Sudan,
> currently living in Nebraska[1]

In tribal and class-divided societies, the routine of daily life is governed above all by tradition.[2] The social movement to modify female genital mutilation (FGM) has confronted tradition and brought about social change and a cultural evolution. There is progress in replacing FGM with new behaviors that will become tradition. Most scholars and most people in Africa whom I interviewed predict continued change as a result of the social movement to move away from the practice of FGM. "Those of us caught up in the change are also caught up in the challenge."[3]

THE CHANGES

Language

Toni Morrison said that the poise of language "arcs toward the place where meaning may lie."[4] "Language can never 'pin down' slavery, genocide, war. Nor should it yearn for the arrogance to be able to do so. Its force, its felicity, is in its reach toward the ineffable."[5] Originally from Malakal in south Sudan and now living in Grand Island, Nebraska, Aban Laamatjok spoke of the impact of language:

> If there is any kind of movement from the global world to stop this surgery, it should be through the societies which are working there actually, which are a part of the people who are there. Because when

the people who are talking with them who are Muslim like them or who know the culture and even the language, they will be more likely to listen. The most important [factor] anywhere you go is the language, because the language can carry your idea or your word. As I said, there is a lack of trust between the West and the Muslim world. If you are American or British and you go there, what you are trying to say, they will not just try to get you on is it false or true, they will say, "Ah, all that comes from you is evil." So, it is better if we can support those of the nation, of communities, who are trying to prevent and to eradicate this surgery in countries like Sudan or Iraq or Egypt, because they are doing a good job. That is why you can see that this surgery is eliminated just in the big cities. Because they lack transportation, funds to hire more people to work or funds for the materials, they don't have the ability to go to the villages. So, if they get support with donations that would help them. In addition to this, those who are working in this field need also more education and more training. These are the most important things. Some organizations like in the Western world send more money to Sudan but they're not concerned about the teaching and training which, to me, are the most important. You cannot send money for me while you did not train me. What am I going to do with this money if I am not trained? If you train me and if you support me after that, it would be good use of this support and these funds.[6]

The Inter-African Committee on Traditional Practices Affecting the Health of Women and Children (IAC) recognizes the value of training and of language. The importance of the role of education and language is illustrated in IAC's campaign material that is offered in more than one language. IAC's 2002 *Activity Report* indicated:

> The IAC produces a series of audiovisual and printed materials and the anatomical model to distribute to the National Committees implementing projects in the field. The IAC also provides support to its Committees in the field for the production and distribution of information and campaign items in national and local languages such as booklets, leaflets, posters, videos, t-shirts, pins, cups and other, considered appropriate by the NCs [National Committees].[7]

Just as advocates in Africa believe that over time FGM will be eradicated there, Mut Ruey, a native of south Sudan, offers insight for the practice decreasing in industrialized nations like the United States:

> A family living in the United States just calls on the custom that they are used to. But the children themselves, they know better. Even though the adults try to send them back to the country where they came from, they would never do it to them. Because they came to the first world, they know better, they know people are to be treated equally. There's no such thing that [circumcision] should be done to any human being.[8]

I asked Colleen Renk Zengotitabengoa, staff attorney at the Tahirih Justice Center in Falls Church, Virginia, about the reasons that a woman might have female genital cutting (FGC) done here in the United States. After all, the woman is in a different culture. She believes cultural assimilation is several generations away. She said:

> She is and she isn't.... Immigrants, when they come to this country tend to stick among their own community, at least in that first generation and possibly the second generation as well. It usually takes a few generations for immigrants to become fully integrated into American society. Even though they are in the United States and may attend school and may be American children in many respects, they're still living amongst their own community and their own ethnic group probably and most definitely amongst people from their same country. There is still a question of social mores and living up to those. For girls, there's always a question of marriageability. It comes down to marriageability almost in every case. The family wants her to make a good marriage.[9]

Lisa Johnson-Firth, Director of Legal Services at the Tahirih Justice Center, suggested another aspect:

> The other aspect might also be, and Alice Walker writes about this in *The Secret Possession of Joy*, that when the West had made attempts to eradicate this process in Africa, it has been interesting to watch that they've, in fact, done it all the more, almost to fly in the face of what the West may be dictating to them. Alice's book does touch on this. It's about a woman who has come to the United States. She's already here and has no reason to go back and do this except her own strong cultural identification issues. That's how she thinks that she can best represent her culture if she does that.[10]

Renk Zengotitabengoa added, "It would make her more African. And not less American. It's a great book."[11]

Toni Morrison believes that the final word or the reach toward the ineffable is in cultural evolution. In 1996, the World Health Organization (WHO) issued a statement with the United Nations Children's Fund (UNICEF) and the United Nations Population Fund (UNFPA), "People will change their behavior when they understand the hazards and indignity of harmful practices and when they realize that it is possible to give up harmful practices without giving up meaningful aspects of their culture."[12] A group based in Washington, DC, Advocates for Youth, echoed the words of WHO, "Efforts to change harmful traditions are most effective when they originate within the culture that practices them."[13] Advocates for Youth creates programs and advocates policies that help young people make informed and responsible decisions about their reproductive and sexual health.

Shell-Duncan and Hernlund's research found that whether FGC might be adaptive or maladaptive might be evaluated by the issue of who benefits. As the practice of FGM evolves, the adaptiveness could be evaluated as it relates to the different reproductive strategies in the context of patriarchy, resource inequality, and the desire of men to control female fertility.[14]

John Wachira, M.D., a urologist and member of the African Medical Research Foundation (AMREF) Flying Doctor Surgical Outreach Program, shared two observations:

> One can hardly find anyone who would say they support FGM. Yet it persists. In the Central Province of Kenya, there is much education of the public. The low infant mortality rates and acceptance of family planning, including vasectomy in males, are similar to even some places in Europe. Yet, FGM is on the rise. It was still high in the 60s, then dropped, but is on the rise again, though maybe not back to 60s levels. So, we see that education alone is not the answer.
>
> Another observation I have is that male circumcision (never called "male genital mutilation, by the way") is never being fought against. Yet, as I said, most of the complications I see as a urologist are from male circumcision, about five or six cases per year.[15]

Sami A. Aldeeb Abdu-Sahlieh believes "there is no valid justification for the distinction made between male and female circumcision."[16] He condemns the attitude of international and nongovernmental organizations (NGOs) saying they dissociate one type of circumcision from the other, giving legitimacy to male circumcision in the process. He also condemns the discriminatory attitude of those Western countries. He maintains they have passed laws against female circumcision but not against male circumcision. Western countries are afraid that they will be considered anti-Semitic.

Clandestine change may indicate a need for new strategies to address change, says Hortense Palm, Permanent Secretary of the National Committee Against the Practice of Circumcision based in Burkina Faso. A "decline in the number of circumcision operations performed on young women in Burkina Faso masks a growing trend to circumcise younger and younger girls," concludes a new survey by the WHO and the Burkina-based National Committee Against the Practice of Circumcision.[17] Baptism ceremonies are sometimes used as a cover for cutting, because the baby is expected to cry at a baptism. Dr. Kebwe explained that in Tanzania the practice of circumcising infants within the first week of birth also occurs.[18] On the compendium of change, areas still exist where the eradication of FGM remains a great challenge.

Examples of positive change are also noted. The Kilimanjaro Inter-

African Committee (KIAC) in Tanzania has been successful in sensitizing some to not perform circumcision. The success is so complete that those people have chosen to celebrate a girl's becoming of age, but without cutting.[19] Another change in Tanzania is the kind of circumcision performed. Dr. Kebwe Stephen Kebwe said, "They are changing the kind [of] circumcision that is done. They do a very small scratch. Once they see blood, they say, 'Oh.' Mainly, that is the kind of circumcision that they do now."[20]

James Emanuel Sichilma, from Arusha, Tanzania, knows first hand that the kind of circumcision being done is changing. He explained:

> I talk with my wife about her tribal customs. She tells me that "we still keep the young woman in the room, but we don't do the circumcision. We just put them in there like in the traditional, and we teach them how to live with their husband, but we don't do 'that.'" At the same time, I asked my friend who is of the same tribe as my wife and he says, "In my tribe we still do that, but we don't cut in deeply like we did before. Just by tradition, we cut some small place to show that this, this and this, but we don't do like we did before. Before we cut so much, but right now just a little thing."[21]

James added that he doesn't know if the little things they cut affect the woman or not.

James believes, "Right now change is coming, but very, very slowly."[22] He considers it good luck that he lives in town, where sometimes the young people get together and talk about circumcision. James does not like it if a woman is circumcised. In the young people's groups, James says, "We have our own opinions. Many people don't like the situation, especially the young right now."[23] He explained:

> Sometimes if you try to ask the woman in a town or city, it's not like asking a woman who lives in the village. In the village, if you ask the young woman, "Do you circumcise?" She will answer, "Yes, I am circumcised and feeling much better." But in town, in the big city, you ask somebody, "Ah, you are circumcised?" "No, I didn't circumcise. I don't like it. I'm not coming from the village. I'm not a villager. I live in town. I know everything." Something like that. So I hope at home there are the changes, but the changes are still coming to the villages slowly. Some women will get it [understand the change] and then come back to their village, so they will try to tell the others about this. The problem is education.[24]

There are positive programs and people are responding in a positive way to reduce female circumcision (FC). Charles Henry Sweke, M.D., C.I. Ord., Ph.D., a consultant and obstetrician and gynecologist at Selian Lutheran Hospital in Arusha, Tanzania, believes that someday it won't be there. He said, "Although it will take long, because the problem is that, in fact, if you are trying to educate somebody who is uneducated about something to do with their tradition that they have been doing for years and years, it is very difficult. But we are optimistic that, in fact, this one will go."[25]

Dr. Kebwe identified other hopeful signs in the Bunda district that he serves. Current villager reasoning is that circumcision is a tradition and there are economic and social benefits for performing it. Dr. Kebwe said that because of the age limits, they get what they want for now, but he believes it is in the young generation that we will see the situation change. Many more people will become more educated; they will become much more aware of society's benefits, including the benefit of law enforcement. He sees the compendium of change bringing a new picture. He said, "I understand in ten years time, the picture will be quite different, but it is lacking in heritage nowadays. Judging [by] the law enforcement massive campaigns in the first ten years, we are not there, but the way you saw the law enforcement about five years ago, you would have said, 'It's going to be a long time.'"[26]

Change in FC is certain, whether the change is cutting less of the body or a decline in the practice. From 1994 to 1995 a study in Southwest Nigeria represents both types of change. It revealed a decline in towns in families where parents had some secondary education. The study's most significant change was a trend toward medicalization. Approximately one-quarter of male and female circumcisions were being performed by doctors. Among the Yoruba the major change was the move toward younger circumcision.[27]

That change will move forward the decline in the practice of FGM as it is now known is also certain. The change is apparent in the literature I was given when visiting UNICEF in Nairobi, Kenya. The UNICEF program on FGM is entitled "Work in Progress." From the title, we understand that the change they seek is not yet complete. Their tenets provide:

1. Give voice to the most vulnerable, for example, women and girls, youth, ethnic minorities

2. Community ownership

3. Harmonization of community values to universal principles of human rights

4. Ensure environment conducive to change and sustainability, and

5. Provide care, support and protection for those affected by FGM/FC.[28]

The future will bring more change as the world grapples with human immunodeficiency virus/acquired immunodeficiency syndrome (HIV/ AIDS) and as training programs gain even more momentum. This book refuses to "sum up"[29] or try to be the final word on the practice of FGM, but it does chronicle hopeful signs of change as the world moves to eliminate FGM. Eliminating FGM is a social movement that is gaining momentum. This book would not have been possible without the spirits that wandered along my road and worked my heart into bolder shape. "I change. Society changes."[30]

Epilogue

I am a girl child
With genital[s] mutilated
  I am unpaid labourer
  Serving my family
  Not sent to school
  But carrying water and wood
On my way back abducted
I am a girl child
I am a mother of child
Forced to marry and give birth
I hate living on this earth
  I am a girl child
  Who doesn't know childhood
  I am a mother and child
  I am a child beaten and raped
  Serving and cooking food
  Considered as no value
To the country or to you
I was a child crying with tears
Without knowing the consequences
Now, I face the results
The result of female genital mutilation
I suffered the real situation
Affected my health, hampered my joy
I wish I were a boy,
But, why would I wish to be a boy
While God has given me equal joy
  I cry to stop the harmful culture
  All in all, all in all
  Not to mutilate female genital
My childhood tears
My motherhood tears
Are floods to erode
Harmful cultures
  I call upon myself

I call upon my mother
Sisters and brothers and father
Government and society
To tackle with unity
To condemn and stop
Early marriage
Cause of fistula at this age
To fight and stop harmful culture
Which is life end torture
We all have lost
The benefit of nature
The right to enjoy love
The right to live happily
And peacefully
We are all losers
Let us be together with God's blessing
And destroy harmful cultures.

— Mulu Solomon[1]

Wanawake Wana Haki Kukataa Kutahiriwa Acha!
Women Have the Right to Say No or To Refuse to Be
Circumcised
Don't do it!

Message on poster of a woman saying
no to a circumciser, Tanzania[2]

I want you to spread the word all over the world saying that you
are writing about female circumcision and that you are against
it.

Nyarieka Ruey from Miywut, Sudan,
currently living in Nebraska[3]

In Africa, men are more powerful. Everything which, in fact,
wouldn't be condemned by men, they are being advised to fight
against it. As long as men are coming up and helping us, trying to give confidence to their women that in fact even if they're
not circumcised, they are to be considered just like other
women, they are going to be married. This would be very
good.... We are trying our best and I think we are going to succeed.

Dr. Charles Henry Sweke, Arusha, Tanzania[4]

Abbreviations
and Glossary

ACOG: American College of Obstetricians and Gynecologists.

AMREF: African Medical Research Foundation.

angurya cuts: scraping of tissue surrounding the vaginal orifice performed on infants to remove the hymen loop.

BAFROW: Foundation for Research on Women's Health, Productivity and the Environment.

BIA: Board of Immigration Appeals in the United States.

boma: Maasai village.

CEDPA: Center for Development and Population Activities.

CHRC: Community Humanitarian Resource Center.

clitoridectomy: a type of excision that removes the prepuce with or without excision of part or all of the clitoris; clitoridectomies are done in the United States so that girls' clitorises are of the appropriate socially acceptable size.

clitoris: small organ at the anterior or ventral part of the vulva that assists women to achieve sexual satisfaction.

CNAPN: National Action Committee to Abandon Harmful Practices (Mali).

CRR: Center for Reproductive Rights; formerly Center for Reproductive Law and Policy (CRLP).

defibulation: enlarging the vaginal opening to make possible sexual intercourse and/or birth of a baby.

DHS: Demographic and Health Surveys.

DMO: District Medical Officer (Tanzania).

ELCT: Evangelical Lutheran Church of Tanzania, Diocese in Arusha Region, Arusha, Tanzania.

ENABLE: Enabling Change for Women's Reproductive Health.

excision: the act or procedure of removing by cutting; used here to mean removal of the prepuce and clitoris together with partial or total removal of the labia minora.

exciser: circumciser.

FC: female circumcision.

FGC: female genital cutting.

FGM: female genital mutilation.

FGS: female genital surgery.

FIGO: International Federation of Gynecology and Obstetrics.

fistula: a vesico-vaginal or recto-vaginal narrow passage or duct that may result from injury during FGM, intercourse, or obstructed labor. Continuous leakage of urine or feces can plague a woman her entire life.

gishiri cuts: cutting of the vagina that is performed when labor is prolonged.

HIV/AIDS: human immunodeficiency virus/acquired immunodeficiency syndrome.

IAC: Inter-African Committee on Traditional Practices Affecting the Health of Women and Children.

IIRIRA: Illegal Immigration Reform and Immigrant Responsibility Act of 1996.

infibulation: removing part or all of the external genitalia and stitching to narrow or close the vaginal opening.

INS: U.S. Immigration and Naturalization Service (USCIS as of 2002).

IPU: Inter-Parliamentary Union.

jambo: hello in Swahili.

keloid formations: an abnormal proliferation of scar tissue that results from a wound or surgical incision.

KIAC: Kilimanjaro Inter—African Committee on Traditional Practices Affecting the Health of Women and Children.

KMT Hospital: Kanisa la Mennonite Tanzania Hospital, Shirati, Tanzania.

labia majora: the outer folds of skin of the external female genitalia; protects the inner structures and orifices.

labia minora: the inner folds of skin of the external female genitalia; protects structures and orifices.

laibon (or ol-oiboni): the Maasai traditional witch doctor, a medical and spiritual healer.

lawalawa: yeast infection.

Maasai: an indigenous African tribe of semi-nomadic people who reside primarily in Kenya and northern Tanzania.

maize: corn.

medicalization: FGM performed by physicians in a clinic or hospital.

mondo: pocket.

Moran (i): circumcised adult male warrior(s).

moruithia: woman specialist in circumcision (Gikuyu people).

ngariba: circumciser.

NGO: nongovernmental organization.

olaiguenani: age-set leader in a Maasai village.

PASAF: Project of support to the fight against the practices prejudicial with the health of the woman and of child.

PATH: Program for Appropriate Technology in Health.

perineum: tissue that supports the pelvic organs and separates the vagina from the anus.

pharaonic circumcision: name given to Type III or infibulation.

PRIME II project: a partnership combining leading global healthcare organizations dedicated to improving the quality and accessibility of family planning and reproductive healthcare services throughout the world.

PvdA: Dutch opposition Labour Party.

RAINBO: Research, Action, and Information Network for Bodily Integrity of Women.

REACH: Reproductive, Education and Community Health program.

rectum: the comparatively straight, terminal section of the intestine, ending in the anus.

re-infibulation: stitching closed or narrowing the vaginal area that was cut during childbirth.

rong'otho: clitoris (Gikuyu people).

rwenji: the Gikuyu razor.

sphincter: a circular band of voluntary or involuntary muscle that encircles an orifice of the body or one of its hollow organs.

SRCO: Sudanese Refugee Community Organization.

sunna: Arabic name given to Type I circumcision.

trichomoniasis vaginalis: a sexually transmitted disease typically asymptomatic in men that results in vaginitis with a copious, frothy discharge and itching in women, caused by a trichomonad, *Trichomonas vaginalis*.

UN: United Nations.

UNDP: United Nations Development Program.

UNESCO: United Nations Educational, Scientific and Cultural Organization.

UNFPA: United Nations Population Fund; began operations in 1969 as the United Nations Fund for Population Activities.

UNHCR: United Nations High Commissioner for Refugees.

UNICEF: United Nations International Children's Emergency Fund; changed to United Nations Children's Fund in 1953.

urethral meatus: passage that allows emptying of the bladder within a few minutes.

USAID: United States Agency for International Development.

USCIS: U.S. Citizenship and Immigration Services; known as INS before 2002.

UTI: urinary tract infection.

Uwane: Councilor.

vaginal orifice: the narrowest part of the canal that allows menstrual flow, sexual intercourse, and birth of a baby.

WHO: World Health Organization.

witch doctor: Maasai healer with divine power.

Appendix 1

Overview of the Practice in Traditional Countries

Country	Prevalence of FGM	Type of FGM	Ethnic Group/Area
Benin	30%-50% IAC 1992 survey is 30%. World Health Organization (WHO) estimates 50%.	Type II	FGM widely practiced. Ethnic groups most affected: Bariba, Peul (Fulani), Boko, Baatonau, Wama, Nago. Found mostly in north in Alibori, Atacora, Borgou, and Zou. Also occurs in south in Oueme.
Burkina Faso	71.6% from 1999 Demographic and Health Survey of 6,445 women nationally	Type II	All but a few of 50 ethnic groups practice FGM. Bella group and castes and some secret societies do not practice any form of FGM.
Cameroon	Less than 5%-20% according to various estimates.	Type I and Type II	FGM practiced in areas of far north, east, and southwest.
Central African Republic	43.4% according to 1995 Demographic and Health Survey of 5,884 women nationally.	Type I and Type II	Practice found in 8 to 10 of 48 ethnic groups.
Chad	60% according to 1995 UN report.	Type II common in all parts of the country. Type III confined to eastern part of country in area	In all areas of the country but strongest in the east and south. Crosses ethnic and religious lines. Practiced by Christians, Muslims, and Animists in roughly equal proportions.

		bordering Sudan.	Frequency higher in rural areas.
Cote d'Ivoire (Ivory Coast)	44.5% according to 1999 Demographic and Health Survey of 3,040 women nationally.	Type II	Prevalent among Muslim women and rooted in Animist initiation rites in western, central, and northern Cote d'Ivoire. Muslim groups practicing FGM include the northern Mande (Malinke, Foula, Bambara, Dioula) and some members of the Voltaic groups of the north (Senuofo, Tagwana, Djimini, Lobi, Birifor, Koulango) and southern Mande of the west (Dan, Yacouba, Toura, Gouro)— many of whom are not Muslim — and the We from the Krou group and Baoule in some villages around city of Bouake.
Democratic Republic of the Congo (formerly Zaire)	5% estimate	Type II	Practiced in ethnic groups living in the northern part of country above the equator.
Djibouti	90%-98% according to various estimates.	Type II and Type III	Afars and Issa practice Type III. Girls of Yemeni extraction subjected to Type II.
Egypt	78%-97%. 2000 Demographic and Health Survey of 15,648 women nationwide showed figure to be 97% among ever married women aged 15–49 and 78% among daughters of the women surveyed aged 11–19.	Type II and Type I throughout country. Type III concentrated in a few ethnic groups in southern part of country.	Practiced by both Muslims and Coptic Christians; across ethnic lines.
Eritrea	90% according to 1997 Demographic and Health Survey of 5,054 women nationally.	Type I, Type II, Type III	Some form of FGM practiced by almost all ethnic and religious groups.

Ethiopia	72.7% according to a 1997 survey published in 1998 by the National Committee on Traditional Practices in Ethiopia.	Type I and Type II. Type III in areas bordering Sudan and Somalia. Mariam Girz (Type IV) blood letting with a sharp needle practiced to lesser extent.	Type I practiced among Amharas, Tigrayans, and Jeberti Muslims living in Tigray. Type II practiced by Gurages, some Tigrayans, Oromos, and Shankilas. Type III practiced among the Afar, the Somali, and the Harari. Mariam Girz (Type IV) practiced in Gojam (the Amhara region). No form of FGM is practiced among Bengas of Wellga, the Azezo, the Dorze, the Bonke, the Shama, and some population groups in Godole, Konso, and Gojam. By region: Afar-94.5%; Harare-81.2%; Amhara-81.1%; Oromia-79.6%; Addis Ababa City-70.2%; Somali-69.7%; Beneshangul Gumuz-52.9%; Tigray-48.1%; Southern-46.3%.
Gambia	60%-90% various estimates. BAFROW reports 7 of 9 ethnic groups practice FGM.	Type I and Type II. Type III in very small percentage of women and girls. Also special "sealing" performed.	Mandikas, Hausas, and Jolas practice Type II. Sarahulis practice modified form of Type II. Fulas practice "sealing" analogous to Type III. Bambaras practice Type III. Wolofs, Akus, Sereres, and Manjangos do not practice any form of FGM.
Ghana	9%-15%. Various estimates. 1998 estimate by Gender Studies and Human Rights Documentation Center is 15%. Recent UNFPA-funded study by Rural Help Integrated estimates between 9% and 12% of women nationwide.	Type I, Type II, Type III. Type II most common.	Practice most common in Upper East Region. Also practiced in remote parts of Northern Region, Upper West Region, and northern Volta Region. Also prevalent among migrants of bordering countries in south. Found in both Muslim and Christian communities. Ethnic groups known to practice FGM include

			Kussasi, Frafra, Kassena, Nankanne, Bussauri, Moshie, Manprusie, Kantansi, Walas, Sissala, Grunshie, Dargati, and Lobi. Less prevalent among the educated in urban areas.
Guinea	98.6% according to 1999 Demographic and Health Survey of 6,753 women nationally.	Type I, Type II, Type III	Peul, Malinke, Soussou, Guerze, Toma, and Nalou practice one of these forms of FGM.
Guinea-Bissau	50% average. Various estimates. 70%-80% in Fula and Mandinka areas; 20%-30% in urban Bissau.	Type I and Type II	Fulas, Mandinkas, Peul practice Type I or Type II. Practiced on adolescent girls and babies as young as 4 months old.
Indonesia	No national figures available. Study by University of Indonesia's Women's Research Graduate Program in 1998 in Jakarta and West Java of 200 mothers found most girls circumcised but often with less invasive procedures used.	Type I and less invasive Type IV forms such as scraping or touching clitoris to draw drop of blood or cutting a plant root symbolically without touching child.	Practiced in parts of East, Central, and West Java; North Sumatra; Aceh; South Sulawesi; and on Madura Island.
Kenya	37.6% according to 1998 Demographic and Health Survey of 7,881 women nationally.	Type I and Type II. Some Type III in far eastern areas bordering Somalia.	FGM practiced in 30 of Kenya's 40 ethnic groups. Not practiced among 2 largest groups in far west: Luos and Luhyas. Examples of ethnic groups include Kisii–97%; Maasai–89%; Kalenjin–62%; Taita and Taveta–59%; Mercu/Embu–54%; Kikuyu–43%; Kamba–33%; Miji Kenda/Swahili–12%. Widely practiced among Muslims of northeastern province, particularly Somalis, Borans, and Gabras. Declining among the educated and in urban areas.

Liberia	50% of females over 18: pre-civil war 1989 estimate. estimate 10% during civil war (1990–1996). Update unavailable.	Type II	Major groups including the Mande-speaking people of Western Liberia such as Gola and Kisii practice Type II. Not practiced by the Kru, Grebo, or Krahn in Southeast; by Americo-Liberians; (Congos) or by Muslim Mandingos.
Mali	93.7% according to USAID-funded Demographic and Health Survey of 9,704 women aged 15–49. Commission for the Promotion of Women estimates 96% rural and 92% urban women have undergone this procedure.	Type I, Type II, Type III (southern part of country)	Most groups, including the Bambara, Dogon, Senoufo, Soninke, and Peul practice some form of FGM. The Songhai, Tuareg, and Moor populations generally do not practice any form. The practice is lowest among ethnic groups in north. In south over 95%. For example, Bamako-95.3%; Koulikoro-99.3%. Very low percentage in north. For example, Tombouctou and Gao-9.3%.
Mauritania	25% according to 1997 Juene Afrique survey and 1996 UN Population Fund report.	Type I (more common among the Soninkes) and Type II (more common among Toucouleurs). Also symbolic Type IV using gum arabic plant-based product mixture to shrink the clitoris.	A 1992 government-funded national survey indicated that 93% of Pulaar women, 78% of Soninke, 69% of Moors (who make up 70% of the population), and 12% of Wolof practiced FGM.
Niger	4.5% according to 1998 Demographic and Health Survey of 7,577 women nationally.	Type II	Most prevalent in the Tillaberi and Dosso areas, along the Niger river, and among Arab communities in the Diffa region. Communities/ethnic groups practicing FGM are Arabs (known locally as Shoua), Kanuris, and Zarma-Son-

			rhais. Also by the Peul, Songhai, Kourtey, and Wago.
Nigeria	25.1% according to 1999 Demographic and Health Survey of 8,206 women nationally.	Type I, Type II, and Type III throughout the country. Type III more predominant in the north. Type I and Type II more predominant in the south. Another Type IV form practiced to a lesser extent uses a corrosive substance on the female genitalia.	Practiced across ethnic groups and religions. Practiced by almost all ethnic groups. Among the largest ethnic groups that practice some form of FGM are the Yoruba, Ibo, Ijaw, Hausa, and Kanuri. The Fulanis do not practice any form. Practice among states of Nigeria varies from 0%-1% in Yobe to 90%-100% in Benue and 90%-98% in Ondo.
Senegal	5%-20%. 20% according to 1988 Environmental Development Action in the Third World study. Various other estimates range as low as 5%.	Type II and Type III	Toucouleur, Sarakole, Peul, Bambara, the Halpular, Mande, Diolas (mostly rural), Mandingos (mostly rural), and the Tenda practice one of these forms. It is not practiced among the Wolof plurality-43%, the Serere-15%, and most Christians, regardless of ethnicity. Minority Halpularen, Puel, and Toucouleur in rural areas of eastern and southern Senegal-88%. Urban Halpularen-20%. Becoming less common in urban areas.
Sierra Leone	80%-90%. Various estimates.	Type II	All ethnic and religious groups except Krios practice FGM.
Somalia	90–98%. UNICEF estimates 90%. Other estimates are 96–98%. 1999 CARE International survey estimates 100% for Somaliland (northwest Somalia).	Type III is most common. Also Type I (also called sunna).	Most if not all ethnic groups. Type I mainly in coastal towns of Mogadishu, Brava, Merca, and Kismayu

Sudan	89% according to 1991 Demographic and Health Survey of 5,860 women nationally. 87% urban — 91% rural of northern Sudanese women and girls according to survey conducted from 1996 to April 2000 by Sudan National Committee on Traditional Practices (SNCTP) and Save the Children Sweden.	Type III predominates. Some are switching to Type I or Type II.	All ethnic and religious groups practice one of these forms throughout the northern, northeastern, and northwestern regions.
Tanzania	17.9% according to 1996 Demographic and Health Survey of 8,120 women nationally. Percentage is between 2.9% in Mtwara to 81.4% in Arusha according to a 1999 report by the Tanzanian Legal and Human Rights Center.	Type II and Type III	Practiced in approximately 20 of country's 130 main ethnic groups. Government data show incidence varies by region with the most affected being: Arusha-81.4%, Dodoma-67.9%, Mara-43.7%, Kilimanjaro-36.9%, Iringa-27%, Singida-25.4%, and Kilosa-20.2%. The percentage in Mtwara is only 2.9%. It is not practiced in Zanzibar. Practice almost nonexistent in rest of the country.
Togo	12% average. Ethnic groups vary. Cotocoli, Tchamba, Mossi, Yanga, and Peul- 85–98%; Moba-22%; Gourma-12%, according to U.S. funded 1996 research carried out by the Demographic Research Unit of Togo's University of Benin.	Type II	Cotocoli, Tchamba, Peul, Mossi, Yanga, Moba, Gourma, Ana-Ife practice Type II. Two of the largest ethnic groups, Adja-Ewe and Akposso-Akebou, do not practice any form. Highest regional incidence is in the Central Region, 33% home of the Cotocoli and Tchamba. By religion: Muslim-63.9%; Christian-3.2%; Animists-6.1%; other-10%.
Uganda	Less than 5% of female population. Number of girls undergoing Type I or Type II in recent years	Type I and Type II	Prevalent in rural district of Kapchorwa in the east among the Sabiny ethnic group. Also practiced by the Pokot group, also

are: 1990–971 girls; 1992–903 girls; 1994–854 girls; 1996–544 girls; 1998–965 girls; 2000–742 girls. Initiation ceremonies for girls between ages of 14 and 16 take place in December of even numbered years.

known as the Upe, located along the remote northeastern border with Kenya. Approximately 10,000 Sabiny and 20,000 Upe live in the country.

Yemen, Republic of

23% of women who have ever been married, according to a USAID-funded 1997 Demographic and Maternal and Child Health Survey.

Type II. Type III practiced only among small community of East African immigrants and refugees.

Primarily women living in coastal areas, but also practiced to lesser extent in the mountainous region and in the plateau and desert region. In the Tihama region along Red Sea coast, 69% of women were circumcised; 15% of women in highlands; 5% in central plateau and desert regions to the east. Ministry of Public Health survey in five governorates. Results show over 96% of women in Hodeidah, Hadraumaut, and Al-Maharah had been circumcised; 82% in Aden and in Sana'a City forty-five and a half percent.

Source: U.S. Department of State, Office of the Senior Coordinator for International Women's Issues, Office of the Under Secretary for Global Affairs, Feb. 1, 2001, K. Chart. Updated June 27, 2001. Available: http://www.state.gov.g/wi/rls/rep/9305.htm. Accessed Dec. 7, 2003.

Appendix 2

Law and Outreach

Country	*Law and Outreach*
Benin	No law against FGM.

The Inter-African Committee on Traditional Practices has Affecting the Health of Women and Children has led campaigns against this practice since 1982 with workshops, and seminars. It collaborates with Ministry of Social Affairs and Health. NGOs "Le Levier du Developpement" and "Dignite Feminine" are also involved in anti-FGM campaigns. FGM treated as a community issue. Government permits distribution of informational materials in government-run clinics and undertakes sensitivity activities in rural areas.

Burkina Faso A 1996 law forbids FGM. It provides prison terms and fines.

Sixty convictions of both excisors and accomplices since its adoption.

Campaign against FGM since 1975. Government has been waging widespread campaign against this practice for years. National Committee set up by Presidential decree in 1990 does extensive work about FGM including workshops, plays, posters, pamphlets, full-length feature film, etc. There is a 24-hour SOS hotline on FGM.

Cameroon No law against FGM.

Women's groups lobby for legislation. IAC-organized conference Aug. 4–5, 1997, called for law against this practice and instruction of men and women and practitioners on the harmful effects. National Committee of IAC actively campaigns against this practice. Their activities are supported by government. Government active against the practice. Public campaign to eradicate this practice in 15–20 years started in March 1997. This includes public discussion and information programs on the subject. State-run television and newspaper have programs and articles about this practice. Ministry of Women's and Social Affairs and Cameroon's NGOs continue to make concrete and strong efforts to combat the practice.

Central African Republic There has been a law against FGM since 1966.

Arrests under the law unknown.

Government is active in campaigns to inform the public about health problems and has taken measures against this practice. Government adopted policy to improve position of women and a program 'Women-Nutrition-Development for Children', which address this problem, in 1989.

Chad   No law specifically makes FGM punishable. Practice might be prosecutable as involuntary physical assault against a minor under existing Penal Code. Draft law expected to go before Parliament in 2001 would criminalize this practice.

In 1995, a government-published policy opposing the practice was enacted into law. This includes provisions to increase awareness of the problem, protect women against this practice and initiate punitive measures against those who continue it. Both the government and NGOs are active in conducting public awareness campaigns and seminars about the practice. Ministry of Social Action and the Family coordinates activities concerning this practice. In FY 2001 budget, line item supports activities of leading NGO, Chadian Association for Family Well Being, in combating this practice. NGOs work for eradication; projects include several NGO-led seminars on the subject. Education programs have been initiated. IAC National Committee active in outreach programs. U.S. Embassy supported local NGO program to get decision makers, traditional leaders, and officials involved. Seminars are planned throughout country about the practice plus publicity campaign on radio and in print media. Conference held March 1997 with widespread media coverage. The World Health Organization is active in mobilizing government and private efforts to halt the practice.

Cote   1998 law against FGM. Punishable by fine and imprisonment. Law enforced.
d'Ivoire   Four excisers arrested and jailed in 2000.
(Ivory
Coast)   After enactment of law and before enforcement, government and NGOs such as the Ivoirian Association for Defense of Women's Rights (AIDF) launched major information campaign about the law for general population, law enforcement authorities, and local government officials. Government heavily involved in campaign to eradicate this practice through Ministry of Women's Affairs and Family and the Ministry of Public Health. NGOs campaign against the practice. AIDF is most active NGO. It works to raise awareness; holds seminars on the subject; leads fight against medicalization of FGM. IAC aims its work of fighting this practice at community institutions—institutions for female education, youth hostels, etc. Gynecological and Obstetrical Society and the National Federation of Midwives and the Association for the Well Being of the Family take action via radio and newspapers to inform public about this practice.

Democratic   No law prohibits FGM.
Republic of   Outreach efforts unknown.
the Congo
(formerly
Zaire)

Djibouti   Effective in 1995, Penal Code outlaws FGM with prison term and fine.

Government incorporated awareness of this practice into national program to promote safe motherhood. NGO outreach groups campaign to eradicate the practice. Government allows use of its facilities; encourages use of the media. The Union Nationale des Femmes de Djibouti (UNFD) holds workshops to increase awareness of health consequences of FGM. Association for the Equilibrium and Promotion of the Family (ADEPF) and UNFD work to raise awareness in schools and women's groups. WHO,

UNICEF, Caritas, and the Red Sea Team International are involved in this work.

Egypt   Ministerial decree in 1959 prohibited FGM, making it punishable by fine and imprisonment. Changes made over the years. In December 1997, the Court of Cassation upheld a government ban on FGM. Issued as a decree in 1996 by Health Minister, ban prohibits medical and nonmedical practitioners from performing FGM in public or private facilities, except for medical reasons certified by head of hospital's obstetric department.

Government committed to eradicating FGM through education and information. Some provisions of Penal Code on "wounding," "intentional infliction of harm leading to death" might be used. Reports of prosecution of at least 13 persons for FGM in 1995, 1996 under the Code. Many NGOs doing outreach to teach about the harmful effects. In 1982, a project by the Population Crisis Committee and Cairo Family Planning Association produced material on harmful effects and carried out training for doctors, nurses, midwives, and social workers. National Committee of IAC active in anti-FGM activities since 1985. Task force targets mothers' clinics, family planning centers, secondary school students, etc. Current efforts focus on community-based approaches and the positive deviance approach that uses individuals who have deviated from tradition and stopped, prevented, oppose the procedure to advocate change. The U.S. Agency for International Development, in cooperation with Egyptian government, is funding projects to train health providers on dangers of the practice and providing grants to NGOs to increase public information about this subject. Government and NGOs use media to disseminate information on health risks.

Eritrea   No law prohibits FGM.

Government uses education and persuasion to eliminate this practice. Ministry of Health carries out campaign to eradicate practice. Government supports groups working to end the practice including National Union of Eritrean Women and the National Union of Eritrean Youth and Students. The Eritrean People's Liberation Front (EPLF), which led fight for independence, has worked since 1988 to eradicate practice. Women fighters (30% of EPLF) are vocal in effort not to re-establish traditions harmful to women, including FGM. In 1996, government policy was enunciated to eliminate this and other harmful traditional practices; to create and enforce legislation prohibiting these practices; to include prevention of practices such as FGM in women's health care, and to provide treatment, counseling, and rehabilitation for women suffering negative effects of this practice. Government makes information on this practice part of its health and general education programs. Ministry of Health carries out government policy on this practice and provides in-service training on the subject to all primary health care coordinators throughout country, including training materials (visual aids and documents). In 1996, workshop on safe motherhood focused on negative health aspects of the practice. Health Ministry, with USAID, UNICEF, and UNFPA, is designing a national and local level campaign against this practice. During independence struggle, EPLF tried to prohibit the practice in areas it controlled. Result was practice went underground. Because of this, government now believes best approach is through education, rather than laws, to eliminate practice.

Ethiopia   No law prohibits any form of FGM. Law being drafted. Constitution pro-
                  hibits harmful traditional practices. Government national policy on women
                  is strongly against FGM and other harmful practices. 1960 Penal Code pro-
                  hibits torture and cutting off any body parts.

                  Wide range of grassroots outreach activities by NGOs. Government very
                  active in outreach. 1993 National Policy on Women takes strong stance
                  against these practices. Government has followed up with support and
                  action by its various ministries and bureaus, including mandating that edu-
                  cational materials discouraging the practices be included in primary school
                  curricula. (Such materials used in curricula since 1994.) The government's
                  National Committee on Traditional Practices in Ethiopia, a chapter of the
                  IAC, does extensive work throughout the country on this subject, includ-
                  ing courses to raise awareness about the practices in secondary schools.
                  Some positive results are being seen in stopping FGM. Ethiopian Women
                  Lawyers Association very active on updating laws, including writing pro-
                  visions into new criminal code (as yet unratified) that will criminalize
                  FGM.

Gambia   No law prohibits any form of FGM. In 1999, the President announced that
                  FGM would not be banned and that FGM is part of the country's culture.

                  NGOs working to provide information to the public and eradicate all forms
                  using workshops, seminars, theater, media, etc. Gambia Committee Against
                  Traditional Practices focuses on community workshops. Foundation for
                  Research on Women's Health, Productivity and the Environment (BAF-
                  FROW) developed curriculum for schools on "initiation without mutila-
                  tion." The government has recognized harmful effects of FGM and supported
                  NGO outreach. After Director of Information and Broadcasting ordered
                  ban on anti-FGM radio and TV programs, Vice President stated that gov-
                  ernment policy was to discourage such harmful practices as FGM. That was
                  before the President's 1999 statement. Government does allow reproductive
                  health issues such as FGM to be discussed on national radio and television
                  networks. NGOs can use government media to address these issues.

Ghana   1994 law prohibits FGM. Sec. 69A of Criminal Code makes it second degree
                  felony with fine and imprisonment. Art. 39 of Constitution abolishes inju-
                  rious and traditional practices.

                  History of enforcement of this criminal law. There have been seven arrests
                  since 1994. Two practitioners convicted of second degree felony. One was
                  sentenced to three years in prison. In a 1995 case, the parents of the girl
                  were also charged for having FGM performed on their daughter.

                  Extensive outreach by groups in collaboration with government to eradi-
                  cate this practice. Government at all levels publicly supports eradication.
                  Ghana Association of Women's Welfare (GAWW) active in projects in the
                  north to inform the public about effects of the practice and for its eradi-
                  cation. WHO, GAWW and Muslim Family Counseling Services in 1997
                  toured and identified 18 practitioners in Volta region to teach them about
                  harmful effects of FGM. They work with Ministry of Education to incor-
                  porate education about practice into public school health curriculum. Vol-
                  untary watchdog committees intervene to stop impending FGM
                  ceremonies. There is little real protection to turn to, however, in many
                  rural areas.

Guinea	Art. 265 of Penal Code prohibits all forms of FGM. Art. 6 of Constitution prohibits cruel and inhumane treatment. Supreme court preparing clause for Constitution prohibiting FGM.

Outreach groups work with government to eradicate the practice through films, TV, seminars, etc. Government initiated a 20-year strategy (1996–2015) to eradicate this practice in collaboration with WHO's Africa regional efforts. This is to reinforce and institutionalize efforts with NGOs using communication and education mediums to inform public about this practice.

Guinea-Bissau   No law prohibits FGM. In 1995, a law proposed to outlaw this practice was defeated. Assembly did approve proposal to hold practitioners criminally responsible if woman dies as result of one of these procedures.

Government, with assistance of the Dutch, Swedish, and UN aid agencies and high-level support from Ministers of Health and of Social Affairs and Women, in January 1997, implemented a 2-year nationwide program targeting female leaders, excisors, traditional and religious leaders, educators, and youth. Government gives support for outreach groups doing informational seminars, publicity, etc. Government formed National Committee to conduct nationwide education campaign to discourage this practice. U.S. Embassy funds are used to finance regional committees to carry out campaigns in rural areas, on radio and TV spots, and by production of a play to be performed in regional centers. The Swedish group Radda Barnen and Plan International as well as domestic NGOs such as Friends of Children and Sinim Mira Nasseque work through the National Committee to eliminate this practice. The efforts of these groups, suspended after outbreak of fighting in June 1998, resumed in many parts of the country in February 1999.

Indonesia   No law against this practice.

Public awareness of this practice is low. Government included this practice as a gender issue in its National Action Plan to End Violence against Women, published in Nov. 2000. Commits Ministry of Women's Empowerment and Ministry of Religion to conduct research on religious teachings that impede women's rights. FGM heads Action Plan's list of religious teachings requiring investigation and modification. Indonesian Government, National Ulemas Council, religious leaders, women's groups, and health practitioners are to develop guidelines for health practitioners and midwives on noninvasive techniques. Awareness campaign planned.

Kenya   No law prohibits FGM. In 1982 and 1989, presidential decrees were issued banning this practice. A vote in 1996 by Parliament defeated a motion to outlaw it. Government forbids government hospitals and medical clinics from performing any of these procedures. Ministries of Health and Culture discourage this practice; encourage adoption of alternative rites of passage. Government encourages enactment of legislation to eradicate practice.

Many NGOs working to eradicate practice. National Committee on Traditional Practices (now the Kenya National Council on Traditional Practices) does outreach to inform population about this subject, as do other groups. Seminars have been held. Materials are provided on the practice. MYWO, the national women's organization closely aligned with the ruling Kanu party, is one of most active organizations working to eradicate the practice. MYWO focuses on informing community about the harmful health effects. It has also developed alternative initiation rites without "the cut" and is retraining excisors in other lines of work. Media helps campaign to eradicate practice. Schools include this subject in curricula. USAID is funding programs for research and eradication of the practice in several targeted areas. UNICEF and UNDP are also working to eradicate this practice. They focus on key local level officials and building local support. In March 1997, UNICEF organized meeting of donors, NGOs, and UN agencies to coordinate eradication campaigns in Kenya. Information, training and persuasion are to be the tools to change practice at grassroots.

Liberia

No law specifically prohibits FGM. Section 242 of Penal Code might cover it.

No cases to date.

The IAC Liberian National Committee conducted research, trained volunteers, and provided health training about harmful effects of this practice. It collaborated with government to integrate awareness of consequences of FGM into programs for mother and child care and primary health care. It continued to provide information and training about the dangers of FGM during the civil war. Liberian Action Network also worked in campaign gathering information and recommending programs, seminars, workshops, and meetings. Media is used to address damage caused by FGM. Campaigns during pre-civil war period had little effect in stopping FGM.

Mali

No specific law prohibits FGM, but Penal Code outlaws assault and grievous bodily harm. Law being drafted to outlaw this practice.

Government formed National Action Committee in 1996 to promote eradication of harmful health practices against women and children. Engages in information activities, training, support of NGOs combating harmful practices, etc. In 1997, Committee devised first phase of Plan of Action for the Eradication of FGM by 2007. Many NGOs campaign and provide extensive programs on subject throughout country. Government regional offices support these activities.

Mauritania

No law prohibits FGM. Secretariat of State for Women's Affairs, a cabinet post, directs government efforts to eliminate this practice. The practice is banned from government hospitals. NGOs, public health workers, and medical doctors provide education and information to women about the harmful effects and the fact that FGM is not a requirement of Islam.

Secretary of State for Women's Affairs formed Committee in June 1997 to coordinate activities against this practice. UNICEF and UNFPA working in country on FGM projects. In 1996, U.S. funded publication and distribution of booklet on women's rights, including information on FGM that was launched through public campaign in all regions of country. Prominent in campaign is an eminent Imam, member of higher Islamic Council of Mauritania, who carries message that this practice are not a religious requirement of Islam.

Niger

No law prohibits FGM at this time. Government has drafted proposed amendment to Penal Code that would outlaw FGM and carry a sentence of 3–20 years prison term. Must now be submitted to Parliament.

Government decree in 1990 established committee to campaign against FGM called Nigerian Committee against Harmful Traditional Practices (Lute Contra les Practices Traditionnelles Nefastes or CONIPRAT). It is the leading NGO in the fight against FGM. It carries out publicity campaigns to raise awareness, disseminates information on this practice in local languages, and participates in research. With UNICEF funding and government participation, CONIPRAT held several seminars on the harmful effects of these and other traditional practices. It is working to strengthen its presence at regional and local levels. Organized ceremony in rural Tillaberi department where excisors turned in their knives and pledged to discontinue practice of FGM. Received prominent coverage in government media. Government participates in information seminars, publicity. March 1997, Minister of Health announced the government will do whatever it can to halt the practice of FGM. Government created a division for protection of women and children in Ministry of Social Development that works closely with CONIPRAT on this issue. UNICEF and Care International support CONIPRAT's efforts.

Nigeria

No federal law prohibits FGM. Opponents use Sec. 34(1) (a) of 1999 Constitution instead. There are state laws against this practice. Edo State banned practice in Oct. 1999. There has been one conviction under Edo State law. States of Ogun, Cross River, Osun, Rivers, and Bayelsa also banned practice since that time.

Government publicly opposes this practice. Federal Health Ministry and Federal Ministry of Women's Affairs support nationwide study of the practice. Many NGOs— international, national, and local organizations, including the National Association of Nigerian Nurses and Midwives, Nigerian Medical Women's Association, Nigerian Medical Association, WHO, and UNICEF —campaign and teach about dangers of this practice. IAC/Nigeria has programs throughout the country on the subject. It is pursuing a state-by-state strategy to criminalize the practice in all 36 states.

Senegal

Law passed in 1999 prohibits FGM.

President has spoken out against this practice. Outreach groups conduct seminars, publicity campaigns, surveys, workshops on the subject. The NGO Tostan, with assistance of the government, UNICEF, and the American Jewish World Service, has sponsored skills-training courses including courses on literacy, problem solving, women's health and hygiene, management, leadership, negotiating, and human rights that provide information about the harmful health effects of this practice. Following these courses, the Bambara village of Malicounda abandoned these practices, with the endorsement of the Imam. As of November 2000, 174 villages had abandoned the practice, following completion of the Tostan program. This affects about 140,000 people. Tostan program being replicated in Sudan, Mali, and Burkina Faso. Ministry of Women, Children and the Family sponsors public awareness programs on the practice.

Sierra Leone   No law prohibits FGM.

NGOs carry out instructional programs and work to eradicate the practice. The Sierra Leone Association on Women's Welfare has advocated instruction and information against FGM since 1984. Grassroots programs include teaching about the harmful effects of FGM and eradication of the practice. Seminars held with primary and secondary school teachers on dangers of this practice.

Somalia   No national law against FGM. However, the administration of Puntland passed law against practice November 1999.

Outreach groups campaigned to eradicate this practice since 1977. Former Barre government appointed group to eradicate the practice. Instructional and learning programs existed since Somalia Academy of Arts and Sciences began studies on the subject in 1980s. Extensive work by former government's Ministry of Education. Institute of Women's Education set up in 1984. It engaged in activities to eradicate FGM in a general health program, Family Planning Project. In 1987, the Italian Association for Women and Development and Somali Women's Democratic Organization founded an anti-FGM project. Information packets and audio visual material were produced; workshops set up; seminars held. Technical basis destroyed in 1991 with overthrow of government. UNICEF conducted workshops in Mogadishu, Galgaddud, and Mudug regions in 1999–2000 to eradicate practice. UNICEF-Somalia has sponsored awareness seminars since 1996 to end FGM. U.S. Embassy in 2000 provided grant to Voice of Midwives Association for public awareness campaign. In 1998, U.S. Embassy provided grant to UNICEF for FGM project in four communities in Somaliland.

Sudan   Today there is no law forbidding FGM per se, although Sudan was the first African country to outlaw this practice in 1946. A 1946 amendment to the 1925 Penal Code prohibited infibulation (Type III) but allowed less severe form. Ratified again in 1956. Prohibited infibulation but allowed removal of projecting part of clitoris; punishment of fine and imprisonment. The 1991 Penal Code does not mention any form of FGM. Other provisions of the Penal Code covering "injury" might cover FGM. Reports that some practitioners arrested, but no further information available.

Outreach groups have been working to eradicate the practices for 50 years. Intensive campaign today. NGOs, government, religious groups, and media work to eradicate practices. Focus on information, workshops, and seminars. Medical profession becoming involved. Eradication of FGM worked into curriculum for community health at Khartoum Nursing College.

Tanzania   Sec. 169A of the Sexual Offences Special Provisions Act of 1998 prohibits FGM. Punishment by fine or imprisonment or both.

Government supports campaign to end this practice. There are government efforts to eradicate this practice. There are extensive programs, surveys, studies, research on this practice. National Committee on Traditional Practices is directed toward awareness raising. It did research to design means to combat this practice. It is seeking to inform youth and incorporate information about it into school curriculum. Instruction on dangers of this practice sometimes included in health science in secondary schools. Ministry of Health conducting campaign to prevent this practice as part of their "Safe Motherhood" initiative. Seminars sponsored by governmental organizations and NGOs regularly held to provide information about the practice. The Dodoma Traditional Practices and Beliefs Committee that received a grant from WHO began a program to eliminate FGM in the region within 20 years. USAID funded the NGO TAMWA to conduct workshops on eradication of this practice. The Legal and Human Rights Center report suggests the practice is on the decline.

Togo

A law banning FGM with prison term and fines was passed on October 30, 1998 by the National Assembly.

One excisor arrested under the law.

Human rights and women's organizations provide information to rural populations on harmful effects of the practice. Since 1984, with help of government, National Committee of IAC holds seminars, workshops to teach about the subject. Anti-FGM documentary shown on national (government-controlled) television. Government held seminars after law passed on enforcement of the law. Also informed public about health problems associated with FGM. Major campaign by Togalese Association for the Well Being of the Family in 1999 to educate public about the law. NGO Group Reflection and Action for Women in Democracy and Development work to protect women from this practice.

Uganda

No law yet prohibits FGM. Government, however, is formulating a law banning this practice throughout the country. Constitution in theory protects women and girls from this practice. Section 8 of the Children Statute, enacted in 1996, makes it unlawful to subject a child to social or customary practices that are harmful to child's health. In 1996, a girl upon whom FGM was to be performed secured intervention of a court and the procedure was prevented under this statute.

Government publicly condemns FGM and says it would protect any woman bringing a claim to its attention. National Committee of IAC works to eradicate this practice and inform the public about its harmful effects. United Nations Population Fund pilot program called "Reach" (Reproductive, Educative and Community Health program) in 1995 in Kapchorwa, focused on information, education, and instruction about this practice. It also focused on rallying support of key members of society (such as Elders Association), informing community youth through peer educators, training health workers, and finally instructing traditional birth attendants and excisors. Program resulted in a substantial decline in the practice from 1994 to 1996. Government has fully supported the UNFPA program. Sabiny Elders Association now is very active in campaign to abolish FGM and replace it with a symbolic ritual. Chairman of the Association was awarded the UN Population Award for work of the Sabiny Elders to eradicate this practice in the remote Kapchorwa region.

Yemen, Republic of

No law prohibits FGM. Ministerial decree effective January 9, 2001, prohibits the practice in both government and private health facilities.

The government published the recent Demographic Health Survey on the incidence of FGM. Some government health workers, including the Minister of Public Health actively and publicly discourage this practice.

Some women are doing research to launch a public campaign against the practice. Ministry of Public Health sponsored two-day seminar January 9–10, 2001, entitled "Female Health" on FGM. Nearly 150 academics, health professionals, government officials, donors, and clerics attended. First time FGM had been publicly discussed in Yemen. Conference Plan of Action includes (1) religious leaders to provide legal opinion on FGM in consultation with doctors; (2) ministries to develop public awareness campaign in areas most affected by practice; (3) Ministry of Public Health to conduct nationwide study to determine extent of the practice; (4) plan to be developed to include FGM in curricula at medical schools, health institutes, and literacy centers; (5) a law to be promulgated to prohibit FGM.

Source: U.S. Department of State, Office of the Senior Coordinator for International Women's Issues, Office of the Under Secretary for Global Affairs, Feb. 1, 2001, K. Chart. Updated June 27, 2001. Available: http://www.state.gov.g/wi/rls/rep/9305.htm. Accessed Dec. 7, 2003.

Appendix 3

Overview of the Practice in Industrialized Countries

Country	Law and Outreach
Australia	Constitution does not include Bill of Rights, but rights and liberties acknowledged in judicial and legislative efforts. Criminal legislation in six of eight Australian states and territories has made FGM a crime. This includes Australian Capital Territory, Northern Territory, New South Wales, South Australia, Tasmania, and Victoria. These laws prohibit the practice within the jurisdiction as well as the removal of the child to another jurisdiction for the performance of the procedure. Punishments range from 7 to 15 years imprisonment. Consent is no defense.

One case of child abuse heard in Magistrates Court in Melbourne in December 1993 involved action against a father of two girls who were infibulated. Information on the outcome is unavailable. Other enforcement information for 1998–1999 not available.

The government has implemented the National Education Program to prevent this practice in Australia. Focus is on community education, information, and support; assistance for women and girls at risk of, or who have been subjected to this practice to minimize adverse health problems; promoting consistent health approach in working with communities; and facilitating support and access to health services. Each State and Territory reports biennially on the work of health departments with communities on this issue.

Royal Australian College of Obstetricians and Gynecologists opposes any form performed for nonmedical reasons and develops materials to assist health professionals.

Canada	Charter of Rights and Freedoms guarantees equality of men and women and right to life, liberty, and security of the person.

Canada passed a law that became effective May 26, 1997, amending the Criminal Code of Canada. Under Section 268, this procedure is considered an aggravated assault that is punishable by imprisonment for a term not exceeding 14 years. Specifically, aggravated assault is committed when one "wounds, maims, disfigures or endangers the life" of a complainant. "Wounds" and "maims" are defined to include "...to excise, infibulate or mutilate, in whole or in part, the labia majora, labia minora or clitoris of a person..." There are limited exceptions. Consent is no defense.

The Criminal Code in Section 273.3(1) also makes it a crime to take a child who ordinarily is resident in Canada out of Canada for the purpose of having FGM performed in another country. Punishment is for a term not exceeding 5 years (Criminal Code, R.S.C. 1985, c. C-46, ss. 268, 273.3(1) (c)).

In addition to legal penalties, medical associations in most Canadian provinces have passed prohibitions against performing this procedure. 1999 — no known instances of arrests.

Canadian NGOs are active in efforts, both in Canada and abroad, to provide education about dangers of this practice and its illegality in Canada. Save the Children Canada focuses on finding an alternative traditional rite of passage for young girls. It promotes the "circumcision through words" rite of passage as an alternative to FGM. This program emphasizes education for younger women and involves the entire community to accept this alternative rite of passage. This program was the focus of a 1999 Canadian documentary "Circumcision Through Words" that has been used by medical associations to educate health care professionals about the cultural beliefs of countries where FGM is commonly practiced. Society of Obstetricians and Gynecologists, Canadian Medical Association, and each provincial college of physicians and surgeons have adopted policies that prohibit medical professionals from performing FC/FGM.

Denmark   Constitution guarantees personal liberty.

FC/FGM is a crime under Danish Criminal Code. 1996 Ministry of Health appointed a working group that wages information campaigns to deter immigrants from going abroad to have the procedure. Refugee Department provides information about prohibition of FC/FGM.

1998–1999 enforcement information not available.

1981 National Board of Health declared it illegal for physicians to perform FC/FGM. Danish Medical Women's Association provides information to medical professions on how to treat women who have undergone procedure.

France   Constitution guarantees equality of women to men and, especially to the child, protection of health.

There is no specific law outlawing FGM in France. From 1978 to 2003 more than 20 cases involving this practice have been successfully prosecuted under existing laws. This has included the conviction and imprisonment of persons performing the procedure as well as parents of girls subjected to it.

In 1983, the French high court recognized that FGM cases can be prosecuted under Article 312 of the Penal Code (comparable Article 222 of current Penal Code). This Article provides that acts of violence toward children that result in mutilation shall be tried in the highest criminal court (court d'assisses). The penalty is 10 to 20 years imprisonment.

The Medical Ethics Code (1979) forbids the practice of FGM by medical doctors except when it is medically required. The French Medical Board is not aware of any breaches of the Code.

The most recent case involving this practice occurred in February 1999. A Paris court sentenced a Malian woman, who had been practicing female circumcision for 15 years in France, to 8 years for cutting 48 girls between the ages of 1 month and 10 years. Twenty-seven mothers and fathers who solicited her services received suspended sentences of from 3 to 5 years. The case was brought by a victim, aged 23, who told a judge in 1995 that the woman had performed this procedure on her and her sisters when they were children.

Previous cases include a 1991 circumcision that resulted in a 5-year prison sentence and the 1983 imprisonment of a woman who performed the procedure on her daughter.

Since 1983 the government and private groups have undertaken a campaign to inform immigrants that this practice is contrary to the law and will be prosecuted. These groups include Groupes des Femmes pour l'Abolition des Mutilations Sexuelles, a group of African women in France who advise, support, and inform African women and families in France about the practice; Commission International pour l'Abolition des Mutilations Sexuelles, an associated member of UNICEF France that fights against this practice by creating educational materials for the African community in France and also provides legal services; Association Nationale des Medecins de Protection Matermelles et Infantiles, an association that provides advice and medical treatment for women and children; Prefecture d'lle de France, an organization concerned with women's rights in general with programs focused on FGM prevention; and Movement Francais pour le Planning Familial, which is also involved in this prevention campaign.

Code of Medical Deontology prohibits physicians from performing FC/FGM.

Germany

Constitution guarantees equality of all people. Recognizes the right to life and to physical integrity and provides the freedom of a person is inviolable.

German Penal Code considers FC/FGM serious and grave bodily harm. 1998 the Bundestag approved a motion that FC/FGM is a serious violation of human rights. 1999 Minister of Justice stated the need for police and prosecutors to become familiar with FC/FGM and investigate the practice.

1999 — reluctance of police to investigate.

1996 and 1997 German Medical Association condemned the participation of physicians in FC/FGM.

Italy

Constitution guarantees the equality of men and women without economic and social obstacles and the right to health; protects children and family and religious freedom.

No law criminalizing FC/FGM, but Penal Code's provisions covering personal injury could apply. Committee to address guidelines for professionals addressing FC/FGM. Reports that hospitals permit performing of FC/FGM to reduce risk.

1998–1999 enforcement information not available.

Netherlands

Constitution guarantees equality of women and men; health protection and religious freedom; right to inviolability of person with no prejudice or restrictions; government is to protect health and freedom of religion.

No law but Penal Code provisions are applicable to FC\FGM. 1993 government officially condemned the practice.

1998–1999 enforcement information not available.

Dutch health professionals believe physicians should not participate in the procedure.

New Zealand   Constitution protects individual rights and freedoms. Bill of rights guarantees equality of men and women, right to life, security of person, and rights of minority.

An amendment to the Crimes Amendment Act of New Zealand making FGM a crime was passed in 1995 and became effective on January 1, 1996. Punishment can result in imprisonment for up to 7 years.

1998 — no criminal investigations based on the law.

A National FGM Education Program was established to prevent the practice through community education, support, and health promotion. Guidelines have been established by this program and the New Zealand College of Obstetricians and Gynecologists for women who have undergone this procedure.

Child Protection Laws.

Norway   Constitution provides the State should respect and ensure human rights.

1995 — Norway enacted a law specifically criminalizing FC/FGM.

1998 — no prosecutions.

Child Protection Laws. Health Department provides funding for education and outreach.

No medical ethics provisions or guidelines.

Sweden   Constitution gives specific protections from discrimination, physical violations, and deprivation of liberty.

Sweden was the first Western European country to outlaw all forms of FGM in 1982. The 1982 law was revised in July 1998 to make the penalties more severe. The penalty is between 2 and 10 years imprisonment. In addition to the performance of the operation on a person being illegal under this law, attempts, preparations, conspiracy, and failure to report crimes are treated as criminal in accordance with Section 23 of the Penal Code.

The law also makes it clear that a person resident in Sweden who arranges for the procedure to be performed in another country can be sentenced in Sweden under the law even if the crime was committed abroad.

1998 — one arrest, but no information on the outcome available. No prosecutions.

In Sweden there are immigrant populations from countries where FGM is practiced including Somalia, Ethiopia, and Eritrea. The government of Sweden supports several education projects about this practice for professionals such as doctors, nurses, teachers, day care center staff, religious leaders, interpreters, social workers, and others who work with immigrants. A number of NGOs work within the immigrant communities to help individuals understand the harmful health consequences of these practices and the fact they are illegal in Sweden.

Child Protection Laws may view it as abuse. National Board of Health activities include prevention and assistance to those who have undergone it. Health professional guidelines exist to help those who have undergone the procedure and to inform parents of health risk and that it is prohibited by law.

United Kingdom

No constitution or bill of rights. Human Rights Act of 1998 (became fully effective Oct. 2000) incorporates European Convention on Human Rights into domestic law ensuring equality of men and women, right to liberty and security of person, right to respect private and family life, and freedom of religion. The United Kingdom's Prohibition of Female Circumcision Act of 1985 makes it an offense for any person to perform this procedure and for other persons to aid, abet, counsel, or procure the performance of these acts. A person guilty of an offense is liable to a fine or to imprisonment for a period not exceeding 5 years or to both.

1998 — no prosecutions. 1993 — a physician charged with contracting to perform FC/FGM. Not prosecuted due to lack of evidence.

The Department of Health has supported NGOs to carry out awareness campaigns about this practice. In 1993, a doctor who was charged with contracting to perform FGM was brought before the General Medical Council, found guilty of 7 charges of serious misconduct, and had his license suspended. The Crown Prosecution Service did not proceed with the prosecution of the case, citing lack of evidence.

United States

Constitution protects against deprivation of life, liberty, and property without due process and gives equal protection. The performance of FGM on a person under the age of 18 was made a crime in the United States under section 116 of the Illegal Immigration Reform and Immigrant Responsibility Act of 1996. (18 U.S.C.A. 116) The law, which was enacted September 30, 1996, provides in part that "whoever knowingly circumcises, excises or infibulates the whole or any part of the labia majora or labia minora or clitoris of another person who has not attained the age of 18 years shall be fined under this title or imprisoned not more than 5 years, or both." The law provides that no account shall be taken of the effect on the person on whom the operation is to be performed, of any belief on the part of that person, or any other person, that the operation is required as a matter of custom or ritual.

At the state level, 16 states have passed legislation outlawing this practice: California, Colorado, Delaware, Illinois, Maryland, Minnesota, Missouri, Nevada, New York, North Dakota, Oregon, Rhode Island, Tennessee, Texas, West Virginia, and Wisconsin.

1991 AMA resolution urged obstetric/gynecologists and urologic societies to develop educational material to address medically necessary modification of female genitalia. AMA policy condemns FC/FGM as a form of child abuse. 1995 American College of Obstetricians and Gynecologists opposed all forms. American Academy of Pediatrics opposed all forms.

Sources: Anika Rahman and Nahid Toubia (eds.). Female Genital Mutilation: A Guide to Laws and Policies Worldwide, *London: Zed Books in association with the Center for Reproductive Law and Policy and the Research, Action and Information Network for the Bodily Integrity of Women; New York: St. Martin's Press, 2000, 121–122, 135–137, 151–154, 159–162, 172–174, 186–189,190–195,*

203–205, 218–221, 231–235, 236–241; Harvard University. *"Laws of the World on Female Genital Mutilation." See* Belgium, South Africa. Available: *http://cyber.law.harvard.edu/population/fgm/fgm. htm; U.S. Department of State, Bureau of Public Affairs, "J. Laws in Countries Where Immigrants from Countries Practicing FGM Now Reside." Available: http://www.state.gov/g/wi/rls/rep/9304.htm. Accessed: Dec. 10, 2003 .*

Notes

PREFACE

1. Esther Kawira, M.D., F.A.A.F.P. (Medical Officer in Charge, Shirati Kanisa la Mennonite Tanzania Hospital, Shirati, Tanzania), interview by the author in Shirati, Tanzania, Jan. 23, 2004.

2. Rosemarie Skaine, *Power and Gender: Issues in Sexual Dominance and Harassment* (Jefferson, N.C.: McFarland, 1996).

3. Alice Walker and Pratibha Parmar, *Warrior Marks: Female Genital Mutilation and Sexual Blinding of Women,* (New York: Harcourt Brace & Co., 1993), 1st ed.3.

4. Walker and Parmar, 4.

5. Juliet Chugulu and Rachael Dixey, "Female Genital Mutilation in Moshi Rural District, Tanzania," *International Quarterly of Community Health Education* 19, no. 2 (1999–2000):103–104.

6. Nahid Toubia in Wanda K. Jones, Jack Smith, Burney Kieke, Jr., and Lynne Wilcox, "Female Genital Mutilation/Female Circumcision: Who Is at Risk in the U.S.," *Public Health Reports* 112, no. 5 (Sept. 1997):368, n6.

7. Amnesty International, "United Nations Initiatives," "Female Genital Mutilation," *Human Rights Information Pack,* 1998, Sec. 7. Available: http://www.amnesty.org/ailib/intcam/femgen/fgm7.htm. Accessed June 12, 2003.

8. Inter-Parliamentary Union, "Parliamentary Campaign 'Stop Violence Against Women': Female Genital Mutilation," June 11, 2003. Available: http://www.ipu.org/wmn-e/fgm-ref.htm. Accessed June 12, 2003.

9. Vanguard, "Nigeria: Rage Against Female Genital Mutilation," *Africa News,* Apr. 11, 2002.

10. Feminist Majority, "FC/FGM," Jun. 15, 2003. Available: http://www.crlp.org/ww_iss_fgm.html. Accessed Jun. 15, 2003.

11. Fran P. Hosken, *The Hosken Report: Genital and Sexual Mutilation of Females* (Lexington, Mass.: Women's International Network News, 1993), 4th rev. ed., 72.

12. Hosken, 72.

13. Peter Rogers, post, "Female Genital Mutilation," Jun. 29, 1996, Jun. 9, 2003, H-Africa Discussion Logs, H-Net, Humanities & Social Sciences OnLine.

14. Molefi Kete Asante, "The Afrocentric Idea," in Charles Lemert, ed., *Social Theory: The Multicultural and Classic Readings* (Boulder, Colo.: Westview Press, 1999), 504.

15. Stanlie M. James and Claire C. Robertson, "Introduction: Reimaging Transnational Sisterhood," in Stanlie M. James and Claire C. Robertson (eds.), *Genital Cutting and Transnational Sisterhood: Disputing U.S. Polemics* (Urbana: University of Illinois Press, 2002), 12–13.

16. Sheila Jeffreys, "'Body Art' and Social Status: Cutting, Tattooing and Piercing from a Feminist Perspective," *Feminism and Psychology* 10, no. 4 (2000): 409.

17. Fred E. Willmott, "Body Piercing: Lifestyle Indicator or Fashion Accessory?" *International Journal of STD and AIDS* 12 (2001):358.

18. Laura M. Koenig and Molly Carnes, "Body Piercing: Medical Concerns with Cutting-Edge Fashion," *Journal Of General Internal Medicine* 14 (June 1999):379.

19. Jeffreys, 409.

20. Jones *et. al.,* 368.

CHAPTER 1

1. Mrs. Berhane Ras-Work, President, Welcome Speech, Inter-African Committee on Traditional Practices, *Report of the International Conference on "Zero Tolerance to FGM,"* Feb. 4–6, 2003, Addis Ababa, Ethiopia, 120.

2. Nahid Toubia, *Female Genital Mutilation: A Call for Global Action* (New York: RAINBO, 1995), 2nd ed., 9.

3. Efua Dorkenoo, *Cutting the Rose: Female Genital Mutilation: the Practice and its Prevention* (London, UK: Minority Rights Group, 1994), 4.

4. Kathleen Sheldon (independent scholar with a research affiliation with the University of California at Los Angeles Center for the Study of Women), email to author Jun. 24, 2003; Stanlie M. James and Claire C. Robertson, "Introduction: Reimaging Transnational Sisterhood," in Stanlie M. James and Claire C. Robertson (eds.), *Genital Cutting and Transnational Sisterhood: Disputing U.S. Polemics* (Urbana: University of Illinois Press, 2002), 7–8.

5. James and Robertson, "Introduction: Reimaging Transnational Sisterhood," in James and Robertson (eds.), 7–8.

6. U.S. Department of Health and Human Services, Office of Women's Health, "Female Genital Cutting: Frequently Asked Questions: What are other terms used ...," Aug. 2001. Available: http://www.4woman.gov/faq/fgc.htm. Accessed: Jun. 29, 2004.

7. Anika Rahman and Nahid Toubia, eds., *Female Genital Mutilation: A Guide to Laws and Policies Worldwide* (New York: St. Martin's Press, 2000), 4.

8. Vanguard, "Nigeria; Rage Against Female Genital Mutilation," *Africa News*, Apr. 11, 2002.

9. World Health Organization, "Female Genital Mutilation," Fact Sheet No 241, Jun. 2000. Available: http://www.who.int/inf-fs/en/fact241.html. Accessed Jun. 18, 2003.

10. Edvige Bilotti, "The Practice of Female Genital Mutilation," n.d. Available: http://www.medmedia.org/review/numero3/en/art2.htm. Accessed Aug. 22, 2003.

11. Leonard J. Kouba and Judith Muasher, "Female Circumcision in Africa: An Overview," *African Studies Review* 28, no. 1, (March 1985):96.

12. World Health Organization, "Management of Pregnancy, Childbirth and the Postpartum Period in the Presence of Female Genital Mutilation," Report of a WHO Technical Consultation, Geneva WHO/FCH/GWH/01.2 and WHO/RHR/01.13 (Oct. 12–17, 1997), 4. Available: http://www.who.int/entity/gender/other_health/ manageofpregnan.pdf. Accessed Feb. 8, 2004.

13. Inter-African Committee, "What is Female Genital Mutilation?" July 2003. Available: http://www.iac-ciaf.ch/. Accessed Jun. 24, 2004.

14. Patroba E. Ondiek, Ph.D. (program co-ordinator of the nongovernmental organization, Save the Children of Tarime, Tarime, Tanzania), interview by the author in Tarime, Tanzania, Jan. 24, 2004.

15. Rachel Carnegie, *Things Change: A Resource Book for Working with Youth and Communities on Female Genital Cutting* (Cape Town, South Africa: Maskey Miller Longman and Nairobi, Kenya: United Nations Children's Fund, 2003), 12.

16. "Female Genital Cutting Practices in Burkina Faso and Mali," News Release, U.S. Population Council, Sept. 29, 1999. Available: http://www.popcouncil.org/mediacenter/newsreleases/sfp999(2).html. Accessed Feb. 2, 2004.

17. World Health Organization, *Female Genital Mutilation: A Teacher's Guide* (Geneva, WHO/FCH/GWH/01.3; WHO/RHR/01.16, 2001), 31. Available: www.who.int/frh-whd. Accessed Jun. 22, 2004.

18. Population Reference Bureau, *Abandoning Female Genital Cutting* (Washington, D.C.: Population Reference Bureau, Aug. 2001, Updated Apr. 2003), 16.

19. Carnegie, 12.

20. Fran P. Hosken, *The Hosken Report: Genital and Sexual Mutilation of Females* (Lexington, Mass.: Women's International Network News, 1993), 4th Rev. Ed., 114–115; Karen Hughes, "Note: The Criminalization of Female Genital Mutilation in the United States," 4 *Journal of Law and Policy* 322 (1995).

21. Dorkenoo, 9.

22. Population Reference Bureau, 16.

23. Dorkenoo, 8.

24. M. Neil Williams, M.D. (retired general surgeon and missionary physician, Cedar Falls, Ia.), interview by the author, Aug. 6, 2003; Kebwe Stephen Kebwe (District Medical Officer Bunda, Regional Chairman, Mara, Inter-African Committee, Tanzania), interview by the author in Bunda, Tanzania, Jan. 25, 2004; and Mary E. Laiser (Head of the Women's Department of the Arusha Diocese of the Evangelical Lutheran Church in Tanzania), "Female Genital Mutilation," report prepared for the author, Arusha, Tanzania: The Evangelical Church Diocese in Arusha Region, Women's Department, Jan. 2004.

25. Maasai Laibon and female village members (Mto Wa Mbu, Arusha, Tanzania), interview by the author, Jan. 18, 2004. Translated by James Emanuel Sichilma, Arusha, Tanzania.

26. Carnegie, 12.

27. Kebwe, interview, Jan. 25, 2004.

28. Carnegie, 12.

29. Head Teacher (Esilalei Primary School,

Mto Wa Mbu, Arusha, Tanzania), interview by the author, Jan. 16, 2004.

30. Aban Laamatjok (from Malakal in south Sudan, currently residing in Grand Island, Neb.), interview by the author and James C. Skaine in Grand Island, Neb., Aug. 30, 2003.

31. Laura Reymond, Asha Mohamud, and Nancy Ali, *Female Genital Mutilation — The Facts* (Washington D.C.: Program for Appropriate Technology in Health, July 25, 2003). Available: http://www.path.org/files/FGM-The-Facts.htm. Accessed Apr. 29, 2004.

32. Rahman and Toubia (eds.), 6.

33. Hanny Lightfoot-Klein, *Prisoners of Ritual: An Odyssey into Female Genital Circumcision in Africa* (New York: Haworth Press, 1989), 27.

34. Philo (d.54), *Questions and Answers on Genesis*, Book III, translated by Marcus (Cambridge, Mass.: Harvard University Press, 1979), 47 in Sami Awad Aldeeb Abu-Sahlieh, *Male and Female Circumcision: among Jews, Christians and Muslims: Religious, Medical, Social and Legal Debate* (Warren Center, Pa.: Shangri-La Publications, 2001), 66.

35. Maurice As'ad, *Al-asl al-usturi li-khitan al-inath fi al-usur al-far'uniyyah* (Cairo: without publisher, 1005), 55–56, in Abu-Sahlieh, 66.

36. Hosken, 74, in Abu-Sahlieh, 66.

37. Lightfoot-Klein, 28.

38. Lightfoot-Klein, 28–29.

39. Bettina Shell-Duncan and Ylva Hernlund, "Female 'Circumcision' in Africa: Dimensions of the Practice and Debates," in Bettina Shell-Duncan and Ylva Hernlund (eds.), *Female "Circumcision" in Africa: Culture, Controversy, and Change.* (Boulder, Colo.: Lynne Rienner Publishers, 2000), 18.

40. Lightfoot-Klein, 28.

41. Nawal M. Nour, "Female Genital Cutting: A Need for Reform," Editorial, *Obstetrics and Gynecology* 101, no. 5, Part 2 (May 2003): 1051.

42. World Health Organization, *A Teacher's Guide*, 37–38.

43. World Health Organization, *A Teacher's Guide*, 37–38.

44. Rahman and Toubia (eds.), 5–6.

45. Laurenti Magesa, *African Religion: The Moral Traditions of Abundant Life* (Maryknoll, N.Y.: Orbis Books, 1997), 98.

46. Magesa, 99, 100.

47. Jomo Kenyatta, *Facing Mount Kenya: the Tribal Life of the Gikuyu* (London: Secker and Warburg, 1991), 145–146, in Magesa, 99, 100.

48. Magesa, 100.

49. Magesa, 101.

50. Magesa, 102.

51. Magesa, 103.

52. Esther Kawira, M.D., F.A.A.F.P. (Medical Officer in Charge, Shirati Kanisa la Mennonite, Tanzania Hospital, Shirati, Tanzania), interview by the author in Shirati, Tanzania, Jan. 23, 2004.

53. Esther Kawira, email to the author, Sept. 25, 2003.

54. Esther Kawira, email to the author, Mar. 5, 2003.

55. Esther Kawira, email to the author, Mar. 5, 2003.

56. Emmanuel Babatunde, *Women's Rites Versus Women's Rights: A Study of Circumcision Among the Ketu Yoruba of South Western Nigeria* (Trenton, N.J.: Africa World Press, 1997), 180.

57. Colleen Renk Zengotitabengoa, M.A., J.D. (staff attorney, Tahirih Justice Center, Falls Church, VA), interview by the author at the Tahirih Justice Center, Falls Church, VA, March 22, 2004.

58. Laiser, report, 4.

59. Laiser, report, 3.

60. Cindy M. Little, "Female Genital Circumcision: Medical and Cultural Considerations," *Journal of Cultural Diversity* 10, no. 1 (Spring 2003):32.

61. Mary E. Laiser interview by the author and James C. Skaine in Arusha, Tanzania, Jan. 15, 2004.

62. Laiser interview, Jan. 15, 2004.

63. Kawira interview, Jan. 23, 2004.

64. Sylvie Epelboin and Alain Epelboin, "Special Report: Female Circumcision," *People* (June 1, 1979):28 in Leonard J. Kouba and Judith Muasher, "Female Circumcision in Africa: An Overview," *African Studies Review* 28, no. 1, (March 1985): 103.

65. Kebwe interview, Jan. 25, 2004.

66. Kebwe interview, Jan. 25, 2004.

67. Kebwe interview, Jan. 25, 2004.

68. Kebwe interview, Jan. 25, 2004.

69. John Wachira, M.D. (urologist and member of the African Medical Research Foundation Flying Doctor Surgical Outreach Program), interview by Esther Kawira for the author, in Shirati, Tanzania, Mar. 19, 2004.

70. Dorkenoo, 2,3.

71. U.S. Agency for International Development, Office of Women in Development, "Female Genital Mutilation Information Bulletin," March 1997. Available: http://www.usaid.gov/wid/pubs/fgm97.htm. Accessed September 20, 2003.

72. Reymond, *et al.*, *Female Genital Mutilation — The Facts.*

73. Bettina Shell-Duncan and Ylva Hernlund, "Female 'Circumcision' in Africa: Di-

mensions of the Practice and Debates," in Bettina Shell-Duncan and Ylva Hernlund (eds.), *Female 'Circumcision' in Africa: Culture, Controversy, and Change* (Boulder, Colo.: Lynne Rienner, 2000), 14–17.

74. Charles Henry Sweke, M.D., C.I. Ord., Ph.D. (consultant obstetrician/gynecologist, Selian Lutheran Hospital, Arusha, Tanzania), interview by the author in Arusha, Tanzania, Jan. 15, 2004.

75. Laiser interview, Jan. 15, 2004.

76. Laiser interview, Jan. 15, 2004.

77. Kawira interview, Jan. 23, 2004.

78. United States Agency for International Development, FGM Information Bulletin.

79. World Health Organization, Fact Sheet No 241.

80. Nour, 1051.

81. World Health Organization, "Management of Pregnancy," 9.

82. Williams interview, Aug. 6, 2003.

83. Williams interview, Aug. 6, 2003.

84. Williams interview, Aug. 6, 2003.

85. Williams interview, Aug. 6, 2003.

86. Williams interview, Aug. 6, 2003.

87. Mohamed Amin, Duncan Willetts, and John Eames, *The Last of the Maasai* (Nairobi, Kenya: Camerapix Publishers International, 1987, Second Impression, 1988), 166.

88. Amna A.R. Hassan, "Sudan, Summary on the Impacts of the Research on: FGM Psycho-social-sexual Consequences and Attitudinal Change in N. Khartoum and E. Nile," *Inter-African Committee on Traditional Practices Affecting the Health of Women and Children*, Newsletter No. 28, Dec. 2000, 6.

89. World Health Organization, Fact Sheet No. 241.

90. Laura Reymond, Asha Mohamud, Nancy Ali, Kalle Makalou, and Zohra Yakoub, *The Facts: Female Genital Mutilation* (Washington, D.C.: Program for Appropriate Technology in Health, Dec. 1997), 3.

91. RAINBO African Immigrant Program, *Female Circumcision and Women's Health*, a brochure, 1999, 9, 10, 11.

92. World Health Organization, *A Teacher's Guide*, 38.

93. World Health Organization, Fact Sheet No. 241.

94. Laiser interview, Jan. 15, 2004.

95. Laiser interview, Jan. 15, 2004.

96. Hulda (employee, Women's Department of the Arusha Diocese of the Evangelical Lutheran Church in Tanzania), interview by the author and James C. Skaine in Arusha, Tanzania, Jan. 15, 2004.

97. Lisa Johnson-Firth, L.L.B., J.D. (Director of Legal Services, Tahirih Justice Center, Falls Church, VA), interview by the author at the Tahirih Justice Center, Falls Church, VA, March 22, 2004.

98. Laiser, report, 3.

99. Hulda interview, Jan. 15, 2004.

100. Laiser, report, 3.

101. Wachira interview with Kawira, Mar. 19, 2004.

102. Kawira interview, Jan. 23, 2004.

103. Kawira interview, Jan. 23, 2004.

104. Kawira interview, Jan. 23, 2004.

105. Kawira interview, Jan. 23, 2004.

106. Population Reference Bureau, 3.

107. Mairo Usman Mandara, "Female Genital Cutting in Nigeria: Views of Nigerian Doctors on the Medicalization Debate," in Shell-Duncan and Hernlund (eds.), 96.

108. Mandara, in Shell-Duncan and Hernlund (eds.), 105–106.

109. World Health Organization, "Preventing Medicalization," Apr. 12, 1994. Available: http://www.who.int/docstore/frh-whd/FGM/infopack/English/fgm_infopack.htm. Accessed May 6, 2004.

110. World Health Organization, *A Teacher's Guide*, 37.

111. Kawira, email to author, Mar. 6, 2003.

112. Wachira interview with Esther Kawira, Mar. 19, 2004.

113. Nawal M. Nour, "Female Circumcision and Genital Mutilation: A Practical and Sensitive Approach," *Contemporary OB/GYN Archive*, Mar. 1, 2000. Available: http://obgyn.pdr.net/be_core/search/show_article_search.jsp?searchurl=/be_core/content/jou.... Accessed Feb. 4, 2004.

114. Reymond *et al.*, *Female Genital Mutilation — The Facts*.

115. Wachira interview with Kawira, Mar. 19, 2004.

116. Sweke interview, Jan. 15, 2004.

117. Laiser, report, 4.

CHAPTER 2

1. Feminist.com, "Inspiring Quotes," 1995–2004. Available: http://www.feminist.com/resources/quotes/index.html. Accessed June 19, 2004.

2. World Health Organization, "Female Genital Mutilation," Fact Sheet No 241, June 2000. Available: http://www.who.int/inf-fs/en/fact241.html Accessed June 18, 2003; United Nations, *The World's Women 2000: Trends and Statistics* (New York: United Nations, 2000), 159.

3. Rachel Carnegie, *Things Change: A Resource Book for Working with Youth and Communities on Female Genital Cutting* (Cape Town, South Africa: Maskey Miller Longman

and Nairobi, Kenya: United Nations Children's Fund, 2003), 13; U.S. Department of State, "Prevalence of the Practice of Female Genital Mutilation (FGM); Laws Prohibiting FGM and Their Enforcement; Recommendations on How to Best Work to Eliminate FGM," *Report on Female Genital Mutilation* as required by Conference Report (H. Rept. 106–997) to Public Law 106–429 (Foreign Operations, Export Financing, and Related Programs Appropriations Act, 2001). Available: http://www.state.gov/documents/organization/9424.pdf. Accessed June 8, 2004.

4. World Health Organization, Fact Sheet No 241; United Nations, *The World's Women 2000*, 159.

5. World Health Organization, "Management of Pregnancy, Childbirth and the Postpartum Period in the Presence of Female Genital Mutilation," Report of a WHO Technical Consultation, Geneva WHO/FCH/GWH/01.2 and WHO/RHR/01.13 (Oct. 12–17, 1997). Available: http://www.who.int/entity/gender/other_health/manageofpregnan.pdf. Accessed Feb. 8, 2004.

6. Amnesty International, "What Is Female Genital Mutilation," and "Geographical Distribution of Female Genital Mutilation," *Human Rights Information Pack*, Sec. 1, 1997. Available: http://www.amnesty.org/ailib/intcam/femgen/fgm1.htm#a3. Accessed Mar. 9, 2004.

7. U.S. Department of State, Office of the Senior Coordinator for International Women's Issues, Office of the Under Secretary for Global Affairs, Feb. 1, 2001, K. Chart. Updated June 27, 2001. Available: http://www.state.gov/g/wi/rls/rep/9305.htm. Accessed Dec. 7, 2003.

8. U.S. Department of State, Bureau of Public Affairs, "Country Prevalence of FGM," Mar. 12, 2004. Available: http://www.state.gov/g/wi/rls/rep/9276.htm. Accessed Mar. 12, 2004.

9. Matthew Moore and Karuni Rompies, "In the Cut," *Sydney Morning Herald*, Jan. 13, 2004. Available: http://www.cirp.org/news/smho1-13-04/. Accessed July 20, 2004.

10. Population Council, Jakarta, "Research Report Female Circumcision in Indonesia: Extent, Implications, and Possible Interventions to Uphold Women's Health Rights," Jakarta, Indonesia, Sept. 2003. Available: http://www.dec.org.pdf_docs/PNACU138.pdf. Accessed July 20, 2004.

11. Population Council, Jakarta, Research Report.

12. Population Council, Jakarta, Research Report.

13. Moore and Rompies.

14. U.S. Department of State, "Country Prevalence of FGM."

15. Center for Reproductive Rights, "Female Circumcision/Female Genital Mutilation," Mar. 12, 2004. Available: http://www.crlp.org/ww_iss_fgm.html. Accessed Mar. 12, 2004,

16. World Health Organization, Fact Sheet No 241; United Nations, *The World's Women 2000*, 159.

17. Center for Reproductive Rights, "FC\ FGM: Legal Prohibitions World Wide," June 2003, Item: F027. Available: http://www.crlp.org/pub_fac_fgmicpd.html. Accessed Dec. 4, 2003.

18. CRLP, Item: F027.

19. "Women's Health: Female Genital Mutilation: Common, Controversial, and Bad for Women's Health," *Population Briefs*, 3, no. 2, (Jun. 1997). Available: http://www.popcouncil.org/publications/popbriefs/pb3(2)_1.html. Accessed June 19, 2003.

20. "Women's Health."

21. "Women's Health."

22. "Women's Health."

23. Population Reference Bureau, *Abandoning Female Genital Cutting* (Washington, D.C.: Population Reference Bureau, Aug. 2001, Updated Apr. 2003), 12.

24. Population Reference Bureau, 12.

25. Population Reference Bureau, 13.

26. Population Reference Bureau, 13.

27. ORC Macro, MEASURE DHS+ STATcompiler, 2003. Available: http://www.measuredhs.com. Accessed Dec. 18 2003.

28. Population Reference Bureau, 16.

29. Population Reference Bureau, 14.

30. Population Reference Bureau, 14.

31. Population Reference Bureau, 15.

32. Anika Rahman and Nahid Toubia (eds.), *Female Genital Mutilation: A Guide to Laws and Policies Worldwide* (New York: St. Martin's Press, 2000), 7.

33. U.S. Department of State, Bureau of Public Affairs, Office of the Senior Coordinator for International Women's Issues, "Female Genital Mutilation (FGM) or Female Genital Cutting (FGC): Individual Country Reports," June 1, 2001. Available: http://www.state.gov/g/wi/rls/rep/crfgm/. Accessed Dec. 11, 2003.

34. Rahman and Toubia (eds.), 104, 121, 136, 152–153, 160–161, 174, 188, 192, 204, 219, 233, 237; U.S. Department of State, Bureau of Public Affairs, "J. Laws in Countries Where Immigrants from Countries Practicing FGM Now Reside," 7. Available: http://www.state.gov/g/wi/rls/rep/9304.htm. Accessed Dec. 10, 2003.

35. U.S. Department of State, "J. Laws in Countries."

36. Afrol.com, "Europe Impotent in Fighting Female Mutilation Among African Women," afrol.com, Nov. 30, 2000. Available: http://www.afrol.com/Categories/women/Women/wom015_fgm_europe2.htm. Accessed Dec. 9, 2004.

37. Rahman and Toubia (eds.), 7.

38. Nahid Toubia, *A Technical Manual for Health Care Providers: Caring for Women with Circumcision* (New York: RAINBO, 1999), 26.

39. Toubia, 28.

40. Joe Costan (demographer, U.S. Census Bureau), telephone conversation, July 9, 2004.

41. United Nations *The World's Women 2000*, 161.

42. United Nations *The World's Women 2000*, 163.

43. United Nations *The World's Women 2000*, 161.

44. United Nations *The World's Women 2000*, 162.

45. Costan telephone conversation, July 9, 2004.

46. Nancy Rytina (U.S. Citizenship and Immigrations Services Office of Immigration Statistics), email to the author, July 16, 2004.

47. Gayle Smith (U.S. Office of Refugee Resettlement, Division Director for Budget, Policy and Data Analysis), email to the author, July 20, 2004.

48. Communicating for Change, *Uncut, Playing With Life, A Film about Female Genital Mutilation Background Information*, 2002. Available: http://cfcnigeria.org/CONTENT/uncut/backgroundinfo.*htm*. Accessed Dec. 7, 2003.

49. World Health Organization, Fact Sheet No 241.

50. Janice Boddy, *Wombs and Alien Spirits: Women, Men and the Zar Cult in Northern Sudan* (Madison, Wis.: University of Wisconsin Press, 1989), 47–75, 100–6.

51. Raqiya Haji Dualeh Abdalla, *Sisters in Affliction: Circumcision and Infibulation of Women in Africa* (New York: Zed, 1982), 10.

52. U.S. Department of State, K. Chart.

53. U.S. Department of State, K. Chart.

54. Amnesty International, "Female Genital Mutilation in Africa: Information by Country, Country Estimate, Percent of Women and Girls Who Undergo FGM, Type of FGM, Practised Female Genital Mutilation," *Human Rights Information Pack*, Sec. 9. Available: http://www.amnesty.org/ailib/intcam/femgen/fgm9.ht*m*. Accessed Jun. 12, 2003.

55. Dara Carr, *Female Genital Mutilation*, Calverton, Md.: Macro International, 1997 in United Nations, *The World's Women 2000*, 161.

56. UNICEF, "Workshop on FGM — The Way Forward," Report "Draft + Comments," Sept. 30–Oct. 2, 2003, given to author at UNICEF, Nairobi, Kenya, Jan. 13, 2004, 4.

57. UNICEF, "Draft + Comments," 4.

58. Nigeria Demographic and Health Survey, 2003, 201.

59. Nigeria Demographic and Health Survey, 2003, 202.

60. Nigeria Demographic and Health Survey, 2003, 203.

61. Nigeria Demographic and Health Survey, 2003, 205.

62. Nigeria Demographic and Health Survey, 2003, 206.

63. Nigeria Demographic and Health Survey, 2003, 207.

64. Nigeria Demographic and Health Survey, 2003, 208.

65. U.S. Congress, Conference report to accompany H. R. 3019, 104–537, § 520 (1996) in Wanda K. Jones, Jack Smith, Burney Kieke Jr., and Lynne Wilcox, "Female Genital Mutilation/Female Circumcision: Who Is at Risk in the U.S.," *Public Health Reports*, 112 no. 5 (Sept. 1997):368.

66. Jones et al., 368.

67. Jones et al., 368.

68. Jones et al., 368.

69. Jones et al., 368.

70. Jones et al., 368.

71. Jones et al., 368.

72. Carnegie, 55.

73. Carnegie, 49.

74. Population Reference Bureau, 8.

75. United Nations Children's Fund, "Draft + Comments," 5

CHAPTER 3

1. William G. Riek (President, Sudanese Refugee Community Organization and Refugee Advocate, Community Humanitarian Resource Center, Refugee Center, Grand Island, Neb.), interview by the author and James C. Skaine, Aug. 29, 2003.

2. Jessica A. Platt, "Note: Female Circumcision: Religious Practice v. Human Rights Violation," 3 *Rutgers Journal of Law and Religion* 3 (2001/2002).

3. Bettina Shell-Duncan and Ylva Hernlund, "Female 'Circumcision' in Africa: Dimensions of the Practice and Debates," in Bettina Shell-Duncan and Ylva Hernlund (eds.), *Female 'Circumcision' in Africa: Culture, Controversy, and Change* (Boulder, Colo.: Lynne Rienner, 2000), 2.

4. Christine J. Walley, "Feminism, Anthropology, and Global Debate," in Stanlie M.

James and Claire C. Robertson (eds.), *Genital Cutting and Transnational Sisterhood: Disputing U.S. Polemics* (Urbana: University of Illinois Press, 2002), 44.

5. Nyarieka Ruey (from Miywut in south Sudan, currently residing in Grand Island, Neb.), interview by the author and James C. Skaine, Aug. 31, 2003.

6. Mut Ruey (from Miywut in south Sudan, currently residing in Grand Island, Neb.), interview by the author and James C. Skaine, Aug. 31, 2003.

7. Laura Reymond, Asha Mohamud, and Nancy Ali, *Female Genital Mutilation—The Facts* (Washington D.C.: Program for Appropriate Technology in Health, July 25, 2003). Available: http://www.path.org/files/FGM-The-Facts.htm. Accessed Apr. 29, 2004.

8. Reymond, et al.

9. Susan Waltz, "Reclaiming and Rebuilding the History of the Universal Declaration of Human Rights," *Third World Quarterly* 23, no. 3 (2002):446.

10. Amnesty International, "United Nations Initiatives," "Female Genital Mutilation," *Human Rights Information Pack*, Sec. 7, 1998. Available: http://www.amnesty.org/ailib/intcam/femgen/fgm7.htm. Accessed Jun. 12, 2003.

11. Waltz, 446.

12. United Nations Blue Book Series, *The United Nations and Human Rights 1945–1995*, 5 (1995) at 24 in Platt, n63.

13. United Nations Blue Book Series, at 25 in Platt, n64.

14. United Nations Blue Book Series, at 25 in Platt, n65.

15. United Nations International Covenant on Civil and Political Rights, 999 U.N.T.S. 171 (1976).

16. United Nations Convention on the Elimination of All Forms of Discrimination Against Women, U.N. GA Res. 34/180 (1979).

17. United Nations Convention on the Elimination of All Forms of Discrimination Against Women, GA General Recommendation 19, Violence Against Women, A/47/38, Chapter I (1992).

18. United Nations Convention on the Rights of the Child, Nov. 20, 1989, GA Res. 44/25, 28 ILM 1448 (1989) (into force Sept. 2, 1990), in Platt, 3, n66.

19. Anika Rahman and Nahid Toubia (eds.), *Female Genital Mutilation: A Guide to Laws and Policies Worldwide* (New York: St. Martin's Press, 2000), 18.

20. Rachel Carnegie, *Things Change: A Resource Book for Working with Youth and Communities on Female Genital Cutting* (Cape Town, South Africa: Maskey Miller Longman and Nairobi, Kenya: United Nations Children's Fund, 2003), 50.

21. Rahman and Toubia, 20.

22. Rahman and Toubia, 19–20.

23. Carnegie, 49.

24. Rahman and Toubia, 17.

25. United Nations International Covenant of Civil and Political Rights.

26. United Nations Convention on the Elimination of All Forms of Discrimination Against Women.

27. United Nations Committee on the Elimination of All Forms of Discrimination Against Women.

28. United Nations Convention on the Rights of the Child.

29. United States Agency for International Development: WID Publication: "Female Genital Mutilation," Information Bulletin, March 1997. Available: http://www.usaid.gov/wid/pubs/fgm97.htm. Accessed Sept. 20, 2003.

30. United Nations Convention on the Rights of the Child, Articles 24.3. Available: http://www.unhchr.ch/html/menu3/b/k2crc.htm. Accessed Feb. 17, 2004.

31. United Nations Declaration on the Elimination of Violence Against Women, U.N. OHCHR (GA Res. 48/104, Dec. 20, 1993) (Feb. 23, 1994, Article 2(a)). Available: http://www.unhchr.ch/huridocda/huridoca.nsf/(Symbol)/A.RES.48.104.En?Opendocument. Accessed Feb. 19, 2004.

32. United States Agency for International Development: WID Publication: "Female Genital Mutilation."

33. United Nations Fourth World Conference on Women, Beijing Declaration (Sept. 4–15, 1995) (1 U.N. Doc. DPI/1766/Wom., 1996), Paragraph 118. Available: http://www.un.org/womenwatch/daw/beijing/platform/declar.htm. Accessed Feb. 19, 2004.

34. United Nations Population Information Network, United Nations Population Division, Department of Economic and Social Affairs, with support from the United Nations Population Fund (Sept. 5–13, 1994), A/CONF.171/13: Report of the ICPD (94/10/18) (385k), (Oct. 18, 1994), Paragraph 4.22. Available: http://www.un.org/popin/icpd/conference/offeng/poa.html. Accessed Feb. 17, 2004.

35. United States Agency for International Development: WID Publication: "Female Genital Mutilation."

36. United Nations Fourth World Conference on Women, Beijing Declaration, Paragraph 124.I.

37. Carnegie, 49, 50; and Rahman and Toubia, 15–16, 18–19.

38. 18 U.S.C., § 116, 2000, *West* 2004.

39. Shell-Duncan and Hernlund, "Female

'Circumcision' in Africa" in Shell-Duncan and Hernlund (eds.), 2.

40. Feminist Majority, "Female Circumcision/Female Genital Mutilation (FC/FGM): Global Laws and Policies Towards Elimination," Item: F027, Nov. 2000. Available: http://www.crlp.org/pub_fac_fgmicpd.html. Accessed Jun. 15, 2003.

41. Susan Izett and Nahid Toubia, *Using Female Circumcision as a Case Study: Learning About Social Change* (New York: RAINBO, 1999), 22.

42. Izett and Toubia, 22.

43. Feminist Majority, "Female Circumcision/Female Genital Mutilation."

44. Population Reference Bureau, *Abandoning Female Genital Cutting* (Washington, D.C.: Population Reference Bureau, Aug. 2001, Updated Apr. 2003), 5.

45. Feminist Majority, "Female Circumcision/Female Genital Mutilation."

46. FGC Education and Networking Project, "Summaries of the Laws of Some African Countries," 2003. Available: http://www.fgmnetwork.org/legisl/interntl/africa.html#Burkina%20Faso. Accessed May 6, 2004.

47. Burkina Faso, Law No. 43/96/ADP, November 13, 1996, Penal Code Articles 380–382; Egypt, Order No. 261, July 8, 1996 of the Minister of Health and Population; Ivory Coast, Law No. 98–757, Dec. 23, 1998 on the repression of certain forms of violence against women; Madagascar, Decree No. 98–945, Dec. 4, 1998 setting forth the Code of Medical Ethics (Article 39); South Africa, Promotion of Equality and Prevention of Unfair Discrimination Act, 2000 (Act No. 4 of 2000) (Section 8); Uganda, The Children Statute 1996 (Statute No. 6 of 1996) (Section 8) and Constitution of the Republic of Uganda, Sept. 22, 1995 (Article 33), "Laws of the World," Harvard Univ. Cyberlaw. Available: http://cyber.law.harvard.edu/population/fgm/fgm.htm. Accessed July 2, 2004.

48. Feminist Majority, "Female Circumcision/Female Genital Mutilation."

49. Center for Reproductive Rights, "Female Circumcision/Female Genital Mutilation (FC/FGM): Legal Prohibitions Worldwide," Item: F027, June 2003. Available: http://www.crlp.org/pub_fac_fgmicpd.html. Accessed Dec. 6, 2003.

50. Fareda Banda, "National Legislation Against Female Genital Mutilation," Eschborn/Germany, Executive Summary, May 2003, 16. Available: http://www.gtz.de/fgm/downloads/fgm-law-long%2016-05–03.pdf. Accessed Apr. 2, 2004.

51. Female Genital Cutting Education and Networking Project, "Summaries."

52. Female Genital Cutting Education and Networking Project, "Summaries."

53. Female Genital Cutting Education and Networking Project, "Summaries."

54. Female Genital Cutting Education and Networking Project, "Summaries."

55. Banda, 23.

56. U.S. Department of State, Office of the Senior Coordinator for International Women's Issues, Office of the Under Secretary for Global Affairs, Feb. 1, 2001, K. Chart. Updated June 27, 2001. Available: http://www.state.gov/g/wi/rls/rep/9305.htm. Accessed Dec. 7, 2003.

57. U.S. Department of State, K. Chart.

58. U.S. Department of State, Bureau of Democracy, Human Rights, and Labor, "Oman," "UAE," "Country Reports on Human Rights Practices," Feb. 25, 2004. Available: http://www.state.gov/g/drl/rls/hrrpt/2003/27935 and 27940.htm. Accessed July 25, 2004.

59. Amnesty International, "What Is Female Genital Mutilation," "Geographical Distribution of Female Genital Mutilation," *Human Rights Information Pack*, Sec. 1, 1997. Available: http://www.amnesty.org/ailib/intcam/femgen/fgm1.htm#a3. Accessed Mar. 9, 2004.

60. Inter-Parliamentary Union, "Female Genital Mutilation: India, Indonesia, Ireland, Israel, Italy, Kenya, Lesotho, Liberia, Libyan Arab Jamahiriya, Luxembourg," Mar. 12, 2004. Available: http://www.ipu.org/wmn-e/fgm-prov-i.htm. Accessed Mar. 12, 2004.

61. Inter-Parliamentary Union, "Female Genital Mutilation."

62. Matthew Moore and Karuni Rompies, "In the Cut," *Sydney Morning Herald*, Jan. 13, 2004. Available: http://www.cirp.org/news/smho1-13-04/. Accessed July 20, 2004.

63. Inter-Parliamentary Union, "Female Genital Mutilation: Madagascar, Malawi, Malaysia, Mali, Mauritania, Mauritius, Mexico, Morocco, Mozambique," Mar. 12, 2004. Available: http://www.ipu.org/wmn-e/fgm-prov-m.htm. Accessed Mar. 12, 2004.

64. Center for Reproductive Rights, "The Power of Law for Every Woman," July 8, 2004. Available: http://www.crlp.org/pub_fac_fgmicpd.html. Accessed July 8, 2004.

65. FGC Education and Networking Project, "Australian Laws," 2003. Available: http://www.fgmnetwork.org/legisl/interntl/austral.*html*. Accessed May 6, 2004.

66. Rahman and Toubia, 133, 160, 173, 187, 191, 203, 232.

67. *Agence Fr. Presse*, Feb. 1, 2004.

68. Rahman and Toubia, 133, 160, 173, 187, 191, 203, 232.

69. "Dutch PvdA Calls for Law Exception

for FGM on Girls from Certain Regions," *Dutch News Digest*, Jan. 30, 2004.

70. Rahman and Toubia, 133, 160, 173, 187, 191, 203, 232.

71. FGC Education and Networking Project, "United Kingdom Prohibition of Female Circumcision Act 1985," 2003. Available: http://www.fgmnetwork.org/legisl/internatl/britcan..html. Accessed May 7, 2004.

72. Holly Maguigan, "Redefining Violence Against Women Symposium: Will Prosecutions for 'Female Genital Mutilation' Stop the Practice in the U.S.?" 8 *Temple Political and Civil Rights Law Review* 400, n95, n97, n98 (Spring 1999).

73. Rahman and Toubia, 102–103, 219.

74. Nahid Toubia, *A Technical Manual for Health Care Providers: Caring for Women with Circumcision* (New York: RAINBO, 1999), 9.

75. France, Decree No. 95–1000, Sept. 6, 1995, setting forth the Code of Medical Ethics (Article 41), "Laws of the World," Harvard Univ. Cyberlaw.

76. Feminist Majority, "Female Circumcision/Female Genital Mutilation."; "Female Circumcision/Female Genital Mutilation."

77. Maguigan, 400.

78. Maguigan, 402.

79. Feminist Majority, "Female Circumcision/Female Genital Mutilation"; "CRR," "Female Circumcision/Female Genital Mutilation."

80. Paul Webster, "Paris Court Convicts Mother of Genital Mutilation," *Observer*, Feb. 1, 2004, 25.

81. Canada, Department of Justice, Jan. 20, 2004, Annual Statute, Ch. 16 (Bill-27), An Act to Amend the Criminal Code, § 268(3)(a)(b) and (4), (assented to Apr. 25, 1997). Available: http://laws.justice.gc.ca/en/1997/16/5277.html. Accessed Feb. 24, 2004.

82. Rahman and Toubia, 120–121.

83. Female Genital Cutting Education and Networking Project, "Legislation Notes on Some Overseas Countries' Laws: Canada," 2003. Available: http://www.fgmnetwork.org/legisl/interntl/britcan.html#Canada. Accessed May 7, 2004.

84. Toubia, 10, 11.

85. Maguigan, 397.

86. Faiza Jama Mohamed (ed.), "United States," Africa Regional: Equality Now, *Awaken* 7, no. 2 (Sept. 2003): News.

87. Karen Hughes, "Note: The Criminalization of Female Genital Mutilation in the United States," 4 *Journal of Law and Policy* 324 (1995).

88. U.S. Department of State, Bureau of Public Affairs, "J. Laws in Countries Where Immigrants from Countries Practicing FGM Now Reside." Available: http://www.state.gov /g/wi/rls/rep/9304.htm. Accessed Dec. 10, 2003.

89. U.S. Department of State, "J. Laws."

90. Lisa Johnson-Firth (Director of Legal Services, Tahirih Justice Center, Falls Church, VA), "The Global Dilemma of FGC," presentation to Zonta International, Feb. 9, 2004, 10.

91. Johnson-Firth, "The Global Dilemma of FGC," 10; *see also* "Couple Indicted on Mutilation Charges," *Los Angeles Times*, Feb. 7, 2004, Home Ed., B4.

92. "Female Genital Mutilation: California Couple Charged with Agreeing to Circumcise Young Girls," *Women's Health Weekly* via NewsRx.com and NewsRx.net, Feb. 5, 2004, Sec: Expanded Reporting; 55.

93. Nawal M. Nour, "Remarks," USAID Health, Population, FGC, "FGC Zero Tolerance Day, Congressional Briefing," Washington, DC, Feb. 6, 2004, Apr. 22, 2004. Available: http://www.usaid.gov/our_work/global_health /pop/news/fgcday.html. Accessed May 24, 2004.

94. Nour, "Remarks."

95. Riek interview, May 29, 2004, and email, June 30, 2004.

96. Patroba E. Ondiek, Ph.D. (Program Coordinator of the nongovernmental organization, Save the Children of Tarime, Tarime, Tanzania), interview by the author in Tarime, Tanzania, Jan. 24, 2004.

97. Center for Reproductive Rights, "Female Circumcision/Female Genital Mutilation"; and U.S. Department of Health and Human Services, Office of Women's Health, "Female Genital Cutting: Frequently Asked Questions: What are other terms used ...," Aug. 2001. Available: http://www.4woman.gov/faq/fgc.htm. Accessed June 29, 2004.

98. Calif. Penal Code § 273.4, *West's* Ann. Calif. Penal Code; Calif. Health and Safety Code D. 106, Pt. 2, Ch. 3, Art 8, Refs and Annos and § 124170, *West's* Ann. Calif. Health and Safety Code; "State of Calif. Bill Text Statement Calif. 1995–96 Regular Session Assembly Bill 2125," FGC and Networking Project, Legis., 2003. Available: http://www.fgmnetwork.org/legisl/US/caab2125.htm. Accessed Feb. 4, 2004.

99. Colo. Legis. 216 (1999), 1999 Colo. Legis. Serv. Ch. 216 (S.B. 99–96) *West*, 2004; Colo. State § 25–30–101, *West's Colo. Rev. Statutes Annotated*, 2004; "State of Colo. A Bill for An Act Concerning Female Genital Mutilation, Senate Bill 96–031 (not passed)," FGC Education and Networking Project, Legis., 2003. Available: http://www.fgmnetwork.org /legisl/US/colo031.html. Accessed: Feb. 4, 2004.

100. Del. State TI 11 § 780, *Del. Code Annotated, West's*, 2004; and "Del. State Senate

138th General Assembly, Bill No. 393, May 14, 1996," FGC Education and Networking Project, Legis., 2003. Available: http://fgmnetwork.org/legisl/US/desb393.html. Accessed Feb. 4, 2004.

101. Ill. State CH 325 § 5/3 and CH 720 § 5/12–34, *West's Smith-Hurd Ill. Compiled Statutes Annotated*, 2004; "State of Ill. 89th General Assembly 1995 and 1996 HB 3572," FGC Education and Networking Project, Legis., 2003. Available: http://fgmnetwork.org/legisl/US/ilhb3572.html. Accessed Feb. 4, 2004.

102. Md. Health General § 20–601, *West's Annotated Code of Md.*, 2004.

103. Minn. State § 609.2245, *Minn. Statutes Annotated, West*, 2004; "State of Minn. Legislation on Female Genital Mutilation 144. 3872," and 609.2245, FGC Education and Networking Project, Legis., 2003. Available: http://www.fgmnetwork.org/legisl/US/mn144.htm. Accessed Feb. 4, 2004.

104. Mo. Revised Statutes § 568–065 August 28, 2003, Cross Reference: Child molestation, first and second degree, RSMo 566.067, 566.068, Mo. General Assembly. Available: http://www.moga.state.mo.us/statutes/c500-599/5680000065.htm. Accessed May 23, 2004.

105. Nev. Revised Statutes: 200.5083, 1997, 678, Nev. State Legislature. Available: http://www.leg.state.nv.us/NRS/NRS-200.html #NRS200Sec5083. Accessed May 23, 2004.

106. N.Y. Penal Law, Ch. 40, Pt. 3, Title H, Art 130, § 130.85, *McKinney's* Penal Law; "State of New York, 5010, 2003–2004 Regular Sessions, In Assembly, Feb. 24, 2003," FGC Education and Networking Project, Legis., 2003. Available: http://www.fgmnetwork.org/legisl/US/nys5010.htm. Accessed May 22, 2004.

107. N. D. State Century Code, Criminal Code, 12.1–36–01, *West* 2004; "Legislative Assembly of N. D. Senate Bill No. 2454," FGC Education and Networking Project, Legis., 2003. Available: http://www.fgmnetwork.org/legisl/US/ndsb2454.html Accessed Feb. 4, 2004.

108. "Ore. Legislative Assembly, 70th Ses. Regular Session, House Bill 3608," 1999. Available: http://www.leg.state.or.us/99reg/measures/hb3600.dir/hb3608.int.html. Accessed May 23, 2004.

109. "State of R. I., General Assembly January Session, A.D. 1996," FGC Education and Networking Project, Legis., 2003. Available: http://www.fgmnetwork.org/legisl/US/ris2317.html. Accessed Feb. 4, 2004.

110. "State of Tenn. Senate Bill 2394 by Cruthfield," July 1, 1996, FGC Education and Networking Project, Legis., 2003. Available:

http://www.fgmnetwork.org/legisl/US/tnsb2394.html. Accessed Feb. 4, 2004.

111. Tex. Legis. 612 (2003), Vernon's Tex. Session Law Service, 2003, Ch. 612 (H.B. 1899) *West* Group, 2004; Tex. Health and Safety § 167.001, Vernon's Tex. Statutes and Codes Annotated, *West* Group 2004; "Tex, Bill on FGM H.B. No. 91 By Giddings, Thompson, Chavez, Clark," FGC Education and Networking Project, Legis., 2003. Available: http://www.fgmnetwork.org/legisl/US/tx91.htm. Accessed Feb. 4, 2004.

112. W. Vir. Code § 61–8D-3A, *West's* Annotated Code of W. Vir.

113. Wisc. State, Health, 146.35, *West's* Wisc. Statutes Annotated and "State of Wisc. 1995, Wisc. Act 365," FGC Education and Networking Project, Legis., 2003. Available: http://www.fgmnetwork.org/legisl/US/wi365.html. Accessed Feb. 4, 2004.

114. "State of Mich. House Bill — HB60 95," FGC Education and Networking Project, Legis., 2003. Available: http://www.fgmnetwork.org/legisl/US/mihb6095.html. Accessed Feb. 4, 2004.

115. Mich. State Law Library, email to the author, July 9, 2004.

116. "N. J. General Assembly ACR 335," FGC Education and Networking Project, Legis., 2003. Available: http://www.fgmnetwork.org/legisl/US/njacr35.html. Accessed Feb. 4, 2004.

117. N. J. State Legislature, Office of Legislative Services, Legislative Information and Bill Room, email to the author July 9, 2004.

118. Equality Now, "FGM Fact Sheet," #1527, New York, 2003. Available: http://www.equalitynow.org/english/about/fgmtour/fgm-factsheet.html. Accessed Dec. 25, 2003.

119. FGC Education and Networking Project, "Complete Legislative Graphic of the United States," 2003. Available: http://www.fgmnetwork.org/legisl/index.html#US. Accessed Mar. 11, 2004.

120. Amnesty International, "Female Genital Mutilation and Asylum, Stop Violence Against Women," *Human Rights Information Pack*, Sec. 6, 1998. Available: http://www.amnesty.org/ailib/intcam/femgen/fgm6.htm. Accessed Feb. 21, 2004.

121. United Nations Office of the High Commissioner for Human Rights, Convention Relating to the Status of Refugees [Adopted July 28, 1951, GA Resolution 429 (V), Dec. 14, 1950] (entry into force April 22, 1954), Article 1 (A) (2)). Available: http://www.unhchr.ch/html/menu3/b/o_c_ref.htm. Accessed Feb. 21, 2004.

122. Heaven Crawley, *Women as Asylum Seekers — A Legal Handbook* (London: Immi-

gration Law Practitioners' Association and Refugee Action, 1997), 71 on Amnesty International, "FGM and Asylum."

123. Amnesty International, "FGM and Asylum."

124. Asylum and Withholding Definitions, 65 Fed. Reg. 76588 (proposed Dec. 7, 2000) (to be codified at 8 C.F.R. pt. 208) in E. Dana Neacsu, "General Article: Gender-based Persecution as a Basis for Asylum: an Annotated Bibliography, 1993–2002," 95 *Law Library Journal* 191, n3, 4 (Spring, 2003).

125. 8 U.S. Code Annotated, § 1374, *West* 2004.

126. U.S. Department of Justice, U.S. Immigration and Naturalization Service, "Notice of Implementation of IIRIRA 1996, 63 FR 13433, 1998; "Aliens and Citizens," 3A American Jurisprudence 2d Aliens and Citizens § 40, § 1171, May 2003, *West*, 2004.

127. Asylum and Withholding Definitions, in Neacsu, 191, n3, 4.

128. *Immigration Business News and Comment Daily* 42 (March 7, 2003) in FED App. 0293P (6th Cir.) (2003), File Name: 03a0293 p.06. Available: http://www.michbar.org/opinions/us_appeals/2003/081803/19969.html. Accessed Feb. 27, 2004.

129. "Aliens and Citizens," 3A American Jurisprudence 2d Aliens and Citizens § 1220, May 2003, *West* 2004.

130. *In re Kasinga* 21 I. & N. Dec. 357 (B.I.A. June 13, 1996) in Neacsu, 191.

131. 8 C.F.R. § 208.18, current through Jan. 12, 2004; 69FR 1891, *West* 2004.

132. Lisa Johnson-Firth, LLB., J.D. (Director of Legal Services, Tahirih Justice Center, Falls Church, VA), interview by the author at the Tahirih Justice Center, Falls Church, VA, March 22, 2004.

133. Johnson-Firth interview, March 22, 2004.

134. Johnson-Firth interview, March 22, 2004.

135. Colleen Renk Zengotitabengoa, M.A., J.D. (staff attorney, Tahirih Justice Center, Falls Church, VA), interview by the author at the Tahirih Justice Center, Falls Church, VA, March 22, 2004.

136. Renk Zengotitabengoa interview, March 22, 2004.

137. Renk Zengotitabengoa interview, March 22, 2004.

138. Renk Zengotitabengoa interview, March 22, 2004.

139. Layli Miller Bashir, "Female Genital Mutilation in the United States: An Examination of Criminal and Asylum Law," 4 *American University Journal of Gender and the Law* 415 (1996).

140. Isabelle R. Gunning, "Global Feminism at the Local Level: Criminal and Asylum Laws Regarding Female Genital Surgeries," 3 *Journal of Gender, Race and Justice* 45 (1999).

141. Stephanie Kaye Pell, "Adjudication of Gender Persecution Cases Under the Canada Guidelines: The United States Has No Reason to Fear an Onslaught of Asylum Claims," 2 *North Carolina Journal of International Law and Commercial Regulation* 655 (1995).

142. John Tochukwu Okwubanego, "Female Circumcision and the Girl Child in Africa and the Middle East: The Eyes of the World Are Blind to the Conquered," 33 *International Law* 159 (Spring, 1999).

143. Peter Margulies, "Democratic Transitions and the Future of Asylum Law," 71 *Colorado Law Review* 45 (2000).

144. Daliah Setareh, "Women Escaping Genital Mutilation — Seeking Asylum in the United States," 6 *UCLA Women's Law Journal* 124, 125 (1995).

145. Susannah Smiley, "Taking the 'Force' out of Enforcement: Giving Effect to International Human Rights Law Using Domestic Immigration Law," 29 *California Western International Law Journal* 344–45 (1999).

146. Smiley, 345.

147. Rahman and Toubia, 21.

148. Caryn L. Weisblat, "Gender-Based Persecution: Does United States Law Provide Women Refugees with a Fair Chance?" 7 *Tulane Journal of International and Comparative Law* 416, (1999).

149. Weisblat, n42, 416.

150. Patricia A. Armstrong, "Female Genital Mutilation: The Move toward the Recognition of Violence against Women as a Basis for Asylum in the United States," 21 *Maryland Journal of International Law and Trade* 95–122 (1997).

151. TiaJuana Jones-Bibbs, "United States Follows Canadian Lead and Takes an Unequivocal Position Against Female Genital Mutilation: In Re Fauziya Kasinga," 4 *Tulane Journal of International and Comparative Law* 275 (1997).

152. Renk Zengotitabengoa interview, March 22, 2004.

153. Johnson-Firth interview, March 22, 2004.

154. United States Agency for International Development, Health, Population, "Congressional Briefing on Female Genital Cutting," Press Release, Feb. 5, 2004.

155. United States Agency for International Development, "Congressional Briefing on Female Genital Cutting."

156. Karen Musalo, "Symposium: Beyond Belonging: Challenging the Boundaries of Na-

tionality: Revisiting Social Group and Nexus in Gender Asylum Claims: A Unifying Rational for Evolving Jurisprudence," 52 *Depaul Law Review* 777 (Spring 2003).

157. Musalo, 778.

158. Musalo, 807.

159. Musalo, 807–808.

160. *Azeez Jimmy Imohi v. INS*, 87 F.3d 1319, 1996 WL 297612 (9th Cir.).

161. *Imohi v. INS.*

162. *Ruth E. Obazee v. John D. Ashcroft*, 79 Fed.Appx. 914, 2003 WL 22473831 (7th Cir.).

163. *Helen Seifu v. John Ashcroft*, 80 Fed. Appx. 323, 2003 WL 22490221 (5th Cir.).

164. Amnesty International, "FGM and Asylum."

165. Amnesty International, "FGM and Asylum."

166. Amnesty International, "FGM and Asylum."

167. Amnesty International, "FGM and Asylum."

CHAPTER 4

1. Robin M. Maher, "Female Genital Mutilation: The Modern Day Struggle to Eradicate a Torturous Rite of Passage," 23:4 Human Rights (Fall 1996):12–15. Available: http://www.abanet.org/irr/hr/fgm.html. Accessed Feb. 29, 2004.

2. "Sweden Says Cosmetic Surgery on Female Genitals May be Illegal," *Agence Fr.-Presse*, Jan. 28, 2004.

3. Stanlie M. James and Claire C. Robertson, "Prologue," in Stanlie M. James and Claire C. Robertson (eds.), *Genital Cutting and Transnational Sisterhood: Disputing U.S. Polemics* (Urbana: University of Illinois Press, 2002), 1–2.

4. James McBride, "'To Make Martyrs of Their Children': 'Female Genital Mutilation,' Religious Legitimation, and the Constitution," in Kathleen M. Sands (ed.), *God Forbid Religion and Sex in American Public Life* (New York: Oxford University Press, 2000), 219–220.

5. *Doris C. Oforji v. John D. Ashcroft*, 354 U.S. F.3d 609 (2003).

6. David Ziemer, "Alien Parent Can't Establish Derivative Claim for Asylum Based on Citizen Children," *Wisconsin Law Journal* (Jan. 4, 2004).

7. Ziemer, "Alien Parent."

8. Maher, "Female Genital Mutilation."

9. McBride, in Sands (ed.), 220.

10. McBride, in Sands (ed.), 220–221.

11. McBride, in Sands (ed.), 225.

12. McBride, in Sands (ed.), 225.

13. McBride, in Sands (ed.), 225.

14. Universalway.org, "The Truth About Circumcision," updated Feb. 10, 2004. Available: http://www.universalway.org/circtruth. html. Accessed July 20, 2004.

15. Federal Prohibition of Female Genital Mutilation Act of 1995," 104th Congress, 1st Ses., S. 1030, 1995, Female Genital Cutting Education and Networking Project, Legislation, 2003. Available: http://www.fgmnetwork.org /legisl/US/federal.html. Accessed May 22, 2004; 18 U.S. Code Annotated § 116; "Assault and Battery," 6 American Jurisprudence, 2d, § 14, May 2003, *West* 2004.

16. Laura Reymond, Asha Mohamud, and Nancy Ali, *Female Genital Mutilation — The Facts* (Washington D.C.: Program for Appropriate Technology in Health, July 25, 2003). Available: http://www.path.org/files/FGM-The-Facts.htm. Accessed Apr. 29, 2004.

17. Reymond, et al.

18. New York City Law, Local Law No. 1066 of 1997, "Laws of the World," Harvard Univ. Cyberlaw. Available: http://cyber.law.harvard. edu/population/fgm/fgm.htm. Accessed July 2, 2004.

19. Joan R. Tarpley, "Bad Witches: A Cut on the Clitoris with the Instruments of Institutional Power and Politics," 100 *West Virginia Law Review* 300, n81 (1997).

20. E. Dana Neacsu, "General Article: Gender-based Persecution as a Basis for Asylum: an Annotated Bibliography, 1993–2002," 95 *Law Library Journal* 213 (Spring, 2003).

21. Neacsu, 213.

22. Holly Maguigan, "Redefining Violence Against Women Symposium: Will Prosecutions for 'Female Genital Mutilation' Stop the Practice in the U.S.?" 8 *Temple Political and Civil Rights Law Review* 391 (Spring 1999).

23. Maguigan, 391.

24. Maguigan, 393–394, 401, 412.

25. Maguigan, 421, 414.

26. Allan Rosenfeld, "Introduction," in Nahid Toubia, *A Technical Manual for Health Care Providers: Caring for Women with Circumcision* (New York: RAINBO, 1999), 12.

27. Donna E. Shalala, "Foreword," in Toubia, *A Technical Manual*, 8.

28. Rita Morris, "The Culture of Female Circumcision," *Advances in Nursing Science* 19, no. 2 (Dec. 1996):43(11).

29. Morris, 43(11).

30. B. Vissandjée, M. Kantiébo, A. Levine, and R. N'Dejuru, "The Cultural Context of Gender, Identity: Female Genital Excision and Infibulation," *Health Care For Women International* 24, no. 2 (Feb. 2003), 115.

31. African Women's Health Center, Brigham and Women's Hospital, Boston, Mass.,

Sept. 13, 2003. Available: http://www.brigham andwomens.org/patient/awhc.asp. Accessed May 21, 2004.

32. Tobe Levin, "Abolition Efforts in the African Diaspora: Two Conferences on Female Genital Mutilation in Europe," *Women's Studies Quarterly* 22, nos. 1 and 2 (Spring/ Summer 1999): 114.

33. Levin, 114.

34. Toubia, *A Technical Manual*, 74.

35. Cheryl Chase, "'Cultural Practice' or 'Reconstructive Surgery'? U.S. Genital Cutting, the Intersex Movement, and Medical Double Standards," in James and Robertson (eds.), 126.

36. Chase, in James and Robertson (eds.), 126.

37. Chase, in James and Robertson (eds.), 126.

38. Chase, in James and Robertson (eds.), 126.

39. Chase, in James and Robertson (eds.), 127.

40. Intersex Society of North America, "ISNA's Recommendations for Treatment," 1994. Available: http://www.isna.org/library/recommendations.html. Accessed Feb. 7, 2004.

41. Hank Hyena, "The Micropenis and the Giant Clitoris," *Health and Body*, Dec. 16, 1999. Available: http://www.salon.com/health /sex/urge/world/1999/12/16/surgery. Accessed Feb. 7, 2004.

42. *Hermaphrodites with Attitude*, Newsletter, Winter 1994–1995, 1. Available: http:// www.isna.org/newsletter/winterr94-95/winter94–95.html. Accessed Feb. 7, 2004.

43. Intersex Society of North America.

44. Alexandra Hall, "Do the Eyes Have It?: Flesh Wounds: The Culture of Cosmetic Surgery," Winter 2003. Available: http://www. msmagazine.com/dec03/fleshwounds_book. asp. Accessed Jan. 7, 2004.

45. W.G. Rathmann, "Female Circumcision: Indications and a New Technique," *General Practitioner* 20, no. 3 (Sept. 1959):115. Available: http://noharmm.org/femcirctech. htm. Accessed July 20, 2004.

46. Lisa Johnson-Firth, LLB., J.D. (Director of Legal Services, Tahirih Justice Center, Falls Church, VA), interview by the author at the Tahirih Justice Center, Falls Church, VA, March 22, 2004.

47. Johnson-Firth interview, March 22, 2004.

48. "The Clitoris at Risk," The-Clitoris. com, n.d. Available: http://www.the-clitoris. com/f_html/risk.htm. Accessed Feb. 7, 2004.

49. "The Clitoris at Risk."

50. L.M. Koenig and M. Carnes, "Body

Piercing: Medical Concerns with Cutting-Edge Fashion," *Journal of General Internal Medicine* 14, no. 6 (June 1999):379.

51. Victoria Pitts, *In the Flesh: the Cultural Politics of Body Modification* (New York: Palgrave Macmillan, 2003), back cover, 57.

52. Pitts, 92–93.

53. W. Handrick, P. Nenoff, H. Müller, and W. Knöfler, "Infektionen durch Piercing und Tattoos— eine Übersicht," *Wiener Medizinische Wochenschrift* 153, no. 9–10 (May 2003): 194.

54. Pitts, 49.

55. Pitts, 55, 77–80.

56. Pitts, 53, 137.

57. Pitts, 74.

58. Pitts, 78.

59. Pitts, back cover, 31, 33.

60. Jean-Chris Miller, *The Body Art Book: A Complete, Illustrated Guide to Tattoos, Piercings, and Other Body Modifications* (New York: Berkley Books, 1997), 36.

61. Miller, 30.

62. Sheila Jeffreys, "'Body Art' and Social Status: Cutting, Tattooing and Piercing from A Feminist Perspective," *Feminism & Psychology* 10, no. 4 (Nov. 2000):409.

63. BME/Piercing, Choose a Gallery, Tweed Ontario, Canada: Bmezine.com LLC., PsyberCity Inc., and/or Shannon Larratt 1994–2004. Available: http://www.bmezine.com/ pierce/10-female/index.html. Accessed Mar. 9, 2004.

64. BME/Piercing, "Princess Albertina, Female Urethral Piercing."

65. BME/Piercing, "Isabella, Deep Clitoral Shaft Piercing."

66. M. Neil Williams (retired general surgeon and missionary physician, Cedar Falls, Ia.), interview by the author, Aug. 6, 2003.

67. Williams interview, Aug. 6, 2003.

68. V. S. Millner and B. H. Eichold II, "Body Piercing and Tattooing Perspectives," *Clinical Nursing Research* 10, no. 4 (Nov. 2001):424.

69. Williams interview, Aug. 6, 2003.

70. P. N. Jervis, N. J. Clifton, and T. J. Woolford, "Ear Deformity in Children Following High Ear-piercing: Current Practice," Consent Issues and Legislation, *Journal of Laryngology and Otology* 115, no. 7 (July 1, 2001):519.

71. J. Niamtu, "Eleven Pearls for Cosmetic Earlobe Repair," *Dermatologic Surgery* 28, no. 2 (Feb. 2002):180.

72. J. Greif, W. Hewitt, and M. L. Armstrong, "Tattooing and Body Piercing: Body Art Practices Among College Students," *Clinical Nursing Research* 8, no. 4 (Nov. 1999):368.

73. Shari Roan, "Erasing the Past," *Los An-*

geles Times, Home Ed., Dec. 8, 2003, Health; Part 6; p. 1.

74. Krzysztof M. Kuczkowski and Jonathan L. Benumof, "Tongue Piercing and Obstetric Anesthesia Is There Cause for Concern?" *Journal of Clinical Anesthesia* 14, Issue 6 (Sept. 2002):447.

75. Painful Pleasures, "Body Piercing Afer-Care," Hints for Particular Areas: Genital, 2001–2002. Available: http://www.painful pleasures.com/xcart/customer/home.php? mode=aftercare#fgenital. Accessed Jun. 21, 2003.

76. C.R.F. Azevedo, G. Spera, and A. P. Silva, "Characterization of Metallic Piercings That Caused Adverse Reactions During Use Practical Failure Analysis," *ASM International* 2, no. 4 (Aug. 1, 2002):47–53(7).

77. G. Ventolini and S. Kleeman, "Adhesions Caused by Umbilical Piercing, *Journal of the American Association of Gynecologic Laparoscopists* 10, no. 2 (May 1, 2003):281.

78. Ronald Braithwaite, Alyssa Robillard, Tammy Woodring, Torrence Stephens, and Kimberly Jacob Arriola, "Tattooing and Body Piercing among Adolescent Detainees Relationship to Alcohol and Other Drug Use," *Journal of Substance Abuse* 13, Issues 1–2, (Sept. 2001):5.

79. Braithwaite et al., 5.

80. Traci L. Brooks, Elizabeth R. Woods, John R. Knight, and Lydia A. Shrier, "Body Modification and Substance Use in Adolescents: Is There a Link?" *Journal of Adolescent Health* 32, Issue 1 (Jan. 2003):44.

81. J. K. Brooks, K. A. Hooper and M. A. Reynolds, "Formation of Mucogingival Defects Associated With Intraoral and Perioral Piercing: Case Reports," *Journal of the American Dental Association* 134, no. 7 (July 2003):837.

82. Kuczkowski and Benumof, "Tongue Piercing and Obstetric Anesthesia."

83. R.J.G. De Moor, A.M.J.C. De Witte, and M.A.A. De Bruyne, "Tongue Piercing and Associated Oral and Dental Complications," *Dental Traumatology* 16, no. 5 (Oct. 2000): 232

CHAPTER 5

1. Poster prepared by The Network of Anti-Female Genital Mutilation Organizations, Arusha Regional, Arusha, Tanzania, in collaboration with the Konrad Adenauer Foundation.

2. Juliet Chugulu R.N., R.M., M.Sc. (Kilimanjaro Christian Medical Centre School of Nursing; Chairperson of the Kilimanjaro

Inter-African Committee on Traditional Practices Affecting the Health of Women and Children, Moshi, Tanzania), interview by the author in Moshi, Tanzania, Jan. 28, 2004.

3. Molefi Kete Asante, *Afrocentricity* (Trenton, N.J.: Africa World Press, Inc., 1988), 95.

4. Asante, 101.

5. Asante, 101.

6. Asante, 94, 101.

7. Kebwe Stephen Kebwe (District Medical Officer, Bunda; Regional Chairman, Mara, Inter African Committee, Tanzania), interview by the author in Bunda, Tanzania, Jan. 25, 2004 and Patroba E. Ondiek, Ph.D. (Program Coordinator of the nongovernmental organization Save the Children of Tarime, Tarime, Tanzania), interview by the author in Tarime, Tanzania, Jan. 24, 2004.

8. Ellen Gruenbaum, *The Female Circumcision Controversy: An Anthropological Perspective* (Philadelphia: University of Pennsylvania Press, 2000), 1.

9. Gruenbaum, 15.

10. Maasai Laibon and female village members (Mto Wa Mbu, Arusha, Tanzania), interview by the author, Jan. 18, 2004.

11. Claudie Gosselin, "Feminism, Anthropology and the Politics of Excision in Mali: Global and Local Debates in a Postcolonial World," *Anthropologica* XLII (2000):56.

12. Gosselin, 56.

13. Sondra Hale, "A Question of Subjects: The 'Female Circumcision' Controversy and the Politics of Knowledge," *Ufahamu* 22, no. 3 (Fall 1994):34.

14. Hale, 26.

15. Hale, 31.

16. Hale, 26, 32–33.

17. Anke Van Der Kwaak, "Female Circumcision and Gender Identity: A Questionable Alliance?" *Social Science and Medicine* 35, no. 6 (1992):785.

18. Christine J. Walley, "Searching for 'Voices': Feminism, Anthropology, and the Global Debate over Female Genital Operations," *Cultural Anthropology* 12, no. 3 (1997):406.

19. Walley, 407.

20. Richard A. Shweder, "'What About Female Genital Mutilation?' and Why Understanding Culture Matters in the First Place," in R. Shweder, M. Minow, and H. Markus (eds.), *Engaging Cultural Differences: The Multicultural Challenge in Liberal Democracies* (New York: Russell Sage Foundation Press, 2002), 218.

21. Carla M. Obermeyer, "Female Genital Surgeries: The Known, the Unknown, and the Unknowable," *Medical Anthropology Quar-*

terly 13 (1999):79, 80, 81 in Shweder, et al. (eds.), 219.

22. Shweder, et al. (eds.), 222–223, 227.

23. Shweder, et al. (eds.), 229.

24. Isabelle R. Gunning, "Female Genital Surgeries and Multicultural Feminism: The Ties that Bind; The Differences That Distance," *Third World Legal Studies* (1994):47.

25. Gunning, 19, 20, 21.

26. Hope Lewis, "Between Irua and 'Female Genital Mutilation': Feminist Human Rights Discourse and the Cultural Divide," 8 *Harvard Human Rights Journal* 28 (Spring 1995).

27. Gosselin, 44.

28. Angela Gilliam, "Women's Equality and National Liberation," in C.T. Mohanty, A. Russo, and L. Torres (eds.), *Third World Women and the Politics of Feminism* (Bloomington and Indianapolis: Indiana University Press, 1991), 217 in Gosselin, 44.

29. Gosselin, 45.

30. Gosselin, 45.

31. Gosselin, 46.

32. Gruenbaum, 24–25.

33. Gruenbaum, 25.

34. Gruenbaum, 26.

35. Gruenbaum, 30.

36. Lewis, 1.

37. Lewis, 1.

38. Lewis, 27, 28.

39. Lewis, 28.

40. M. Neil Williams (retired general surgeon and missionary physician, Cedar Falls, Ia.), interview by the author, Aug. 6, 2003.

41. Williams interview, Aug. 6, 2003.

42. Williams interview, Aug. 6, 2003.

43. Williams interview, Aug. 6, 2003.

44. Radhika Coomaraswamy, "Article: Identity Within: Cultural Relativism, Minority Rights and the Empowerment of Women," 34 *George Washington International Law Review* 490 (2002).

45. Coomaraswamy, 490, n38.

46. Coomaraswamy, 491, n38.

47. Coomaraswamy, 492, 493.

48. Gruenbaum, 30.

49. Birgit Leyendecker and Michael E. Lamb, "Latino Families," in Michael E. Lamb (ed.), *Parenting and Child Development in 'Nontraditional' Families* (Mahwah, N.J.: Lawrence Erlbaum Associates, 1999), 247–262.

50. Lisa Johnson-Firth, LLB., J.D. (Director of Legal Services, Tahirih Justice Center, Falls Church, VA, "The Global Dilemma of FGC," presentation to Zonta International, Feb. 9, 2004, 7.

51. Johnson-Firth, "The Global Dilemma of FGC," 8.

52. Jon Heinrich (Director of Missions, Trinity Lutheran Church, Grand Island, Neb.). Interview by the author, Aug. 30, 2003.

53. Heinrich interview, Aug. 30, 2003.

54. Heinrich interview, Aug. 30, 2003.

55. Heinrich interview, Aug. 30, 2003.

56. Heinrich interview, Aug. 30, 2003.

57. Aban Laamatjok (from Malakal in south Sudan, currently residing in Grand Island, Neb.), interview by the author and James C. Skaine in Grand Island, Neb., Aug. 30, 2003.

58. Laamatjok interview, Aug. 30, 2003.

59. Jenty Nawal Chacha Kosta (from Juba in south Sudan, currently residing in Grand Island, Neb.), interview by the author and James C. Skaine in Grand Island, Neb., Aug. 30, 2003.

60. Laamatjok interview, Aug. 30, 2003.

61. Laamatjok interview, Aug. 30, 2003.

62. Kosta interview, Aug. 30, 2003.

63. Laamatjok interview, Aug. 30, 2003.

64. Laamatjok interview, Aug. 30, 2003.

65. Mut Ruey (from Miywut in south Sudan, currently residing in Grand Island, Neb.), interview by the author and James C. Skaine, Aug. 31, 2003.

66. Ruey interview, Aug. 31, 2003.

67. William G. Riek (President, Sudanese Refugee Community Organization and Refugee Advocate, Community Humanitarian Resource Center, Grand Island, Nebraska), interview by the author and James C. Skaine, May 29, 2004.

68. Riek interview, May 29, 2004.

69. Riek, email follow-up, June 30, 2004.

70. Riek interview, May 29, 2004.

71. Riek, email follow-up, June 30, 2004.

72. Riek, email follow-up, June 30, 2004.

73. Riek, email follow-up, June 30, 2004.

74. Riek interview, May 29, 2004.

75. Riek interview, May 29, 2004.

76. Riek interview, May 29, 2004.

77. Riek, email follow-up, June 30, 2004.

78. Emmanuel Babatunde, *Women's Rites Versus Women's Rights: A Study of Circumcision Among the Ketu Yoruba of South Western Nigeria* (Trenton, N.J.: Africa World Press, 1997), xvi.

79. Babatunde, 180.

80. Efu Dorkenoo, *Cutting the Rose, Female Genital Mutilation: The Practice and its Prevention* (London: Minority Rights Publications, 1994), 45.

81. Charles Henry Sweke, M.D., C.I. Ord., Ph.D. (consultant obstetrician/gynecologist, Selian Lutheran Hospital, Arusha, Tanzania), interview by the author, Jan. 15, 2004.

82. Mary E. Laiser (Head of the Women's Department of the Arusha Diocese of the Evangelical Lutheran Church in Tanzania) in-

terview by the author and James C. Skaine in Arusha, Tanzania, Jan. 15, 2004.

83. Laiser interview, Jan. 15, 2004.

84. Laiser interview, Jan. 15, 2004.

85. Dorkenoo, 45.

86. James Emanuel Sichilma (driver, guide, interpreter, Arusha, Tanzania), interview by the author and James C. Skaine, Shirati, Tanzania, Jan. 25, 2004.

87. Sichilma interview, Jan. 25, 2004.

88. Sichilma interview, Jan. 25, 2004.

89. Sichilma interview, Jan. 25, 2004.

90. Sichilma interview, Jan. 25, 2004.

91. Friedrich Engels (1884), "The Patriarchal Family," in Charles Lemert (ed.), *Social Theory: The Multicultural and Classic Readings* (Boulder, Colo.: Westview Press, 1999), 66–67.

92. Engels, in Lemert (ed.), 67–68.

93. Engels, in Lemert (ed.), 69.

94. Sweke interview, Jan. 15, 2004.

95. Patricia Dysart Rudloff, "In Re Oluloro: Risk of Female Genital Mutilation as 'Extreme Hardship' in Immigration Proceedings," 26 St. *Mary's Law Journal* 877–903 (1995).

96. James A. Lazarus, "Note: In Through the Side Door: Analyzing In Re Anikwata Under U.S. Asylum Law and the Torture Convention," 32 *Case Western Reserve Journal of International Law* 113, 86 (Winter, 2000).

97. Lazarus, 113, 86.

98. Jane Wright, "Female Genital Mutilation: An Overview," *Journal of Advanced Nursing*: 24, no. 2 (1996):251–259, para. 6 in Cindy M. Little, "Female Genital Circumcision: Medical and Cultural Considerations," *Journal of Cultural Diversity*: 10, no. 1 (Spring 2003):30(5).

99. Fareda Banda, "National Legislation Against Female Genital Mutilation," Eschborn/Germany, May 2003, 19. Available: http://www.gtz.de/fgm/downloads/fgm-law-long%2016-05-03.pdf. Accessed Apr. 2, 2004.

100. Paul Jimbo, "Govt. Issues Ultimatum to Circumcisers," *The East African Standard/All Africa*, Mar 13, 2004, *Africa News Service*, March 15, 2004, pNA.

101. "Kenya: Boost for Anti-FGM Effort As 200 Circumcisers Quit," *Africa News Service*, March 11, 2004, pNA.

102. "Kenya: Boost for Anti-FGM Effort."

103. "70-Year Old Woman Jailed for FGM," *Africa News Service*, Jan. 28, 2004 pNA.

104. Vanguard, "Nigeria; Rage Against Female Genital Mutilation," *Africa News*, Apr. 11, 2002.

105. Vanguard.

106. Inter-African Committee on Traditional Practices Affecting the Health of Women and Children, *Female Genital Mutilation: Zero Tolerance Eighteen Years of Action 1984–2002* (Addis Ababa, Ethiopia: Jan. 2003), 30.

107. Ondiek interview, Jan. 24, 2004.

108. Ondiek interview, Jan. 24, 2004.

109. Laiser interview, Jan. 15, 2004.

110. Laiser interview, Jan. 15, 2004.

111. Laurenti Magesa, *African Religion: The Moral Traditions of Abundant Life* (Maryknoll, N.Y.: Orbis Books, 1997), 98–103.

112. Babatunde, 25, 45.

113. Babatunde, 45.

114. Babatunde, 166.

115. Babatunde, 167–168.

116. Babatunde, 168.

117. Babatunde, 169.

118. Kay L. Levine, "Article: Negotiating the Boundaries of Crime and Culture: a Sociolegal Perspective on Cultural Defense Strategies," 28 *Law and Social Inquiry* 63 (Winter 2003).

119. Alison D. Renteln, "Is the Cultural Defense Detrimental to the Health of Children?" *Law and Anthropology: International Yearbook for Legal Anthropology*, vol. 7, ed., Rene Kuppe and Richard Potz, 27–105, Dordrecht, the Netherlands: Martinus Nijoff, 1994 in Levine, 63.

120. Kay Boulware-Miller, "Dimensions of the Practice and Debates," in Bettina Shell-Duncan and Ylva Hernlund (eds.), *Female 'Circumcision' in Africa: Culture, Controversy, and Change* (Boulder, Colo.: Lynne Rienner, 2000), 23–24.

121. Boulware-Miller, in Shell-Duncan and Hernlund (eds.), 27.

122. Boulware-Miller, in Shell-Duncan and Hernlund (eds.), 27.

123. Boulware-Miller, in Shell-Duncan and Hernlund (eds.), 30.

124. Ylva Hernlund, "Cutting Without Ritual and Ritual Without Cutting: Female 'Circumcision' and the Re-ritualization of Initiation in Gambia," in Shell-Duncan and Hernlund (eds.), 236.

125. Hernlund, in Shell-Duncan and Hernlund (eds.), 236, 249.

126. Hernlund, in Shell-Duncan and Hernlund (eds.), 238.

127. Hernlund, in Shell-Duncan and Hernlund (eds.), 242–243.

128. Hernlund, in Shell-Duncan and Hernlund (eds.), 245.

129. "Kenya: New Ritual May Replace FGM," *Off our Backs*, May-June 2003, 4(2).

130. B. A. Robinson, "Female Genital Mutilation Female (Circumcision) in Africa, Middle East and Far East," Nov. 13, 2001. Available: http://www.religioustolerance.org/fem_cirm.htm. Accessed April 15, 2004.

131. John Wachira, M.D. (urologist and member of the African Medical Research Foundation, Flying Doctor Surgical Outreach Program), interview by Esther Kawira for the author in Shirati, Tanzania Mar. 19, 2004.

132. Anika Rahman and Nahid Toubia (eds.), *Female Genital Mutilation: A Guide to Laws and Policies Worldwide* (New York: St. Martin's Press, 2000), 6.

133. Rahman and Toubia (eds.), 6.

134. Sami A. Aldeeb Abu-Sahlieh, "Islamic Law and the Issue of Male and Female Circumcision," *Third World Legal Studies* (1994):75.

135. Rahman and Toubia (eds.), 6.

136. Abu-Sahlieh, "Islamic Law," 101.

137. Strabo, *The Geography of Strabo*, translated by William Heinemann Hones, vol. 7, London, 1966, 323 (16.4.9) in Abu-Sahlieh, *Male and Female Circumcision: Among Jews, Christians and Muslims: Religious, Medical, Social and Legal Debate* (Warren Center, Pa.: Shangri-La Publications, 2001), 66.

138. Abu-Sahlieh, *Male and Female Circumcision*, 66–67.

139. W. G. Rathmann, "Female Circumcision, Indications and A New Technique," *General Practitioner*, Kansas City, vol. 20. no. 3, Sept. 1959, 115–120 in Abu-Sahlieh, *Male and Female Circumcision*, 66–68.

140. Abu-Sahlieh, *Male and Female Circumcision*, 67–68.

141. Abu-Sahlieh, *Male and Female Circumcision*, 83.

142. Otto F.A. Meinardus, *Christian Egypt: Faith and Life* (Cairo: The American University Press, 1970), 325 in Abu-Sahlieh, *Male and Female Circumcision*, 83.

143. Abu-Sahlieh, *Male and Female Circumcision*, 83–84.

144. Abu-Sahlieh, *Male and Female Circumcision*, 84.

145. Abu-Sahlieh, *Male and Female Circumcision*, 68.

146. Abu-Sahlieh, *Male and Female Circumcision*, 68.

147. Abu-Sahlieh, "Islamic Law," 77.

148. Abu-Sahlieh, "Islamic Law," 77.

149. Abu-Sahlieh, "Islamic Law," 78.

150. Abu-Sahlieh, "Islamic Law," 80.

151. Abu-Sahlieh, "Islamic Law," 80.

152. Abu-Sahlieh, "Islamic Law," 81.

153. Abu-Sahlieh, "Islamic Law," 81.

154. Abu-Sahlieh, "Islamic Law," 81.

155. Abu-Sahlieh, "Islamic Law," 82, 83.

156. Abu-Sahlieh, "Islamic Law," 85.

157. "Female Genital Mutilation: A Vanquished Tradition?" *Africa News Service*, Feb. 09, 2004.

158. Amnesty International, "United Nations Initiatives," "Female Genital Mutilation," *Human Rights Information Pack*, Sec. 7, 1998. Available: http://www.amnesty.org/ailib /intcam/femgen/fgm7.htm. Accessed Jun. 12, 2003.

159. Jessica A. Platt, "Note: Female Circumcision: Religious Practice v. Human Rights Violation," 3 *Rutgers Journal of Law and Religion* 3 (2001/2002).

160. Mary Nyangweso, "Christ's Salvific Message and the Nandi Ritual of Female Circumcision," *Theological Studies* 63 no. 3 (Sept. 2002):579(22).

161. Nyangweso, 579(22).

162. Nyangweso, 579(22).

163. Robinson, "Female Genital Mutilation."

164. Robinson, "Female Genital Mutilation."

165. Robinson, "Female Genital Mutilation."

166. Robinson, "Female Genital Mutilation."

167. Robinson, "Female Genital Mutilation."

168. Michelle C. Johnson, "Becoming a Muslim, Becoming a Person: Female 'Circumcision,' Religious Identity, and Personhood in Guinea-Bissau," in Shell-Duncan and Hernlund (eds.), 219, 231, 232.

169. Charles P. Wallace, "The Scars of Tradition: (Society/Culture Clash/Female Circumcision), *Time International* 161, no. 17 (May 5, 2003):42+.

170. Wallace, 42+.

171. Wallace, 42+.

172. "The Challenges Faced By Our Women," *Africa News Service* (News Provided by Comtex, Mar 19, 2004 (Addis Tribune/All Africa Global Media via COMTEX), March 21, 2004, pNA.

173. "The Challenges Faced By Our Women," pNA

CHAPTER 6

1. "Give the Spirit Time to Ripen," Washington, D.C.: Program for Appropriate Technology in Health, n.d.

2. Laura Reymond, Asha Mohamud, Nancy Ali, Kalle Makalou, and Zohra Yakoub, "The Facts: Female Genital Mutilation" (Washington, D.C.: Program for Appropriate Technology in Health, Dec. 1997), 3.

3. Program for Appropriate Technology in Health, "FGM Programmes to Date: What Works and What Doesn't," Executive Summary, Sept. 31, 1998.

4. PRIME II, "Research Summary: Ethiopian FGC Project," Jan. 2004, 3.

5. Program for Appropriate Technology in Health, "FGM Programmes to Date."

6. Mary E. Laiser (Head of the Women's Department of the Arusha Diocese of the Evangelical Lutheran Church in Tanzania) interview by the author and James C. Skaine in Arusha, Tanzania, Jan. 15, 2004.

7. World Health Organization, *Female Genital Mutilation: A Teacher's Guide* (Geneva, WHO/FCH/GWH/01.3; WHO/RHR/01.16, 2001), 47. Available: http://www.who.int/reproductive-health/publications/rhr_01_16_fgm_teacher_guide/fgm_teacher_guide.pdf. Accessed: June 22, 2004.

8. World Health Organization, *Female Genital Mutilation: A Teacher's Guide*, 47.

9. Salem Mekuria, "Female Genital Mutilation in Africa: Some African Views," in Meredeth Turshen (ed.), Special Issue on Health and Africa, *Bulletin of the Association of Concerned Africa Scholars*, nos. 44/45 (Winter/Spring 1995) in Chris Lowe, at H-Africa Discussion Logs, June 29, 1996. Available: http://www.h-net.org/~africa/. Accessed June 9, 2003.

10. Lowe, H-Africa Discussion Logs.

11. Seble Dawit and Salem Mekuria, "The West Just Doesn't Get It," *N.Y. Times*, Dec. 7, 1993, A27.

12. Lowe, H-Africa Discussion Logs.

13. Lowe, H-Africa Discussion Logs.

14. Mekuria, "Female Genital Mutilation in Africa," in Turshen (ed.), in Lowe.

15. Lowe, H-Africa Discussion Logs.

16. Lowe, H-Africa Discussion Logs.

17. Veronica English, Gillian Romano-Critchley, Julian Sheather, and Ann Sommerville, "Concerns Are Raised about the Sudanese Government's Plans to Legalize Female Genital Mutilation," *Journal of Medical Ethics* 29, no. 1 (Feb. 2003):57(1).

18. English et al., "Concerns Are Raised," 57(1).

19. R. J. Cook, B. M. Dickens and M. F. Fathalla, "Female Genital Cutting (Mutilation/circumcision): Ethical and Legal Dimensions," *International Journal of Gynecology and Obstetrics* 79 (2002):283.

20. Cook et al., 284.

21. Population Reference Bureau, *Abandoning Female Genital Cutting* (Washington, D.C.: Population Reference Bureau, Aug. 2001, Updated Apr. 2003), 15.

22. International Federation of Gynecology and Obstetrics, "Recommendations on Ethical Issues in Obstetrics and Gynecology," London: International Federation of Gynecology and Obstetrics, 2000, S. 2, p.7 in Cook et al., 285.

23. Cook et al., 285.

24. Cook et al., 285.

25. Cook et al., 286.

26. Population Reference Bureau, 16.

27. Cindy M. Little, "Female Genital Circumcision: Medical and Cultural Considerations," *Journal of Cultural Diversity* 10, no. 1 (Spring 2003):30(5).

28. Little, 30(5).

29. Population Reference Bureau, 24.

30. Population Reference Bureau, 21.

31. World Health Organization, "Management of Pregnancy, Childbirth and the Postpartum Period in the Presence of Female Genital Mutilation," Report of a WHO Technical Consultation, Geneva WHO/FCH/GWH/01.2 and WHO/RHR/01.13 (Oct. 12–17, 1997), p. 3. Available: http://www.who.int/entity/gender/other_health/ manageofpregnan.pdf. Accessed Feb. 8, 2004.

32. Population Reference Bureau, 21.

33. Population Reference Bureau, 21.

34. Pamela A. McCloud, Shahira Aly, and Sara Goltz, *Promoting FGM Abandonment in Egypt: Introduction of Positive Deviance* (Washington, D.C.: Center for Development and Population Activities, n.d.). Available: http://www.cedpa.org/publications/pdf/egypt_fgmabandonment.pdf. Accessed May 9, 2004.

35. McCloud, et al.

36. McCloud, et al.

37. McCloud, et al.

38. Faiza Jama Mohamed (ed.), "Egypt," Africa Regional: Equality Now, *Awaken* 7, no. 2 (Sept. 2003):News.

39. Population Reference Bureau, 13.

40. The Nation, "Kenya; Challenges Abound Over Ban On FGM," *Africa News*, Dec. 21, 2001.

41. The Nation, "Kenya."

42. The Nation, "Kenya."

43. Faiza Jama Mohamed (ed.), "Religious Leaders Form Committee to End FGM," Africa Regional: Equality Now, *Awaken* 7, no. 2 (Sept. 2003):News.

44. Faiza Jama Mohamed (ed.), "Workshop Inspires Boni Women to Call for an End to FGM," Africa Regional: Equality Now, *Awaken* 7, no. 2 (Sept. 2003):News.

45. Abraham Odeke, "Kenyan Men Reject 'Mutilated' Women," BBC, eastern Uganda, June 21, 2004. Available: http://news.bbc.co.uk/2/hi/africa/3826149.stm. Accessed June 21, 2004.

46. "Kenya: Rights Organization 'Locked in Dispute' with Local Community over FGM," BBC Monitoring Africa, Jan. 30, 2004.

47. Faiza Jama Mohamed (ed.), "FGM Blamed on Girls' Poor Performance in Schools," Africa Regional: Equality Now, *Awaken* 7, no. 2 (Sept. 2003):News.

48. Population Reference Bureau, 22.

49. Population Reference Bureau, 22.

50. Reymond et al., 5.

51. Population Reference Bureau, 23.

52. Julia M. Masterson and Julie Hanson Swanson, "Female Genital Cutting: Breaking the Silence, Enabling Change," ICRW Research Report, 2000, 1–35. Available: http://www.icrw.org/docs/FGCfinalpdf.pdf. Accessed May 18, 2004.

53. Alison T. Slack, "Female Circumcision: A Critical Appraisal," *Human Rights Quarterly* 10 (1988):453.

54. Maggie Black, "Mutilation The Facts: The Time Has Come to Disarm," *The Guardian*, Jan. 26, 2004.

55. Black, "Mutilation."

56. Black, "Mutilation."

57. Black, "Mutilation."

58. Black, "Mutilation."

59. Black, "Mutilation."

60. Gaye P. Wertheimer, "Malian Leaders Join Movement to Abandon Female Genital Cutting," *PRIME Pages: Mali*, Nov. 2001.

61. Wertheimer, "Malian Leaders."

62. Program for Appropriate Technology in Health, "Project to Support the Abandonment of Harmful Practices to the Health of Women and Children (PASAF) [Initials for French], n.d.

63. "Give the Spirit Time to Ripen."

64. "Give the Spirit Time to Ripen."

65. PRIME II, "Research Summary: Ethiopian FGC Project," Jan. 2004, 1.

66. PRIME II, 1.

67. PRIME II, 1.

68. Sonny Inbaraj, "Health-Ethiopia: Fistula makes Social Outcasts of Child Brides," Addis Ababa, Feb. 4, 2004. Available: http://www.ipsnews.net. Accessed Feb. 9, 2004.

69. Inbaraj, "Health-Ethiopia."

70. Inbaraj, "Health-Ethiopia."

71. U. S. Agency for International Development, "Working to Eradicate Female Genital Cutting," November 2003.

72. United States Agency for International Development, "Working to Eradicate Female Genital Cutting."

73. World Health Organization, "Management of Pregnancy, Childbirth," 3.

74. P. Stanley Yoder, Papa Ousmane Camara, and Baba Soumaoro, *Female Genital Cutting and Coming of Age in Guinea*, "Summary," (Calverton, Md.: Macro International Inc. and Conakry, Guinea: Université de Conakry, Dec. 1999).

75. Yoder et al.

76. Yoder et al.

77. Yoder et al.

78. Yoder et al.

79. Yoder et al.

80. Yoder et al.

81. Reymond et al., 5.

82. Ahmed Abdel Magied and Suad Musa Ahmed, "Sexual Experiences and Psychosexual Effect of Female Genital Mutilation (FGM) or Female Circumcision (FC) on Sudanese Women," *Ahfad Journal* 19, no. 1 (June 2002): 21–23.

83. Magied and Ahmed, 21–23.

84. Slack, 453.

85. Aban Laamatjok (from Malakal in south Sudan, currently residing in Grand Island, Neb.), interview by the author and James C. Skaine in Grand Island, Neb., Aug. 30, 2003.

86. Jenty Nawal Chacha Kosta (from Juba in south Sudan, currently residing in Grand Island, Neb.), interview by the author and James C. Skaine in Grand Island, Neb., Aug. 30, 2003.

87. Kosta interview, Aug. 30, 2003.

88. Laamatjok interview, Aug. 30, 2003.

89. Laamatjok interview, Aug. 30, 2003.

90. Laamatjok interview, Aug. 30, 2003.

91. Mut Ruey (from Miywut in south Sudan, currently residing in Grand Island, Neb.), interview by the author and James C. Skaine, Aug. 31, 2003.

92. Laamatjok interview, Aug. 30, 2003.

93. Laamatjok interview, Aug. 30, 2003.

94. Laamatjok interview, Aug. 30, 2003.

95. Kosta interview, Aug. 30, 2003.

96. Laamatjok interview, Aug. 30, 2003.

97. Kosta interview, Aug. 30, 2003.

98. Laamatjok interview, Aug. 30, 2003.

99. Kosta interview, Aug. 30, 2003.

100. Laamatjok interview, Aug. 30, 2003.

101. Laamatjok interview, Aug. 30, 2003.

102. Laamatjok interview, Aug. 30, 2003.

103. Nyarieka Ruey (from Miywut in south Sudan, currently residing in Grand Island, Neb.), interview by the author and James C. Skaine, Aug. 31, 2003.

104. Ruey interview, Aug. 31, 2003.

105. William G. Riek (President, Sudanese Refugee Community Organization and Refugee Advocate, Community Humanitarian Resource Center, Grand Island, Nebraska), interview by the author and James C. Skaine August 29, 2003.

106. Riek interview, August 29, 2003.

107. Riek interview, August 29, 2003.

108. Riek interview, August 29, 2003.

109. Riek interview, August 29, 2003.

110. Lowe, H-Africa Discussion Logs.

111. Inter-Parliamentary Union, "Parliamentary Campaign 'Stop Violence Against Women': Female Genital Mutilation," June 11, 2003. Available: http://www.ipu.org/wmn-e/fgm-ref.htm. Accessed June 12, 2003.

112. Associated Press Worldstream, "Inter-African Committee Wants Feb. 6 Named International Day of Zero Tolerance of Female Genital Cutting Aa/sl," Feb. 6, 2003, Sec.: International News, Dateline: Addis Ababa, Ethiopia.

113. Inter-African Committee on Traditional Practices Affecting the Health of Women and Children, Newsletter No. 28, Dec. 2000, 3. Available: http://www.iac-ciaf.ch/IAC_English.28.pdf. Accessed Feb. 2, 2004.

114. Inter-African Committee on Traditional Practices Affecting the Health of Women and Children, Newsletter No. 28.

115. Inter-African Committee on Traditional Practices Affecting the Health of Women and Children, Newsletter No. 28.

116. Inter-African Committee on Traditional Practices Affecting the Health of Women and Children, Newsletter No. 30, Feb. 2002, 7. Available: http://www.iac-ciaf.ch/IAC_English.30.pdf. Accessed Feb. 20, 2004.

117. "Kenyan Bishops Have Joined Other Faith Groups in Forming A Committee to Help End the Practice of Female Genital Mutilation," *America*, Apr. 28, 2003, v. 188, no. 15, 5.

118. RAINBO, "Caring for Women with Circumcision: Fact Sheet for Physicians," n.d. Available: http://www.rainbo.org/factsheet.html. Accessed Oct. 7, 2003.

119. Nawal M. Nour, "Female Circumcision and Genital Mutilation: A Practical and Sensitive Approach," *Contemporary OB/GYN Archive*, Mar. 1, 2000. Available: http://obgyn.pdr.net/be_core/search/show_article_search.jsp?searchurl=/be_core/content/jou.... Accessed Feb. 4, 2004.

120. Nour, "Female Circumcision."

121. RAINBO, "Caring for Women with Circumcision."

122. American Academy of Pediatrics, Committee on Bioethics, "Female Genital Mutilation," *Pediatrics* 102, no. 1 (July 1998): 153–156. Available: http://pediatrics.aapublications.org/cgi/content/full/102/1/153. Accessed Feb. 4, 2004.

123. American Academy of Pediatrics, 153–156.

124. Nour, "Female Circumcision."

125. RAINBO African Immigrant Program, *Female Circumcision and Women's Health*, a brochure, 1999, 9.

126. United States Agency for International Development Health, Population, FGC, "FGC Zero Tolerance Day, Congressional Briefing," Washington, D.C., Feb. 6, 2004, Apr. 22, 2004. Available: http://www.usaid.gov/our_work/global_health/pop/news/fgcday.html. Accessed May 24, 2004.

127. United States Agency for International Development Health, "FGC Zero Tolerance Day."

128. Nawal M. Nour, "Remarks," United States Agency for International Development Health, Population, FGC, "FGC Zero Tolerance Day, Congressional Briefing," Washington, D.C., Feb. 6, 2004, Apr. 22, 2004. Available: http://www.usaid.gov/our_work/global_health/pop/news/fgcday.html. Accessed May 24, 2004.

129. Nour, "Remarks."

130. Nour, "Remarks."

131. Inter-Parliamentary Union, "Parliamentary Campaign."

132. Parliamentary Assembly of the Council of Europe, "Female Genital Mutilation," Resolution 1247 (2001)[1], May 22 2001. Available: http://assembly.coe.int/Main.asp?link=http%3A%2F%2Fassembly.coe.int%2FDocuments%2FAdoptedText%2Fta01%2FERES1247.htm. Accessed Apr. 25, 2004.

133. Report 2001/2035 (INI) on female genital mutilation. Doc. A5–0285/2001 of 17 July 2001.

134. Resolution 2001/2035 (INI) on female genital mutilation, of 20 September 2001.

135. United Nations High Commissioner for Refugees Newsletter, "Separated Children in Europe Programme," Issue 6, August–September 2001, 3–4. Available: http://www.separated-children-europe-programme.org/Global/Documents/Eng/Newsletters/Newsletter6.pdf. Accessed April 25, 2004.

136. United Nations High Commissioner for Refugees Newsletter, "Separated Children," 3–4.

137. United Nations High Commissioner for Refugees Newsletter, "Separated Children," 3–4.

138. 1994 Resolution of the Forty-seventh World Health Assembly WHA47.10 at Inter-Parliamentary Union, "Parliamentary Campaign."

139. "Give the Spirit Time to Ripen."

CHAPTER 7

1. Maasai Laibon and female village members (Mto Wa Mbu, Arusha, Tanzania), interview by the author, Jan. 18, 2004. Translated by James Emanuel Sichilma, Arusha, Tanzania.

2. D. Lee Roper, *The Proud Maasai* (El Cajon, Cal.: Grossmont College, 1978), 1.

3. "Maasai People," Olympia, Wa.: Maasai Assoc., 2004. Available: http://www.maa-

sai-infoline.org/TheMaasaipeople.html. Accessed May 18, 2004.

4. Sevingi R.S.A. (Councilor, Tanzanian Government, Mto Wa Mbu, Arusha, Tanzania), conversation with the author, Jan. 19, 2004.

5. Elspeth Huxley, "Foreword," in Mohamed Amin, Duncan Willetts, and John Eames, *The Last of the Maasai* (Nairobi, Kenya: Camerapix Publishers International, 1987, Second Impression, 1988).

6. Roper, 62.

7. Huxley, "Foreword."

8. Sevingi R.S.A., letter to the author, Jan. 19, 2004.

9. Les Huth, Ph.D. (Professor Emeritus, Director of the Walter Cunningham Memorial Teacher's Project, Wartburg College, Waverly, Ia.), interview by the author Aug. 20, 2003.

10. Huth interview, Aug. 20, 2003.

11. Huth interview, Aug. 20, 2003.

12. Huth interview, Aug. 20, 2003.

13. Huth interview, Aug. 20, 2003.

14. M. Neil Williams (retired general surgeon and missionary physician, Cedar Falls, Ia.), interview by the author, Aug. 6, 2003.

15. Sevingi R.S.A., conversation, Jan. 19, 2004.

16. Sevingi R.S.A., conversation, Jan. 19, 2004.

17. Sevingi R.S.A., email to the author, Mar. 11, 2004.

18. Sevingi R.S.A., email to the author, Mar. 11, 2004.

19. Sevingi R.S.A., letter to the author, Jan. 19, 2004.

20. Sevingi R.S.A., letter to the author and James C. Skaine, Jan. 18, 2004.

21. Maasai Olaiguenani and cabinet (Mto Wa Mbu, Arusha, Tanzania), interview by the author, Jan. 17, 2004. Translated by James Emanuel Sichilma, Arusha, Tanzania.

22. Olaiguenani and cabinet interview, Jan. 17, 2004.

23. Olaiguenani and cabinet interview, Jan. 17, 2004.

24. Olaiguenani and cabinet interview, Jan. 17, 2004.

25. Olaiguenani and cabinet interview, Jan. 17, 2004.

26. Olaiguenani and cabinet interview, Jan. 17, 2004.

27. Olaiguenani and cabinet interview, Jan. 17, 2004.

28. Olaiguenani and cabinet interview, Jan. 17, 2004.

29. Olaiguenani and cabinet interview, Jan. 17, 2004.

30. Olaiguenani and cabinet interview, Jan. 17, 2004.

31. Olaiguenani and cabinet interview, Jan. 17, 2004.

32. Olaiguenani and cabinet interview, Jan. 17, 2004.

33. Olaiguenani and cabinet interview, Jan. 17, 2004.

34. "Ethnologue Report for Language Code: Metmaasai: A Language of Kenya," Ethnologue data from *Ethnologue: Languages of the World, 14th Ed.*, Copyright 2004 SIL International, Nov. 2003. Available: http://www.ethnologue.com/show_language.asp?code=MET. Accessed May 16, 2004.

35. Olaiguenani and cabinet interview, Jan. 17, 2004.

36. Olaiguenani and cabinet interview, Jan. 17, 2004.

37. Olaiguenani and cabinet interview, Jan. 17, 2004.

38. Olaiguenani and cabinet interview, Jan. 17, 2004.

39. Olaiguenani and cabinet interview, Jan. 17, 2004.

40. Olaiguenani and cabinet interview, Jan. 17, 2004.

41. Olaiguenani and cabinet interview, Jan. 17, 2004.

42. Olaiguenani and cabinet interview, Jan. 17, 2004.

43. Olaiguenani and cabinet interview, Jan. 17, 2004.

44. Olaiguenani and cabinet interview, Jan. 17, 2004.

45. Olaiguenani and cabinet interview, Jan. 17, 2004.

46. Olaiguenani and cabinet interview, Jan. 17, 2004.

47. Olaiguenani and cabinet interview, Jan. 17, 2004.

48. Roper, 56.

49. Roper, 56.

50. Laibon and female village members interview, Jan. 18, 2004.

51. Laibon and female village members interview, Jan. 18, 2004.

52. Laibon and female village members interview, Jan. 18, 2004.

53. Roper, 56.

54. Laibon and female village members interview, Jan. 18, 2004.

55. Laibon and female village members interview, Jan. 18, 2004.

56. Laibon and female village members interview, Jan. 18, 2004.

57. Laibon and female village members interview, Jan. 18, 2004.

58. Laibon and female village members interview, Jan. 18, 2004.

59. Mary E. Laiser (Head of the Women's Department of the Arusha Diocese of the Evangelical Lutheran Church in Tanzania), interview by the author and James C. Skaine in Arusha, Tanzania, Jan. 15, 2004.

60. Laiser interview, Jan. 15, 2004.

61. Charles Henry Sweke, M.D., C.I., Ord, Ph.D. (consultant obstetrician/gynecologist, Selian Lutheran Hospital, Arusha, Tanzania), interview by the author in Arusha, Tanzania, Jan. 15, 2004.

62. Sweke interview, Jan. 15, 2004.

63. Sweke interview, Jan. 15, 2004.

64. Laibon and female village members interview, Jan. 18, 2004.

65. Laibon and female village members interview, Jan. 18, 2004.

66. Laibon and female village members interview, Jan. 18, 2004.

67. Laibon and female village members interview, Jan. 18, 2004.

68. Laibon and female village members interview, Jan. 18, 2004.

69. Laibon and female village members interview, Jan. 18, 2004.

70. Laibon and female village members interview, Jan. 18, 2004.

71. Mohamed Amin, Duncan Willetts, and John Eames, *The Last of the Maasai* (Nairobi, Kenya: Camerapix Publishers International, 1987, Second Impression, 1988), 166.

72. Laibon and female village members interview, Jan. 18, 2004.

73. Kebwe Stephen Kebwe (District Medical Officer Bunda, Regional Chairman, Mara, Inter African Committee, Tanzania), interview by author Jan. 25, 2004.

74. Laibon and female village members interview, Jan. 18, 2004.

75. Laibon and female village members interview, Jan. 18, 2004.

76. Laibon and female village members interview, Jan. 18, 2004.

77. Laibon and female village members interview, Jan. 18, 2004.

78. Laibon and female village members interview, Jan. 18, 2004.

79. Laibon and female village members interview, Jan. 18, 2004.

80. Laibon and female village members interview, Jan. 18, 2004.

81. Laibon and female village members interview, Jan. 18, 2004.

82. Laibon and female village members interview, Jan. 18, 2004.

83. Laibon and female village members interview, Jan. 18, 2004.

84. Laibon and female village members interview, Jan. 18, 2004.

85. Laibon and female village members interview, Jan. 18, 2004.

86. Laibon and female village members interview, Jan. 18, 2004.

87. Laibon and female village members interview, Jan. 18, 2004.

88. Laibon and female village members interview, Jan. 18, 2004.

89. Laibon and female village members interview, Jan. 18, 2004.

90. Amin et al., 166.

91. Aud Talle, "The Making of Female Fertility: Anthropological Perspectives on a Bodily Tissue," *Acta Obstetria et Gynecologica Scandinavica* 773 (1994):280–281.

92. Talle, 281.

93. Talle, 281.

94. Talle, 281.

95. Talle, 282.

96. Talle, 282.

97. Talle, 282.

98. Talle, 283

CHAPTER 8

1. Patroba E. Ondiek, Ph.D. (Program Coordinator of the nongovernmental organization Save the Children of Tarime, Tarime, Tanzania, interview by the author in Tarime, Tanzania, Jan. 24, 2004.

2. Kebwe Stephen Kebwe (District Medical Officer Bunda, Regional Chairman, Mara, Inter African Committee, Tanzania), interview with author in Bunda, Tanzania, Jan. 25, 2004.

3. Mary E. Laiser, "Female Genital Mutilation," report prepared for the author (Arusha, Tanzania: The Evangelical Church Diocese in Arusha Region, Women's Department, Jan. 2004), 4.

4. Juliet Chugulu R.N., R.M., M.Sc. (Kilimanjaro Christian Medical Centre School of Nursing, Chairperson, Kilimanjaro Inter-African Committee on Traditional Practices Affecting the Health of Women and Children, Moshi, Tanzania), interview by the author in Moshi, Tanzania, Jan. 28, 2004.

5. Hulda (employee, Women's Department of the Arusha Diocese of the Evangelical Lutheran Church in Tanzania), interview by the author and James C. Skaine in Arusha, Tanzania, Jan. 15, 2004.

6. Hulda interview, Jan. 15, 2004.

7. James Emanuel Sichilma (driver, guide, interpreter, Arusha, Tanzania), interview by the author and James C. Skaine, near Shirati, Tanzania, Jan. 28, 2004.

8. Sichilma interview, Jan. 28, 2004.

9. Mary E. Laiser (Head of the Women's

Department of the Arusha Diocese of the Evangelical Lutheran Church in Tanzania, Tanzania), interview by the author and James C. Skaine in Arusha, Tanzania, Jan. 15, 2004.

10. Laiser interview, Jan. 15, 2004.
11. Laiser interview, Jan. 15, 2004.
12. Laiser interview, Jan. 15, 2004.
13. Laiser interview, Jan. 15, 2004.
14. Laiser interview, Jan. 15, 2004.
15. Laiser interview, Jan. 15, 2004.
16. Laiser interview, Jan. 15, 2004.
17. Laiser interview, Jan. 15, 2004.
18. Laiser interview, Jan. 15, 2004.
19. Laiser interview, Jan. 15, 2004.
20. Hulda interview, Jan. 15, 2004.
21. Laiser interview, Jan. 15, 2004.
22. Laiser interview, Jan. 15, 2004.
23. Laiser interview, Jan. 15, 2004.
24. Laiser interview, Jan. 15, 2004.
25. Kebwe interview, Jan. 25, 2004.
26. Kebwe interview, Jan. 25, 2004.
27. Esther Kawira, M.D., F.A.A.F.P. (Medical Officer in Charge, Shirati Kanisa la Mennonite Tanzania Hospital, Shirati, Tanzania), discussion; Kebwe interview, Jan. 25, 2004.
28. Kebwe interview, Jan. 25, 2004.
29. Kebwe interview, Jan. 25, 2004.
30. Kebwe interview, Jan. 25, 2004.
31. Kebwe interview, Jan. 25, 2004.
32. Kebwe interview, Jan. 25, 2004.
33. Network of Anti-Female Genital Mutilation Organizations Arusha Regional, Arusha, Tanzania, Eradicate Female Genital Mutilation, "Anti-Female Genital Mutilation Law." Translated by Israel Msengi (School of Health, Physical Education and Leisure Services, University of Northern Iowa, Cedar Falls), Apr. 9, 2004.
34. Kebwe interview, Jan. 25, 2004.
35. Kebwe interview, Jan. 25, 2004.
36. Kebwe interview, Jan. 25, 2004.
37. Kebwe interview, Jan. 25, 2004.
38. Kebwe interview, Jan. 25, 2004.
39. Kebwe interview, Jan. 25, 2004.
40. Kebwe interview, Jan. 25, 2004.
41. Kebwe interview, Jan. 25, 2004.
42. Kebwe interview, Jan. 25, 2004.
43. Kebwe interview, Jan. 25, 2004.
44. Kebwe interview, Jan. 25, 2004.
45. "Society Requested to Disclose Traditional Mutilators," Lake Zone News/Announcement, no. 774, Sept. 24–26, 2003. Translated by Israel Msengi (School of Health, Physical Education and Leisure Services, University of Northern Iowa, Cedar Falls), Apr. 8, 2004.
46. "Society Requested to Disclose Traditional Mutilators," Lake Zone News/Announcement, no. 774, Sept. 24–26, 2003. Translated by Israel Msengi (School of Health, Physical

Education and Leisure Services, University of Northern Iowa, Cedar Falls), Apr. 8, 2004.
47. Kawira, discussion; Kebwe, interview, Jan. 25, 2004.
48. Ahmed Makongo, Bunda, "Mara comes up with New Genital Mutilating Strategies," Lake Zone News, NA 680, Oct. 26–29, 2002. Translated by Israel Msengi (School of Health, Physical Education and Leisure Services, University of Northern Iowa, Cedar Falls), Apr. 8, 2004.
49. Kebwe interview, Jan. 25, 2004.
50. Ahmed Makongo, Bunda, "Poligamy, Widows Succession Spreads HIV/AIDS," Lake Zone News, NA 679, Oct. 23–25, 2002, 5. Translated by Israel Msengi (School of Health, Physical Education and Leisure Services, University of Northern Iowa, Cedar Falls), Apr. 8, 2004.
51. Kebwe interview, Jan. 25, 2004.
52. Kebwe interview, Jan. 25, 2004.
53. Kebwe interview, Jan. 25, 2004.
54. Kawira, discussion; Kebwe interview, Jan. 25, 2004.
55. Kebwe interview, Jan. 25, 2004.
56. Kebwe interview, Jan. 25, 2004.
57. Kebwe interview, Jan. 25, 2004.
58. Kebwe interview, Jan. 25, 2004.
59. Juliet Chugulu, Study of Factors which Militate Against the Elimination of Female Genital Mutilation in Singakati and Singachini Villages, Kibosho Ward, Moshi Rural District, Tanzania, Masters Thesis, Leeds Metropolitan University, Leeds, United Kingdom, 1998.
60. Sia E. Msuya, Elizabeth Mbizvo, Akhtar Hussain, Johanne Sundby, Noel E. Sam, and Babill Stray-Pedersen, "Female Genital Cutting in Kilimanjaro, Tanzania: Changing Attitudes?" Tropical Medicine and International Health 7, No. 2 (Feb. 2002):160.
61. Juliet Chugulu and Rachael Dixey, "Female Genital Mutilation in Moshi Rural District, Tanzania," International Quarterly of Community Health Education 19, no. 2 (1999–2000):103.
62. Chugulu interview, Jan. 28, 2004.
63. Chugulu interview, Jan. 28, 2004.
64. Chugulu interview, Jan. 28, 2004.
65. Chugulu interview, Jan. 28, 2004.
66. Chugulu interview, Jan. 28, 2004.
67. Chugulu interview, Jan. 28, 2004.
68. Chugulu interview, Jan. 28, 2004.
69. Chugulu interview, Jan. 28, 2004.
70. Chugulu interview, Jan. 28, 2004.
71. Chugulu interview, Jan. 28, 2004.
72. Chugulu interview, Jan. 28, 2004.
73. Chugulu interview, Jan. 28, 2004.
74. Chugulu interview, Jan. 28, 2004.
75. Sjaak Van der Geest, "The Elder and His Elbow: Twelve Interpretations of an

Akan," *Research in African Literatures* 27, no. 3 (Fall 1996):110(9).

76. Van der Geest, 110(9).
77. Chugulu interview, Jan. 28, 2004.
78. Chugulu interview, Jan. 28, 2004.
79. Chugulu interview, Jan. 28, 2004.
80. Patroba E. Ondiek, *Curriculum Vita*, 2004.
81. Ondiek interview, Jan. 24, 2004.
82. Ondiek interview, Jan. 24, 2004.
83. Catholic Relief Services, "Our Work At A Glance," Spring 2003. Available: http://www.catholicrelief.org/where_we_work/africa/tanzania/index.cfm. Accessed Apr. 6, 2004.
84. Ondiek interview, Jan. 24, 2004.
85. Ondiek interview, Jan. 24, 2004.
86. Ondiek interview, Jan. 24, 2004.
87. Ondiek interview, Jan. 24, 2004.
88. Ondiek interview, Jan. 24, 2004.
89. Ondiek interview, Jan. 24, 2004.
90. Ondiek interview, Jan. 24, 2004.
91. Alakok Mayombo, "Tanzania: Emergency FGM Rescue Operation Fails in Tanzania," Afrol News/Panos, May 29 2002. Available: http://www.afrol.com/index.php. Accessed Apr. 6, 2004.
92. Ondiek interview, Jan. 24, 2004.
93. Josiah Kawira (Projects Officer, Shirati Kanisa la Mennonite Tanzania Hospital, Shirati, Tanzania), discussion; Ondiek interview, Jan. 24, 2004.
94. Ondiek interview, Jan. 24, 2004.
95. Josiah Kawira, discussion; Ondiek interview, Jan. 24, 2004.
96. Ondiek interview, Jan. 24, 2004.
97. Charles Henry Sweke, M.D., C.I., Ord., Ph.D. (consultant obstetrician/gynecologist, Selian Lutheran Hospital, Arusha, Tanzania), interview by the author in Arusha, Tanzania, Jan. 15, 2004.
98. Sweke interview, Jan. 15, 2004.
99. Sweke interview, Jan. 15, 2004.
100. Sweke interview, Jan. 15, 2004

CHAPTER 9

1. Mary E. Laiser (Head of the Women's Department of the Arusha Diocese of the Evangelical Lutheran Church in Tanzania, Tanzania), interview by the author and James C. Skaine in Arusha, Tanzania, Jan. 15, 2004.
2. World Health Organization, "Statement of the Director-General to the World Health Organization's Global Commission on Women's Health," Apr. 12, 1994. Available: http://www.who.int/docstore/frh-whd/FGM/infopack/English/fgm_infopack.htm. Accessed May 6, 2004.

3. World Health Organization, "Statement of the Director-General."
4. Program for Appropriate Technology in Health, "FGM Programmes to Date: What Works and What Doesn't," Executive Summary, Sept. 31, 1998.
5. Program for Appropriate Technology in Health, "FGM Programmes to Date."
6. Laura Reymond, Asha Mohamud, and Nancy Ali, *Female Genital Mutilation — The Facts* (Washington D.C.: Program for Appropriate Technology in Health, July 25, 2003). Available: http://www.path.org/files/FGM-The-Facts.htm. Accessed Apr. 29, 2004.
7. E. Herieka and J. Dhar, "Female Genital Mutilation in Sudan: A Survey of the Attitude of Khartoum University Students Towards This Practice," *Sexually Transmitted Infections* 79, no. 3 (June 2003):220–224.
8. Faiza Jama Mohamed (ed.), "Sudan," Africa Regional: Equality Now, *Awaken* 7, no. 2 (Sept. 2003):News.
9. Reymond, et al.
10. Charles H. Anderson, *Toward A New Sociology* (Homewood, Ill.: The Dorsey Press, 1978), Rev. Ed., 26.
11. Anderson, 27.
12. Anderson, 27–29.
13. Anderson, 29.
14. Anderson, 55.
15. Anderson, 56.
16. Anderson, 56.
17. Susan Izett and Nahid Toubia, *Using Female Circumcision as a Case Study: Learning About Social Change* (New York: RAINBO, 1999), 14.
18. Izett and Toubia, 14.
19. PRIME II, "Mali: Advocacy to Eliminate Female Genital Cutting," *Voices*, No. 23, Chapel Hill, N.C.: Univ. Of N.C., Oct. 13, 2003.
20. PRIME II, "Mali."
21. Na Ahmed Makongo, Bunda, "A Woman Claims Genital Mutilation Led to Her Infertility," *Local News/Home News*, 6 Tanzanian, Wed., Oct. 24, 2002. Translated by Israel Msengi (School of Health, Physical Education and Leisure Services, University of Northern Iowa, Cedar Falls), Apr. 8, 2004.
22. Makongo, "A Woman Claims."
23. Makongo, "A Woman Claims."
24. Makongo, "A Woman Claims."
25. "A Fight Against the Knife," in Yvette Collymore (ed.), *Conveying Concerns: Women Report on Gender-based Violence*, Women's Edition Project (Washington, D.C.: Population Reference Bureau, April 2000), 22.
26. "A Fight Against the Knife," 22.
27. "A Fight Against the Knife," 22.
28. "A Fight Against the Knife," 22.

29. "A Fight Against the Knife," 22.

30. "A Fight Against the Knife," 22.

31. Hawa Aden Mohamed, "Somali Circumciser Shares Her FGM Experience and Views," Faiza Jama Mohamed (ed.): Feature Article.

32. Hawa Aden Mohamed, "Somali Circumciser."

33. Hawa Aden Mohamed, "Somali Circumciser."

34. Hawa Aden Mohamed, "Somali Circumciser."

35. Hawa Aden Mohamed, "Somali Circumciser."

36. Julia M. Masterson and Julie Hanson Swanson, "Female Genital Cutting: Breaking the Silence, Enabling Change," ICRW Research Report, 2000, 1–35. Available: http://www.icrw.org/docs/FGCfinalpdf.pdf. Accessed May 18, 2004.

37. Masterson and Swanson, 1–35.

38. Nawal M. Nour, "Remarks," United States Agency for International Development Health, Population, FGC, "FGC Zero Tolerance Day, Congressional Briefing," Washington, D.C., Feb. 6, 2004, Apr. 22, 2004. Available: http://www.usaid.gov/our_work/global_health/pop/news/fgcday.html. Accessed May 24, 2004.

39. Nour, "Remarks."

40. Nour, "Remarks."

41. Inter-African Committee on Traditional Practices Affecting the Health of Women and Children, *Female Genital Mutilation: Zero Tolerance Eighteen Years of Action 1984–2002* (Addis Ababa, Ethiopia: Inter-African Committee, Jan. 2003), 10–11.

42. Inter-African Committee on Traditional Practices Affecting the Health of Women and Children, "About IAC, Our Mandate," July 2003. Available: http://www.iac-ciaf.ch/. Accessed Apr. 23, 2004.

43. Inter-African Committee on Traditional Practices Affecting the Health of Women and Children, *Zero Tolerance to FGM: Common Agenda for Action for the Elimination of Female Genital Mutilation, 2003–2010* (Addis Ababa, Ethiopia: Inter-African Committee on Traditional Practices Affecting the Health of Women and Children, Feb. 2003), 3.

44. Inter-African Committee on Traditional Practices Affecting the Health of Women and Children, *Zero Tolerance to FGM*, 3.

45. Inter-African Committee on Traditional Practices Affecting the Health of Women and Children, *Zero Tolerance to FGM*, 26.

46. Inter-African Committee on Traditional Practices Affecting the Health of Women and Children, *Report of the International Conference on "Zero Tolerance to FGM,"* Feb. 4–6, 2003, Addis Ababa, Ethiopia, 100–101.

47. "Tostan—Our Mission Statement, About Tostan," n.d. Available: http://www.tostan.org/about.htm. Accessed Apr. 22, 2004.

48. "Tostan—Our Mission Statement."

49. Molly Melching, letter to friends of Tostan in "Tostan Program Chosen as Best Practice by World Health Organization," Tostan News, Oct. 27, 2003. Available: http://www.tostan.org/news-october27_03.htm. Accessed Apr. 20, 2004.

50. Melching, letter to friends, Oct. 27, 2003.

51. "Army Organizes Event To Encourage The Abandonment Of FGC," Tostan, Mar. 22, 2004. Available: http://www.tostan.org/news-03-22-04.htm. Accessed Apr. 20, 2004.

52. "Senegalese Women Remake Their Culture," Washington: D.C.: IK Notes Knowledge and Learning Center Africa Region, World Bank, No. 3, Dec. 1998 at H-Africa Discussion Logs, Jan. 5, 1999. Available: http://www.h-net.org/~africa/. Accessed June 9, 2003.

53. "Senegalese Women Remake Their Culture."

54. "Senegalese Women Remake Their Culture."

55. "Senegalese Women Remake Their Culture."

56. "Senegalese Women Remake Their Culture."

57. "Senegalese Women Remake Their Culture."

58. "Senegalese Women Remake Their Culture."

59. "Female Genital Mutilation: Part II," Washington, D.C.: IK Notes Knowledge and Learning Center Africa Region, World Bank at H-Africa Discussion Logs, Jan. 5, 1999. Available: http://www.h-net.org/~africa/. Accessed June 9, 2003.

60. "FGM: Part II."

61. "FGM: Part II."

62. "FGM: Part II."

63. "Tostan—Our Mission Statement."

64. U.S. Department of State, Office of the Senior Coordinator for International Women's Issues, Office of the Under Secretary for Global Affairs, "Chart: Overview of Practice of Female Genital Mutilation," Sec. K., Feb. 1, 2001, updated June 27, 2001. Available: http://www.state.gov/g/wi/rls/rep/9305.htm. Accessed Apr. 20, 2004.

65. "West African State to Fight Female Genital Mutilation," *Agence France Presse*, Dakar, Sec. International News, Jan. 23, 2002.

66. "Tostan Activities," n.d. Available: http://www.tostan.org/activities.htm. Accessed Apr. 22, 2004.

67. Nirit Ben-Ari, "Villagers Join Campaigns Against FGM," *Herizons Magazine* 16, no. 4 (Spring 2003):6(3).

68. Ben-Ari, 6(3).

69. "Tostan Activities."

70. "Experts to Brief Reporters on Female Genital Cutting, a Global Violation of Health and Human Rights," Washington D.C., U.S. Newswire, Jan. 30, 2004.

71. Molly Melching, "Remarks," United States Agency for International Development Health, Population, FGC, "FGC Zero Tolerance Day, Congressional Briefing," Washington, D.C., Feb. 6, 2004, Apr. 22, 2004. Available: http://www.usaid.gov/our_work/global_health/pop/news/fgcday.html. Accessed May 24, 2004.

72. Melching, "Remarks."

73. Kerthio Diarra, in Molly Melching, "Remarks."

74. Faiza Jama Mohamed (ed.), "Burkina Faso," Africa Regional: Equality Now, *Awaken* 7, no. 2 (Sept. 2003):News.

75. Faiza Jama Mohamed (ed.), "Ghana," Africa Regional: Equality Now, *Awaken* 7, no. 2 (Sept. 2003):News.

CHAPTER 10

1. Mut Ruey (from Miywut in south Sudan, currently residing in Grand Island, Neb.), interview by the author and James C. Skaine, Aug. 31, 2003.

2. Ruth A. Wallace and Alison Wolf, *Contemporary Sociological Theory: Expanding the Classical Tradition* (Upper Saddle River, N.J.: Prentice Hall, 1999), 3rd ed., 183.

3. Rosemarie Skaine, *Power and Gender: Issues in Sexual Dominance and Harassment* (Jefferson, N.C.: McFarland & Co., Inc., Publishers, 1996), 407.

4. Toni Morrison (1993), "Reach Toward the Ineffable," in Charles Lemert (ed.), *Social Theory: The Multicultural and Classic Readings* (Boulder, Colo.: Westview Press, 1999), 664.

5. Morrison, 664.

6. Aban Laamatjok (from Malakal in south Sudan, currently residing in Grand Island, Neb.), interview by the author and James C. Skaine in Grand Island, Neb., Aug. 30, 2003.

7. Inter-African Committee on Traditional Practices Affecting The Health of Women And Children, *Activity Report*, 2002. Available: http://www.risk.org.se/dokument/aktivitets_rapport.doc. Accessed June 17, 2004.

8. Mut Ruey interview, Aug. 31, 2003.

9. Colleen Renk Zengotitabengoa, M.A., J.D. (staff attorney, Tahirih Justice Center, Falls Church, VA), interview by the author at the Tahirih Justice Center, Falls Church, VA, March 22, 2004.

10. Lisa Johnson-Firth, LLB., J.D. (Director of Legal Services, Tahirih Justice Center, Falls Church, VA), interview by the author at the Tahirih Justice Center, Falls Church, VA, March 22, 2004.

11. Renk Zengotitabengoa interview, March 22, 2004.

12. World Health Organization, "Female Genital Cutting: A Joint WHO/UNICEF /UNFPA Statement," 1996. Available: http://www.advocatesforyouth.org/publications /iag/*harmprac.htm.* Accessed June 17, 2004.

13. Advocates for Youth, "Giving Up Harmful Practices, Not Culture," Washington, D.C., 2001. Available: http://www.advocatesforyouth.org/publications/iag/*harmprac.htm.* Accessed June 17, 2004.

14. Bettina Shell-Duncan and Ylva Hernlund, "Female 'Circumcision' in Africa: Dimensions of the Practice and Debates," in Bettina Shell-Duncan and Ylva Hernlund (eds.), *Female 'Circumcision' in Africa: Culture, Controversy, and Change* (Boulder, Colo.: Lynne Rienner, 2000), 18.

15. John Wachira, M.D. (urologist and member of the African Medical Research Foundation, Flying Doctor Surgical Outreach Program), interview by Esther Kawira (M.D., F.A.A.F.P., Medical Officer in Charge, Shirati KMT Hospital, Shirati, Tanzania) for the author, in Shirati, Tanzania Mar. 19, 2004.

16. Sami A. Aldeeb Abu-Sahlieh, "Islamic Law and the Issue of Male and Female Circumcision," *Third World Legal Studies* (1994):101.

17. IRINnews.org, United Nations Office for the Coordination of Human Affairs, "Burkina Faso: Circumcisers Are Operating on Baby Girls to Evade Law," Ouagadougou, May 19, 2004. Available: http://www.irinnews.org/report.asp?ReportID=41157&SelectRegion=West_Africa. Accessed June 17, 2004.

18. "Society Requested to Disclose Traditional Mutilators," *Lake Zone News/Announcement*, No. 774, Sept. 24–26, 2003. Translated by Israel Msengi (School of Health, Physical Education and Leisure Services, University of Northern Iowa, Cedar Falls), Apr. 8, 2004.

19. Juliet Chugulu, R.N., R.M., M.Sc. (Kilimanjaro Christian Medical Centre School of Nursing, Chairperson, Kilimanjaro Inter-African Committee on Traditional Practices Affecting the Health of Women and Children,

Moshi, Tanzania), interview by the author in Moshi, Tanzania, Jan. 28, 2004.

20. Kebwe Stephen Kebwe (District Medical Officer Bunda, Regional Chairman, Mara, Inter African Committee, Tanzania), interview by author in Bunda, Tanzania, Jan. 25, 2004.

21. James Emanuel Sichilma (driver, guide, interpreter, Arusha, Tanzania), interview by the author and James C. Skaine, near Shirati, Tanzania, Jan. 28, 2004.

22. Sichilma interview, Jan. 28, 2004.

23. Sichilma interview, Jan. 28, 2004.

24. Sichilma interview, Jan. 28, 2004.

25. Charles Henry Sweke, M.D., C.I., Ord., Ph.D. (consultant obstetrician/gynecologist, Selian Lutheran Hospital, Arusha, Tanzania), interview by the author in Arusha, Tanzania, Jan. 15, 2004.

26. Kebwe interview, Jan. 25, 2004.

27. John C. Caldwell, I.O. Orubuloye, and Pat Caldwell, "Male and Female Circumcision in Africa from a Regional to a Specific Nigerian Examination," *Social Science and Medicine* 44, No. 8 (April 1997):1189–1190.

28. United Nations Children's Fund, "Work in Progress, UNICEF FGM: The Way Forward-Principles and Processes," Draft pamphlet given to author while at UNICEF, Nairobi, Kenya, Jan. 13, 2004.

29. Morrison, 664.

30. Skaine, 408

EPILOGUE

1. The poem "I Am a Girl Child." Reprinted with permission from the Inter-African Committee on Traditional Practices Affecting the Health of Women and Children, "Report of the International Conference on 'Zero Tolerance to FGM,'" Addis Ababa, Ethiopia, Feb. 4–6, 2003, 107–108.

2. Network of Anti-Female Genital Mutilation Organizations, Arusha Regional, Arusha, Tanzania, collaboration with the Konrad Adenauer Foundation (KAF), poster words, given to the author by Mary E. Laiser (Head of Women's Department Evangelical Lutheran Church in Tanzania (ELCT)-Diocese in Arusha Region), Jan. 28, 2004.

3. Nyarieka Ruey (from Miywut in south Sudan, currently residing in Grand Island, Neb.), interview by the author and James C. Skaine, Aug. 31, 2003.

4. Charles Henry Sweke, M.D., C.I. Ord., Ph.D. (consultant obstetrician/gynecologist, Selian Lutheran Hospital, Arusha, Tanzania), interview by the author in Arusha, Tanzania, Jan. 15, 2004.

Bibliography

Abdalla, Raqiya Haji Dualeh. *Sisters in Affliction: Circumcision and Infibulation of Women in Africa.* New York: Zed, 1982.

Abu-Sahlieh, Sami A. Aldeeb. "Islamic Law and the Issue of Male and Female Circumcision," *Third World Legal Studies* (1994):73–101.

_____. *Male and Female Circumcision: among Jews, Christians and Muslims: Religious, Medical, Social and Legal Debate.* Warren Center, Pa.: Shangri-La Publications, 2001.

Advocates for Youth. "Giving Up Harmful Practices, Not Culture," Washington, D.C., 2001. Available: http://www.advocatesforyouth.org/publications/iag/*harmprac.htm.*

African Charter on Human and Peoples' Rights. Adopted June 26, 1981, Organization of African Unity Doc. CAB/LEG/67/3/Rev. 5, 21 ILM 58 (1982) (into force Sept. 3, 1986). Also known as Banjul Charter.

African Charter on the Rights and Welfare of the Child. Adopted by the Organization of African Unity (1990), OAU Doc. CAB/LEG/24.9/49 (into force Nov. 29, 1999), Minneapolis, Minn: Univ. of Minn., HR Library. Available: http://www1.umn.edu /humanrts/africa/afchild.htm.

African Women's Health Center. Brigham and Women's Hospital, Boston, Mass., Sept. 13, 2003. Available: http://www.brighamandwomens.org/patient/awhc.asp.

Afrol.com. "Europe Impotent in Fighting Female Mutilation Among African Women," afrol.com, Nov. 30, 2000. Available: http://www.afrol.com/Categories/women/ Women/wom015_fgm_europe2.htm.

Agence Fr. Presse. Feb. 1, 2004.

"Aliens and Citizens." 3A American Jurisprudence 2d Aliens and Citizens § 40, § 1171, § 1220, May 2003, *West,* 2004.

American Academy of Pediatrics, Committee on Bioethics. "Female Genital Mutilation," *Pediatrics* 102, no. 1 (July 1998):153–156. Available: http://pediatrics.aapublications.org/cgi/content/f*ull/102/1/153.*

American Convention on Human Rights. Nov. 22, 1969, OAS Treaty Ser. No. 36, OEA/Ser.L./V/II.23.doc.21, Rev. 6 (1979), 9 ILM 673 (1970) (into force July 18, 1978).

Amin, Mohamed, Duncan Willetts and John Eames. *The Last of the Maasai.* Nairobi, Kenya: Camerapix Publishers International, 1987; Second Impression, 1988.

Amnesty International. "Female Genital Mutilation in Africa: Information by Country, Estimated Percent of Women and Girls Who Undergo FGM, Type of FGM Practised," *Human Rights Information Pack,* Sec. 9. Jun. 12, 2003. Available: http://www. amnesty.org/ailib/intcam/femgen/fgm9.htm.

_____. "Female Genital Mutilation and Asylum, Stop Violence Against Women," *Human Rights Information Pack,* Sec. 6, 1998. Available: http://www.amnesty.org/ ailib/intcam/femgen/fgm6.htm.

_____. "What Is Female Genital Mutilation," "Geographical Distribution of Female

Genital Mutilation," *Human Rights Information Pack*, Sec. 1, 1997. Available: http://www.amnesty.org/ailib/intcam/femgen/fgm1.htm#a3.
_____. "United Nations Initiatives," "Female Genital Mutilation," *Human Rights Information Pack*, Sec. 7, 1998. Available: http://www.amnesty.org/ailib/intcam/femgen/fgm7.htm.
Anderson, Charles H. *Toward A New Sociology*. rev. ed. Homewood, Ill.: Dorsey Press, 1978.
Armstrong, Patricia A. "Female Genital Mutilation: The Move toward the Recognition of Violence against Women as a Basis for Asylum in the United States," 21 *Maryland Journal of International Law and Trade* (1997): 95–122.
"Army Organizes Event To Encourage The Abandonment Of FGC." Tostan, Mar. 22, 2004. Available: http://www.tostan.org/news-03-22-04.htm.
As'ad, Maurice. "Al-asl al-usturi li-khitan al-inath fi al-usur al-far'uniyyah." In Sami Awad Aldeeb Abu-Sahlieh, *Male and Female Circumcision: Among Jews, Christians and Muslims: Religious, Medical, Social and Legal Debate*, 66. Cairo: without publisher, 1005.
Asante, Molefi Kete. "The Afrocentric Idea." In *Social Theory: The Multicultural and Classic Readings*, edited by Charles Lemert, pp. 504–506. Boulder, Colo.: Westview Press, 1999.
_____. *Afrocentricity*. Trenton, N.J.: Africa World Press, 1988.
"Assault and Battery." 6 American Jurisprudence, 2d, § 14, May 2003, *West* 2004.
Associated Press Worldstream. "Inter-African Committee Wants Feb. 6 Named International Day of Zero Tolerance of Female Genital Cutting Aa/sl," Feb. 6, 2003, Sec.: International News, Dateline: Addis Ababa, Ethiopia.
Azeez Jimmy Imohi v. INS. 87 F.3d 1319, 1996 WL 297612 (9th Cir.).
Azevedo, C.R.F., G. Spera and A.P. Silva. "Characterization of Metallic Piercings That Caused Adverse Reactions During Use Practical Failure Analysis," *ASM International* 2, no. 4 (Aug. 1, 2002):47–53(7).
Babatunde, Emmanuel. *Women's Rites Versus Women's Rights: A Study of Circumcision Among the Ketu Yoruba of South Western Nigeria*. Trenton, N.J.: Africa World Press, 1997.
Banda, Fareda. "National Legislation Against Female Genital Mutilation," Eschborn, Germany, May 2003, 1–32. Available: http://www.gtz.de/fgm/downloads/fgm-law-long%2016-05-03.pdf.
Banjul Charter. *See African Charter on Human and Peoples' Rights*.
Bashir, Layli Miller. "Female Genital Mutilation in the United States: An Examination of Criminal and Asylum Law," 4 *American University Journal of Gender and the Law* (1996): 415–54.
Beijing Declaration and Platform for Action. Fourth World Conference on Women, Beijing, China, Sept. 4–15, 1995, 1 UN Doc. DPI/1766/Wom. (1996).
Ben-Ari, Nirit. "Villagers Join Campaigns Against FGM," *Herizons Magazine* 16, no. 4 (Spring 2003):6(3).
Berhane, Ras-Work. Welcome Speech, IAC, *Report of the International Conference on "Zero Tolerance to FGM,"* Feb. 4–6, 2003, Addis Ababa, Ethiopia, pp. 120–122.
Bilotti, Edvige. "The Practice of Female Genital Mutilation," n.d. Available: *http://www.medmedia.org/review/numero3/en/art2.htm*.
Black, Maggie. "Mutilation The Facts: The Time Has Come to Disarm." *The Guardian*, Jan. 26, 2004.
BME/Piercing. "Choose a Gallery," Tweed Ontario, Canada: Bmezine.com LLC., PsyberCity Inc., and/or Shannon Larratt 1994–2004. Available: http://www.bmezine.com/pierce/10-female/index.html.
Boddy, Janice. *Wombs and Alien Spirits: Women, Men and the Zar Cult in Northern Sudan*. Madison, Wisconsin: University of Wisconsin Press, 1989.
Boulware-Miller, Kay. "Dimensions of the Practice and Debates." In *Female 'Circum-*

cision' in Africa: Culture, Controversy, and Change, edited by Bettina Shell-Duncan and Ylva Hernlund, pp. 1–40. Boulder, Colo.: Lynne Rienner, 2000.

Braithwaite, Ronald, Alyssa Robillard, Tammy Woodring, Torrence Stephens and Kimberly Jacob Arriola. "Tattooing and Body Piercing among Adolescent Detainees Relationship to Alcohol and Other Drug Use," *Journal of Substance Abuse* 13, Issues 1–2 (Sept. 2001):5–16.

Brooks, J. K., K. A. Hooper and M. A. Reynolds. "Formation of Mucogingival Defects Associated With Intraoral and Perioral Piercing: Case Reports," *Journal of the American Dental Association* 134, no. 7 (July 2003):837–843(7).

Brooks, Traci L., Elizabeth R. Woods, John R. Knight and Lydia A. Shrier. "Body Modification and Substance Use in Adolescents: Is There a Link?" *Journal of Adolescent Health* 32, Issue 1 (Jan. 2003):44–49.

Caldwell, John C., I. O. Orubuloye and Pat Caldwell. "Male and Female Circumcision in Africa from a Regional to a Specific Nigerian Examination," *Social Science and Medicine* 44, no. 8 (April 1997):1181–1193.

Calif. Health and Safety Code. D. 106, Pt. 2, Ch. 3, Art 8, Refs and Annos and § 124170, *West's* Ann. Cal. Health and Safety Code.

Calif. Penal Code. § 273.4, *West's* Ann. Cal. Penal Code.

Canada, Dept. of Justice. Jan. 20, 2004, Annual Statute, Ch. 16 (Bill-27), An Act to Amend the Criminal Code, § 268(3)(a)(b) and (4), (assented to Apr. 25, 1997). Available: http://laws.justice.gc.ca/en/1997/16/5277.html.

Carnegie, Rachel. *Things Change: A Resource Book for Working with Youth and Communities on Female Genital Cutting.* Cape Town, South Africa: Maskey Miller Longman and Nairobi, Kenya: UNICEF, 2003.

Carr, Dara. *Female Genital Mutilation.* Calverton, Md.: Macro International, 1997.

Catholic Relief Services. "Our Work At A Glance," Spring 2003. Available: http://www.catholicrelief.org/where_we_work/africa/tanzania/index.cfm.

Center for Reproductive Rights. "Female Circumcision/Female Genital Mutilation," Mar. 12, 2004. Available: http://www.crlp.org/ww_iss_fgm.html.

_____. "Female Circumcision/Female Genital Mutilation: Legal Prohibitions Worldwide," June 2003, Item: F027. Available: http://www.crlp.org/pub_fac_fgmicpd.html.

"Challenges Faced By Our Women." *Africa News Service* [News Provided by Comtex, Mar 19, 2004 (*Addis Tribune/All Africa Global Media* via COMTEX)], March 21, 2004 pNA.

Chase, Cheryl. "'Cultural Practice' or 'Reconstructive Surgery?' U.S. Genital Cutting, the Intersex Movement, and Medical Double Standards." In *Genital Cutting and Transnational Sisterhood: Disputing U.S. Polemics*, edited by Stanlie M. James and Claire C. Robertson, pp. 126–151. Urbana: University of Illinois Press, 2002.

Chugulu, Juliet. (Kilimanjaro Christian Medical Centre School of Nursing, Chairperson, Kilimanjaro Inter-African Committee on Traditional Practices Affecting the Health of Women and Children, Moshi, Tanzania), interview by the author in Moshi, Tanzania, Jan. 28, 2004.

_____. *Study of Factors which Militate Against the Elimination of Female Genital Mutilation in Singakati and Singachini Villages, Kibosho Ward, Moshi Rural District, Tanzania.* Masters Thesis, Leeds Metropolitan University, 1998.

Chugulu, Juliet, and Rachael Dixey. "Female Genital Mutilation in Moshi Rural District, Tanzania," *International Quarterly of Community Health Education* 19, no. 2 (1999–2000):103–118.

"The Clitoris at Risk." The-Clitoris.com, n.d. Available: http://www.the-clitoris.com/f_html/risk.htm.

Coello, Isabel. "Female Genital Mutilation: Marked by Tradition," 7 *Cardozo Journal of International and Comparative Law* (1999):213–26.

Colorado Legislature 216 (1999). 1999 Colo. Legis. Serv. Ch. 216 (S.B. 99–96) *West*, 2004.

Colorado State § 25–30–101. *West's Colo. Rev. Statutes Annotated*, 2004.

Communicating for Change. *Uncut, Playing With Life.* A film About Female Genital

Mutilation Background Information, 2002. Available: http://cfcnigeria.org/CON-TENT/uncut/backgroundinfo.*htm*.

Coren, C. "Genital Cutting May Alter, Rather than Eliminate, Women's Sexual Sensations," *International Family Planning Perspectives* 29, no. 3 (Mar. 2003):51.

Cook, R. J., B. M. Dickens and M. F. Fathalla. "Female Genital Cutting (Mutilation/circumcision): Ethical and Legal Dimensions," *International Journal of Gynecology and Obstetrics* 79 (2002):281–287.

Coomaraswamy, Radhika. "Identity Within: Cultural Relativism, Minority Rights and the Empowerment of Women," 34 *George Washington International Law Review* (2002):483.

"Couple Indicted on Mutilation Charges." *Los Angeles Times*, Feb. 7, 2004, Home Ed., B4.

Crawley, Heaven. *Women as Asylum Seekers — A Legal Handbook*. London: Immigration Law Practitioners' Association and Refugee Action, 1997, 71 on Amnesty International, "Female Genital Mutilation and Asylum," "Stop Violence Against Women," *Human Rights Information Pack* Sec. 6, 1998. Available: http://www.amnesty.org/ailib/intcam/femgen/fgm6.ht*m*.

Dawit, Seble, and Salem Mekuria. "The West Just Doesn't Get It." *New York Times*, Dec. 7, 1993, p. A27.

"Delaware State Senate 138th General Assembly, Bill No. 393, May 14, 1996." The Female Genital Cutting Education and Networking Project, Legislation, 2003. Available: http://fgmnetwork.org/legisl/US/desb393.html.

Delaware State TI 11 § 780. *Delaware Code Annotated, West*, 2004.

De Moor, R.J.G., A.M.J.C. De Witte and M.A.A. De Bruyne. "Tongue Piercing and Associated Oral and Dental Complications," *Dental Traumatology* 16, no. 5 (Oct. 2000):232–237(6).

Diarra, Kerthio, and Molly Melching. "Remarks," USAID Health, Population, FGC, "FGC Zero Tolerance Day, Congressional Briefing," Washington, D.C., Feb. 6, 2004, Apr. 22, 2004. Available: http://www.usaid.gov/our_work/global_health/pop/news/fgcday.html.

Dorkenoo, Efua. *Cutting the Rose: Female Genital Mutilation: The Practice and its Prevention*. London, UK: Minority Rights Group, 1994.

"Dutch PvdA Calls for Law Exception for FGM on Girls from Certain Regions." *Dutch News Digest*, Jan. 30, 2004.

Engels, Friedrich. "The Patriarchal Family." In *Social Theory: The Multicultural and Classic Readings*, edited by Charles Lemert, pp. 66–69. Boulder, Colo.: Westview Press, 1999.

English, Veronica, Gillian Romano-Critchley, Julian Sheather, and Ann Sommerville. "Concerns Are Raised about the Sudanese Government's Plans to Legalize Female Genital Mutilation," *Journal of Medical Ethics* 29, no. 1 (Feb. 2003):57(1).

Epelboin, Sylvie, and Alain Epelboin. "Special Report: Female Circumcision." *People*, June 1, 1979, pp. 24–29.

Equality Now. "FGM Fact Sheet," no. 1527, New York: Equality Now, 2003. Available: http://www.equalitynow.org/english/about/fgm-tour/fgm-factsheet.html.

"Ethnologue Report for Language Code: Metmaasai: A Language of Kenya." In *Ethnologue: Languages of the World*, 14th ed., edited by Barbara Grimes. SIL International, 2003. Available: http://www.ethnologue.com/show_language.asp?code=MET.

"Experts to Brief Reporters on Female Genital Cutting, a Global Violation of Health and Human Rights." *U.S. Newswire*, Jan. 30, 2004.

Federal Prohibition of Female Genital Mutilation Act of 1995. 104th Congress, 1st Ses., S. 1030 1995, The Female Genital Cutting Education and Networking Project, Legislation, 2003. Available: http://www.fgmnetwork.org/legisl/US/federal.html.

Female Genital Cutting Education and Networking Project. "Complete Legislative Graphic of the United States," 2003. Available: http://www.fgmnetwork.org/legisl/index.html#US.

_____. "International Listing," 2003. Available: http://www.fgmnetwork.org/legisl/index.html#International.

_____. "Summaries of the Laws of Some African Countries," 2003. Available: http://www.fgmnetwork.org/legisl/interntl/africa.html#Burkina%20Faso.

"Female Genital Cutting Practices in Burkina Faso and Mali." News Release, U.S. Population Council, Sept. 29, 1999. Available: http://www.popcouncil.org/mediacenter/newsreleases/sfp999(2).html.

"Female Genital Mutilation: A Vanquished Tradition?" *Africa News Service*, Feb. 09, 2004.

"Female Genital Mutilation: California Couple Charged with Agreeing to Circumcise Young Girls." *Women's Health Weekly* via NewsRx.com and NewsRx.net, Feb. 5, 2004, Expanded Reporting, p. 55.

"Female Genital Mutilation: Part II." Washington, D.C.: *IK Notes* Knowledge and Learning Center Africa Region, World Bank at H-Africa Discussion Logs, Jan. 5, 1999. Available: http://www.h-net.org/~africa/.

Feminist Majority. "FC/FGM," Jun. 15, 2003. Available: http://www.crlp.org/ww_iss_fgm.html.

_____. "Female Circumcision/Female Genital Mutilation (FC/FGM): Global Laws and Policies Towards Elimination," International Factsheets, Item: F027, Nov. 2000. Available: http://www.crlp.org/pub_fac_fgmicpd.html.

"A Fight Against the Knife." In *Conveying Concerns: Women Report on Gender-based Violence*, edited by Yvette Collymore. Washington, D.C.: Population Reference Bureau, 2000.

France, Decree. No. 95–1000, Sept. 6, 1995 setting forth the Code of Medical Ethics [Article 41], "Laws of the World," Harvard University Cyberlaw. Available: http://cyber.law.harvard.edu/population/fgm/fgm.htm.

Gilliam, Angela. "Women's Equality and National Liberation." In *Third World Women and the Politics of Feminism*, edited by C.T. Mohanty, A. Russo, and L. Torres, pp. 215–236. Bloomington and Indianapolis: Indiana University Press, 1991.

"Give the Spirit Time to Ripen." Washington, D.C.: PATH, n.d.

Gosselin, Claudie. "Feminism, Anthropology and the Politics of Excision in Mali: Global and Local Debates in a Postcolonial World," *Anthropologica* XLII (2000):43–60.

Greif, J., W. Hewitt and M. L. Armstrong. "Tattooing and Body Piercing: Body Art Practices Among College Students," *Clinical Nursing Research* 8, no. 4 (Nov. 1999):368–385(18).

Gruenbaum, Ellen. *The Female Circumcision Controversy: An Anthropological Perspective*. Philadelphia: University of Pennsylvania Press, 2000.

_____. "The Movement Against Clitoridectomy and Infibulation in Sudan: Public Health Policy and the Women's Movement," *Medical Anthropology Newsletter* 13, no. 2 (1982):4–12.

Gunning, Isabelle R. "Female Genital Surgeries and Multicultural Feminism: The Ties that Bind; The Differences That Distance," *Third World Legal Studies* (1994):17–48.

_____. "Global Feminism at the Local Level: Criminal and Asylum Laws Regarding Female Genital Surgeries," *Journal of Gender, Race and Justice* 3 (1999):45–62.

Hale, Sondra. "A Question of Subjects: The 'Female Circumcision' Controversy and the Politics of Knowledge," *Ufahamu* 22, no. 3 (Fall 1994):26–35.

Hall, Alexandra. "Do the Eyes Have It?: Flesh Wounds: The Culture of Cosmetic Surgery," Winter 2003. Available: http://www.msmagazine.com/dec03/flesh-wounds_book.asp.

Handrick, W., P. Nenoff, H. Müller and W. Knöfler. "Infektionen durch Piercing und Tattoos—eine Übersicht," *Wiener Medizinische Wochenschrift* 153, no. 9–10 (May 2003):194–197(4).

Harvard University. "Laws of the World on Female Genital Mutilation, France," Decree

No. 95–1000, Article 41 (Sept. 6, 1995). Available: http://cyber.law.harvard.edu/pop-ulation/fgm/fgm.htm.

Hassan, Amna A.R. "Sudan, Summary on the Impacts of the Research on: FGM Psy-cho-social-sexual Consequences and Attitudinal Change in N. Khartoum and E. Nile," *Inter-African Committee on Traditional Practices Affecting the Health of Women and Children*," Newsletter no. 28 (Dec. 2000):6–8.

Head Teacher (Esilalei Primary School, Mto Wa Mbu, Arusha, Tanzania), interview by the author, Jan. 16, 2004.

Heinrich, Jon (Director of Missions, Trinity Lutheran Church, Grand Island, Neb.), interview by the author, Aug. 30, 2003.

Herieka, E., and J. Dhar. "Female Genital Mutilation in Sudan: A Survey of the Atti-tude of Khartoum University Students Towards This Practice," *Sexually Transmit-ted Infections* 79, no. 3 (June 2003):220–224.

Hermaphrodites with Attitude. Newsletter, Winter 1994–1995. Available: http://www.isna.org/newsletter/winterr94-95/winter94–95.html.

Hernlund, Ylva. "Cutting Without Ritual and Ritual Without Cutting: Female 'Cir-cumcision' and the Re-ritualization of Initiation in the Gambia." In *Female "Cir-cumcision" in Africa: Culture, Controversy, and Change*, edited by Bettina Shell-Duncan and Ylva Hernlund, pp. 235–252.

Hosken, Fran P. *The Hosken Report: Genital and Sexual Mutilation of Females*. 4th rev. ed., Lexington, Mass.: Women's International Network News, 1993.

HR-Net, Hellenic Resources Network. "Council of Europe The European Convention on Human Rights, Rome 4 November 1950 and its Five Protocols," Nov. 4, 1950. Available: http://www.hri.org/docs/ECHR50.html#C.Art8.

Hughes, Karen. "The Criminalization of Female Genital Mutilation in the United States," 4 *Journal of Law and Policy* (1995):321.

Hulda (Employee, Women's Department Evangelical Lutheran Church in Tanzania Diocese in Arusha Region), interview by the author and James C. Skaine in Arusha, Tanzania, Jan. 15, 2004.

Huth, Les (Professor Emeritus, Director of the Walter Cunningham Memorial Teacher's Project, Wartburg College, Waverly, Iowa), interview by the author, Aug. 20, 2003.

Huxley, Elspeth. "Foreword." In Mohamed Amin, Duncan Willetts, and John Eames, *The Last of the Maasai*. Nairobi, Kenya: Camerapix Publishers International, 1987, Second Impression, 1988.

Hyena, Hank. "The Micropenis and the Giant Clitoris," *Health and Body*, Dec. 16, 1999. Available: http://www.salaon.com/health/sex/urge/world/1999/12/16/surgery.

Hymon, Steve. "No Victims Found in Genital Mutilation Case; Authorities Say Evi-dence Shows That Couple Conspired to Violate Law Barring the Procedure." *L.A. Times*, Jan. 11, 2004, p. B3.

Illinois State CH 325 § 5/3 and CH 720 § 5/12–34. *West's Smith-Hurd Illinois Compiled Statutes Annotated*, 2004.

Immigration Business News and Comment Daily. 42 (March 7, 2003) in FED App. 0293P (6th Cir.) (2003), File Name: 03a0293 p.06. Available: http://www.michbar.org/opinions/us_appeals/2003/081803/19969.html.

In re Kasinga. 21 I. & N. Dec. 357 (B.I.A. June 13, 1996).

Inbaraj, Sonny. "Health-Ethiopia: Fistula makes Social Outcasts of Child Brides," Inter Press Service News Agency Addis Ababa, Feb. 4, 2004. Available: http://www.ipsnews.net.

Inter-African Committee on Traditional Practices Affecting the Health of Women and Children. "About IAC, Our Mandate," July 2003. Available: http://www.iac-ciaf.ch/.

_____. *Activity Report*, 2002. Available: http://www.risk.org.se/dokument/aktivitets_rapport.doc.

_____. *Female Genital Mutilation: Zero Tolerance Eighteen Years of Action 1984–2002*. Addis Ababa, Ethiopia: IAC, Jan. 2003.

_____. Newsletter no. 28, Dec. 2000. Available: http://www.iac-ciaf.ch/IAC_English. 28.pdf.

_____. Newsletter no. 30, Feb. 2002. Available: http://www.iac-ciaf.ch/IAC_English. 30.pdf.

_____. *Report of the International Conference on "Zero Tolerance to FGM,"* Feb. 4–6, 2003, Addis Ababa, Ethiopia, pp. 100–101.

_____. "What is Female Genital Mutilation?" July 2003. Available: http://www.iac-ciaf .ch/.

_____. *Zero Tolerance to FGM: Common Agenda for Action for the Elimination of Female Genital Mutilation, 2003–2010.* Addis Ababa, Ethiopia: IAC, Feb. 2003.

International Federation of Gynecology and Obstetrics (FIGO). "Recommendations on Ethical Issues in Obstetrics and Gynecology," London: FIGO, 2000, S. 2, p.7 in Cook *et al.*, 285.

Inter-Parliamentary Union. "Parliamentary Campaign 'Stop Violence Against Women': Female Genital Mutilation," June 11, 2003. Available: http://www.ipu.org/wmn-e/fgm-ref.htm.

Intersex Society of North America. "ISNA's Recommendations for Treatment," 1994. Available: http://www.isna.org/library/recommendations.html.

IRINnews.org, United Nations Office for the Coordination of Human Affairs. "Burkina Faso: Circumcisers Are Operating on Baby Girls to Evade Law," Ouagadougou, May 19, 2004. Available: http://www.irinnews.org/report.asp?ReportID=41157& SelectRegion=West_Africa.

Izett, Susan, and Nahid Toubia. *Using Female Circumcision as a Case Study: Learning About Social Change.* New York: RAINBO, 1999.

James, Stanlie M., and Claire C. Robertson (eds.). *Genital Cutting and Transnational Sisterhood: Disputing U.S. Polemics.* Urbana, Ill.: University of Illinois Press, 2002.

_____. "Introduction: Reimaging Transnational Sisterhood," In *Genital Cutting and Transnational Sisterhood: Disputing U.S. Polemics,* edited by Stanlie M. James and Claire C. Robertson, pp. 5–15. Urbana, Ill.: University of Illinois Press, 2002.

Jeffreys, Sheila. "'Body Art' and Social Status: Cutting, Tattooing and Piercing from a Feminist Perspective," *Feminism and Psychology* 10, no. 4 (2000):409–429.

Jervis, P. N., N. J. Clifton, T. J. Woolford. "Ear Deformity in Children Following High Ear-piercing: Current Practice," *Journal of Laryngology and Otology* 115, no. 7 (July 1, 2001):519–521(3).

Jimbo, Paul. "Govt. Issues Ultimatum to Circumcisers." *The East African Standard/All Africa,* Mar 13, 2004; *Africa* News *Service,* March 15, 2004, pNA.

Johnson, Michelle C. "Becoming a Muslim, Becoming a Person: Female 'Circumcision,' Religious Identity, and Personhood in Guinea-Bissau." In *Female "Circumcision" in Africa: Culture, Controversy, and Change* edited by Bettina Shell-Duncan and Ylva Hernlund, pp. 215–233.

Johnson-Firth, Lisa (Director of Legal Services, Tahirih Justice Center, Falls Church, VA). "The Global Dilemma of FGC," presentation to Zonta International, Feb. 9, 2004, pp. 1–15.

_____, interview by author at the Tahirih Justice Center, Falls Church, Vir., March 22, 2004.

Jones-Bibbs, TiaJuana. "United States Follows Canadian Lead and Takes an Unequivocal Position Against Female Genital Mutilation: In Re Fauziya Kasinga," 4 *Tulane Journal of International and Comparative Law* (1997):275–304.

Jones, Wanda K., Jack Smith, Burney Kieke Jr. and Lynne Wilcox. "Female Genital Mutilation/Female Circumcision: Who Is at Risk in the U.S.," *Public Health Reports,* 112 no. 5 (Sept. 1997):368.

Kajtazi, Besnik. "International Human Rights Law and Standards." Armedcon: International Human Rights Law, Feb. 12, 2004, updated daily. Available: http://www. essex.ac.uk/armedcon/international/legal/ihr/default.htm.

Kawira, Esther (Medical Officer in Charge, Shirati Kanisa la Mennonite Hospital, Shirati, Tanzania), interview by the author in Shirati, Tanzania, Jan. 23, 2004; emails to the author, Sept. 25, 2003, Mar. 5, 2004 and Mar. 6, 2004.

Kawira, Josiah (Projects Officer, Shirati Kanisa la Mennonite Hospital, Shirati, Tanzania), interview by the author in Tarime, Tanzania, Jan. 24, 2004.

Kebwe, Kebwe Stephen (District Medical Officer Bunda, Regional Chairman, Mara, Inter-African Committee, Tanzania), interview with author in Bunda, Tanzania, Jan. 25, 2004.

"Kenya: Boost for Anti-FGM Effort As 200 Circumcisers Quit." *Africa News Service*, March 11, 2004, pNA.

"Kenya: New Ritual May Replace FGM." *Off our Backs*, May–June 2003, 4(2).

"Kenya: Rights Organization 'Locked in Dispute' with Local Community over FGM." *BBC Monitoring Africa*, Jan. 30, 2004.

"Kenyan Bishops Have Joined Other Faith Groups in Forming A Committee to Help End the Practice of Female Genital Mutilation." *America*, Apr. 28, 2003, v. 188, no. 15, 5.

Kenyatta, Jomo. *Facing Mount Kenya: The Tribal Life of the Gikuyu.* London: Secker and Warburg, 1991.

Koenig, Laura M. and Molly Carnes. "Body Piercing: Medical Concerns with Cutting-Edge Fashion," *Journal Of General Internal Medicine* 14, no. 6 (June 1999):379–385.

Kosta, Jenty Nawal Chacha (from Juba in south Sudan, currently residing in Grand Island, Neb.), interview by the author and James C. Skaine in Grand Island, Neb., Aug. 30, 2003.

Kouba, Leonard J., and Judith Muasher. "Female Circumcision in Africa: An Overview," *African Studies Review* 28, no. 1, (March 1985):95–110.

Kuczkowski, Krzysztof M., and Jonathan L. Benumof. "Tongue Piercing and Obstetric Anesthesia Is There Cause for Concern?" *Journal of Clinical Anesthesia* 14, Issue 6 (Sept. 2002):447–448.

Laamatjok, Aban (from Malakal in south Sudan, currently residing in Grand Island, Neb.), interview by the author and James C. Skaine in Grand Island, Neb., Aug. 30, 2003.

Laiser, Mary E. "Female Genital Mutilation." Report prepared for the author, Arusha, Tanzania: The Evangelical Church Diocese in Arusha Region, Women's Department, Jan. 2004.

_____. (Head of Women's Department, Arusha Diocese of the Evangelical Lutheran Church in Tanzania), interview by the author and James C. Skaine in Arusha, Tanzania, Jan. 15, 2004.

"Laws of the World." Harvard University Cyberlaw. Available: http://cyber.law.harvard.edu/population/fgm/fgm.htm.

Lazarus, James A. "In Through the Side Door: Analyzing In Re Anikwata Under U.S. Asylum Law and the Torture Convention," 32 *Case Western Reserve Journal of International Law* 101, n86 (Winter, 2000).

"Legislative Assembly of North Dakota Senate Bill No. 2454." The Female Genital Cutting Education and Networking Project, Legislation, 2003. Available: http://www.fgmnetwork.org/legisl/US/ndsb2454.html.

Levin, Tobe. "Abolition Efforts in the African Diaspora: Two Conferences on Female Genital Mutilation in Europe," *Women's Studies Quarterly* 22, nos. 1 and 2 (Spring/Summer 1999):109–116.

Levine, Kay L. "Negotiating the Boundaries of Crime and Culture: a Sociolegal Perspective on Cultural Defense Strategies," 28 *Law and Social Inquiry* 39 (Winter 2003).

Lewis, Hope. "Between Irua and 'Female Genital Mutilation': Feminist Human Rights Discourse and the Cultural Divide," 8 *Harvard Human Rights Journal* (1995):1–31.

Leyendecker, Birgit, and Michael E. Lamb. "Latino Families." In *Parenting and Child Development in 'Nontraditional' Families*, edited by Michael E. Lamb, pp. 247–262. Mahwah, N.J.: Lawrence Erlbaum Associates, 1999.

Lightfoot-Klein, Hanny. *Prisoners of Ritual: An Odyssey into Female Genital Circumcision in Africa.* New York: Haworth Press, 1989.

Little, Cindy M. "Female Genital Circumcision: Medical and Cultural Considerations," *Journal of Cultural Diversity* 10, no. 1 (Spring 2003):30(5).

Lowe, Chris. At H-Africa Discussion Logs, June 29, 1996. Available: http://www.h-net.org/~africa/.

Maasai Laibon and female village members (Mto Wa Mbu, Arusha, Tanzania), interview by the author, Jan. 18, 2004.

Maasai Olaiguenani and cabinet (Mto Wa Mbu, Arusha, Tanzania), interview with the author, Jan. 17, 2004; translated by James Emanuel Sichilma.

"Maasai People." Olympia, Wa.: Maasai Association, 2004. Available: http://www.maasai-infoline.org/TheMaasaipeople.html.

Magesa, Laurenti. *African Religion: The Moral Traditions of Abundant Life.* Maryknoll, N.Y.: Orbis Books, 1997.

Magied, Ahmed Abdel, and Suad Musa Ahmed. "Sexual Experiences and Psychosexual Effect of Female Genital Mutilation (FGM) or Female Circumcision (FC) on Sudanese Women," *Ahfad Journal* 19, no. 1 (June 2002):21–29.

Maguigan, Holly. "Redefining Violence Against Women Symposium: Will Prosecutions for 'Female Genital Mutilation' Stop the Practice in the U.S.?" 8 *Temple Political and Civil Rights Law Review* 391 (Spring 1999).

Maher, Robin M. "Female Genital Mutilation: The Modern Day Struggle to Eradicate a Torturous Rite of Passage," 23:4 *Human Rights* (Fall 1996):12–15. Available: http://www.abanet.org/irr/hr/fgm.html.

Makongo, Ahmed. "Mara comes up with New Genital Mutilating Strategies." *Lake Zone News,* NA 680, Oct. 26–29, 2002. Translated by Israel Msengi (School of Health, Physical Education and Leisure Services, University of Northern Iowa, Cedar Falls), Apr. 8, 2004.

_____. "Poligamy, Widows Succession Spreads HIV/AIDS." *Lake Zone News,* NA 679, Oct. 23–25, 2002, 5. Translated by Israel Msengi, Apr. 8, 2004.

_____. "A Woman Claims Genital Mutilation Led to Her Infertility." *Local News/Home News,* 6 Tanzanian, Oct. 24, 2002. Translated by Israel Msengi, Apr. 8, 2004.

Mandara, Mairo Usman. "Female Genital Cutting in Nigeria: Views of Nigerian Doctors on the Medicalization Debate." In *Female 'Circumcision' in Africa: Culture, Controversy, and Change,* edited by Bettina Shell-Duncan and Ylva Hernlund, pp. 95–108.

Margulies, Peter. "Democratic Transitions and the Future of Asylum Law," 71 *Colorado Law Review* (2000):3–49.

Maryland Health General § 20–601. *West's Annotated Code of Maryland,* 2004.

Masterson, Julia M., and Julie Hanson Swanson. "Female Genital Cutting: Breaking the Silence, Enabling Change," *ICRW Research Report* (2000):1–35. Available: http://www.icrw.org/docs/FGCfinalpdf.pdf.

Mayombo, Alakok. "Tanzania: Emergency FGM Rescue Operation Fails in Tanzania." *Afrol News/Panos,* May 29 2002. Available: http://www.afrol.com/index.php.

McBride, James. "'To Make Martyrs of Their Children': 'Female Genital Mutilation,' Religious Legitimation, and the Constitution." In *God Forbid Religion and Sex in American Public Life,* edited by Kathleen M. Sands, pp. 219–244. New York: Oxford University Press, 2000.

McCloud, Pamela A., Shahira Aly, and Sara Goltz. "Promoting FGM Abandonment in Egypt: Introduction of Positive Deviance." Washington, D.C.: CEPDA, n.d. Available: http://www.cedpa.org/publications/pdf/egypt_fgmabandoment.pdf.

Meinardus, Otto F.A. "Christian Egypt: Faith and Life." In Sami A. Aldeeb Abu-Sahlieh, *Male and Female Circumcision: among Jews, Christians and Muslims: Religious, Medical, Social and Legal Debate.* Warren Center, Pa.: Shangri-La Publications, 200.

Mekuria, Salem. "Female Genital Mutilation in Africa: Some African Views," Association of Concerned Africa Scholars, *ACAS Bulletin,* nos. 44/45 (Winter/Spring 1995) in Chris Lowe, at H-Africa Discussion Logs, June 29, 1996. Available: http://www.h-net.org/~africa/.

Melching, Molly. Letter to friends of Tostan in "Tostan Program chosen as Best Practice by World Health Organization." Tostan News, Oct. 27, 2003. Available: http://www.tostan.org/news-october27_03.htm.

_____. "Remarks," USAID Health, Population, FGC, "Female Genital Cutting (FGC) Zero Tolerance Day, Congressional Briefing," Washington, D.C., Feb. 6, 2004, Apr. 22, 2004. Available: http://www.usaid.gov/our_work/global_health/pop/news/fgc-day.html.

Michigan State Law Library, email to the author, July 9, 2004.

Miller, Jean-Chris. The Body Art Book: A Complete, Illustrated Guide to Tattoos, Piercings, and Other Body Modifications. New York: Berkeley Books, 1997.

Millner, V.S., and B.H. Eichold II. "Body Piercing and Tattooing Perspectives," Clinical Nursing Research 10, no. 4 (Nov. 2001):424–441(18).

Minnesota State § 609.2245. Minn. Statutes Annotated, West, 2004.

Missouri Revised Statutes § 568–065. August 28, 2003, Cross Reference: Child molestation, first and second degree, RSMo 566.067, 566.068, Missouri General Assembly. Available: http://www.moga.state.mo.us/statutes/c500-599/5680000065.htm.

Mohamed, Faiza Jama (ed.). "Africa Regional: Equality Now," Awaken 7, no. 2 (Sept. 2003):News.

Mohamed, Hawa Aden. "Somali Circumciser Shares Her FGM Experience and Views," Awaken 7, no.2 (Sept. 2003):6–8.

Moore, Matthew, and Karuni Rompies. "In the Cut." Sydney Morning Herald, Jan. 13, 2004. Available: http://www.cirp.org/news/smho1-13-04/.

Morris, Rita. "The Culture of Female Circumcision," Advances in Nursing Science 19, no. 2 (Dec. 1996):43(11).

Morrison, Toni. "Reach Toward the Ineffable." In Social Theory: The Multicultural and Classic Readings, edited by Charles Lemert, pp. 663–664. Boulder, Colo.: Westview Press, 1999.

Musalo, Karen. "Beyond Belonging: Challenging the Boundaries of Nationality: Revisiting Social Group and Nexus in Gender Asylum Claims: A Unifying Rational for Evolving Jurisprudence," 52 Depaul Law Review (Spring 2003):777.

Msuya, Sia E., Elizabeth Mbizvo, Akhtar Hussain, Johanne Sundby, Noel E. Sam and Babill Stray-Pedersen. "Female Genital Cutting in Kilimanjaro, Tanzania: Changing Attitudes?" Tropical Medicine and International Health 7, no. 2 (Feb. 2002):159–165.

Nation, The. "Kenya; Challenges Abound Over Ban On FGM." Africa News, Dec. 21, 2001.

Neacsu, E. Dana. "Gender-based Persecution as a Basis for Asylum: an Annotated Bibliography, 1993–2002," 95 Law Library Journal (Spring, 2003):191.

Network of Anti-Female Genital Mutilation Organizations, Arusha Regional, Arusha, Tanzania. Eradicate Female Genital Mutilation, "Anti-Female Genital Mutilation Law." Translated by Israel Msengi (School of Health, Physical Education and Leisure Services, University of Northern Iowa, Cedar Falls), Apr. 9, 2004.

_____. Collaboration with the Konrad Adenauer Foundation. Poster words, given to the author by Mary E. Laiser, Jan. 28, 2004.

Nevada Revised Statutes. 200.5083, 1997. 678, Nev. State Legislature. Available: http://www.leg.state.nv.us/NRS/NRS-200.html#NRS200Sec5083.

"New Jersey General Assembly ACR 335." The Female Genital Cutting Education and Networking Project, Legislation, 2003. Available: http://www.fgmnetwork.org/legisl/US/njacr35.html.

New Jersey State Legislature, Office of Legislative Services, Legislative Information and Bill Room. Email to the author July 9, 2004.

New York City Law. Local Law No. 1066 of 1997, "Laws of the World," Harvard Uni-

versity Cyberlaw. Available: http://cyber.law.harvard.edu/population/fgm/fgm.
htm.

New York Penal Law. Ch. 40, Pt. 3, Title H, Art 130, § 130.85, *McKinney's* Penal Law.

Niamtu, J. "Eleven Pearls for Cosmetic Earlobe Repair," *Dermatologic Surgery* 28, no.
2 (Feb. 2002):180–185(6).

Nigeria Demographic and Health Survey. 2003.

North Dakota State Century Code. Criminal Code, 12.1–36–01, *West* 2004.

Nour, Nawal M. "Female Circumcision and Genital Mutilation: A Practical and Sensitive Approach," *Contemporary OB/GYN Archive*, Mar. 1, 2000. Available: http://
obgyn.pdr.net/be_core/search/show_article_search.jsp ?searchurl=/be_core/con-
tent/jou....

_____. "Female Genital Cutting: A Need for Reform," Editorial, *Obstetrics and Gyne-
cology* 101, no. 5, Part 2 (May 2003):1051–1052.

_____. "Remarks," USAID Health, Population, FGC, "Female Genital Cutting (FGC)
Zero Tolerance Day, Congressional Briefing," Washington, D.C., Feb. 6, 2004. Available: http://www.usaid.gov/our_work/global_health/pop/news/fgcday.html.

Nyangweso, Mary. "Christ's Salvific Message and the Nandi Ritual of Female Circumcision," *Theological Studies* 63 no. 3 (Sept. 2002):579(22).

Obazee, Ruth E. v. John D. Ashcroft. 79 Fed.Appx. 914, 2003 WL 22473831 (7th Cir.).

Obermeyer, Carla M. "Female Genital Surgeries: The Known, the Unknown, and the
Unknowable," *Medical Anthropology Quarterly* 13 (1999):79–106.

Odeke, Abraham. "Kenyan Men Reject 'Mutilated' Women," BBC, eastern Uganda,
June 21, 2004. Available: http://news.bbc.co.uk/2/hi/africa/3826149.stm.

Oforji, Doris C. v. John D. Ashcroft. 354 U.S. F.3d 609 (2003).

Okwubanego, John Tochukwu. "Female Circumcision and the Girl Child in Africa
and the Middle East: The Eyes of the World Are Blind to the Conquered," 33 *International Law* (Spring, 1999):159.

Ondiek, Patroba E. *Curriculum Vita*, 2004.

_____. (Program Coordinator of the nongovernmental organization, Save the Children
of Tarime, Tarime, Tanzania), interview by the author in Tarime, Tanzania, Jan.
24, 2004.

ORC Macro. MEASURE DHS+ STATcompiler, 2003. Available: http://www.mea-
suredhs.com.

Oregon Legislative Assembly. 70th Ses. Regular Session, House Bill 3608, 1999. Available: http://www.leg.state.or.us/99reg/measures/hb3600.dir/hb3608.int.html.

Orubuloye, I. O., Pat Caldwell and John C. Caldwell. "Female 'Circumcision' Among
the Yoruba of Southwestern Nigeria: The Beginning of Change." In *Female 'Circumcision' in Africa: Culture, Controversy, and Change*, edited by Bettina Shell-Duncan and Ylva Hernlund, pp. 73–94.

Painful Pleasures. "Female Body Piercing: Labia Genital Piercing, Piercings, Pierced
Nipple Jewelry, Jewelry Rings." 2001–2002. Available: http://www.bodyjewelry.us/
body_piercing_peircing/female-body-piercing.html.

Parliamentary Assembly of the Council of Europe. "Female Genital Mutilation," Resolution 1247 (2001)[1], May 22 2001. Available: http://assembly.coe.int/Main.asp?
link=http%3A%2F%2Fassembly.coe.int%2FDocuments%2FAdoptedText%2Fta01
%2FERES1247.htm.

Pitts, Victoria. *In the Flesh: the Cultural Politics of Body Modification.* New York: Palgrave Macmillan, 2003.

Platt, Jessica A. "Female Circumcision: Religious Practice v. Human Rights Violation,"
3 *Rutgers Journal of Law and Religion* (2001/2002):3.

Population Council, Jakarta. *Research Report Female Circumcision in Indonesia: Extent,
Implications and Possible Interventions to Uphold Women's Health Rights.* Jakarta,
Indonesia: Population Council, 2003. Available: http://www.dec.org/pdf_docs/
PNACU138.pdf.

Population Reference Bureau. *Abandoning Female Genital Cutting*. Washington, D.C.: Population Reference Bureau, Aug. 2001, Updated Apr. 2003.

PRIME II. "Mali: Advocacy to Eliminate Female Genital Cutting," *Voices*, no. 23, Chapel Hill: University of North Carolina, Oct. 13, 2003.

_____. "Research Summary: Ethiopian FGC Project," Jan. 2004, pp. 1–3.

Program for Appropriate Technology in Health. *Evaluating Efforts to Eliminate the Practice of Female Genital Mutilation: Raising Awareness and Changing Harmful Norms in Kenya*. Washington, D.C.: PATH, 2002.

_____. "FGM Programmes to Date: What Works and What Doesn't," Executive Summary, Sept. 31, 1998.

_____. "Project to Support the Abandonment of Harmful Practices to the Health of Women and Children," n.d.

_____. *Reproductive Health and Rights: Reaching the Hardly Reached*. Washington, D.C.: PATH, 2002.

Rahman, Anika and Nahid Toubia (eds.). *Female Genital Mutilation: A Guide to Laws and Policies Worldwide*. New York: St. Martin's Press, 2000.

RAINBO. African Immigrant Program. *Female Circumcision and Women's Health*, a brochure, 1999.

_____. "Caring for Women with Circumcision: Fact Sheet for Physicians." n.d. Available: http://www.rainbo.org/factsheet.html.

Rathmann, W. G. "Female Circumcision, Indications and A New Technique," *General Practicioner* 20, no. 3 (Sept. 1959):115–120. Available: http://noharmm.org/femcirc tech.htm.

Renk Zengotitabengoa, Colleen (staff attorney, Tahirih Justice Center, Falls Church, VA), interview with the author at the Tahirih Justice Center, Falls Church, Vir., March 22, 2004.

Renteln, Alison D. "Is the Cultural Defense Detrimental to the Health of Children?" In *Law and Anthropology: International Yearbook for Legal Anthropology*, vol. 7, edited by Rene Kuppe and Richard Potz, pp. 27–105. Dordrecht, the Netherlands: Martinus Nijoff, 1994.

Reymond, Laura, Asha Mohamud and Nancy Ali. *Female Genital Mutilation — The Facts*. Washington D.C.: PATH, 2003. Available: http://www.path.org/files/FGM-The-Facts.htm.

Reymond, Laura, Asha Mohamud, Nancy Ali, Kalle Makalou and Zohra Yakoub. *The Facts: Female Genital Mutilation*. Washington, D.C.: PATH, 1997.

Riek, William G. (President, Sudanese Refugee Community Organization and Refugee Advocate, Community Humanitarian Resource Center, Grand Island, Nebraska), interview by the author and James C. Skaine August 29, 2003 and May 29, 2004; email follow-up, June 30, 2004.

Roan, Shari. "Erasing the Past." *Los Angeles Times*, Home Ed., Dec. 8, 2003, Health; Part 6; p. 1.

Robinson, B.A. "Female Genital Mutilation Female (Circumcision) in Africa, Middle East and Far East." Nov. 13, 2001. Available: http://www.religioustolerance.org/fem_cirm.htm.

Rogers, Peter. Post, "Female Genital Mutilation," Jun 29, 1996. Jun. 9, 2003, H-Africa Discussion Logs, H-Net, Humanities & Social Sciences OnLine.

Roper, D. Lee. *The Proud Maasai*. El Cajon, Cal.: Grossmont College, 1978.

Rosenfeld, Allan, "Introduction." In Nahid Toubia, *A Technical Manual for Health Care Providers: Caring for Women with Circumcision*. New York: RAINO, 1999.

Rytina, Nancy (U.S. Citizenship and Immigrations Services, Office of Immigration Statistics) email to the author, July 16, 2004.

Rudloff, Patricia Dysart. "In Re Oluloro: Risk of Female Genital Mutilation as 'Extreme Hardship' *in* Immigration Proceedings." 26 *St. Mary's Law Journal* (1995):877–903.

Ruey, Mut (from Miywut in south Sudan, currently residing in Grand Island, Neb.), interview by the author and James C. Skaine, Aug. 31, 2003.

Ruey, Nyarieka (from Miywut in south Sudan, currently residing in Grand Island, Neb.), interview by the author and James C. Skaine, Aug. 31, 2003.

Seifu, Helen v. John Ashcroft. 80 Fed.Appx. 323, 2003 WL 22490221 (5th Cir.).

"Senegalese Women Remake Their Culture." Washington: D.C.: *IK Notes* Knowledge and Learning Center Africa Region, World Bank, no. 3, Dec. 1998 at H-Africa Discussion Logs, Jan. 5, 1999. Available: http://www.h-net.org/~africa/.

Setareh, Daliah. "Women Escaping Genital Mutilation — Seeking Asylum in the United States," 6 *UCLA Women's Law Journal* (1995):123.

"70-Year Old Woman Jailed for FGM." *Africa News Service,* Jan. 28, 2004 pNA.

Sevingi R.S.A. (Councilor, Tanzanian Government, Mto Wa Mbu, Arusha, Tanzania), conversation with the author, Jan. 19, 2004; email to the author, Mar. 11, 2004; letter to the author and James C. Skaine, Jan. 18, 2004; and letter to the author, Jan. 19, 2004.

Shalala, Donna E. "Foreword," In Nahid Toubia, *A Technical Manual for Health Care Providers: Caring for Women with Circumcision.* New York: RAINBO, 1999.

Sheldon, Kathleen (independent scholar with a research affiliation with the University of California Los Angeles Center for the Study of Women), email to author June 24, 2003.

Shell-Duncan, Bettina, and Ylva Hernlund. "Female 'Circumcision' in Africa: Dimensions of the Practice and Debates." In *Female "Circumcision" in Africa: Culture, Controversy and Change* edited by Bettina Shell-Duncan and Ylva Hernlund, pp. 1–40.

Shweder, Richard A. "'What About Female Genital Mutilation?' and Why Understanding Culture Matters in the First Place." In *Engaging Cultural Differences: The Multicultural Challenge in Liberal Democracies,* edited by R. Schweder, M. Minow, and H. Markus, pp. 216–251. New York: Russell Sage Foundation Press, 2002.

Sichilma, James Emanuel (driver, guide, interpreter, Arusha, Tanzania), interview by the author and James C. Skaine, Shirati, Tanzania, Jan. 25, 2004 and Jan. 28, 2004.

Skaine, Rosemarie. *Power and Gender: Issues in Sexual Dominance and Harassment.* Jefferson, N.C.: McFarland, 1996.

Slack, Alison T. "Female Circumcision: A Critical Appraisal," *Human Rights Quarterly* 10 (1988):437–486.

Smiley, Susannah. "Taking the 'Force' out of Enforcement: Giving Effect to International Human Rights Law Using Domestic Immigration Law," 29 *California Western International Law Journal* (1999):339–356.

Smith, Gayle (U.S. Office of Refugee Resettlement, Division Director for Budget, Policy and Data Analysis), email to the author, July 20, 2004.

"Society Requested to Disclose Traditional Mutilators." *Lake Zone News/Announcement,* no. 774, Sept. 24–26, 2003. Translated by Israel Msengi, Apr. 8, 2004.

"State of California Bill Text Statement California 1995–96 Regular Session Assembly Bill 2125, 1995." Female Genital Cutting Education and Networking Project, Legislation, 2003. Available: http://www.fgmnetwork.org/legisl/US/caab2125.htm.

"State of Illinois 89th General Assembly 1995 and 1996 HB 3572." The Female Genital Cutting Education and Networking Project, Legislation, 2003. Available: http://fgmnetwork.org/legisl/US/ilhb3572.html.

"State of Michigan House Bill — HB6095." The Female Genital Cutting Education and Networking Project, Legislation, 2003. Available: http://www.fgmnetwork.org/legisl/US/mihb6095.html.

"State of Minnesota Legislation on FGC 144.3872 and 609.2245." The Female Genital Cutting and Networking Project, Legislation, 2003. Available: http://www.fgmnetwork.org/legisl/US/mn144.htm.

"State of New York, 5010, 2003–2004 Regular Sessions, In Assembly, Feb. 24, 2003." The Female Genital Cutting Education and Networking Project, Legislation, 2003. Available: http://www.fgmnetwork.org/legisl/US/nys5010.htm.

"State of Rhode Island In General Assembly January Session, A.D. 1996." The Female Genital Cutting Education and Networking Project, Legislation, 2003. Available: http://www.fgmnetwork.org/legisl/US/ris2317.html.

"State of Tennessee Senate Bill 2394 by Cruthfield." July 1, 1996. The Female Genital Cutting Education and Networking Project, Legislation, 2003. Available: http://www.fgmnetwork.org/legisl/US/tnsb2394.html.

"State of Wisconsin 1995, Wisconsin Act 365." The Female Genital Cutting Education and Networking Project, Legislation, 2003. Available: http://www.fgmnetwork.org/legisl/US/wi365.html.

"Sweden Says Cosmetic Surgery on Female Genitals May be Illegal." *Agence Fr.-Presse*, Jan. 28, 2004.

Sweke, Charles Henry (consultant obstetrician/gynecologist, Selian Lutheran Hospital, Arusha, Tanzania), interview by the author in Arusha, Tanzania, Jan. 15, 2004.

Talle, Aud. "The Making of Female Fertility: Anthropological Perspectives on a Bodily Tissue," *Acta Obstetria et Gynecologica Scandinavica* 773 (1994):280–283.

Tarpley, Joan R. "Bad Witches: A Cut on the Clitoris with the Instruments of Institutional Power and Politics," 100 *West Virginia Law Review* (1997):297–352.

"Texas Bill on FGM H.B. No. 91 By Giddings, Thompson, Chavez, Clark." The Female Genital Cutting Education and Networking Project, Legislation, 2003. Available: http://www.fgmnetwork.org/legisl/US/tx91.htm.

Texas Health and Safety § 167.001. Vernon's Texas Statutes and Codes Annotated, *West* Group 2004.

Texas Legis 612 (2003). Vernon's Texas Session Law Service, 2003, Ch. 612 (H.B. 1899) *West* Group, 2004.

Thiam, Awa. *Black Sisters, Speak Out: Feminism and Oppression in Black Africa*. London: Pluto, 1986.

"Tostan Activities." n.d. Available: http://www.tostan.org/activities.htm.

"Tostan — Our Mission Statement, About Tostan." n.d. Available: http://www.tostan.org/about.htm.

Toubia, Nahid. *A Technical Manual for Health Care Providers: Caring for Women with Circumcision*. New York: RAINBO, 1999.

_____. *Female Genital Mutilation: A Call for Global Action*. 2nd ed. New York: RAINBO, 1995.

United Nations. Charter. "Table of Contents," signed, San Francisco, June 26, 1945: 1996–2002. Available: http://www.unhchr.ch/html/menu3/b/ch-cont.htm.

_____. Convention Against Torture and other Cruel, Inhuman or Degrading Treatment or Punishment. GA Res. 39/46 (Dec. 10, 1984) (into force June 26, 1987).

_____. Convention on the Elimination of All Forms of Discrimination Against Women. G.A. Res. 34/180 (Dec. 18, 1979), 1249 UNTS (Treaty Series) 13 (into force Sept. 3, 1981).

_____. Convention on the Elimination of All Forms of Discrimination Against Women. GA General Recommendation 19 on violence against women, A/47/38, Chapter I (1992).

_____. Convention on the Elimination of All Forms of Racial Discrimination. GA Res. 2106 (XX) (Dec. 21, 1965) (into force Jan. 4, 1969)

_____. Convention on the Rights of the Child. Nov. 20, 1989, GA Res. 44/25, 28 ILM 1448 (1989) (into force Sept. 2, 1990).

_____. Convention Relating to the Status of Refugees. Adopted, July 28, 1951 by the United Nations Conference of Plenipotentiaries on the Status of Refugees and Stateless Persons, GA Res. 429 (V) (Dec. 14, 1950) (into force Apr. 22, 1954). Available: http://www.unhchr.ch/html/menu3/b/o_c_ref.htm.

_____. Declaration on the Elimination of Violence Against Women. GA/RES/48/104, (Dec. 20, 1993) (into force Feb. 23, 1994). Available: http://www.unhchr.ch/huridocda/huridoca.nsf/(Symbol)/A.RES.48.104.En?Opendocument.

_____. Declaration of the Principles of International Cultural Co-operation. Gen. Conference of UNESCO, 14TH Session (Nov. 4, 1966).

_____. Declaration on the Rights of Persons Belonging to National or Ethnic, Religious and Linguistic Minorities. GA Res. 47/135 (Dec. 18, 1992).

_____. European Convention for the Protection of Human Rights and Fundamental Freedoms. Adopted Nov. 4, 1950, 213 UNTS 222 (into force Sept. 3, 1953).

_____. HCR Newsletter. "Separated Children in Europe Programme," Issue 6, August–September 2001, pp. 3–4. Available: http://www.separated-children-europe-programme.org/Global/Documents/Eng/Newsletters/Newsletter6.pdf.

_____. International Covenant of Civil and Political Rights. (1966), 999 U.N.T.S. (Treaty Series) 171 (1976).

_____. International Covenant on Economic, Cultural and Social Rights. GA Res. 2200A (XXI) (Dec. 16, 1966), 993 UNTS 3 (into force Jan. 3, 1976).

_____. Programme of Action, International Conference of Population and Development. Cairo, Egypt, (Sept. 1994).

_____. *The United Nations and Human Rights, 1945–1995.* Blue Book Series, 1995.

_____. Universal Declaration of Human Rights. Adopted Dec. 10, 1948, GA Resolution 217A (III), UN Doc. A/810 (1948).

_____. "Workshop on FGM — The Way Forward," Report "Draft + Comments," Sept. 30–Oct. 2, 2003, pp. 1–63. Given to author at UNICEF in Nairobi, Kenya, Jan. 13, 2004.

_____. *The World's Women 2000: Trends and Statistics.* New York: United Nations, 2000. United Nations Children's Fund. "Work in Progress, UNICEF FGM: The Way Forward-Principles and Processes," Draft pamphlet given to author at UNICEF in Nairobi, Kenya, Jan. 13, 2004.

U.S. Agency for International Development, Bureau for Global Health. "Issue Brief: Population and Reproductive Health, Female Genital Cutting: Legislation and the Cairo Declaration," Jan. 2004.

_____. Health, Population. "Congressional Briefing on Female Genital Cutting," Press Release, Feb. 5, 2004.

_____. Health, Population. "FGC Zero Tolerance Day, Congressional Briefing," Washington, D.C., Feb. 6, 2004, Apr. 22, 2004. Available: http://www.usaid.gov/our_work /global_health/pop/news/fgcday.html.

_____. Office of Women in Development. "Female Genital Mutilation Information Bulletin," March 1997. Available: http://www.usaid.gov/wid/pubs/fgm97.htm.

_____. "Working to Eradicate Female Genital Cutting," November 2003.

U.S. Citizenship and Immigrations Services. Dept. of Homeland Security, Apr. 16, 2004. Available: http://uscis.gov/graphics/aboutus/thisisimm/index.*htm.*

_____. Table 9, "Immigrants Admitted by Selected Class of Admission and Region and Country of Last Permanent Residence, Fiscal Year 2002." Available: http://uscis. gov/graphics/shared/aboutus/statistics/Yearbook2002.pdf.

U. S. Code Annotated. Title 8, Ch. 12, SubCh II, Part IX, § 1374, *West* 2004.

_____. Title 18, Part I, Ch. 7, § 116, *West* 2004.

U.S. Code of Federal Regulations. Title 8, Ch. 1, SubCh B, Part 208.18, SubPart A, current through Jan. 12, 2004; 69FR 1891, *West* 2004.

U.S. Congress. Conference report to accompany H. R. 3019, 104–537, § 520 (1996).

U.S. Department of Health and Human Services, Office of Women's Health. "Female Genital Cutting: Frequently Asked Questions: What are other terms used ...," Aug. 2001. Available: http://www.4woman.gov/faq/fgc.htm.

U.S. Department of Homeland Security, Office of Immigration Statistics. *2002 Yearbook of Immigration Statistics,* Table 9, Oct. 2003, 34. Available: http://uscis.gov/ graphics/shared/aboutus/statistics/Yearbook2002.pdf.

U.S. Department of Justice, U.S. Immigration and Naturalization Service. "Notice of Implementation of IIRIRA 1996, 63 FR 13433, 1998.

U.S. Department of State. "Prevalence of the Practice of Female Genital Mutilation (FGM); Laws Prohibiting FGM and Their Enforcement; Recommendations on How to Best Work to Eliminate FGM," *Report on Female Genital Mutilation* as required by Conference Report (H. Rept. 106–997) to Public Law 106–429 (Foreign Operations, Export Financing, and Related Programs Appropriations Act, 2001). Available: http://www.state.gov/documents/organization/9424.p*df.*

_____. Bureau of Democracy, Human Rights, and Labor. "Oman," "Country Reports on Human Rights Practices," Feb. 25, 2004. Available: http://www.state.gov/g/drl/rls/hrrpt/2003/27935.ht*m.*

_____. Bureau of Public Affairs. "J. Laws in Countries Where Immigrants from Countries Practicing FGM Now Reside." Available: http://www.state.gov/g/wi/rls/rep/9304.htm.

_____. Bureau of Public Affairs, Office of the Senior Coordinator for International Women's Issues. "Female Genital Mutilation (FGM) or Female Genital Cutting (FGC): Individual Country Reports," June 1, 2001. Available: http://www.state.gov/g/wi/rls/rep/crfgm/.

_____. Bureau of Public Affairs. "Prevalence of FGM," Mar. 12, 2004. Available: http://www.state.gov/g/wi/rls/rep/9276.htm.

_____. Office of the Senior Coordinator for International Women's Issues, Office of the Under Secretary for Global Affairs. "Chart: Overview of Practice of Female Genital Mutilation," Sec. K., Feb. 1, 2001, updated June 27, 2001. Available: http://www.state.gov/g/wi/rls/rep/9305.htm.

Universalway.org. "The Truth About Circumcision." Updated Feb. 10, 2004. Available: http://www.universalway.org/circtruth.html.

Van der Geest, Sjaak. "The Elder and His Elbow: Twelve Interpretations of an Akan," *Research in African Literatures* 27, no. 3 (Fall 1996):110(9).

Van Der Kwaak, Anke. "Female Circumcision and Gender Identity: A Questionable Alliance?" *Social Science and Medicine* 35, no. 6 (1992):777–787.

Vanguard. "Nigeria; Rage Against Female Genital Mutilation." *Africa News*, Apr. 11, 2002.

Ventolini G., and S. Kleeman. "Adhesions Caused by Umbilical Piercing," *Journal of the American Association of Gynecologic Laparoscopists* 10, no. 2 (May 1, 2003):281–281 (1).

Vissandjée B., M. Kantiébo, A. Levine and R. N'Dejuru. "The Cultural Context of Gender, Identity: Female Genital, Excision and Infibulation," *Health Care For Women International* 24, no. 2 (Feb. 2003):115–124.

Wachira, John (urologist and member of the African Medical Research Foundation Flying Doctor Surgical Outreach Program), interview by Esther Kawira for the author in Shirati, Tanzania Mar. 19, 2004.

Walker, Alice, and Pratibha Parmar. *Warrior Marks: Female Genital Mutilation and Sexual Blinding of Women.* 1st ed. New York: Harcourt Brace, 1993.

Wallace, Charles P. "The Scars of Tradition: (Society/Culture Clash/Female Circumcision)," *Time International* 161, no. 17 (May 5, 2003):42+.

Wallace, Ruth A. and Alison Wolf. *Contemporary Sociological Theory: Expanding the Classical Tradition.* 3rd ed. Upper Saddle River, N.J.: Prentice Hall, 1999.

Walley, Christine J. "Feminism, Anthropology, and Global Debate." In *Genital Cutting and Transnational Sisterhood: Disputing U.S. Polemics,* edited by Stanlie M. James and Claire C. Robertson, pp. 17–53. Urbana: University of Illinois Press, 2002.

_____. "Searching for 'Voices': Feminism, Anthropology, and the Global Debate over Female Genital Operations," *Cultural Anthropology* 12, no. 3 (1997):405–438.

Waltz, Susan. "Reclaiming and Rebuilding the History of the Universal Declaration of Human Rights," *Third World Quarterly* 23, no. 3 (2002):437–448.

Webster, Paul. "Paris Court Convicts Mother of Genital Mutilation." *Observer,* Feb. 1, 2004, p. 25.

Weisblat, Caryn L. "Gender-Based Persecution: Does United States Law Provide

Women Refugees with a Fair Chance?" 7 *Tulane Journal of International and Comparative Law* (1999):407–430.

Wertheimer, Gaye P. "Malian Leaders Join Movement to Abandon Female Genital Cutting," *PRIME Pages: Mali*, Nov. 2001.

"West African State to Fight Female Genital Mutilation." *Agence France Presse*, Jan. 23, 2002, Sec. International News.

West Virginia Code § 61–8D-3A. *West's* Annotated Code of West Virginia.

Williams, M. Neil (retired general surgeon and missionary physician, Cedar Falls, Ia.) interview by the author, Aug. 6, 2003.

Willmott, Fred E. "Body Piercing: Lifestyle Indicator or Fashion Accessory?" *International Journal of STD and AIDS* 12 (2001):358–360s.

Wisconsin State, Health, 146.35. *West's* Wisconsin Statutes Annotated.

World Health Organization. "Female Genital Cutting: A Joint WHO/UNICEF/UNFPA Statement," 1996. Available: http://www.advocatesforyouth.org/publications/iag/harmprac.htm.

_____. Female Genital Mutilation: A Teacher's Guide," Geneva, WHO/FCH/GWH/01.3; WHO/RHR/01.16, 2001. Available: www.who.int/frh-whd.

_____. Female Genital Mutilation: An Overview. Geneva: World Health Organization, 1998.

_____. "Female Genital Mutilation," Fact Sheet No 241, Jun. 2000. Available: http://www.who.int/inf-fs/en/fact241.html.

_____. "Management of Pregnancy, Childbirth and the Postpartum Period in the Presence of Female Genital Mutilation," Report of a WHO Technical Consultation, Geneva WHO/FCH/GWH/01.2 and WHO/RHR/01.13 (Oct. 12–17, 1997). Available: http://www.who.int/entity/gender/other_health/ manageofpregnan.pdf.

_____. "Preventing Medicalization," Apr. 12, 1994. Available: http://www.who.int/docstore/frh-whd/FGM/infopack/English/fgm_infopack.htm.

_____. "Statement of the Director-General to the World Health Organization's Global Commission on Women's Health," Apr. 12, 1994. Available: http://www.who.int/docstore/frh-whd/FGM/infopack/English/fgm_infopack.htm.

_____. "United Nations Estimated Prevalence Rates for FGM," updated May 2001. Available: http://www.who.int/docstore/frh-whd/FGM/FGM%20prev%20update.html.

"Women's Health: Female Genital Mutilation: Common, Controversial, and Bad for Women's Health." *Population Briefs*, 3, no. 2, (Jun. 1997). Available: http://www.popcouncil.org/publications/popbriefs/pb3(2)_1.h tml.

Wright, Jane. "Female Genital Mutilation: An Overview," *Journal of Advanced Nursing*: 24, no. 2 (1996):251–259; para. 6 in Little, 30(5).

Yoder, P. Stanley, Papa Ousmane Camara and Baba Soumaoro. *Female Genital Cutting and Coming of Age in Guinea*. Calverton, Md.: Macro International and Conakry, Guinea: Université de Conakry, 1999.

Ziemer, David. "Alien Parent Can't Establish Derivative Claim for Asylum Based on Citizen Children," *Wisconsin Law Journal* (Jan. 4, 2004).

Index

299

3 1119   01138   0582